REA's Test Prep Books Are The Best!
(a sample of the <u>hundreds of letters</u> REA receives each year)

" I found [REA's *The Best Test Preparation for the AP Examinations in Both U.S. & Comparative Government & Politics*] to be an invaluable help to my review and I highly recommend that you get it. "
Student, Long Island, NY

" My students report your chapters of review as the most valuable single resource they used for review and preparation. "
Teacher, American Fork, UT

" Your book was such a better value and was so much more complete than anything your competition has produced — and I have them all! "
Teacher, Virginia Beach, VA

" Compared to the other books that my fellow students had, your book was the most helpful in helping me get a great score. "
Student, North Hollywood, CA

" Your book was responsible for my success on the exam, which helped me get into the college of my choice... I will look for REA the next time I need help. "
Student, Chesterfield, MO

" Just a short note to say thanks for the great support your book gave me in helping me pass the test... I'm on my way to a B.S. degree because of you! "
Student, Orlando, FL

(more on next page)

(continued from front page)

" I did well because of your wonderful prep books... I just wanted to thank you for helping me prepare for these tests. "
Student, San Diego, CA

" The [REA] book is great for independent study for the exam... From [it], I gained test confidence and a positive attitude. "
Student, Jackson, MS

" I'm a student at a Canadian high school. I really wanted to go to school in the U.S., so I got this book. I was really going into it without knowing what to expect. This product really helped. I went into the test confident. "
Student, Winnipeg, Manitoba

" The best thing about this book is that it's updated and the information is accurate... I would rate it an 11 out of 10. "
Student, Chicago, IL

" The [REA] practice tests are very much like the real thing... [and] are stated in a logical manner [that is] superior [to the competition]. "
Student, Freeville, NY

" I am fond of your books and have found them to be of tremendous assistance in preparing for all classes — not just this [AP Government & Politics test prep]. "
Student, Spartanburg, SC

THE BEST TEST PREPARATION FOR THE

AP

U.S. & Comparative
Government & Politics Exams

8th Edition

Keith Mitchell
AP Instructor
Table Leader for the College Board
Franklin Central High School, Indianapolis, IN

Elliot Kalner, M.A.
Former Social Studies Instructor
Greenwich High School, Greenwich, CT

Paul R. Babbitt, Ph.D.
Instructor
Rutgers University, New Brunswick, NJ

Anita C. Danker, M.A., M.Ed.
Social Studies Instructor
Hopkinton Jr./Sr. High School, Hopkinton, MA

Robert F. Gorman, Ph.D.
Associate Professor of Political Science
Southwest Texas State University,
San Marcos, TX

Scott J. Hammond, Ph.D.
Assistant Professor of Political Science
James Madison University, Harrisonburg, VA

Jack Hamilton, Ph.D.
Professor of Political Science
University of Montevallo, Montevallo, AL

Wesley G. Phelan, Ph.D.
Assistant Professor of Political Science
Eureka College, Eureka, IL

Gerald G. Watson, Ph.D., J.D.
Former Associate Professor and Director
Political Science and Legal Studies Program
University of Portland, Portland, OR

Research & Education Association, Inc.
Visit our website at
www.rea.com

Research & Education Association
61 Ethel Road West
Piscataway, New Jersey 08854
E-mail: info@rea.com

The Best Test Preparation for the
**AP U.S. & COMPARATIVE
GOVERNMENT & POLITICS EXAMS**

Published 2009
Copyright © 2006, 2004, 2003, 2001, 1998, 1995, 1994,
1993 by Research & Education Association, Inc. All
rights reserved. No part of this book may be reproduced
in any form without permission of the publisher.

Printed in the United States of America

Library of Congress Control Number 2006900902

ISBN 13: 978-0-7386-0046-8
ISBN 10: 0-7386-0046-6

REA® is a registered trademark of
Research & Education Association, Inc.

CONTENTS

Chapter 3

ABOUT OUR AUTHOR

Keith Mitchell teaches AP Comparative Government & Politics at Franklin Central High School in Indianapolis, Indiana. Since the course's inception in 1995, more than 85% of his students have achieved scores of "4" (well qualified) or "5" (extremely well qualified) on the AP exam.

In addition to teaching the course, Mitchell has served as an AP Reader and Table Leader, evaluating essays for the College Board during its annual reading period since 1998. He also presents a weeklong workshop on AP Comparative Government & Politics at St. Mary's College, Notre Dame, Indiana, each summer.

ABOUT RESEARCH & EDUCATION ASSOCIATION

Founded in 1959, Research & Education Association (REA) is dedicated to publishing the finest and most effective educational materials–including software, study guides, and test preps—for students in middle school, high school, college, graduate school, and beyond. REA's test preparation series includes books and software for all academic levels in almost all disciplines. REA publishes test preps for students who have not yet entered high school, as well as high school students preparing to enter college. We invite you to visit us at *www.rea.com* to find out how "REA is making the world smarter."

ACKNOWLEDGMENTS

In addition to our author, we would like to thank Larry B. Kling, Vice President, Editorial, for his overall guidance; Pam Weston, Vice President, Publishing, for setting the quality standards for production integrity and managing the publication to completion; Molly Solanki, Associate Editor, for coordinating revisions to this edition; Diane Goldschmidt, Senior Editor, for post-production editorial quality assurance; Kathy Caratozzolo, for typesetting revisions; and Christine Saul, Senior Graphic Artist, for designing our cover. We also extend our thanks to Aquent Publishing Services, for typesetting this edition.

STUDY SCHEDULE FOR THE AP EXAM IN U.S. GOVERNMENT AND POLITICS

The following study schedule will help you become thoroughly prepared for the U.S. Government and Politics exam. Although the schedule is designed as a six-week study program, it can be condensed into three weeks if less time is available by combining two weeks into one. Be sure to set aside enough time each day for studying purposes. If you choose the six-week program, you should plan to study for at least one hour per day. If you choose the three-week program, you should plan to study for at least two hours per day. Keep in mind that the more time you devote to studying for the U.S. Government and Politics exam, the more prepared and confident you will be on the day of the exam.

Week	Activity
1	Go through the introduction on the following pages. Then, take and score U.S. Government and Politics Practice Test 1 to determine your strengths and weaknesses. It's best to have someone who's objective and has broad knowledge of U.S. Government and Politics score your essay. When you grade your exam, you should determine what types of questions cause you the most difficulty, as this will help you determine which review areas to concentrate on. For example, if you incorrectly answer a number of questions dealing with the Constitution, you should carefully study the section on Constitutional Framework. Begin studying this book's U.S. Government and Politics Review, starting with the first sections on American Political Literacy and Constitutional Framework.
2	Continue studying with the section on The Federal Government and the Public Policy section of the review. Make sure to answer all of the drill questions.
3	Study the Political Institutions and Special Interests section and the Public Opinion and Voter Behavior Section of the review and answer the drill questions.
4	Study the Civil Rights and the Supreme Court section, and the George W. Bush Administration section of the review, and answer the drill questions.
5	Study the glossary of U.S. Government and Politics terms.
6	Take and score U.S. Government and Politics Practice Test 2. Make sure to review all of the detailed explanations of answers. Restudy the section(s) of the review for any area(s) in which you are still weak. Then take Practice Test 3. Be sure to review all of the explanations of answers and restudy the areas in which you are still weak.

STUDY SCHEDULE FOR THE AP EXAM IN COMPARATIVE GOVERNMENT AND POLITICS

The following study schedule will help you become thoroughly prepared for the Comparative Government and Politics exam. Although the schedule is designed as a six-week study program, it can be condensed into three weeks if less time is available by combining two weeks into one. Be sure to set aside enough time each day for studying purposes. If you choose the six-week program, you should plan to study for at least one hour per day. If you choose the three-week program, you should plan to study for at least two hours per day. Keep in mind that the more time you devote to studying for the Comparative Government and Politics exam, the more prepared and confident you will be on the day of the exam.

Week	Activity
1	Read and study the introduction on the following pages. Then, take and score Practice Test 4 to determine your strengths and weaknesses. You should have someone with knowledge of Comparative Government and Politics score your essay. When you grade your exam, you should determine what types of questions cause you the most difficulty, as this will help you determine which review areas to study most thoroughly. For example, if you incorrectly answer a number of questions dealing with the government of China, you should carefully study the section on The People's Republic of China.
2	Begin studying the Comparative Government and Politics Review starting with the sections on Comparative Political Literacy and The United Kingdom. Make sure to answer all of the drill questions.
3	Study the sections of the review on The European Union and the Russian Federation and answer the drill questions.
4	Study the sections of the review on the People's Republic of China and Mexico and answer the drill questions.
5	Study the sections of the review on Nigeria and The Islamic Republic of Iran and answer the drill questions.
6	Study the glossary of Comparative Government and Politics terms. Then, take and score Practice Test 5. Make sure to review all of the detailed explanations of answers. Restudy the section(s) of the review for any area(s) in which you are still weak.

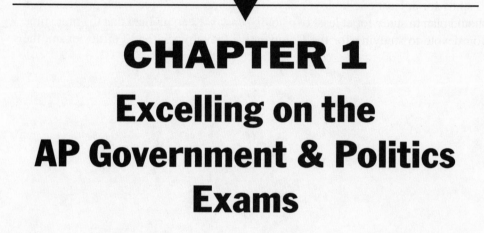

CHAPTER 1
Excelling on the
AP Government & Politics
Exams

Chapter 1

EXCELLING ON THE AP GOVERNMENT & POLITICS EXAMS

This book will prepare you for the Advanced Placement Examinations in Government and Politics by giving you, first and foremost, an accurate and complete representation of the actual exams for both United States Government and Politics and Comparative Government and Politics. But REA doesn't stop there: we give you thorough yet concise subject reviews, a series of targeted drills, and an up-to-date glossary that comprises the full range of terminology with which you should be familiar.

If you are taking the United States Government and Politics exam, you'll want to concentrate on Chapter 2. Chapter 3 is devoted to the Comparative Government and Politics exam. In both cases, you'll find a lively course review keyed to exactly the material you'll need to know to score well on the test, complemented by our handy glossary to help you get the most out of your study time. Three complete practice exams are provided for U.S. Government and Politics, while two full-length practice exams are provided for Comparative Government and Politics.

Each REA practice exam features an answer key and detailed explanations for every question. The explanations not only provide the correct response but also tell you why the remaining answers shouldn't be chosen.

By going over the appropriate review section(s), taking the corresponding exam(s), and studying our detailed explanations, you will discover your strengths and weaknesses and prepare yourself to score well on the AP Government and Politics exams.

ABOUT THE ADVANCED PLACEMENT PROGRAM

The Advanced Placement Program is designed to provide high school students with the opportunity to pursue college-level studies while still attending high school. The program consists of two components: an AP course and an AP exam. In addition, the AP Government and Politics curriculum is divided into two courses: United States Government & Politics and Comparative Government & Politics.

If you wish to pursue an Advanced Placement Government and Politics course you may enroll in the United States course, the Comparative course, or both. You will be expected to leave the course(s) with college-level writing skills and knowledge of government and politics. Upon completion of the course(s), you may then take the corresponding AP exam(s). Test results are then used to grant course credit and/or determine placement level in the subject when you enter college.

AP exams are administered every May. The exam schedule has been designed to allow you the opportunity to take both exams, if you are enrolled in both courses. If the United States exam is given during the morning administration, the Comparative exam will be given during the afternoon administration.

THE AP UNITED STATES GOVERNMENT & POLITICS EXAM

The United States exam is 145 minutes in length and is divided into two sections:

I. **Multiple-Choice (50% of your grade):** This 45-minute section is composed of 60 questions designed to measure your understanding of facts, concepts, and theories pertinent to United States government and politics. Your ability to analyze and understand data, and the patterns and consequences involved with political processes and behaviors will also be tested. In addition you must have knowledge of the various institutions, groups, beliefs, and ideas relevant to United States government and politics.

II. **Free-Response (50% of your grade):** This 100-minute section consists of four mandatory questions, each of which accounts for one-fourth of your total free-response score. You should allot roughly 25 minutes—or one-quarter of the total time in the free-response segment—for each essay. Each question normally asks you to interrelate ideas from different content areas from among the topics listed below. In addition, you may also be asked to evaluate and define fundamental concepts in the study of United States politics, and possibly to analyze case studies that bear on political relationships and events in the United States. You will be required to demonstrate mastery of political interpretation, and analytic and organizational skills through writing. In addition, you may be presented with graphs, charts and tables from whose data you would be asked to draw logical conclusions.

Here's a breakdown of coverage on the United States exam:

	Topics	% of Exam
I.	Constitutional Underpinnings of United States Government	5-15%
II.	Political Beliefs and Behaviors	10-20%
III.	Political Parties, Interest Groups, and Mass Media	10-20%
IV.	Institutions of National Government: The Congress, the Presidency, the Bureaucracy, and the Federal Courts	35-45%
V.	Public Policy	5-15%
VI.	Civil Rights and Civil Liberties	5-15%

THE AP COMPARATIVE GOVERNMENT & POLITICS EXAM

The Comparative exam is 145 minutes long and is divided into two sections:

I. **Multiple-Choice (50% of your grade):** This 45-minute section is composed of 55 questions designed to measure your understanding of facts, concepts, and theories pertinent to Comparative government and politics. Your ability to analyze and understand data, and the patterns and consequences involved with political processes and behaviors will also be tested. Six countries, referred to as core countries, are covered: The United Kingdom, The Russian Federation, The People's Republic of China, Mexico, Nigeria, and Iran. For certain questions, basic knowledge of the United States will be assumed.

II. **Free-Response (50% of your grade):** This 100-minute section consists of eight mandatory questions. Comparative Free-Response questions require you to provide brief definitions or descriptions of five concepts or terms, and their significance; to identify and explain relationships using major concepts from comparative politics, and to discuss the causes and implications of politics and policy; and to use core concepts in an analysis of one or more of the countries studied during the course. In answering the definitions and descriptions questions, the student will note that the responses are confined to a single paragraph. They key to this type of essay is to illustrate the concept completely, yet with brevity. Also, if the concept can be further illustrated by an event in one of the case study countries, then it should be referred to, preferably as a closing sentence in the response.

Here's a breakdown of coverage on the Comparative exam:

	Topics	% of Exam
I.	Introduction to Comparative Politics	5%
II.	Sovereignty, Authority, and Power	20%
III.	Political Institutions	35%
IV.	Citizens, Society, and the State	15%
V.	Political and Economic Change	15%
VI.	Public Policy	10%

ABOUT THE REVIEW SECTIONS

As mentioned earlier, this book includes two reviews: one for United States Government and Politics, the other for Comparative Government and Politics.

The United States Government and Politics Review covers all of the key information you'll need to score well on the United States exam. These topics include:
- American Political Literacy
- Constitutional Framework

- The Federal Government
- Public Policy
- Political Institutions and Special Interests
- Public Opinion and Voter Behavior
- Civil Rights and the Supreme Court

We also provide a glossary for the United States Government and Politics exam. Included are the key historical figures, court cases, programs, laws, etc., that often appear on this AP exam.

The Comparative Review provides a thorough discussion of the material most often tested on the Comparative exam. Special emphasis is placed on the governments and politics of:

- The United Kingdom
- The European Union
- The Russian Federation
- The People's Republic of China
- Mexico
- Nigeria
- Iran

A glossary for the Comparative Government and Politics exam enables you to brush up on terms that you are likely to encounter on this test.

EXAM SCORING

After the AP administrations, college professors and secondary school teachers are brought together to grade the exams during June. These readers are chosen from around the United States for their familiarity with the AP program.

Scoring the Multiple-Choice Section

The multiple-choice sections of the Comparative Government & Politics and U.S. Government & Politics exams are scored by granting one point for each correct answer and deducting one-fourth of a point for each incorrect answer. Unanswered questions receive neither credit nor deduction. Therefore, it is advisable to answer as many questions as possible. Only leave blanks if you have *no idea whatsoever* about a question or if you run out of time. Blank answers are not counted either for or against a student. Thus, wild guessing is not advisable, but moreover, taking reasonable chances *is* advisable. Losing a quarter point on a question you have partial knowledge about is worth the risk of gaining a full point for being correct. Generally, if you can eliminate one answer as "definitely not right," it is advisable to attempt to answer the question. To build up a high score, a student must attempt the vast majority of the questions presented. Prepare well, attend study sessions outside of class that your teacher may offer, use this guide as practice and review, and then trust yourself when testing.

Scoring the Free-Response Section

The free-response answers are read and scored using a specific set of objective criteria, but the actual points available for each question may vary from administration to administration. Therefore, the sample essays written for the practice tests in this book have all been written to model what a top essay might consist of regardless of the particular numeric rubric employed on that question.

To score the free-response answers on your practice tests, it is suggested that you have a teacher read your essay and provide a letter grade consistent with that employed in the classroom. It is safe to assume that a "C" grade on an essay equates with passing. Obviously to score an overall high grade on an AP exam (see the chart that follows), you would want to improve your essay grade. For tips on how to improve your essay writing, see the Essay Writing Tips at the end of this chapter.

AP EXAM SCORES

The AP scale for these exams extends from 5 down to 1:

5: Extremely well qualified
4: Well qualified
3: Qualified
2: Possibly qualified
1: No recommendation

A score of 4 or 5 will generally ensure that students receive three hours of college credit in an introductory course in American Government and/or Comparative Government at their eventual college or university. Scores of 3 are accepted for credit by some institutions, but not all. Students should question admissions offices about their policies regarding AP credit upon applying to colleges and universities.

STUDYING FOR YOUR AP EXAMINATION

It is never too early to start studying. The earlier you begin, the more time you will have to sharpen your skills. Do not procrastinate! Cramming is not an effective way to study, since it does not allow you the time needed to learn the test material.

It is very important for you to choose the time and place for studying that works best for you. Some students may set aside a certain number of hours every morning to study, while others may choose to study at night before going to sleep. Other students may study during the day, while waiting on a line, or even while eating lunch. Only you can determine when and where your study time will be most effective. However you go about it, be consistent and use your time wisely. Work out a study routine and stick to it!

When you take our practice exams, try to make your testing conditions as much like the actual test as possible. Turn your television and radio off, and sit down at a quiet table free from distraction. Make sure to time yourself.

As you complete the practice test(s), score your test(s) and thoroughly review the explanations to the questions you answered incorrectly, but do not review too much during any one sitting. Concentrate on one problem area at a time by reviewing the question and explanation, and by studying our review(s) until you are confident that you completely understand the material.

Since you will be allowed to write in your test booklet during the actual exam, you may want to write in the margins and spaces of this book when practicing. However, do not make miscellaneous notes on your answer sheet. Mark your answers clearly and make sure the answer you have chosen corresponds to the question you are answering.

Keep track of your scores! By doing so, you will be able to gauge your progress and discover general weaknesses in particular sections. You should carefully study the reviews that cover the topics causing you difficulty, as this will build your skills in those areas.

To get the most out of your studying time, we recommend that you follow the Study Schedule which corresponds to the exam you are taking. It details how you can best budget your time. If you are taking both exams, do not try to study for each at the same time. Try alternating days by studying for the United States exam one day and the Comparative exam the next.

TEST-TAKING TIPS

Although you may be unfamiliar with tests such as the Advanced Placement exams, there are many ways to acquaint yourself with this type of examination and help alleviate your test-taking anxieties. Listed below are ways to help yourself become accustomed to the AP exam; these may also be applied to other standardized tests.

Bring two No. 2 pencils with erasers and two working pens, blue or black ink, with you to the testing room.

Don't bring any books related to the test, or other "study aids."

Become comfortable with the format of the AP Examination in Government and Politics that you are taking. When you are practicing to take the exam(s), simulate the conditions under which you will be taking the actual test(s). You should practice under the same time constraints as well. Stay calm and pace yourself. After simulating the test only a couple of times, you will boost your chances of doing well, and you will be able to sit down for the actual test much more confidently.

Know the directions and format for each section of the exam. Familiarizing yourself with the directions and format of the different test sections will not only save you time, but will also ensure that you are familiar enough with the AP exam to avoid nervousness (and the mistakes caused by being nervous).

Work on the easier questions first. If you find yourself working too long on one question, make a mark next to it in your test booklet and continue. After you have answered all of the questions that you can, go back to the ones you have skipped.

Use the process of elimination when you are unsure of an answer. If you can eliminate three of the answer choices, you have given yourself a fifty-fifty chance of getting the item correct since there will only be two choices left from which to make a guess. If you cannot eliminate at least three of the answer choices, you may choose not to guess, as you will be penalized one-quarter of a point for every incorrect answer. Questions not answered will not be counted.

Be sure that you are marking your answer in the circle that corresponds to the number of the question in the test booklet. Since the multiple-choice section is graded by machine, marking the wrong answer will throw off your score.

ESSAY WRITING TIPS

Analysis of Essay Strategies to Achieve a Top AP Exam Score

As shown in the sample essays, it is a very good idea to follow the "a, b, c" format given in a free-response question. The College Board typically uses this format on most questions. Answer the "a" portion in its entirety before advancing to the "b" portion, and so on. This will help ensure that your response is complete and organized.

Attempt to balance your response. For example, at a recent AP Reading a question dealt with a comparison of the electoral systems of Great Britain and the Russian Federation. Many students answered the British portion of the question with great insight and detail, but on the Russian portion, responses were much thinner and vague in detailed support. A comparison calls for a balanced presentation in terms of depth of knowledge.

Detailed support is a must. Know the names of key figures in the state you are referencing. Know relevant political parties, electoral and executive systems, media realities, cultural traits, and the details that make a state unique. "God is in the details," it has been often said, and that axiom holds true here. Rather than writing, "Nigeria has many ethnicities," go deeper. "Nigeria has some 300 nations, led by the 'big three,' the Hausa-Fulani in the Muslim north, the Yoruba mainly in the southwest near Lagos, and the Ibo concentrated in the southeast". It is always better to be specific than vague. Often, the opening sentence of each paragraph will be a generalization, such as "Under Vladimir Putin, the Russian executive has become stronger." The generalization must be supported with specifics to prove that it is valid. For example, the next sentences in the paragraph might read, "Putin's pro-Kremlin United Russia Party has gained much strength and holds the largest amount of seats in the Duma, ensuring Putin's legislation will pass easily. Also, Putin has greatly censored the media to the point where only state-run outlets now exist on television. Thus, Russian viewers are likely to hear praise and not criticism of the current administration."

Notice that in the sentences above, not only is specific vocabulary used, such as the *Duma* or *United Russia*, but explanations are included linking the terms with their importance. You'd then want to explain the effects of censoring the media or controlling the oligarchs.

Bring two pens with you when taking the AP test. Only ink is allowed in your response booklet and if one of your pens fail, you'll have a backup ready. (You will use a pencil on the objective portion of the test; make sure yours has a good eraser.) Do not use first person—*I, me, my*—when writing. It is understood that the essay is "your informed opinion," so don't waste words explaining this. Don't recopy the question into your booklet. Time is precious on the writing portion of the Government & Politics AP exam. In both the U.S. and Comparative portions, you will face four questions that must be answered in a 100-minute period, and to excel, you must be on task.

Make certain you stay focused on the question asked. Answers that heavily editorialize a particular political view do not score well because they are not relevant to the essay question asked. Also, avoid a "shrapnel" approach where you use all the vocabulary terms and names you know about Mexico when the question asks you to analyze how the Mexican government has handled its U.S. immigration question, for example. In such a question, explaining corporatism, *la mordida*, or, say, the *dedazo* aren't going to earn a student any merit because they have nothing to do with what's being asked. Clear your head and stay focused on the given topic. Following the "a, b, c," format will help with this task.

Legibility helps. Make your essay readable. If it looks like hieroglyphics, your AP evaluator may miss important points that you have made. However, spelling and grammatical errors are not deducted from a student's score. And in the interest of time, you certainly may simply cross out mistakes or draw an arrow indicating what portion of the essay should next be read. Logically, since you're attempting to gain college credit, spelling errors and grammatical mistakes should be minimized.

A final strategic point: Of the four essay questions given, a student should handle the ones he or she knows best first. There is no specific rule that limits a student to a strict 25 minutes per essay. You will simply have a total of 100 minutes to complete all four essays. Use more time on an essay question you know well and slightly less time on an essay on which you have less knowledge.

Read the sample essays in this guide carefully. They model the qualities that have been described above.

CHAPTER 2

United States Government & Politics Review

Chapter 2

AMERICAN POLITICAL LITERACY

In this unit, we'll introduce some essential basic concepts and terms. Remember, AP success will get you university credit at the introductory course level. This means that you will have to illustrate an atypically high level of American political insight.

The universities and colleges who grant credit for AP excellence—scores of 5, 4, and sometimes 3—will expect and assume you have a solid fundamental knowledge of American political science: both the theory and the reality.

A good place to start is with the key terms "liberal" and "conservative." In American political parlance, a conservative is apt to oppose change, to be more religious, to prefer smaller government and the Republican Party. A conservative believes that people themselves, not government, should solve their own problems. Since conservatives generally support less government, they also support lower taxes. Finally, a conservative view places the needs of state (national government) over the rights of the individual.

(GOP, by the way, is a synonym for the Republican Party. It simply stands for "grand old party" even though the Democratic Party is the older of the two parties in their current incarnations.)

A liberal philosophy generally opposes most of these ideas. Liberals believe that government can and should help solve social problems. This requires higher taxation to fund government services and programs. Liberals are more prone to prefer change and political experimentation, champion the rights of the individual over the needs of the state. The Democratic Party is traditionally a moderately liberal party.

Remember, "change" is all relative. For instance, you, as a high school student, have grown up with ideas such as racially motivated school busing, affirmative action, and the legality of abortion. To you, then, these ideas seem "old," and thus possibly conservative. But in the scope of the country's history these are relatively new ideas. The United States was born in 1776; busing only began in the 1970s, *Roe vs. Wade* legalizing abortion occurred in 1973, and affirmative action was enacted around this same time. These are each liberal ideas representing change from the political norm that had preceded them for our country's first two centuries.

Refer to the following chart on specific issues:

KEY ISSUES

Viewed From The Left And The Right

More liberal views:	More conservative views:
• Higher budget for Environmental Protection Agency and Department of Housing and Urban Development	• Higher budget for the Departments of Defense and Homeland Security
• Opposes capital punishment	• Supports capital punishment
• Contents that government can and should help people via programs; favors larger government (e.g., supports raising the minimum wage or implementing "equal pay for equal work" laws)	• Believes that government should remain smaller; that people can and should solve their own problems without government interference (e.g., opposed to minimum wage or "equal pay for equal work" laws; prefers to let the market dictate wages)
• Pro-choice; supports a woman's right to choose regarding abortion	• Pro-life; opposed to abortion
• Supports gun control measures	• Opposed to gun control measures
• Pro-labor; supports increases in minimum wage	• Pro-business; opposed to higher minimum wage
• Believes affirmative action is a positive, if temporary, step	• Opposed to affirmative action

An AP United States Government teacher recently commented that the word "litigation" had thrown his students when used on the AP test. Use of such terminology is not only fair and reasonable by the College Board, but it is to be expected on a test of understanding at this level. Litigation is simply a lawsuit. A litigant is a person involved in a lawsuit—the plaintiff is the litigant who brings the case to court; the defendant is the person being tried.

An acronym that you will cross in this course and on the exam often is PAC, which stands for political action committee. PACs are set up by labor unions, corporations, or other special interest groups to support candidates via campaign contributions in order (they hope) to eventually influence policy in their favor.

In general, a student at this level must have basic American "political literacy." You cannot expect a university to grant you credit if you don't know the basics. For instance, you will be expected to know that capital punishment is the death penalty and in which states it is common (Florida and Texas) and in which it is not utilized (New York, among others), and that "pro-life" means a person is opposed to abortion; that the GOP's symbol is the elephant and the Democratic symbol is the donkey.

"Equal pay for equal work" is a measure by which men and women are paid equally given similar job descriptions and similar performance evaluations. While women have closed this gap over the past few decades, a pay gap still exists. The "glass ceiling" is a reference to the perceived limits that a woman can reach compared her to male counterparts, especially in corporate America.

An understanding of the media as it relates to politics is another must. The major television networks—ABC, NBC, and CBS—along with the most respected newspapers, such as the *New York Times* and *Washington Post*, are considered to have a liberal bias. Conservatives are not shut out by the media, though—see Rush Limbaugh and the FOX News Network as examples. A related term is "spin control," more often simply called spin. This is the attempt by a candidate or his or her staff to frame a message a certain way, generally ignoring the potential negatives to a particular policy.

KEY TERMS

CEO (Chief Executive Officer)—Top officer of a corporation. CEOs have been increasingly noteworthy with corporate scandals involving Enron, Arthur Andersen, WorldCom, and Martha Stewart and ImClone.

Incumbent—A candidate currently holding a given office.

"Lame duck"—A candidate holding office, but not retaining it. The "lame duck" period then occurs after a general election and before the politician exits office. This could occur due to term limits for a particular office, because of defeat in a general (or primary) election, or more rarely because the incumbent simply decides not to seek re-election.

Plea bargain—An agreement between a prosecutor's office and the accused to avoid a trial. The accused generally pleads (admits guilt) to a lesser charge in return for a more lenient sentence. Often, this involves an agreement on the part of the accused to cooperate with law enforcement as an informant, undercover "agent," etc. Plea bargains help to alleviate the choked American court system.

While this introductory unit is far from exhaustive, it will give you a solid footing toward American political literacy.

DRILL

AMERICAN POLITICAL LITERACY

DIRECTIONS: Carefully read and answer each of the following questions, which are based on the information that you have just read.

1.   A candidate's efforts to use the media to frame a message or an event in a positive light is called

   (A)   franking   (D)   spin

   (B)   pork   (E)   plea bargaining

   (C)   logrolling

2.   A plea bargain is designed to potentially benefit all of the following EXCEPT

   (A)   the courts   (D)   the prosecutor's office

   (B)   law enforcement   (E)   the victim

   (C)   the defendant

3.   Which of the following is NOT typically a view held by a staunch Republican?

   (A)   Religion should be strictly separated from government, whether it's a Ten Commandments display or "In God We Trust" inscribed upon currency.

   (B)   Ronald Reagan was a great President.

   (C)   Immigration should be open to provide a cheap labor pool to America business.

   (D)   Abortions should either be outlawed or greatly restricted.

   (E)   The less government, the better.

4. A liberal would be likely to support all of the following EXCEPT

    (A) affirmative action

    (B) gun control

    (C) capital punishment

    (D) the Democratic Party

    (E) harsh punishment of corporate scandals

5. Mainstream American media are generally considered to have

    (A) no bias

    (B) a liberal bias

    (C) a conservative bias

    (D) a bias against females

    (E) a pro-elderly agenda

AP United States Government & Politics Review

CONSTITUTIONAL FRAMEWORK

HISTORICAL BACKGROUND

The United States Constitution was the result of a conscious effort on the part of several distinguished American political leaders to remedy the obvious defects of the Articles of Confederation. The Articles served as the national government from 1781 to 1787. Power was vested in a unicameral legislature that was clearly subordinate to the states. Representatives to the national Congress were appointed and paid by their state legislatures, and their mission was to protect the interests of their respective home states. Each state had one vote in the Congress, which could request, but could not order, states to provide financial and military support. Key weaknesses of the government included:

1) its inability to regulate interstate and foreign trade,
2) its lack of a chief executive and a national court system, and
3) its requirement that laws be passed by a majority of nine of the thirteen states and amendments be ratified by unanimous consent.

Sometimes referred to as the "critical period," the 1780s was a decade marked by internal conflict. With little power to impose control, the Congress presided over a deteriorating economic and political crisis that saw individual states print their own currency, tax the products of their neighbors, and ignore trade agreements with foreign nations. Inflation soared, many small farmers lost their property, and wealthy commercial interests were targeted as the villains. The most serious manifestation of the discontent of the agrarian population occurred in 1786 in rural western Massachusetts when Revolutionary War veteran Daniel Shays led a rebellion against foreclosures by seizing the courts and attacking the tax collectors. Shays' Rebellion symbolized the inability of the national government to promote order and to control unrest.

A series of meetings to consider reform of the Articles led to the calling of the Constitutional Convention in Philadelphia in 1787. Fifty-five delegates participated, with every state represented except Rhode Island. Among the most prominent of the Founding Fathers were James Madison, who recorded the debate proceedings; George Washington, who was named President of the body, Gouverneur Morris, who wrote the final version of the Constitution; and elder statesman Benjamin Franklin.

Several issues divided the delegates, including:

1) representation in the Congress,
2) regulation of interstate and foreign trade,
3) regulation of slavery, and
4) the method of choosing a chief executive.

Edmund Randolph offered the Virginia Plan, which called for a strong national government with representation favoring the larger states. William Paterson of New Jersey countered with a plan that retained some of the state control of the national legislature featured in the Articles and that appealed to the smaller states because it called for equal representation in Congress. The dispute was resolved when the Connecticut delegation offered a compromise that included:

1) a bicameral legislature,
2) equal representation in the Senate, and
3) representation in the House of Representatives based on population.

The Connecticut Compromise is sometimes called the "Great Compromise."

Other controversial questions were similarly resolved by compromises. The Commerce and Slave Trade Compromise gave Congress the power to regulate interstate and foreign trade but denied it the right to tax exports or to interfere with the slave trade for twenty years. The Three-Fifths Compromise allowed three out of every five slaves to be counted for the purpose of determining both representation and taxation. The Electoral College, which provides for an indirect method of choosing a President, was established to pacify those who desired an independent executive branch.

According to Article VII of the Constitution, nine of the thirteen states had to approve of the new government in order for it to become the law of the land. A battle ensued between those favoring the new plan, the Federalists, and those opposed to it, the Anti-Federalists. The disputed issues involved the increased power of the central government at the expense of the states and the lack of a bill of rights guaranteeing individual protections to the citizens. Pro-Constitution leaders James Madison, John Jay, and Alexander Hamilton published a series of articles known collectively as *The Federalist* to explain the Constitution and to persuade its opponents that their fears about a tyrannical central government were unfounded. One of the most quoted of the essays is James Madison's *Federalist 10*, which expresses the Founding Fathers' fear of factions and their belief that the Constitution would control the effects of such factions. The Constitution was ratified in 1788, and the new government convened in the spring of 1789.

DRILL

HISTORICAL BACKGROUND

DIRECTIONS: Carefully read and answer each of the following questions, which are based on the information that you have just read.

6. The national government under the Articles of Confederation

    (A) consisted of three branches

    (B) promoted unity among the states

    (C) had a bicameral legislature

    (D) consisted of a unicameral legislature

    (E) required unanimous passage of all legislation

7. Shays' Rebellion was significant because it

    (A) allowed commercial interests to express their disenchantment with the status quo

    (B) symbolized the weakness of the central government under the Articles

    (C) was the first organized protest against the system of slavery in the South

    (D) expressed the discontent of the upper class

    (E) was a great victory for the agrarian interests

8. The following were all prominent among the leaders at the Constitutional Convention of 1787 EXCEPT

    (A) Thomas Jefferson   (D) Gouverneur Morris

    (B) Benjamin Franklin   (E) George Washington

    (C) James Madison

9. The Connecticut Compromise resolved the controversy at the Constitutional Convention involving

    (A) the method of choosing a President

    (B) the regulation of interstate and foreign trade

(C) representation in Congress

(D) the protection of the institution of slavery

(E) ratification of the Constitution

10. One purpose of the Electoral College was to

(A) ensure that only qualified candidates would run for the presidency

(B) ensure an independent executive branch

(C) promote democracy

(D) provide for a direct method of choosing the chief executive

(E) give the small states an equal voice in choosing the President

11. The stated purpose of the delegates to the Constitutional Convention of 1787 was to

(A) write a new plan of government

(B) eliminate the growth of the institution of slavery

(C) raise more money by taxing exports

(D) construct a more democratic form of government

(E) reform the Articles of Confederation

12. Congress under the Articles of Confederation

(A) could require the states to provide financial support

(B) represented the interests of the individual states

(C) could conscript individuals for military service

(D) was dominated by a strong chief executive

(E) forcefully dealt with Shays' Rebellion

13. James Madison's *Federalist 10* articulated the belief of the Founding Fathers that the Constitution would

(A) lead to a tyranny of the majority

(B) promote the growth of political parties

(C) control the effects of factions

(D) allow the states to maintain their preeminence

(E) lead to a tyranny of the minority

14. A major concern of the Anti-Federalists involved

    (A) their desire to strengthen the central government

    (B) their fear that the states would maintain their dominance under the new government

    (C) their fear that foreign governments would try to overpower the new nation

    (D) their belief that a strong chief executive was necessary

    (E) their desire to see a bill of rights guaranteeing individual protections added to the Constitution

FUNDAMENTAL PRINCIPLES EMBODIED IN THE CONSTITUTION

The Founding Fathers drew upon a variety of sources to shape the government that was outlined in the Constitution. British documents such as the Magna Carta (1215), the Petition of Right (1628), and the Bill of Rights (1689), all of which promoted the concept of limited government, were influential in shaping the fundamental principles embodied in the Constitution. British philosopher John Locke, who wrote about the social contract concept of government and the right of people to alter or abolish a government that did not protect their interests, was a guiding force.

One of the most significant of the basic principles embodied in the Constitution is the concept of a federal system that divides the powers of government between the states and the national government. Local matters are handled on a local level, and those issues that affect all citizens are the responsibility of the federal government. Such a system was a natural outgrowth of the colonial relationship between the Americans and the mother country of England. It is clearly stated in the Tenth Amendment, which declares: "Those powers not delegated to the United States by the Constitution, nor prohibited by it to the States, are reserved to the States respectively, or to the people." The federal government and those of the separate states have powers that may in practice overlap, but in cases where they conflict, the federal government is supreme.

Another key principle is separation of powers. The national government is divided into three branches that have separate functions (legislative, executive, and judicial), but they are not entirely independent. These functions are outlined in Articles I, II, and III of the main body of the Constitution. Closely related to the concept of separation of powers is the system of checks and balances in which each of the branches has the ability to limit the actions of the other branches. The legislative branch can check the executive by refusing to confirm his appointments or by passing laws over his veto (by a two-thirds majority in both houses). The executive can check the legislative by use of the veto and on the judicial by appointing his choices to the federal bench. The judicial can check the other two branches by declaring laws to be unconstitutional.

Additional fundamental principles include:

1) the establishment of a representative government (a republic),
2) the belief in popular sovereignty or a government that derives its power from the people (the Preamble opens with the words, "We the People"), and
3) the enforcement of a government with limits, sometimes referred to as the "rule of law."

DRILL

FUNDAMENTAL PRINCIPLES EMBODIED IN THE CONSTITUTION

DIRECTIONS: Carefully read and answer each of the following questions, which are based on the information that you have just read.

15. British documents such as the Magna Carta, the Petition of Right, and the Bill of Rights

   (A) stressed the supremacy of the monarch

   (B) advanced the concept of limited government

   (C) were written by John Locke

   (D) were rejected by the Founding Fathers

   (E) were rejected by the British Parliament

16. Under a federal system of government, all of the following are true EXCEPT

   (A) local matters are largely handled on a local level

   (B) national matters are the responsibility of the federal government

   (C) federal and state governments have powers that sometimes overlap

(D)   in cases where powers are in conflict, the state government is supreme

(E)   in cases where powers are in conflict, the national government is supreme

17.   The system under which each branch can limit the actions of the other branches is called

(A)   separation of powers   (D)   limited government

(B)   checks and balances   (E)   representative government

(C)   federalism

18.   The opening words of the Constitution, "We the People," express the fundamental principle of

(A)   popular sovereignty   (D)   federalism

(B)   rule of law   (E)   republicanism

(C)   constitutionalism

19.   The section of the Constitution that clearly states the concept of federalism is

(A)   Article I   (D)   the Tenth Amendment

(B)   Article II   (E)   the Preamble

(C)   Article III

20.   Under the system of checks and balances, all of the following are allowed EXCEPT

(A)   the Senate's refusal to approve the President's appointment of a justice to the Supreme Court

(B)   the Senate's refusal to ratify a treaty negotiated by the President and his foreign policy advisors

(C)   the Senate's dismissal of a Cabinet member accused of accepting bribes

(D)   the President's lobbying for a new crime bill to be passed in Congress

(E)   the Supreme Court's ruling that an executive order is unconstitutional

CONSTITUTIONAL LAW

In reality, the Constitution equals much more than the Preamble, seven Articles and twenty-seven Amendments that are written. The written U.S. Constitution is, in fact, a paper-thin document that can be read in roughly a half hour. It is, purposely, rather vague in many regards.

Thus, "Constitutional Law" is a more complete view of what actually makes up a legal view of what is and isn't "constitutional" today. United States constitutional law is comprised of the following four components:

1) The formally written United States Constitution described above
2) Informal amendments
3) The most important acts of Congress
4) Current Supreme Court case precedents

Informal constitutional amendments are actually more important than the twenty-seven formal ones. For one reason, there are thousands of informal amendments, so they more greatly shape U.S. constitutional law. An informal amendment is defined as an accepted (meaning understood and applied), but *unwritten*, change to the constitution.

Some important examples of informal amendments include the following:

- The electoral college would be winner-take-all in converting a state's popular vote.
- A President would have a Cabinet of advisors.
- That a two-party system would develop.
- That the committee system would emerge in Congress.
- There would be a two-term limit for Vice Presidents.
- That members of Congress must reside in the district they represent.
- The presidential use of executive agreements in place of treaties.
- The presidential ability to wage war without a Congressional declaration.

When an informal amendment is violated or threatened, one of two things will happen:

1) Congress and the states will make the amendment formal. This happened with presidential term limits (Twenty-second Amendment) and the succession of the Vice President to the presidency (Twenty-fifth Amendment).
2) More commonly, a violated or threatened informal amendment will simply be discarded. For example, one informal amendment

stated that men only could realistically serve in the U.S. Senate. That informal amendment obviously no longer exists, so in effect, it has been eradicated. This shows the beauty of the informal amendments—it is much easier to amend the constitution this way as opposed to the 2/3 of Congress plus 3/4 of all state legislatures required in the ratification of a formal amendment. This is a main reason why so many more informal amendments exist than formal ones.

A final point of interest: several of the twenty-seven formal amendments themselves have been informally amended. An example is the Second Amendment. The initial portion, which reads, "A well regulated militia, being necessary to the security of a free state," is rendered meaningless and thus has been informally erased. The might of the United States military and various branches, weapons, and personnel, plus the state national guard units, obviously render a homemade army of citizens shooting out their windows a preposterous notion. Thus this portion of the Second Amendment is no longer valid and is removed in terms of a legal view of the U.S. Constitution.

However, the second half of the amendment—"the right of the people to bear arms shall not be infringed"—is very much alive, although somewhat limited by law.

An examination of other amendments in the Bill of Rights will reveal this same phenomenon: informal amendment of the formal amendment. For instance, the Third Amendment has been *completely* repealed informally. It holds no relevance for twenty-first century reality. But why not formally repeal it? That would take legislative time, money, and effort. It is much easier just to ignore the amendment informally.

The most important acts of Congress also become part of constitutional law. One example would be the War Powers Act of 1973, which allows Congress (as a reaction to the Vietnam War) to rein in the President's ability to wage war. Other examples include the banning of literacy tests as a suffrage qualification, the establishment of a minimum wage, and the number of seats that exist in the federal House of Representatives (435) and Supreme Court (nine).

Supreme Court precedents literally determine what is and is not constitutional. Thus, they play an integral and fluid role in shaping the body of U.S. constitutional law. In the landmark case of *Marbury vs. Madison*, the Court gave itself the power of judicial review, or the power to determine what is and is not constitutional.

Other examples of landmark cases include the *Brown vs. Board of Education* decision concerning the racial integration of public schools in 1954 and the *Roe vs. Wade* case legalizing abortion in 1973.

DRILL

CONSTITUTIONAL LAW

DIRECTIONS: Carefully read and answer each of the following questions, which are based on the information that you have just read.

21. Which of the following is NOT considered a component of U.S. constitutional law?

    (A) All previous acts of Congress

    (B) Current Supreme Court precedent

    (C) The formal articles and amendments of the constitution

    (D) Important congressional laws

    (E) Thousands of unwritten informal amendments

22. Formal amendments require which of the following?

    I. Bi-partisan support

    II. Presidential support

    III. Regional support

    IV. National support

    (A) I, II, III, and IV   (D) II and III only

    (B) I, II, and IV   (E) IV only

    (C) I only

23. Which of the following is NOT an informal amendment to the Constitution?

    (A) The President will have a Cabinet of advisors.

    (B) The electoral college will be winner-take-all in each state.

    (C) The President may use an executive agreement instead of signing a treaty with a foreign country.

    (D) A two-party system will exist in the United States.

    (E) The House of Representatives will have 435 members.

24. When an informal amendment is violated, what is most likely to occur?

    (A) It will become a formal amendment.

    (B) The Supreme Court will review the issue.

    (C) Congress will pass a law covering the issue in question.

    (D) The informal amendment will simply be discarded and, in effect, repealed.

    (E) The President will publicly speak in favor of the violated amendment.

25. Which of the following best describes the body of American constitutional law?

    (A) It is rigid and inflexible.

    (B) It is completely fluid and easily changeable.

    (C) It combines elements of long-lasting consistency with needed flexibility.

    (D) It includes only a Preamble, seven Articles and twenty-seven Amendments.

    (E) Informal amendments are permanent; more can be added but none can be subtracted.

AP United States Government & Politics Review

THE FEDERAL GOVERNMENT

THE LEGISLATIVE BRANCH

Legislative power is vested in a bicameral Congress, which is the subject of Article I of the Constitution. The expressed or delegated powers are set forth in Section 8 and can be divided into several broad categories. Economic powers include:

1) to lay and collect taxes,
2) to borrow money,
3) to regulate foreign and interstate commerce,
4) to coin money and regulate its value, and
5) to establish rules concerning bankruptcy.

Judicial powers are comprised of the following:

1) to establish courts inferior to the Supreme Court,
2) to provide punishment for counterfeiting, and
3) to define and punish piracies and felonies committed on the high seas.

War powers of Congress are enumerated as follows:

1) to declare war,
2) to raise and support armies,
3) to provide and maintain a navy, and
4) to provide for organizing, arming, and calling forth the militia.

Other general peace powers include:

1) to establish uniform rules on naturalization,
2) to establish post offices and post roads,
3) to promote science and the arts by issuing patents and copyrights, and
4) to exercise jurisdiction over the seat of the federal government (District of Columbia).

In addition, the Constitution includes the so-called "elastic clause," which grants Congress implied powers to implement the delegated powers.

The Constitution also grants Congress the power to discipline federal officials through impeachment and removal from office. The House of Representatives has the power to charge officials (impeach), and the Senate is empowered to conduct the trials. These powers have been invoked infrequently. More significant is the Senate's power to confirm presidential appointments (to the Cabinet, federal judiciary, and major bureaucracies) and to ratify treaties. Both houses are involved in choosing a President and Vice-President if no majority is achieved in the Electoral College. The House of Representatives votes for the President from among the top three electoral candidates, with each state delegation casting one vote. The Senate votes for Vice-President. This power has been exercised only twice, in the disputed elections of 1800 and 1824.

In Article V, the Constitution empowers Congress to propose amendments. A two-thirds majority in both houses is necessary for passage. In addition, amendments may be proposed by the legislatures of two-thirds of the states. In order to be ratified, three-fourths of the states must approve (through their legislatures or by way of special conventions, as in the case of the repeal of Prohibition).

Article I, Section 9, specifically denies certain powers to the national legislature. Congress is prohibited from suspending the privilege of *habeas corpus* unless the nation is in a state of rebellion or has been invaded. Other prohibitions include: 1) the passage of export taxes, 2) the passage of *ex post facto* laws, 3) the withdrawal of money from the national treasury without an appropriations law, and 4) the favored treatment of one port or state over another with respect to commerce.

The Committee System

The work of Congress is organized around a committee system. The standing committees are permanent and deal with such matters as agriculture, the armed services, the budget, energy, finance, and foreign policy. Special, or select, committees are established to deal with specific issues and usually have a limited duration. An example from recent history of a powerful select committee was the Senate Select Committee on Presidential Campaign Activities, which investigated the Watergate scandal. Joint committees comprise members from both the House and the Senate, and they often deal with routine matters. The most short-lived yet often the most significant committees are the conference committees which must iron out differences between House and Senate versions of a bill.

One committee unique to the House of Representatives is the powerful Rules Committee. Thousands of bills are introduced on the floor of the House each term, and the Rules Committee acts as a clearinghouse to weed out those that are deemed unworthy of consideration before the full House.

Constitutionally, all revenue-raising bills must originate in the House of Representatives. Consequently, all tax measures are sent to the powerful House Ways and Means Committee.

Committee membership is organized on party lines, with seniority being a key factor, although in recent years length of service in the Congress has diminished in importance in the determination of chairmanships. The Democrats and the Republicans have special committees (e.g., the Senate Democratic Steering Committee) to consider assignments. The composition of each committee is largely based on the ratio of each party in the Congress as a whole. The party with the majority has a larger number of members on each committee. The chairmen of the standing committees are selected by the leaders of the majority party. Since the 1970s, committees have been required by law to adhere to written rules of procedure. This reform has diminished somewhat the power of committee chairmen, some of whom had previously behaved like virtual dictators in the control they exercised over their members. Generally though, committee chairs (and subcommittee chairs) are granted along the following criteria:

1) Member of the majority party in their chamber of Congress, the Senate or the House of Representatives
2) Hold committee seniority (not total congressional seniority) among the members of their own party in the committee
3) Hold no other chair positions

The Legislative Process

The legislative process is at once cumbersome and time-consuming. A bill can be introduced in either Chamber (with the exception of revenue bills, which must originate in the House), where it is referred to the appropriate committee. Next, the bill travels to a subcommittee which will schedule a hearing if the members deem that it has merit. The bill is reported back to the full committee, which must then decide whether or not to send it to the full chamber to be debated. A bill originating in the House must pass through the Rules Committee before going on to the full House. If the bill passes in the full chamber, it is then sent on to the other chamber to begin the process all over again. Any differences in the House and Senate versions of a bill must be resolved in a conference committee before being passed along to the President for consideration. Most of the thousands of bills introduced in Congress die in committee, with *less than five percent* becoming law.

Debate on major bills is a key step in the legislative process because of the tradition of attaching amendments at this stage. In the House, the rules of debate are designed to enforce limits necessitated by the size of the body (435 members). On the other hand, in the substantially smaller Senate (100 members), unlimited debate is allowed. Here, the filibuster, a tactic to block legislation, can delay action indefinitely. It was used on several occasions in the 1950s and 1960s by southern Senators seeking to kill civil rights legislation. Cloture is a parliamentary procedure that can be invoked by three-fifths of the membership to limit debate and bring a filibuster to conclusion.

House of Representatives

Constitutional qualifications for the House of Representatives state that members must be at least twenty-five years of age, must have been U.S. citizens for at least seven years, and must be residents of the state that sends them to Congress. Tradition, but not law, dictates that members of the House live in the districts they represent. According to the Reapportionment Act of 1929, the size of the House is fixed at 435 members who serve terms of two years in length. The presiding officer in the House and generally the most powerful member is the Speaker, who is the leader of the political party of the majority. In recent history, the post has been dominated by Democrats. Sam Rayburn of Texas dominated the position throughout most of the 1940s and 1950s. Congressman Thomas "Tip" O'Neill, a colorful Democrat from Massachusetts, presided over the House during the Carter and Reagan administrations. Another Democrat, Texas's Jim Wright, succeeded O'Neill, serving from 1987 to 1989, when he was forced into retirement by charges that stemmed from an ethics complaint that had been lodged against him by Minority Whip Newt Gingrich. The Democratic majority then voted in Thomas S. Foley of Washington, who held the Speakership through 1995. The mid-term election in 1994 saw the House shift to a Republican majority for the first time since the Eisenhower administration in 1954—a feat credited largely to a campaign strategy (known as the Contract With America) devised by Gingrich—and, as a result, his colleagues elected him Speaker. Like Wright, Gingrich, too, would be charged, in 1996, with House ethics violations. He was reprimanded and fined. Though he continued to serve as Speaker in 1997, the Georgian was weakened politically.

In 1998, much of the American public perceived Republicans in Congress as more interested in attacking President Clinton than in working to solve more pressing problems. In the 1998 congressional elections, the Republicans lost seats in the House of Representatives, an extremely unusual event for the party that did not hold the executive branch during a mid-term election. Gingrich and his leadership were blamed for this outcome, and he was removed as Speaker of the House. Replacing Gingrich led to something of a power struggle. The first candidate for Speaker of the House, Rep. Robert Livingston, did not take the post due to revelations about his personal life. Rep. J. Dennis Hastert ultimately became House Speaker, but could do little to change the focus of the House of Representatives to other issues. Throughout 1998 and into 1999, Clinton's scandals continued to dominate the agenda of the House of Representatives, and its reputation (as well as that of the President) suffered as a result.

The Senate

Members of the Senate are elected to terms of six years in length on a staggered basis so that one-third of the body is up for re-election in each national election year. The President of the Senate is the Vice-President of the U.S., and as such he has a largely symbolic role, voting only in case of a tie. The presiding officer is the President *pro tempore*, an honor customarily conferred on the senior member of the party of the majority. More visible and generally recognized as the leaders of the Senate are the majority and minority leaders.

DRILL

THE LEGISLATIVE BRANCH

DIRECTIONS: Carefully read and answer each of the following questions, which are based on the information that you have just read.

26. The chairmen of the standing committees of Congress are chosen

    (A) by the voters

    (B) according to a strict seniority system

    (C) by the President

    (D) by the leaders of both political parties

    (E) by the leaders of the majority party

27. Bills may be introduced in either house of Congress with the exception of _____ bills, which must originate in the House of Representatives.

(A)   agricultural   (D)   military

(B)   revenue   (E)   education

(C)   foreign aid

28.   Article I grants Congress the power to do all of the following EXCEPT

(A)   declare war   (D)   regulate interstate trade

(B)   collect taxes   (E)   establish federal courts

(C)   appoint federal judges

29.   The "elastic clause" grants Congress

(A)   delegated powers   (D)   expressed powers

(B)   inherent powers   (E)   war powers

(C)   implied powers

30.   Permanent committees dealing with such matters as agriculture, finance, and foreign policy are known as

(A)   select committees   (D)   standing committees

(B)   conference committees (E)   *ad hoc* committees

(C)   joint committees

31.   The House Committee that acts as a "clearinghouse" for the thousands of bills introduced each term is called the

(A)   Rules Committee

(B)   Ways and Means Committee

(C)   Steering Committee

(D)   Legislative Committee

(E)   Clearing Committee

32.   Constitutional Amendments must pass in both houses of Congress by

(A)   a simple majority   (D)   a three-fourths majority

(B)   a three-fifths majority (E)   unanimous consent

(C)   a two-thirds majority

33. Article I, Section 9 prohibits Congress from exercising all of the following powers EXCEPT

   (A) the passage of import taxes

   (B) the passage of export taxes

   (C) the passage of *ex post facto* laws

   (D) the withdrawal of money from the Treasury without an appropriations law

   (E) the favored treatment of one port or state over another in matters of commerce

34. The use of the filibuster, a tactic to block the passage of legislation,

   (A) has been declared unconstitutional by the Supreme Court

   (B) is allowed in the both the House and the Senate

   (C) can be ended by a majority vote

   (D) was used in the 1950s and 1960s to stall civil rights legislation

   (E) can be ended by executive order

35. The number of members in the House of Representatives

   (A) changes after each national census

   (B) was fixed at 435 by the Constitution

   (C) is based on an equal number from each house

   (D) was fixed at 435 by the Reapportionment Act of 1929

   (E) was fixed at 435 by a constitutional amendment

36. All of the following are true about the office of the Speaker of the House EXCEPT

   (A) the Speaker is the leader of the majority party in the House of Representatives

   (B) the Speaker is chosen directly by the American people

   (C) the Speaker is the most powerful individual member of the House of Representatives

   (D) the Speaker presides over the House of Representatives

   (E) the Speaker serves a six-year term

THE EXECUTIVE BRANCH

Article II of the Constitution deals with the powers and duties of the President. The chief executive's constitutional responsibilities include the following:

1) to serve as Commander-in-Chief,
2) to negotiate treaties (with the approval of two-thirds of the Senate),
3) to appoint ambassadors, judges, and other high officials (with the consent of the Senate),
4) to grant pardons and reprieves for those convicted of federal crimes (except in impeachment cases),
5) to seek counsel of department heads (Cabinet secretaries),
6) to recommend legislation,
7) to meet with representatives of foreign states, and
8) to see that federal laws are "faithfully executed."

The President's powers with respect to foreign policy are paramount. Civilian control of the military is a fundamental concept embodied in the naming of the President as Commander-in-Chief: in essence, the nation's leading general. As such, he can make battlefield decisions as well as shape military policy. This role has expanded in the twentieth century, particularly with respect to such recent conflicts as Korea and Vietnam, where Presidents Truman, Eisenhower, Kennedy, Johnson, and Nixon, respectively, made war without formal declarations from Congress. Although the War Powers Act of 1973 was designed to limit the President's ability to commit American troops to foreign soil without informing Congress within forty-eight hours and prohibits him from leaving them engaged in conflict for more than sixty days without authorization from Congress, three contemporary Presidents—Reagan and both Presidents Bush—have still exercised broad military powers, as in Grenada, Panama, and Iraq.

In 1990, Iraq, led by Saddam Hussein, invaded Kuwait. President Bush led an international coalition to pressure Iraq to withdraw. The United States sent a large military force to the region. Since it was possible that a military action would extend beyond the time limits of the War Powers Act, Bush sought and received Senate authorization for military action. An invasion that drove Iraq's forces from Kuwait followed. Though there was never a formal declaration of war, the authorization of force from the Senate gave the President the ability to use force as part of his foreign policy. More recently, President Clinton has used U.S. troops in Somalia, Haiti, and the former Republic of Yugoslavia.

Foreign Policy

The President, in essence, shapes American foreign policy with his treaty-making and diplomatic powers. Treaties are usually negotiated with representatives of foreign states through the efforts of the Secretary of State, and they must be ratified by a majority of two-thirds in the Senate. An example of a controversial treaty which was rejected by the Senate despite the President's extraordinary efforts to garner support was that ending World War I. Despite President Wilson's unprecedented involvement in the negotiations that produced the Versailles Treaty, an isolationist circle within the Senate refused to pass it due to the inclusion of a clause calling for American membership in the League of Nations. Presidents can circumvent the Senate by executive agreements with other nations. These must relate to treaties that have been previously negotiated. President Johnson used this power extensively to conduct the Vietnam War with minimal congressional involvement.

As a world diplomat, the President of the United States receives foreign heads of state and their representatives and formally acknowledges the existence of a government through the power of recognition. In recent years, U.S. presidents have attended a series of highly publicized summit conferences with foreign heads of state, particularly those of the former Soviet Union. These meetings have produced mixed results, although some, as in the case of the Nixon and Brezhnev summit in 1972 which led to SALT I, have been historically significant.

The Presidency

Attaining the presidency has evolved into an arduous, costly, and at times painful process despite the relatively simple constitutional requirements for qualifying for the office. Candidates must be at least thirty-five years of age, must be natural-born citizens, and must have resided in the United States for a minimum of fourteen years. Article II provides for an Electoral College in which each state has as many votes as it has members of Congress to formally select the President. Over time, the Electoral College has become a ceremonial body due to the control the major political parties have over the election process. After the political parties have selected their nominees via caucuses, primaries, and conventions, the general election is held in November every four years. The electors are chosen by popular vote on a winner-take-all basis (with the exception of Maine, which has a district plan), so that the candidate who receives a majority of the popular votes in each state receives all of the state's electoral votes. Electors meet in their respective state capitals in December and cast their ballots for President and Vice-President. A majority of 270 electoral votes is needed for election. If no majority is achieved, the House of Representatives is empowered to choose a President from among the top three candidates. In this case, each state casts one ballot, with a majority of 26 needed to win.

Presidential succession has become a key issue in recent years. The Constitution states that if the President dies or cannot perform his duties, the "powers and duties" of the office shall "devolve" on the Vice-President. Until recently, when the Vice-President assumed the Office of President, his former position was left vacant. Since the passage of the Twenty-Fifth Amendment in 1967, the

President has the power to appoint a new Vice-President (with the approval of a majority of both houses of Congress). In 1973, President Nixon invoked this power when Vice-President Spiro Agnew resigned due to criminal allegations and appointed Congressman Gerald Ford as his replacement. Ford in turn assumed the Office of President when Nixon resigned under threat of impeachment. Ford then appointed Governor Nelson Rockefeller of New York as his own replacement. The Twenty-Fifth Amendment also provides for the Vice-President to serve as acting President if the President is disabled or otherwise unable to carry out the duties of his office.

The Cabinet

Although the Constitution makes no mention of a formal Cabinet as such, since the days of George Washington, chief executives have relied on department heads to aid in the decision-making process. Washington's Cabinet[*] was composed of a Secretary of State, a Secretary of the Treasury, a Secretary of War, and an Attorney-General. Today there are fifteen Cabinet departments, with Homeland Security being the most recently created post in October 2001. Traditionally, the heads of the State and Defense departments are highly visible and indispensable in helping the President to formulate foreign policy. The Cabinet also has an important role in setting domestic policy. For instance, the Department of Education administers most federal education programs. The Department of Treasury and the Department of Labor have a great deal of influence over economic policy.

The President also has broad powers in domestic policy. The most significant domestic policy tool is the President's budget, which he submits to Congress. Though Congress must approve all spending, the President has a great deal of power in budget negotiations. The President can use also use considerable resources in persuading Congress to enact legislation, and he also has opportunities, such as the State of the Union Address, to reach out directly to the American people to convince them to support these presidential policies.

DRILL

THE EXECUTIVE BRANCH

DIRECTIONS: Carefully read and answer each of the following questions, which are based on the information that you have just read.

37. Characteristics of executive agreements include all of the following EXCEPT that

    (A) they are similar to treaties

[*]The term *Cabinet* was coined by James Madison in 1793.

    (B)   they must be ratified by the Senate

    (C)   they must be related to treaties previously negotiated

    (D)   presidents use them to circumvent the Senate

    (E)   they were used extensively to conduct the war in Vietnam

38.   The War Powers Act of 1973

    (A)   enlarges the President's power to commit troops to foreign soil

    (B)   calls for the President to notify Congress within twenty-four hours of ordering military forces into operation

    (C)   prohibits the President from leaving troops engaged in combat for more than thirty days without authorization from Congress

    (D)   has crippled the President's power to exercise his constitutional military powers

    (E)   prohibits the President from leaving troops engaged in conflict for more than sixty days without authorization from Congress

39.   All of the following are true of the Twenty-Fifth Amendment EXCEPT that

    (A)   it allows the President to appoint a Vice-President if a vacancy occurs

    (B)   it allows the President to name a successor of his own choice if he leaves office prematurely

    (C)   it provides for the Vice-President to serve as acting President if the President is temporarily unable to perform his duties

    (D)   it was invoked by President Nixon when Vice-President Agnew resigned from office

    (E)   under its terms Gerald Ford became the first appointed President

40.   The President's constitutional duties include all of the following EXCEPT

    (A)   negotiating treaties

    (B)   granting pardons and reprieves in federal cases

    (C)   passing legislation

    (D)   appointing high-ranking federal officials

    (E)   executing the laws

41.   Candidates for the Offices of President and Vice-President

   (A)   must be at least 30 years of age

   (B)   must run in all of the presidential primaries

   (C)   must be lifelong residents of the United States

   (D)   must be native-born citizens

   (E)   must be members of an established political party

42.   The Electoral College

   (A)   functions largely independently of the major political parties

   (B)   provides for a winner-take-all system of election in all fifty states

   (C)   requires that the candidate who receives a plurality of the votes will be elected to the Office of the President

   (D)   meets continuously until a President is chosen

   (E)   requires that a candidate receive a majority of 270 electoral votes in order to be elected

43.   Members of the Cabinet are nominated by

   (A)   the President

   (B)   members of the President's party in Congress

   (C)   the Electoral College

   (D)   the party's convention

   (E)   the Vice-President

THE JUDICIAL BRANCH

Article III of the Constitution states that "the judicial power of the United States shall be vested in one Supreme Court, and in such inferior courts as the Congress may from time to time ordain and establish." Hence, the Supreme Court is the only court mentioned specifically in the document. Yet our contemporary judicial branch consists of thousands of courts and is, in essence, a dual system, with each state having its own judicial structure functioning simultaneously with a complete set of federal courts. The most significant piece of legislation with reference to establishing a federal court network was the Judiciary Act of 1789. This law organized the Supreme Court and set up the federal district courts (13) and the circuit (appeal) courts (3). In 1891, the U.S. Court of Appeals was created to relieve the Supreme Court of some of its heavy case load. The district courts have original jurisdiction to hear federal cases involving both civil and criminal law. Each state has at least one federal district court, while the larger states are divided into two or more jurisdictions. These courts handle thousands of cases annually and are plagued by long delays. Federal cases on appeal are heard in one of the Courts of Appeals. The decisions of these courts are final, except for those cases that are accepted for review by the Supreme Court.

The Supreme Court today is made up of a Chief Justice and eight Associate Justices. They are appointed for life by the President with the approval of the Senate, and they are routinely, but not exclusively, drawn from the ranks of the federal judiciary. In recent years, the appointment of Supreme Court justices has been the focus of intense scrutiny and in the cases of Robert Bork and Clarence Thomas, the center of heated political controversy.

Each year, thousands of cases are appealed to the Supreme Court, but relatively few are accepted for consideration. The Court chooses its cases based on whether or not they address substantial federal issues. If four of the nine justices vote to consider a case, then it will be added to the agenda. This is known as the "Rule of Four." In such cases, writs of certiorari are issued, calling up the records from a lower court. The justices are given detailed briefs and hear oral arguments. Reaching a decision is a complicated process. The justices may scrutinize the details of the case with reference to the provisions of the Constitution. Precedence (*stare decisis*) is a key concept borrowed from the British legal tradition. If two cases are generally similar, then the decision in the earlier controversy usually stands. Breaks with the concept of precedence have sometimes had historic ramifications, as when the 1954 Warren Court reversed *Plessy vs. Ferguson* (1896) and declared "separate but equal" accommodations to be unconstitutional. This decision (*Brown vs. Board of Education*) led to the school desegregation crises of the Civil Rights Era.

Judicial Review

The authority of courts to declare laws and executive actions to be unconstitutional is known as judicial review. This procedure was established in 1803 with the case of *Marbury vs. Madison.* In the last days of his term, Federalist President John Adams hastily appointed several justices of the peace for Washington, D.C., the so-called midnight judges. The incoming Democratic-Republican President Thomas Jefferson instructed his Secretary of State James Madison not to deliver the appointments. One of the disappointed justices, William Marbury, petitioned the Supreme Court to issue a writ of mandamus (a court order instructing a public official to perform his duties) to compel Jefferson to deliver the commissions. Chief Justice John Marshall, himself a Federalist, wrote the unanimous opinion refusing Marbury's request on the grounds that the section of the Judiciary Act of 1789 empowering the Supreme Court to issue writs of mandamus was unconstitutional. Hence, the power of judicial review was established. The Supreme Court is not alone in this power, as most state and federal courts may also exercise judicial review.

When all of the justices on the Supreme Court agree, the opinion issued is unanimous. In the case of split decisions, a majority opinion is written by one of the justices in agreement. Sometimes a justice will agree with the majority but for a different principle, in which case he/she can write a concurring opinion explaining the different point of view. Justices who do not vote with the majority may choose to write dissenting opinions to air their conflicting arguments. Dissenting opinions are often the basis for the majority opinion in cases where the Supreme Court reverses a previous decision.

According to Article III of the Constitution, the Supreme Court may exercise both original and appellate jurisdiction. Original jurisdiction relates to cases in which a state is a party to cases involving consuls, ambassadors, and other public ministers. By and large, the vast majority of cases that reach the Supreme Court do so on appeal from both lower federal courts and state supreme courts. It is the "court of last resort" in the appeals process, and its decisions stand.

Article III also outlines those conditions under which federal (as opposed to state) courts have original jurisdiction. These include:

1) cases in which the Constitution is involved,
2) cases involving federal laws,
3) cases dealing with treaties with foreign states and with Native American tribes,
4) cases arising out of crimes committed on the high seas or disputes over maritime transactions,
5) cases in which the U.S. government is a party,
6) cases stemming from disputes between two or more states,
7) controversies between citizens of different states,
8) conflicts between a state and citizens of another state,
9) disputes involving U.S. citizens and foreign nations, and
10) cases affecting public ministers and consuls.

In addition to the Supreme Court, the federal district courts, and the courts of appeals, several special courts at the federal level have been created by Congress. These courts are not addressed in Article III, for they deal with matters within the realm of congressional responsibility. The U.S. Tax Court handles conflicts between citizens and the Internal Revenue Service. The Court of

Claims was designed to hear cases in which citizens bring suit against the U.S. government. Other special courts include the Court of International Trade, the Court of Customs and Patent Appeals, and the Court of Military Appeals.

Though the Federal courts—especially the Supreme Court—have the final authority in interpretation of the Constitution, the judicial branch has no enforcement mechanism. It relies on the executive and the legislative branches to respect and abide its decisions. Because justices are appointed for life, they need not consider public opinion in deciding cases. However, the extent to which the Court responds to public opinion and the positions of the other branches of government is a matter of some controversy among political scientists and other observers. Some argue that the Supreme Court cannot stray too far from public opinion in deciding cases, while others argue that Court decisions are an important factor in changing public opinion.

Another important controversy is how the Court interprets the Constitution. Some argue that the Court should be guided by the original intent of the authors of the Constitution, while others argue that because of social changes and modern conditions, the Court should interpret Constitutional provisions broadly.

DRILL

THE JUDICIAL BRANCH

DIRECTIONS: Carefully read and answer each of the following questions, which are based on the information that you have just read.

44. Article III of the Constitution

    (A) set up the federal district court system

    (B) organized the U.S. Supreme Court

    (C) established the legislative courts

    (D) set forth the instances in which federal courts have jurisdiction

    (E) organized the courts of appeal

45. The dual court system refers to

    (A) the district courts and the federal appeals courts

    (B) the constitutional and the legislative courts

    (C) civil and criminal courts

(D) the Supreme Court and the U.S. Courts of Appeals

(E) separate federal and state court systems

46. The term *stare decisis* means

(A) "separate but equal"   (D) "a concurring opinion"

(B) "let the decision stand"   (E) "original jurisdiction"

(C) "judicial review"

47. The Supreme Court decides to hear cases on appeal

(A) whenever a state supreme court requests an opinion

(B) in all capital cases

(C) if they address substantial federal issues

(D) if a writ of mandamus is issued

(E) if a writ of certiorari is submitted for consideration

48. The Supreme Court's jurisdiction encompasses all of the following situations EXCEPT

(A) a case involving an ambassador

(B) review of a federal executive order

(C) review of a piece of federal legislation

(D) a Secret Service agent suspected of internal espionage

(E) a case in which a state is a party

49. The procedure of judicial review was clearly established in

(A) Article III of the Constitution

(B) *Plessy vs. Ferguson*

(C) *Marbury vs. Madison*

(D) the Preamble to the Constitution

(E) *Brown vs. Board of Education*

50. The case of a U.S. citizen bringing suit against the federal government would be heard first in the

(A)   Court of Claims   (D)   District Court

(B)   Supreme Court   (E)   Court of Appeals

(C)   Tax Court

51.   Dissenting opinions of the Supreme Court are important because

(A)   they are usually written by the Chief Justice

(B)   they are often used by Congress to guide legislation

(C)   they can be used as a basis for the Supreme Court to reverse precedent

(D)   they express the President's opinion on a Supreme Court decision

(E)   they help the Supreme Court decide which cases it will hear

THE CLINTON IMPEACHMENT

The Constitution provides for the removal of a President by a process called impeachment. Though an exceptional event, the impeachment of President Clinton in 1998 reveals a great deal about the interaction of the various branches of government, and how the separation of powers works, and how public opinion can influence the outcome of events.

Kenneth Starr, an independent counsel originally appointed to investigate possible wrongdoing by President Clinton in the Whitewater real estate development, investigated charges of perjury and obstruction of justice by the President in connection with testimony in the Paula Jones sexual harassment lawsuit. After Starr presented his report to the House of Representatives, it began impeachment proceedings. First, the Articles of Impeachment were passed in the Judiciary Committee and were then sent to the full House. The House impeached the President when it voted to approve the Articles of Impeachment.

The Senate became the court where the President would be tried. Supreme Court Chief Justice William Rehnquist presided over the trial. The House Managers, members selected by the House of Representatives, served as the prosecuting attorneys, while the President used his own lawyers as defense attorneys. Though the Constitution provides the general outline for impeachment proceedings, since it had occurred only one other time in U.S. history, the Senate had to make a number of decisions about specific aspects of the trial.

After both sides presented their case, the Senate voted to acquit Clinton on the charges of perjury and obstruction of justice. Throughout the process, several factors influenced the outcome of the event. Public opinion polls showed that though most Americans believed that Clinton had done wrong, his wrongdoings did not warrant removal from office. Many members of Congress paid close attention to these polls during the process. Some Republican members of the House of Representatives believed they had an obligation to make sure the President was impeached to answer the charges against him. Much of the process was broadcast by television, which gave Americans an opportunity to see it as it happened. Finally, though the President was acquitted, his reputation and public image were damaged by the scrutiny of his actions while he was in the White House.

DRILL

THE CLINTON IMPEACHMENT

DIRECTIONS: Carefully read and answer each of the following questions, which are based on the information that you have just read.

52. President Clinton was not removed from office following impeachment because

   (A) the independent counsel, Kenneth Starr, was found to be guilty of wrongdoing

   (B) the House of Representatives did not approve the Articles of Impeachment

   (C) the Supreme Court decided that the charges against President Clinton did not warrant impeachment

   (D) the Senate did not have the two-thirds majority necessary to convict the President

   (E) Newt Gingrich was defeated in his 1998 Congressional election

THE FEDERAL BUREAUCRACY

In addition to the President's Cabinet, a series of independent agencies, as well as the Executive Office of the President, make up the so-called federal bureaucracy. The term itself, often used derisively, refers to a large body of government administrators. The federal bureaucracy has grown from less than one thousand employees in the 1790s to an unwieldy body of close to three million in 2006.

Among the most important of the independent agencies are the regulatory commissions. The administrators of these powerful agencies are appointed by the President with the approval of the Senate. But unlike the Cabinet secretaries and other high appointees, they cannot be dismissed by the chief executive. These agencies were established to police big business, the first one being the Interstate Commerce Commission, which was created in 1887 in response to popular protest against the abuses of the powerful railway industry. Today it also regulates surface and water transportation, as well as some pipelines. Other major regulatory agencies of the federal government include:

1) the Federal Trade Commission, which is the main consumer protection agency of the federal government,
2) the Consumer Product Safety Commission, which sets standards of safety for manufactured products,
3) the Securities and Exchange Commission, which monitors the sale of stocks and bonds,
4) the Commodity Futures Trading Commission, which oversees practices in the sale of agricultural and mining resources,
5) the Federal Reserve System, which is responsible for the nation's banking industry,
6) the Federal Communications Commission, which regulates the airwaves,
7) the National Labor Relations Board, which supervises labor-management practices, and
8) the Nuclear Regulatory Commission, which licenses and inspects nuclear power plants.

These independent agencies wield so much power that they have been referred to as the "fourth branch of the federal government." In recent years, under the administrations of Carter and Reagan, and both Bush administrations, however, the trend has been toward deregulation.

Government Corporations

Another category of bureaucratic agencies includes the independent executive agencies and the government corporations. Some of the key executive agencies include the Central Intelligence Agency, the National Aeronautics and Space Administration, the Civil Rights Commission, and the Environmental Protection Agency. These agencies do not enjoy Cabinet status, but nonetheless are powerful entities with large workforces and impressive budgets. The President appoints their top-level executives with the approval of the Senate.

Government corporations are commercial enterprises established by Congress to perform certain necessary services. They trace their historical roots back to the First Bank of the United States, which was established under Secretary of the Treasury Alexander Hamilton in 1791. A more recent example of the government corporation is the Federal Deposit Insurance Corporation (FDIC), which insures bank deposits and which has been unusually active during the 2001–2002 recession due to a rash of bank failures. The Tennessee Valley Authority was established under the New Deal of Franklin Roosevelt. Originally, it was conceived as a project to revive a depressed region, and today it oversees the generation of electric power in the states of the Tennessee Valley. The largest of the government corporations and the most familiar to the general public is the U.S. Postal Service, which was originally a Cabinet department.

The Executive Office

The Executive Office of the President comprises several critical agencies and departments which oversee important administrative functions. Among the most powerful are the Office of Management and Budget, the Council of Economic Advisors, the Council on Environmental Quality, and the National Security Council, which advises the President on matters both domestic and foreign that threaten the safety of the nation.

The large and powerful federal bureaucracy shapes and administers government policy. It is inherently political despite sporadic efforts throughout the years to maintain the integrity of the bureaucratic staff. Dating back to the administrations of Andrew Jackson in the late 1820s, the practice of handing out government jobs in return for political favors (the spoils system) had been the rule. In response to a drive for reform in the 1870s, Congress passed the Civil Service Act (the Pendleton Act) in 1883 which established the framework for the modern-day civil service. Under this law, the government is required to recruit federal workers on the basis of merit related to a competitive exam and to provide job security. A "veterans preference" policy does exist which boosts the scores of those who were honorably discharged from the military. The Hatch Act of 1939 placed restrictions on the political activities of civil service employees in an attempt to ensure the neutrality of government workers.

In recent years, as with the regulatory agencies, there has been a drive to streamline the bureaucracy. Presidents Carter and Reagan both made efforts to downsize the amount of paperwork stemming from bureaucratic agencies and to reduce the size of the federal workforce. More recently, former Vice-President Gore dedicated himself to monitoring the number of rules emanating from federal agencies in a continuing effort to "streamline" government.

Meanwhile, President Clinton, the first Democrat to be returned to the White House since Franklin Delano Roosevelt, told the nation that the days of a large, all-encompassing federal government—in so many aspects the legacy of FDR's New Deal—were over.

DRILL

THE FEDERAL BUREAUCRACY

DIRECTIONS: Carefully read and answer each of the following questions, which are based on the information that you have just read.

53. The largest of the government corporations is the

   (A) Tennessee Valley Authority

   (B) Bank of the United States

   (C) U.S. Postal Service

   (D) Federal Deposit Insurance Corporation

   (E) Environmental Protection Agency

54. The civil service system was originally established to

   (A) provide jobs for veterans

   (B) eliminate the abuses of the spoils system

   (C) provide equal opportunities for women and minorities

   (D) restrict the political activities of government employees

   (E) investigate civil rights abuses

55. In recent years presidential policy with respect to the federal bureaucracy has been to

   (A) favor an increase in the number of workers to cope with the complexity of federal programs

   (B) favor significant budget increases to fund new programs

   (C) favor a downsizing of the workforce

    (D)   request the creation of new agencies to regulate the transportation industry

    (E)   request the elimination of the Central Intelligence Agency

56.   All of the following are true of the administrators of the regulatory commissions EXCEPT that

    (A)   they are appointed by the President

    (B)   they must be approved by the Senate

    (C)   they are expected to be non-political in their recommendations

    (D)   they can be dismissed by the President

    (E)   they serve for a fixed number of years

57.   The first regulatory agency to be created (1887) was the

    (A)   Interstate Commerce Commission

    (B)   Federal Trade Commission

    (C)   National Labor Relations Board

    (D)   Federal Reserve System

    (E)   Securities and Exchange Commission

58.   All of the following are categorized as independent executive agencies EXCEPT the

    (A)   Central Intelligence Agency

    (B)   National Aeronautics and Space Administration

    (C)   Civil Rights Commission

    (D)   Environmental Protection Agency

    (E)   Federal Deposit Insurance Corporation

AP United States Government & Politics Review

PUBLIC POLICY

Public policy is how the government implements the decisions of the public and politicians. In a modern state, once a law is passed, it is up to professional officials to find the best way to implement the law. The government has established a network of bureaus, offices, and departments in order for this to happen. In general, except at the highest levels, policy-makers are part of the civil service, and do not owe their positions to elected officials. These professionals are often called bureaucrats. Even though they do not officially have the authority to make law, in the process of implementing laws through policy, they may have a great deal of discretion. In addition, lawmakers may consult with policy-makers to work out complex policy directives. In many cases, legislation establishes an agency and charges it with a responsibility, but the agency determines how it will fulfill its mission. For instance, the Food and Drug Administration determines whether a drug is "safe and effective" by examining scientific evidence, and does not require legislative approval. That is why the bureaucracy is often called the "fourth branch" of government.

POLICY-MAKING IN THE FEDERAL SYSTEM

In the United States, the federal bureaucracy is the largest, most complex, and most important policy-making apparatus. Its tasks range from national defense to providing grants for the performing arts. In addition, it can also have a significant impact on policy-making at the state and local level. The federal government provides a great deal of funding to state and local agencies, and that funding often comes with specific requirements that states and localities must follow to receive it. For the most part, the federal government has more resources, especially funding and expertise, to implement policy than states, and states, therefore, rely on the federal government to acquire these resources.

The interaction between the federal government and state and local governments can be quite complex. In many cases, state governments have agencies that duplicate federal agencies. This is because states often have their own policies, so they must have agencies to implement them. Federal agencies, on the other hand, make sure that, throughout all the states, certain policies are consistent. The federal government, for instance, must regulate interstate commerce. Since food is often processed in one state but purchased in another, federal food safety guidelines ensure that all food meets minimum standards.

State, local, and federal governments also interact in funding programs. Some programs are funded by the federal government, but administered by the states. In some cases, states can choose to supplement the federal funding of these programs with their own money. The federal government usually regulates how the states can spend the money. However, in recent years, "block grants" have been used more often. The federal government provides money to a state or local government for a general purpose, such as reducing crime or improving education, but imposes relatively few requirements on how the states can spend the money. In the case of matching grants, the federal government provides money to a state in proportion to the money the state itself will spend on a program. State and local governments also make policy independent of the federal government, especially in areas such as education.

For the most part, policy-making in a federal system is a function of the executive branch. Most of the federal government is organized in what are called Cabinet-level organizations, such as the Department of Health and Human Services or the Department of the Treasury. Congress exercises influence through legislation, which can establish agencies, or in rare cases, disband agencies. Its largest impact, however, is through funding. Through the budget, Congress allocates resources. For instance, the Defense Department must receive budgetary approval before it can build, design, or purchase a new weapons system. Congress can cut an agency's budget, which will reduce its ability to carry out its tasks.

Courts also have a role in policy, though their impact can be less direct. In interpreting the law, courts determine whether a policy does indeed satisfy legislative and constitutional requirements. Courts can also require the legislative and executive branches to make policy in order to meet constitutional requirements. One prominent example of the court's influence on policy was when it ordered school districts to bus students outside of their neighborhood in order to desegregate schools. Courts can also require the other two branches of government to end a policy it deems to be in violation of other laws or the Constitution. In some cases, federal courts have restricted states' ability to make policy by deciding that state policies violate constitutional principles. The court's policymaking activities have been controversial, because some people argue that the court's involvement in policy areas, especially when it specifies a remedy, is a usurpation of the powers of the executive and legislative branches.

DRILL

POLICY-MAKING IN THE FEDERAL SYSTEM

DIRECTIONS: Carefully read and answer each of the following questions, which are based on the information that you have just read.

59. Which statement best describes the Supreme Court's role in public policy?

    (A) The Supreme Court makes recommendations to Congress and the President about policies regarding education.

    (B) The Supreme Court is responsible for policy regarding law enforcement.

    (C) The Supreme Court rules on the constitutionality of specific policies.

    (D) The Supreme Court provides block grants to states.

    (E) When the President and Congress cannot agree about a policy, the Supreme Court makes the decision.

60. Most public policy is the responsibility of

    (A) the executive branch

    (B) Senate committees

    (C) state governors

    (D) the legislative branch

    (E) the Vice-President

61. The federal government influences public policy at the state level by all of the following EXCEPT

    (A) providing funding for state programs

    (B) providing expertise to state agencies

    (C) providing block grants

    (D) mandating that states establish specific policies as a requirement for federal programs

    (E) requiring that states hire policy experts named by the federal government

62. Which of the following is true of most policy-makers?

    (A) They are elected by the people of various states.

    (B) They are members of the civil service, and are not political appointees.

    (C) They are appointed by the President.

    (D) Their appointments are confirmed by the Senate.

    (E) They are appointed for life.

63. Resources are allocated to various government agencies

    (A) through the federal budget

    (B) based on the President's decision

    (C) according to public opinion

    (D) through hearings conducted by the House of Representatives

    (E) by a committee composed of the President, Vice-President, and the Speaker of the House

---

FOREIGN POLICY

In the United States, foreign policy is exclusively in the domain of the federal government. The State Department, the Defense Department, and the National Security Council largely direct foreign policy. The National Security Council, or NSC, is not actually an agency, but a means to coordinating foreign policy. It includes a National Security Advisor, the President, the Vice President, the Secretary of State, and the Secretary of Defense.

Congress has relatively little influence in foreign policy. Of course, Congress does hold the "power of the purse." That is, it must agree to fund a President's foreign policy agenda, including war. Another traditionally important power has been to ratify treaties, and pick up with words "for instance" the Senate's power to ratify any treaty; for instance, the Senate refused to ratify the Versailles Treaty at the end of World War I. The War Powers Act is another tool Congress has to influence foreign policy. The Act requires Congress to approve the stationing of American troops overseas for more than 90 days. However, it has proven difficult for Congress to enforce the terms of the Act, in part because it can be perceived as opposing the American troops who are at risk. Even though Congress can do little if it opposes a particular foreign policy initiative, the President usually seeks Congressional support, in part to convince foreign nations that the United States is committed to a course of action. Thus, prior to the U.S. invasion of Iraq in 2003, George W. Bush sought and received congressional support for his proposed actions.

Unlike domestic policy, the conduct of foreign policy occurs in an environment of inconsistent rules. Enforcing international law can be difficult and costly. Foreign policy is complex, involving economic, military, and cultural factors. In addition to nations, significant foreign policy actors include the United Nations, other multi-national organizations such as the North Atlantic Treaty Organization (NATO), transnational corporations, and non-state political organizations, such as the Palestine Liberation Organization. An effective foreign policy seeks to achieve the strategic goals of the United States through understanding the goals and capabilities of other international organizations. Doing this requires accurate information, as well as an effective set of tools.

In conducting foreign policy, the President has a number of tools. International trade is an increasingly significant element in international relations, and economic sanctions are used to isolate nations that oppose United States policy. Most nations with which the United States trades enjoy most-favored-nation status, and the revocation of this status can be a significant part of U.S. policy. On the other hand, the United States can offer economic assistance to nations, especially if there is a perception that economic turmoil in another nation could have an impact on the economy of the United States. Other forms of assistance to nations can include arms sales or other forms of military aid (though this is used less frequently since the end of the Cold War) and other military assistance.

DRILL

FOREIGN POLICY

DIRECTIONS: Carefully read and answer each of the following questions, which are based on the information that you have just read.

64. Which of the following is the most important means of restricting the President's power in conducting foreign policy?

   (A) The role of the Senate in approving treaties

   (B) The role of public opinion

   (C) The National Security Council's advice to the President

(D)   The need to coordinate foreign policy with organizations such as the North Atlantic Treaty Organization and the United Nations

(E)   The ability of the states to limit the time American soldiers can be stationed overseas

65.   The President can use all of the following in conducting foreign policy EXCEPT

(A)   providing arms sales and other forms of military aid

(B)   providing economic aid

(C)   granting nations "most-favored-nation" status in conducting trade with the U.S.

(D)   allowing U.S. citizens to join other nations' armies

(E)   calling for international sanctions

66.   The War Powers Act

(A)   requires congressional approval for placing American troops in a combat situation for more than 90 days

(B)   requires congressional approval before the U.S. formally declares war

(C)   grants the National Security Council nearly unlimited power in time of war

(D)   prohibits United States troops from cooperation with United Nations operations

(E)   established the Department of State and Department of Defense

HOW POLICY AGENDAS ARE FORMED

In most cases, public policy is a response to the perception of a problem that requires action by a government. The policy could be a response to public pressure, or it could be the result of a crisis. A policy agenda is formed when one or more specific solutions to a problem are articulated and promoted. Public opinion can be a catalyst for the formation of a policy, but it cannot usually shape the policy itself. Many areas of policy are technical and complex, and require a great deal of expertise to fully understand. Public opinion may be adequate for identifying a problem, but cannot usually be used to craft a solution.

Often, public policy is initiated by an interest group. In some cases, the policy is specifically targeted to benefit a specific group, such as agricultural programs designed to help farmers. In other cases, a group advocates a policy to promote a public good, such as education programs.

Public policy differs from politics in that policy is not about deciding what ends the government should pursue; instead, it is about how government ought to achieve those ends. For instance, once the political process forms a decision that toxic waste sites must be cleaned up, it is up to policy-makers to decide how best to clean the sites, who will clean the sites, and the best way to pay for it. Good public policy is effective—that is, it achieves its ends, and it is efficient, in that it uses the fewest resources possible to achieve those ends. Good policy also avoids or minimizes negative, unintended consequences. Anticipating how well a policy will work is difficult, since most policy is an attempt to do something that has not been done before. Even when a policy has been tried before with the desired results, other factors can change the outcome. Therefore, once a policy is in place, it should be evaluated in order to find out if it is having the desired effects, that its costs do not outweigh its benefits, and that unintended or undesired effects are minimal.

Often the first step to forming a policy agenda is mobilizing public opinion. The public may not be aware that a problem exists. Only when a significant number of people recognize a problem can they be motivated to take action, or demand that government take action. This "grass roots" approach can be used by groups that work to promote the public interest, but it has also been used by interest groups that seek to shape policy by enlisting public support. Policy-makers must be convinced that a specific policy will provide a public benefit. A specific group that seeks a benefit must usually persuade decision-makers that the public in general will benefit as well. Other means to forming a policy agenda can include lobbying, working in coalition with other interest groups, and working directly with agencies charged with policy to influence the policy outcomes.

Individuals and organizations directly affected by the policy in question often try to influence policy outcomes. In addition to lobbying, interest groups can conduct research, develop approaches to public policy, and are often called upon by government officials to provide expertise and input regarding how the policy would affect an organization. In this way, groups or organizations directly affected by a policy can have a significant role in shaping policy. Groups directly affected by a policy will often testify to Congress or other policy-making bodies. Research can be an important part of the policy-making process. The government sponsors a great deal of research in order to help it make sound policy decisions. Common examples of government-sponsored research include unemployment figures, epidemiological studies, and product safety studies. Independent groups also conduct research in order to influence policy.

Experts and specialists usually make public policy. Elected officials also rely on experts to help them make decisions. It is often difficult for citizens to make informed judgments about the best course to take to achieve a desired end. However, experts frequently disagree with each other, and research findings can be contradictory. Organizations employ experts to promote a particular view and debate the issue with other experts. At times, policy debates are less about the most effective policy and more about who should receive the benefits or pay the costs of a policy decision. Hence, policy debates are often not much different from other kinds of political debates.

DRILL

HOW POLICY AGENDAS ARE FORMED

DIRECTIONS: Carefully read and answer each of the following questions, which are based on the information that you have just read.

67. Public opinion can have all of the following roles in the formation of a policy agenda EXCEPT

    (A) electing politicians who endorse a particular policy

    (B) putting pressure on government to solve a particular problem

    (C) providing experts to help develop policy

    (D) supporting "grass-roots" organizations that advocate a specific policy

    (E) writing letters to officials to try to influence policy

68. Which is the most important barrier to greater public participation in policy formation?

    (A) Most members of the public do not have sufficient time.

    (B) Most members of the public lack the expertise to makes public policy.

    (C) The public is largely indifferent to public policy issues.

    (D) The public is not usually aware of the kinds of problems public policy solves.

    (E) Most members of the public would only consider their own self-interest.

69. Evaluating whether a policy is efficient and effective is the role of

    (A) public opinion

    (B) the U.S. Senate

    (C) elections

    (D) policy researchers

    (E) lobbyists

70. In order to be implemented, in most cases, public policy should result in

    (A) a public benefit

    (B) support of the public

    (C) campaign contributions for its sponsors

    (D) consensus of expert opinion

    (E) grass roots support

POLICY AND POLITICAL PROCESS

Since policy involves the distribution of goods, it is part of a political process. The most rational or effective plan does not always become policy. Political institutions, including the executive and legislative branches and, to a lesser extent, the courts, are responsible for the general direction and content of policy. Often, politicians support a policy because their constituents favor it. Some policy alternatives are easier to explain and understand than others, and, therefore, receive more attention and support. Policy decisions also depend on the priorities of those in office. A President who favors a specific education program can be expected to try to generate support for the program by promoting it to the public and working with Congress and other branches of government to implement the policy. Getting policy passed into law usually requires compromises and deals. Many reluctant members of Congress have come to favor a policy when one result of the policy is significant federal spending in the home district or state.

Another significant aspect of public policy is who pays for the policy. Every policy has some cost associated with it. Determining who will bear the cost of a policy is usually a political process, not a function of bureaucratic institutions. A common option is called a "user fee," where those who benefit from a particular program will pay for all or part of it. Entrance fees at national parks to pay for park maintenance, and taxes added to the purchase of airline tickets to pay for federal aviation programs are common examples of user fees. Often, these fees are hidden, such as taxes on cigarettes that are included in the purchase price. Other ways to pay for programs are through taxes on specific industries or products.

The Policy Process

The formation of public policy can be understood as a two-part process. First, the political process determines the broad policy objectives. Second, the bureaucracy develops plans to implement that policy. For instance, the Environmental Protection Agency (EPA) cannot do much to improve air quality until Congress and the President enact legislation allowing it to do so. The interaction between the participants in policy formation is more complex. Individual members of Congress can request that the EPA relax its enforcement for certain industries or corporations, or they can request that the EPA investigate a specific corporation. The EPA may not have sufficient resources or technical expertise to implement all the elements of a policy, so it may choose to emphasize some at the expense of others.

In choosing one party over the other, voters can be understood as expressing a broad set of policy preferences. In general, the Republican Party favors fewer and smaller federal government programs, allowing the private sector more independence from government regulation and shifting government functions to state and local governments. The Democratic Party, on the other hand, tends to favor larger programs, is more willing to use governmental authority to regulate business, and is more willing to have the federal government responsible for programs than the states. Though there are many exceptions to these general characterizations, it is useful to help understand how elections influence policy outcomes, even when voters are unaware of the specific policy platforms of the party.

Party is not the only predictor of policy orientation. Politicians from rural areas tend to support programs that benefit agriculture, while politicians from urban areas tend to favor programs, such as mass transportation, that favor those areas. These kinds of policy orientations can help to form coalitions, where individuals and groups work to promote common interests, despite opposition on other issues. Labor unions and automobile manufacturers often work together to support policies that benefit the industry as a whole. Elected officials look to their constituents and other supporters, as well as their party, to guide their policy choices.

Elections themselves are often used as measures of the success or failure of a policy. Voting for a specific candidate is seen as approval of the candidate's policy. During an election, the voter has an opportunity to counter the influence of experts and other interest groups by voting for a candidate who favors a specific policy. However, the relationship between policy and elections is indirect. Rarely is a voter aware of all of a candidate's positions on policy. Many policy positions do not emerge as issues in elections, which makes it difficult for voters to learn about positions that may be important to the voter. Even if the information is available, the average voter will usually not expend the effort that may be required to learn about it.

Public policy is the consequence, or the output, of the political process. In a democracy, policy expertise is subordinate to the preferences of voters and their representatives. From time to time, this results in inefficient or ineffective policy. But most political observers believe that the problems of public policy in a democracy are outweighed by democratic accountability of public officials, both elected representatives and civil servants.

DRILL

POLICY AND POLITICAL PROCESS

DIRECTIONS: Carefully read and answer each of the following questions, which are based on the information that you have just read.

71. User fees are

    (A) money that goes directly to a program or agency, paid by those who use the program or agency

    (B) money which is paid at the discretion of taxpayer, indicated by a check-off on an income tax form

    (C) forbidden by the Constitution

    (D) fees paid by lobbyists

    (E) public financing of political campaigns

72. In the formation of public policy, broad goals are determined by

    (A) the Senate

    (B) the President and the Cabinet

    (C) the political process

    (D) public opinion

    (E) state governments

73. All of the following are predictors of a candidate's policy orientation EXCEPT

    (A) political party

    (B) home region

(C)   personality characteristics

(D)   political ideology

(E)   important industries in the candidate's district

74.   Which of the following statements about the relationship between public policy and democracy is most true?

(A)   Democracies tend to choose less effective public policies than authoritarian regimes.

(B)   In a democracy, policy expertise is subordinate to voter preference.

(C)   Voters in a democracy should know all of a candidate's policy preferences.

(D)   Voters cannot tell much about a candidate's policy preferences based on political party.

(E)   Voting is not a good way to express dissatisfaction with a public policy.

AP United States Government & Politics Review

POLITICAL PARTIES AND SPECIAL INTERESTS

A political party is an organization that seeks to influence the government and to determine public policy by electing officials from within its ranks. The Constitution does not mention political parties, and the Founding Fathers in general were opposed to them. Yet they developed simultaneously with the organization of the new government. In fact, it was the initial conflict over the interpretation of the powers assigned to the federal government by the Constitution that gave rise to the first organized American political parties.

The Federalist Party evolved around the policies of President Washington's Secretary of the Treasury, Alexander Hamilton. Hamilton and his supporters favored a "loose construction" approach to the interpretation of the Constitution, meaning that they advocated a strong federal government with the power to assume any duties and responsibilities not prohibited to it in the text of the doctrine. They generally supported programs designed to benefit the banking and commercial interests, and in foreign policy the Federalists were pro-British.

In opposition to the Federalists were the Democratic or Jeffersonian Republicans, who rallied around the Secretary of State. The modern Democratic Party traces its roots to the Jeffersonians. They were backed by those who believed in a "strict constructionist" approach, interpreting the Constitution in a narrow, limited sense. The Democratic-Republicans were mistrustful of a powerful central government, and sympathized with the needs of the "common man." They believed the small agrarian interests were the backbone of the nation along with shopkeepers and laborers. In the realm of foreign affairs, the Democratic-Republicans were pro-French. They wrested power from the Federalists in the election of 1800 when Jefferson narrowly defeated incumbent John Adams.

By the 1820s, the Democrats had divided into factions led by Andrew Jackson (Democrats) and John Quincy Adams (National Republicans). The Jacksonians continued the Jeffersonian tradition of supporting policies designed to enhance the power of the common man. Their support was largely rural, with both small farmers and some large planters in their camp. The National

Republicans, on the other hand, like their Federalist predecessors, represented the interests of Eastern bankers, merchants, and some planters. Eventually, a new party was formed from the remnants of the old Federalists and the National Republicans. They called themselves the Whigs after a British party of the same name and were dedicated to opposing the policies of the Jacksonians. The Whigs wielded power throughout the decade of the 1840s, but like their Democratic rivals, they split apart in the 1850s over the divisive slavery issue. The modern Republican Party was born in 1854 as Whigs and anti-slavery Democrats sought to halt the spread of slavery. The Republicans built their constituency around the interests of businesses, farmers, laborers, and the newly emancipated slaves in the post–Civil War era.

According to Robert Weissberg in *Understanding American Government*, the history of the evolution of political parties in the United States illustrates three consistent patterns. First, there is the fact that there is an almost rhythmic "ebb and flow" to their power and effectiveness. One party rises, the other regroups only to increase in vitality as the other declines. A second characteristic of our modern political parties is their ability to resist the challenges of third-party threats and, indeed, to co-opt their-themes and appeal. Lastly, Weissberg observes that American political parties are resilient and powerful, because historically they have been able to adapt to ever-changing economic and social forces such as urbanization, industrialization, immigration, and reform movements.

How Political Parties Function

Over the years, political parties have exerted a variety of functions essential to our democratic tradition. The most obvious function is the nomination of suitable candidates for local, state, and national office. This function, particularly at the national level, has been diluted to some extent by the popularity of primary elections to allow voters to express their preference for candidates. Gone are the days of raucous conventions and "smoke-filled rooms" from which such "dark horse" candidates as Warren G. Harding emerged from obscurity to capture national elections. Political parties stimulate interest by focusing on their own strengths and on the weaknesses of their opposition. They also provide a framework for keeping the machinery of government functioning as seen in the way Congress is organized strictly on party lines. They raise money to support candidates and provide a forum for airing public issues.

American political parties appear in theory to be highly organized, but due to our geographic size and the federal system of government, they are in practice largely decentralized. At the local level, the fundamental unit of organization is the precinct. At the precinct level, there is usually a captain, leader, or committee to handle routine tasks such as registering voters, distributing party literature, organizing "grass-roots" meetings, and getting out the vote on election day.

The next unit of party organization is the county. States vary considerably with respect to the selection of party officials at this level. Some are elected by their precincts, others elected at the county level, and in some states, they are selected by party conventions. County committees/county party leaders are often in positions to hand out patronage jobs to those who work for the election of party candidates.

State central committees are critical to fund-raising activities, and they are responsible for the organization of state party conventions. As with the counties, there is great variation from state to state concerning selection and composition of committees at this level. Like the county party leaders, these officials distribute party patronage jobs. State committees often formulate policies and traditions independently of the national committee.

In presidential election years, the national party committees are most visible. They plan the national nominating convention, write the party platform (a summary of positions on major issues), raise money to finance political activities, and carry out the election campaign. Representatives from each state serve on the national committees, and the presidential nominee chooses one individual to serve as party chairperson. Since the 1970s, the national committees have been more active in activities other than those strictly associated with the presidential campaign. Both the Democrats and Republicans have utilized the national committees to train would-be candidates and to recruit potential office holders.

The popularity of primary elections to screen and select the final party candidates has blunted the effect of party bosses and indeed the organizations themselves in controlling the political process. Closed primaries allow voters who are registered in a particular party to express their preferences for the party's candidates in the final election. Open primaries, on the other hand, allow voters to decide at the polls which party they will support. A few states allow "crossover" voting, which permits voters registered in one party to vote for the candidates in the other party. This practice can lead to such devious practices as voting for the weakest choice in the opposition party to give an advantage in the final election to the candidate and the party a voter in actuality supports. By the time the long presidential primary season is over (from the New Hampshire primary in February to the California primary in June), the final nominees of the respective parties are well-known to voters, hence the national party conventions are anti-climactic.

The national nominating conventions were introduced in the 1830s by the Anti-Masonic Party and quickly adopted by the Democrats and the newly organized Whig Party. Other "third parties" leaving their marks on the American political scene include: 1) the American or Know Nothing Party, which opposed Catholic immigration in the 1850s, 2) the Prohibition Party, which opposed the use of alcohol and worked for the adoption of the Eighteenth Amendment, 3) the Populist Party of the 1890s, which championed the cause of the farmers and workers and advocated the free coinage of silver, public ownership of major utilities, and electoral reforms such as the initiative and the referendum, 4) the Progressive or Bull Moose Party of Theodore Roosevelt (a splinter party which broke away from the Republican Party in 1912), which was built around the personality of the former President, and 5) the Socialist Party, which was founded in the 1890s and which advocates economic planning and government ownership of major industries and resources. These parties have wielded considerable influence over the years, and although they have not captured the White House, they have highlighted important issues and have often influenced the programs and platforms of the major parties.

DRILL

POLITICAL PARTIES

DIRECTIONS: Carefully read and answer each of the following questions, which are based on the information that you have just read.

75. An important characteristic of American political parties is the fact that they

    (A) are highly organized

    (B) function independently of the federal system

    (C) largely bypass local politics

    (D) are highly decentralized

    (E) enforce strict policies concerning membership and participation

76. America's first political party was the

    (A) Democratic Party   (D) Whig Party

    (B) Democratic-Republican Party   (E) Federalist Party

    (C) National-Republican Party

77. With reference to political parties, the U.S. Constitution

    (A) provided a general framework for their development

    (B) made no mention of them

    (C) provided a detailed plan for their organization

(D) specified that Congress be organized along party lines

(E) had to be amended to allow for their development

78. All of the following are true of the Whig Party EXCEPT

(A) it was popular during the 1840s

(B) it fragmented over the slavery issue

(C) it was created from the remnants of the Federalists and the National Republicans

(D) it traced its roots to the Jeffersonians

(E) it was dedicated to opposing the policies of the Jacksonians

79. One characteristic NOT associated with the major American political parties is

(A) a clear division between liberals and conservatives as seen in their affiliation with different parties

(B) their ability to resist third party threats

(C) their ability to cope with changing economic and social forces

(D) the cyclical nature of their popularity and effectiveness

(E) their evolution from the division within Washington's first Cabinet

80. A type of election that encourages voters to support weak candidates is the

(A) open primary   (D) "off-year" election

(B) closed primary   (E) party caucus

(C) crossover primary

81. National nominating conventions to choose final presidential candidates were first introduced by which of the following third parties?

(A) Bull Moose Party   (D) Prohibition Party

(B) Know Nothing Party   (E) Populist Party

(C) Anti-Masonic Party

INTEREST GROUPS

American officials and political leaders are continually subjected to pressure from a variety of interest groups to enact or quash policies friendly or hostile to their respective causes. These groups may be loosely organized (informal) with no real structure or regulations. A group of neighbors united in opposition to the building of a shopping mall on a wooded lot is an example of this type of interest group. They may hold meetings, distribute literature, circulate petitions, collect funds for legal fees, pack zoning board meetings, and command the attention of the local media. Using these techniques, such an informal interest group may effectively influence appropriate town politicians and accomplish the limited goal of halting the development of the woodland acreage.

Other interest groups are much more formal and permanent in nature. This type of interest group may have a large staff, suites of offices, and a broad agenda with clearly defined political objectives. Usually such a group has an economic interest, which may range from agricultural to financial to industrial. Some formal interest groups are more altruistic, with a reform agenda such as that of Common Cause or Massachusetts Fair Share. This type of pressure group may be classified as a public-interest group.

Some formal interest groups are dedicated to the advancement or protection of a single issue. The National Rifle Association, which fights gun control legislation, and the National Right to Life Committee, which seeks to roll back *Roe vs. Wade* and end legalized abortion, are examples of powerful single-issue pressure groups.

Interest groups use a variety of tactics to accomplish their goals. The most obvious strategy utilized by such groups is to lobby elected officials, particularly members of Congress, to advocate or to oppose policies favorable or unfriendly to their agendas. The majority of America's organized interest groups employ lobbyists in Washington. Business, labor, professionals, religious groups, environmentalists, consumer groups, and a host of others employ representatives to work for their benefit. They provide reports, statistics, and other forms of data to members of Congress to persuade them of the legitimacy of their respective positions. They may present expert testimony at public hearings, and they commonly manipulate the media to disseminate information favorable to their employers. They are not allowed to resort to such illegal tactics as presenting false and misleading information or bribing public officials. Since 1946, when Congress passed legislation regulating the activities of professional lobbyists, they have been required to register in Washington and to make their positions public. Such legislation cannot, of course, curb all abuses and underhanded practices inherent to a system of organized persuasion.

In recent years, in an attempt to circumvent legislation limiting contributions to political campaigns, a new type of pressure group, the political action committee (PAC), has evolved. Under current election laws, individuals may legally contribute $1,000 to candidates for national office. Interest groups such as PACs, on the other hand, can contribute $5,000 to candidates, and individuals may donate up to $5,000 a year to a political action committee. PACs have become increasingly popular and powerful in recent years. By the mid-1980s, there were over three thousand recognized political action committees. Despite their power and proliferation on the American political scene, political action committees have engendered a measure of controversy. Critics see these interest groups as just another means of diluting the influence the individual voter may realistically have on his/her elected representatives. Hence, some politicians refuse to accept PAC money.

In the mid-1990s, campaign finance reform edged ever closer to center stage until 1997, when charges of questionable fund-raising practices by both parties led to a call for congressional hearings into the matter.

DRILL

INTEREST GROUPS

DIRECTIONS: Carefully read and answer each of the following questions, which are based on the information that you have just read.

82. Which of the following is an example of a single-interest group?

    (A) National Right to Life Committee

    (B) Greenpeace

    (C) National Education Association

    (D) American Medical Association

    (E) National Organization for Women

83. All of the following are legitimate functions of registered lobbyists EXCEPT

    (A) testifying at public hearings

    (B) providing members of Congress with statistical data

    (C) preparing reports

    (D)   presenting media spots

    (E)   nominating candidates for political office

84.   Common Cause and the League of Women Voters are examples of

    (A)   informal interest groups   (D) ideological groups

    (B)   single-issue groups   (E) professional groups

    (C)   public interest groups

85.   Political action committees (PACs)

    (A)   have roots that originated in the nineteenth century

    (B)   have declined in popularity in recent years

    (C)   may contribute up to $1,000 a year to a political candidate

    (D)   may accept contributions of up to $5,000 from individuals

    (E)   may make unlimited contributions to political candidates

86.   The principal function of a pressure group is to

    (A)   provide campaign money to candidates for public office who favor its programs

    (B)   draw media attention to its cause

    (C)   obtain favorable policies from government for the cause it supports

    (D)   win congressional seats for its members

    (E)   unseat incumbent political office-holders

MEDIA

In the modern political arena, one of the most important means of political communication is the mass media. Television, radio, and newspapers all present information to the public and help the public understand political issues. Though most people consider news and commentary the most significant element of the media in political communication, popular culture, such as music and film, can also influence how members of the public understand their political world. The basic function of the media is to transmit information. For politics and government, the most relevant mode of transmission is through newspapers and news programs. In addition to presenting information, reporters and other members of the media analyze news. Analysis provides background and context for events, and can help people draw parallels to similar events.

News organizations are supposed to present and analyze information in a fair, accurate, and unbiased manner. (Newspapers have editorial and op-ed pages where readers can learn editors' and columnists' opinions on matters of the day.) Even in the news section, however, several factors can interfere with the achievement of this standard. Editors and others must make decisions about how newspapers or news programs will allocate space or time to specific stories. Competition to come out first with a news story can result in the reporting of information that has not been confirmed. Finally, those reporting and editing the news can never completely eliminate their own biases. Even with these obstacles, most people who work in the news subscribe to a set of professional ethics and standards that allow citizens to have confidence in the objectivity of journalists.

Though both print media and electronic media transmit news, their function is quite different. Electronic media—that is, radio, television, and increasingly the Internet—transmit information quickly, sometimes as the events themselves are unfolding. At times, reporters and viewers are learning about the events simultaneously. Print media, such as newspapers and magazines, allow for more opportunities to analyze the information and for more careful review of stories and sources.

Especially in a democratic society, media have an important function. Independent news organizations keep government officials accountable by reporting on their activities. By presenting news, they ensure that the population can make informed decisions when they vote or otherwise participate in the political process. In order to properly inform the public, the media is protected from government interference by the First Amendment of the Constitution. In this sense, the media are a political institution, with an assigned function and guaranteed independence from the institutions and individuals on which they are to report.

Media seen as having a liberal bias:	Media seen as having a conservative bias:
New York Times	Rush Limbaugh
Washington Post	Fox News Channel
CBS	Wall Street Journal

DRILL

MEDIA

DIRECTIONS: Carefully read and answer each of the following questions, which are based on the information that you have just read.

87. All of the following are part of the media EXCEPT

    (A) popular music

    (B) newsmagazines

    (C) the Internet

    (D) campaign slogans

    (E) radio talk shows

88. Which of the following statements about the media is TRUE?

    (A) Since true objectivity is impossible, news stories are always biased.

    (B) Though complete objectivity is impossible, most news organizations hold it as an important standard.

    (C) Media have very little influence on political attitudes.

    (D) News organizations are prohibited from being overly critical of public officials.

    (E) Television networks present news programs as a public service, not for profit.

PUBLIC OPINION AND VOTER BEHAVIOR

THE NATURE OF PUBLIC OPINION

Public opinion is a misleading term, but generally it refers to the attitudes and preferences expressed by a significant number of individuals about an issue that involves the government or society at large. It does not necessarily represent the sentiments of all or even most of the citizenry. Public opinion, nonetheless, is an important component of any society, particularly a democratic republic such as the United States where the government in both theory and practice is based on the concept of popular sovereignty.

In general, Americans are less apt to base their opinions on a set ideology than they are to respond to a public issue or concern by considering what will work and then supporting the most expedient solution. Still, there are labels applied to politically active individuals based on tradition and loosely related to party affiliation. Those who consider themselves to be conservatives usually are hesitant to espouse change and seek to preserve time-honored values and political traditions. They are sometimes labeled as "right-wing." Leftists or liberals are more receptive to change, and they are willing to use government to reform society. Moderates, or those in the political center, are somewhere in between these two. In reality, both the Republican and Democratic parties are moderate political institutions, but the former tends to support a conservative approach to governing while the latter is somewhat more liberal in philosophy.

An individual's public opinions are rooted in his/her family, ethnicity, religious heritage, and socio-economic group. Although the family is not generally regarded as a political institution, young people see the outside world first through the eyes of their parents and caregivers. Youngsters who participate in mock elections and straw polls generally support the candidates that their parents favor. This rule may change as the young person enters the sometimes rebellious years of adolescence and young adulthood. In the tumultuous 1960s, when the term "generation gap" was coined, many anti-establishment radicals were indeed the children of traditional, patriotic, middle-class conservatives or moderates.

Schools are also important agents in molding politically conscious young people, particularly those from homes where public issues may be downplayed or ignored. Schools foster patriotism by opening the day with a salute to the flag, studying civic holidays, and requiring curriculum treatment of American history and government as an integral component of public education. Young people are encouraged to learn about the heroes of the republic and, at the secondary level, to express their informed opinions about contemporary issues.

In today's technological society, the influence of the mass media in molding public opinion cannot be over-emphasized. Radio, television, newspapers, and newsmagazines all play a critical part in informing the public about major issues, and the biases of those who make decisions about how to present information quite naturally affect the nature of the final product. The electronic media in particular have been criticized for over-simplification of complicated issues and for reducing major speeches to sound bites lasting for less than a minute. On a positive note, the media can be credited with heightening general interest about public affairs.

Political candidates often exploit the media to transmit their respective messages to the public and in so doing utilize a number of common propaganda techniques most often employed by corporate advertising campaigns. These techniques include:

1) the testimonial, in which a well-known celebrity lends credibility to a candidate by endorsing his/her campaign,
2) the plain-folks approach, in which the candidate mingles with working-class voters in an attempt to convince voters that he/she is one of them,
3) the band-wagon approach, where the candidate tries to create the impression that individuals who do not support him/her will be left out because everyone else is doing so,
4) name-calling, which consists of labeling the opponent with terms that carry negative connotations, such as "extremist" or, in the election of 2004, "tax and spend liberal," or "flip-flopper."
5) employing glittering generalities, such as "life, liberty, and the pursuit of happiness" and "peace and prosperity," to sway voters.

Polls

Measuring the effects of the media on public opinion is indeed difficult and pinpointing where the public stands on a given issue is a difficult assignment, but certainly polls such as those administered by the Gallup and Harris organizations are fairly accurate in predicting voter behavior. Pollsters usually address a random sample of the population reflecting a cross-section of society with carefully constructed questions designed to elicit responses that do not mirror the biases of the interviewer. Results are tabulated and generalizations presented to the media.

Public opinion polls have been criticized on a variety of fronts. Some observers suggest that despite the sophistication of professional pollsters, many polls are poorly designed and/or the answers of the subjects are improperly interpreted. Another criticism is that they oversimplify complicated issues and encourage pat answers to complex problems. One type of election poll that has been severely criticized is the so-called exit poll, in which an interviewer questions voters about their preferences as they leave polling places. These polls may be accurate, although, with reference to sensitive issues, voters may avoid being candid and respond only as they think is proper. Another problem with exit polls arises if the media present the results while voting is still in progress and predict the outcome before all potential voters have had the opportunity to express their choices. In the election of 1980, Ronald Reagan was declared the victor over Jimmy Carter by some of the major news outlets before the polls closed on the West Coast, thereby robbing a large segment of the electorate of the sense that its participation mattered.

In the 1990s, exit polling continued to engender controversy, with critics urging the media to exercise self-restraint by keeping their projections to themselves until all ballots were cast.

Public opinion is about more than the popularity of politicians and candidates for office; it has come to play an increasingly important role in the political process. Most elected officials watch polls closely even though they may decide to take a position contrary to public opinion. Polls help politicians decide how to present issues to the public and which issues are most important to the public. Interest groups, lobbyists, and others use public opinion polls to help determine strategy and to gauge the success of their efforts to enact or defeat legislation.

Focus groups are another important tool used to understand public opinion. Focus groups are usually about ten to fifteen people and a moderator who have an opportunity to discuss their opinions about issues and candidates in depth. Since the groups are small, the opinions cannot be generalized to the public at large as in a sample survey, but the discussion can reveal why and how people think as they do.

As important as polls and focus groups have become in the political process, public opinion is more than the latest poll results. It also refers to broad trends. For instance, no one needs to take a poll to know that raising taxes tends to be unpopular. More significantly, public opinion lies at the heart of support for the laws and institutions of any political system. This kind of public opinion is known by political scientists as "diffuse support," because it does not refer to support for specific candidates or policy preferences, but to support for the means by which the political system elects candidates and forms policy.

DRILL

THE NATURE OF PUBLIC OPINION

DIRECTIONS: Carefully read and answer each of the following questions, which are based on the information that you have just read.

89. The LEAST important agent in molding public opinion among the young would probably be

    (A) older family members   (D) socio-economic groups

    (B) school curriculum   (E) religious role models

    (C) peer group members

90. Media influence on the formation of public opinion has been criticized for all of the following reasons EXCEPT

    (A) oversimplification of complicated issues

    (B) reducing major speeches to brief sound bites

    (C) biased presentations

    (D) heightening general interest in public issues

    (E) focusing on the trivial and the sensational

91. All of the following are characterizations of public opinion EXCEPT

    (A) it reflects the attitudes of a majority of the population

    (B) it involves attitudes about public issues

    (C) it influences the decisions of public officials

    (D) it is measured by pollsters

    (E) it is an important component of any society

92. Both the Republican and Democratic parties

    (A) appeal mainly to conservative voters

    (B) appeal principally to liberals

    (C) are based on clearly defined ideologies

    (D) usually embrace a moderate approach to solving society's problems

    (E) eschew a pragmatic approach to problem-solving

93. A propaganda device in which a candidate advertises an endorsement from a celebrity figure is called

    (A) "the band-wagon approach"

    (B) "the testimonial"

    (C) "a glittering generality"

    (D) "the plain-folks technique"

    (E) "name-calling"

POLITICAL PARTICIPATION

Though public opinion is critical in a democratic regime, only through elections and other forms of participation can citizens directly influence the conduct of government. Voting is the most common form of political participation in the United States. In national elections, citizens elect Senators and Members of the House of Representatives to represent their state or congressional district. Voters also indirectly elect the President through the Electoral College. At the state and local level, elected offices vary. In some states, for instance, judges are elected, and in others they are appointed. In addition to voting for candidates for office, voters in states that have "Initiative and Referendum" can vote to pass or reject laws directly. In this way, laws are approved directly by voters, not through representatives.

Citizens base their voting decisions on a variety of factors. The political party is usually among the first things a voter learns about the candidate. Though an increase of independent voters has made partisanship less significant than in the past, it remains an important piece of information, as many independent voters tend to prefer one party to the other. Other factors voters use in deciding which candidate to support include (a) agreement on issues important to the voter, (b) the candidate's personality traits, such as honesty or integrity, or (c) the candidate's identification with groups important to the voter, such as ethnic or religious groups.

Campaigns attempt to persuade voters to support a candidate. Campaigns try to communicate information about the candidates to voters. In some cases, campaigns inform voters about the accomplishments and achievements of a candidate. In other cases, campaigns focus on an opponent's supposed failings or shortcomings. Some observers believe that an increase in negative campaigns or campaign messages that attack an opponent reduces participation because negative campaigns diminish the appeal of both candidates. Regardless of the impact of negative campaigns, it is important to recognize that a campaign may attempt to persuade likely supporters of an opponent to abstain from voting. Another critical factor in modern campaigns is the role of money. Campaign costs have increased over the past years, as campaigns have become more focused on television and other forms of mass communication. In order to raise the large sums of money candidates believe they need in order to win elections, some observers believe candidates have no choice but to pay close attention to the desires of those capable of making large campaign contributions.

Beyond Voting

Though voting is the most common form of political participation, it is not the only form. Citizens have other opportunities to influence government. One common form of participation is writing to representatives and other government officials. People often contact elected representatives in order to address a problem they are having with a government agency. In other cases, citizens are trying to persuade a representative to support a particular position. Interest groups often organize campaigns to write letters to officials, soliciting members and other citizens. Technology has made it easier for citizens to contact representatives. Phone, faxes, and e-mail are used to communicate with elected officials. Most Members of Congress have websites where constituents and other interested citizens can learn about issues and provide feedback.

Involvement in political campaigns is another important way for citizens to participate in politics. Displaying a lawn sign or bumper sticker, wearing a button, or simply trying to persuade friends and neighbors can be considered political participation. Most political campaigns use volunteers for tasks such as stuffing envelopes, canvassing neighborhoods to generate support, running phone banks, and transporting supporters to the polls. Contributing money to a candidate running for office is also a form of political participation.

Citizens can participate by joining political groups that are not associated with a particular candidate or party—dubbed interest groups. These groups coordinate letter-writing campaigns, provide information about candidate positions, and can even channel campaign funds to favored candidates. In addition, citizens often organize themselves to confront local problems. Such problems can range from a nearby toxic waste site to inadequate street lighting. These groups rarely support candidates for office or attempt to influence elections. Instead, they try to get public officials to focus on the issue of concern.

Public demonstrations and protests provide yet another vehicle for political participation. This kind of activity has several strategic functions. Public demonstrations provide an opportunity to make a case for a cause or issue public.

Protests receive media attention and, thus, attention for a cause. This way, demonstrators hope to persuade other citizens and politicians. Large demonstrations can show that a significant number of people are committed to an issue.

DRILL
POLITICAL PARTICIPATION

DIRECTIONS: Carefully read and answer each of the following questions, which are based on the information that you have just read.

94. All of the following are forms of political participation EXCEPT

   (A) voting

   (B) writing letters to a representative

   (C) participating in a protest

   (D) serving in the military

   (E) contributing money to a campaign

95. Only citizens of states with Initiative and Referendum

   (A) vote on state and local laws directly

   (B) vote for President without the electoral college

   (C) vote in primaries

   (D) have term limits for all elected offices

   (E) have a flat income tax

96. All of the following statements about public opinion are true EXCEPT

   (A) public opinion is especially important in a democracy

   (B) legislators must consult public opinion before deciding how to vote on an issue

(C)   politicians often consult public opinion in order to decide which issues to focus on

(D)   public opinion is commonly measured by polls

(E)   public opinion is used to help predict elections

97.   Which of the following is the most important reason campaign costs have increased?

(A)   Rising mail costs

(B)   The increased amount of negative campaigning

(C)   The increase reliance of campaigns on television advertising

(D)   The increase importance of interest groups

(E)   The use of computer technology, such as e-mail and web-sites

98.   The term "diffuse support" refers to

(A)   the President's public opinion rankings

(B)   support for the laws and institutions of the political system

(C)   the decline in turnout that results from negative campaigning

(D)   support for a third-party candidate

(E)   people who do not vote because they do not support any candidates

99.   Political protests and demonstrations are

(A)   usually favorable to unpopular causes

(B)   a violation of the law

(C)   though legal, always disruptive of legitimate political participation

(D)   a form of civil disobedience

(E)   an unusual but legitimate form of political participation

VOTER BEHAVIOR

Suffrage (the right to vote) qualifications in the United States have historically been determined by the individual states, but in response to a variety of reform efforts, amendments have been added to the Constitution to broaden the size of the electorate. In 1870, following the Civil War, the Fifteenth Amendment was ratified making it illegal to deny a citizen the right to vote due to "race, color, or previous condition of servitude." Despite the intent to enfranchise the former slaves, a number of legal devices were utilized to deny blacks the right to vote. Among these were the poll tax, literacy test, and the infamous "grandfather clause," which denied suffrage to those whose grandfathers had not been legally entitled to vote. In the spirit of the modern civil rights movement, in 1964 the Twenty-fourth Amendment was passed, outlawing the poll tax as a voting qualification in federal elections. Women had gained the vote in 1920 with the ratification of the Nineteenth Amendment which barred the federal government as well as the separate states from denying women access to the polls. During the Vietnam War, when eighteen-year-olds were subject to the draft, the Twenty-sixth Amendment was added to the Constitution, granting them the vote in both federal and state elections.

In recent years much attention has been focused on the topic of voter apathy, for despite historic efforts to extend suffrage to all segments of the adult population, participation in the electoral process has been on the decline. Several theories have been advanced to explain this trend. There is a widespread belief that Americans are dissatisfied with their elected officials and mistrust all politicians; therefore, they have been "turned off" to the system and refuse to participate. Of course, some Americans do not vote because they are ill, handicapped, incarcerated, or homeless and do not have access to the ballot. Others, such as college students, who do not live at home find it cumbersome and inconvenient to register and use absentee ballots. While most of the attempts to explain voter apathy in the United States focus on it as a negative aspect of our civic culture, some analysts disagree and see disinterest in the ballot as a sign that the majority of the citizenry are satisfied with the system and with life in America in general; hence, they feel no sense of urgency about participating in the political process.

Voting Trends

Attempts to explain how people vote as they do in American elections have produced few consistent generalizations because each election has its own unique character. However, a few suggestions can be offered to explain some of the factors that determine how Americans vote. One obvious consideration is party identification. For those who harbor a strong sense of loyalty to the Democratic or Republican party, the choice of whom to support, particularly in presidential elections, is fairly predictable. Still, only one-termer Jimmy Carter, in 1976, broke the Republicans' lock on the White House between 1968 and 1992, despite the fact that there are more registered Democrats. (It is well to note, too, that Bill Clinton's successful Democratic campaigns in 1992 and 1996 at times co-opted traditional GOP issues.) In addition, the number of voters who register with no party affiliation is on the rise. Another factor that may explain the vote in a particular election is related to a candidate's stand on a controversial issue such as abortion rights. Many pro-choice and right-to-life voters use this issue as a so-called litmus test to determine which candidates they will support. Factors such as age, sex, education, socio-economic group, religion, occupation, and geography also play a part in shaping voter behavior.

DRILL

VOTER BEHAVIOR

DIRECTIONS: Carefully read and answer each of the following questions, which are based on the information that you have just read.

100. Which of the following generalizations is true of the American electorate?

(A) Voter indifference is always an indication of dissatisfaction with public officials.

(B) Participation in the political process is on the rise.

(C) Party identification is insignificant in explaining why Americans vote as they do.

(D) Some voters use a "litmus test" with reference to a single critical issue to determine whom they will support.

(E) Young people vote in large numbers because they have a comparatively greater amount of free time than middle-aged voters.

101. Which of the following amendments to the Constitution outlawed the poll tax in federal elections?

(A) The Twenty-sixth   (D) The Fourteenth

(B) The Twenty-fourth   (E) The Fifteenth

(C) The Nineteenth

102. Which of the following factors is probably most significant in determining how an individual will vote in a presidential election?

(A) Occupation

(D) Geography

(B) Income level

(E) Religion

(C) Party loyalty

103. The principal reason why eighteen-year-olds were enfranchised in 1971 was

(A) universal education

(B) the Vietnam War

(C) higher income levels

(D) availability of information via the electronic media

(E) the civil rights movement

AP United States Government & Politics Review

CIVIL RIGHTS AND THE SUPREME COURT

HISTORICAL BACKGROUND AND THE BILL OF RIGHTS

As with other traditional aspects of the American civic culture, the origins of the concept of fundamental freedoms and unalienable rights can be traced to the British heritage and to the thinkers of the Enlightenment. In crafting the Declaration of Independence in 1776, Thomas Jefferson and his comrades coined the phrases "all men are created equal" and "life, liberty and the pursuit of happiness" to indicate why governments exist—to ensure the protection of these basic rights. The list of grievances which makes up the body of the Declaration contains several references to King George III's failure to uphold the civic rights that subjects of the British crown considered their birthright. The signers of the document complained that the King refused to accept laws that were passed for their common good, that he deprived many of them of trial by jury, that he obstructed justice, that he kept standing armies among them in times of peace, that he taxed them without their consent, and that, in general, he behaved like a tyrant.

When constructing the Constitution, the Founding Fathers attempted to include passages to ensure the protection of civil liberties such as in Article I, Section 9 where specific provisions are set down for maintaining the right of habeas corpus. Similarly, in Article III, Section 2, trial by jury for all federal crimes with the exception of cases involving impeachment is affirmed. However, one criticism of the document voiced by some of the Anti-Federalists who opposed its ratification was its lack of a bill of rights protecting the civil liberties of individual citizens.

During the first session of Congress in 1789, the first ten amendments were adopted and sent to the states for ratification. They were formally added to the Constitution as a package in 1791. These amendments are known collectively as the Bill of Rights, and they contain protections of those individual freedoms which in many ways define what it is to be an American. However, most of the rights enumerated in the Bill of Rights are extended to "all persons" living in the United States, including aliens.

The amendment that Americans in general hold most dear is undoubtedly the First Amendment, which protects our freedom of expression and which specifically guarantees the following rights:

- freedom of religion
- freedom of speech
- freedom of the press
- freedom of assembly and
- freedom to petition the government

In the case of religion, Congress is barred from establishing a state religion and from preventing individuals from worshipping freely. The right to assemble must be carried out "peaceably."

Another category of fundamental freedoms protected by the Bill of Rights involves due process, or the rights of the accused. The Fourth Amendment outlaws "unreasonable searches and seizures" and mandates that warrants be granted only "upon probable cause." The section of the amendment that affirms the "right of the people to be secure in their persons" has been cited by abortion rights activists as a source of constitutional protection for women to make private decisions concerning reproduction. The broad provisions of the Fifth Amendment call for grand juries, bar double jeopardy, insist that defendants not be compelled to testify against themselves, protect due process in general, and require the government to compensate anyone whose private property is taken for public use (eminent domain). The Sixth Amendment guarantees to those accused of criminal offenses a speedy trial by a jury of peers, the right to be informed of the charges, and the right to be represented by an attorney. The Eighth Amendment prohibits "excessive bail and fines" and restrains the state from imposing "cruel and unusual punishments." The "cruel and unusual" clause has been invoked by opponents of capital punishment to justify their position.

As originally formulated, the provisions of the Bill of Rights were geared to the federal government. For the most part, the separate states have constitutions that include lists of protections similar to the Bill of Rights. Following the Civil War, the Fourteenth Amendment was added to the Constitution to extend the rights of citizenship to the former slave. In so doing, the framers of this amendment specified that no state could abridge the rights of citizenship nor "deprive any person of life, liberty, or property, without due process of law, nor deny to any person within its jurisdiction the equal protection of the laws." States now must conform to the federal concept of civil liberties.

DRILL

HISTORICAL BACKGROUND AND
THE BILL OF RIGHTS

DIRECTIONS: Carefully read and answer each of the following questions, which are based on the information that you have just read.

104. The First Amendment protects all of the following freedoms EXCEPT

    (A)   freedom of religion   (D)   freedom of speech

    (B)   freedom of choice   (E)   freedom of assembly

    (C)   freedom of the press

105. Jefferson's reference to "unalienable rights" in the Declaration of Independence relates to

    (A)   laws passed by Parliament

    (B)   laws passed by the colonial legislatures

    (C)   laws that did not protect aliens

    (D)   traditions of the Enlightenment

    (E)   rights that cannot legally be taken away

106. When creating the Constitution, the Founding Fathers did not include a bill of rights because

    (A)   the Anti-Federalists opposed such a bill

    (B)   they had too many other issues to consider

    (C)   they were unsure of what to include

    (D)   they believed such a bill was unnecessary because the states already had such protections

    (E)   James Madison lobbied against such a bill

107. The Fifth Amendment guarantees all of the following legal protections EXCEPT

    (A)   freedom from double jeopardy

(B)   freedom from being compelled to testify against oneself

(C)   freedom from cruel and unusual punishments

(D)   indictment by a grand jury

(E)   compensation for land taken by eminent domain

108.   States are now prohibited from infringing upon the rights protected by the federal Bill of Rights because of

(A)   an executive order issued by President Washington

(B)   a provision in the Fourteenth Amendment

(C)   legislative action by the first Congress

(D)   an introduction to the document which mandates it

(E)   their state constitutions which require it

KEY FACTS: LANDMARK U.S. SUPREME COURT CASES

Over the years the American judicial system, particularly the U.S. Supreme Court, has been responsible for enforcing the protections originally listed in the Constitution, those guaranteed in the Bill of Rights, and those specified in other legislation and amendments. Numerous landmark decisions have been rendered by the Supreme Court in its mission to protect the rights of the people of the United States. Among the most significant are the following:

Gitlow vs. New York **(1925)** – A Socialist lost his free speech case but the Court affirmed the contention that the states could be required to adhere to the Bill of Rights.

Brown vs. Board of Education **(1954)** – An equal protection case which over-turned *Plessy vs. Ferguson* (1896) and which declared school segregation to be unconstitutional.

Engel vs. Vitale **(1962)** – Outlawed school-sponsored, or "captive audience" prayer in public schools.

Abington Township vs. Schempp **(1963)** – Abolished Bible reading in public schools.

West Virginia Board of Education vs. Barnette **(1943)** – Overturned *Minersville School District vs. Gobitis* and which ruled that a law that mandated compulsory saluting of the flag was unconstitutional.

***Near vs. Minnesota* (1931)** – A freedom of the press case which forbade states to use the concept of prior restraint (outlawing something before it has taken place) to limit publication of objectionable material except during wartime or in cases of obscenity or incitement to violence.

***New York Times vs. United States* (1971)** – Another freedom of the press case, this ruling allowed the publication of the controversial Pentagon Papers during the Vietnam War.

***Tinker vs. Des Moines School District* (1969)** – The Court ruled that wearing black armbands in protest against the Vietnam War was protected by the First Amendment. More recently, the Court has expanded the concept of "symbolic speech" and has protected such activities as burning the flag and cross burning by the KKK.

***Mapp vs. Ohio* (1961)** – Upheld and extended to states the Court's exclusionary rule which bars at trial the introduction of evidence which has not been obtained legally. Recently, particularly with reference to drug cases, the Court has modified this ruling so that evidence that might not have been initially obtained legally but which would eventually have turned up through lawful procedures can be introduced.

***Gideon vs. Wainwright* (1963)** – Ruled that courts must provide legal counsel to poor defendants in all felony cases. A later ruling extended this right to all defendants facing possible prison sentences.

***Escobedo vs. Illinois* (1964)** – Extended the right to counsel to include consultation prior to questioning by authorities.

***Miranda vs. Arizona* (1966)** – The Court mandated that all suspects be informed of their due process rights before police interrogate them.

***Korematsu vs. United States* (1944)** – Upheld the constitutionality of a 1942 order that all persons of Japanese ancestry including American citizens be relocated and detained. This measure was viewed as a wartime necessity. The Court also ruled (in the *Endo* case) that it *was* unconstitutional for any individual whose loyalty to the nation had been established to be restricted in his/her freedom of movement.

***Bakke vs. The Regents of the University of California* (1978)** – A reverse discrimination case in which the Court declared the University's quota system for minority students to be unconstitutional while it at the same time upheld the legitimacy of affirmative action policies in which institutions consider race as a factor when determining admissions.

***Roe vs. Wade* (1973)** – The Court legalized abortion so long as the fetus is not viable (able to survive outside the womb).

***Webster vs. Reproductive Health Services* (1989)** – An abortion rights case which allowed states more discretion and upheld their right to limit the use of public funds, buildings, or personnel in administering abortions. Recently, a Pennsylvania law calling for a twenty-four-hour waiting period for abortions, for unmarried women under eighteen years of age to receive the consent of one parent or from a judge in order to obtain an abortion, and for women to be informed by medical personnel of the specifics of the procedure and of alternatives was upheld. However, a provision of the law requiring that married women inform their spouses of their decision to have an abortion was struck down.

After more than eleven years with the same nine justices, 2005 saw several important changes. With the death of Chief Justice William Rehnquist, President George W. Bush was able to nominate his first justice, federal court judge John Roberts, for the post of Chief Justice. Roberts was confirmed by a Senate vote of 78-22. Additionally, Sandra Day O'Connor announced her retirement that same year. President Bush originally tabbed White House counsel Harriet Miers, who had no previous experience as a judge, to fill this vacancy. Criticism of Miers' lack of judicial experience, her close ties to Bush, and her perceived moderate views led GOP hard-liners to push for her ouster. Subsequently, Miers pulled her name from nomination, freeing Bush to choose a conservative federal court judge, Samuel Alito. Both Roberts and Alito are expected to rule on cases in the staunch conservative camp with justices Scalia and Thomas. It seems clear the court will remain widely split into two camps with many key votes likely to remain 5-4.

DRILL

THE SUPREME COURT AND INDIVIDUAL RIGHTS

DIRECTIONS: Carefully read and answer each of the following questions, which are based on the information that you have just read.

109. The *Gideon, Escobedo,* and *Miranda* cases all concerned which of the following issues?

(A) School prayer

(B) Saluting the flag

(C) The rights of the accused

(D) Eminent domain

(E) Freedom of speech

110. A case that expanded the concept of symbolic speech to include wearing armbands in protest was

    (A) *Tinker vs. Des Moines*   (D) *Mapp vs. Ohio*

    (B) *Engel vs. Vitale*   (E) *Bakke vs. Regents*

    (C) *Abington Township vs. Schempp*

111. The significance of the *Gitlow* case was that it

    (A) affirmed the right of a Socialist to make inflammatory speeches

    (B) mandated that state governments uphold the provisions of the federal Bill of Rights

    (C) interpreted the death penalty as a cruel and unusual punishment

    (D) upheld the constitutionality of the exclusionary rule

    (E) outlawed reverse discrimination

112. In a recent ruling concerning a Pennsylvania law restricting abortion rights, the Court upheld all of the following EXCEPT

    (A) the legality of abortions if the fetus is not viable

    (B) parental notification in the case of an unmarried minor

    (C) spousal notification in the case of a married woman

    (D) a twenty-four-hour waiting period before obtaining an abortion

    (E) requiring that medical personnel provide information about alternatives

113. In the *Korematsu* case (1944) the Supreme Court

    (A) declared the Japanese relocation to be unlawful

    (B) declared that U.S. citizens of Japanese origin be exempted from the relocation order

    (C) upheld the measure as reasonable in wartime

    (D) ruled that Japanese residents of the West Coast were entitled to equal protection

    (E) ruled that reverse discrimination was a major factor in the decision

AP United States Government & Politics Review

THE GEORGE W. BUSH ADMINISTRATION

George W. Bush has proven to be a memorable and controversial President. Even before his inauguration in 2001, Bush's disputed victory over Democrat Al Gore had largely polarized the country into separate liberal and conservative camps. The vote tally in Florida was widely held in contention, with that state's 27 electoral votes left to determine the presidency. Eventually, the Supreme Court—itself widely divided—voted 5–4 in favor of ending Florida recounts, thus handing the White House to Mr. Bush.

That polarization only intensified in the subsequent years of the Bush administration. The Iraq War has remained Bush's most scrutinized policy, but both his domestic and foreign policy in general continue to fuel much passion, pro and con, among the American electorate. A general "unilateralist" style of governing has not endeared Bush to either foreign heads of state or to political critics here at home. The sometimes abrasive personalities of top aids like Defense Secretary Donald Rumsfeld has only heightened this effect.

The 2004 election saw the country nearly evenly divided between "red states" (those favoring Republicans) and "blue states" (those favoring the Democrats). Bush defeated former Vietnam War veteran and current Massachusetts Senator John Kerry in the campaign, with Florida and Ohio being key states that fell Bush's way—again, not without various charges of electoral fraud. Michael Moore's unabashed criticism of Bush in the 2004 film *Fahrenheit 9/11* is illustrative of the gap between Bush's supporters and detractors as the election approached.

In his second term, Bush has struggled to retain his first-term popularity. As the memory of the Sept. 11, 2001, terrorist attacks on the U.S. recedes into the background and the Iraq War lingers, polling numbers were increasingly critical of the President. In the late summer of 2005, the President faced widespread criticism for the federal government's perceived lax response in the wake of the devastation wrought by Hurricane Katrina.

Originally Bush stated the United States would avoid the "nation building" experiments of the Clinton years, such as Somalia, Haiti, and the Balkans. A definite change occurred in the wake of 9/11, when the administration promoted "regime change" in Iraq, which by its very definition would lead to nation building. The U.S. is also engaged in "nation building" in Afghanistan supporting the government of Hamad Karzhai.

In terms of foreign policy, Bush is the most unilateralist President since fellow Texan Lyndon Johnson. Examples include:

- Singling out Iran, Iraq, and North Korea as an "axis of evil" in 2002.
- Dropping U.S. support of two widely held international treaties: the Kyoto Accords on global warming and the ABM Treaty with Russia on defensive weapons.
- Leading the 2003 invasion of Iraq even though this opposed world opinion and the wishes of the United Nations in the name of U.S. national interest.
- Raising tariffs against foreign steel in an attempt to protect the U.S. steel industry, yet speaking glowingly of free trade.

KEY TERMS

- "Fast track" capability—Means that when an administration negotiates a trade agreement, Congress cannot change it. They either vote yes or no as is. Bush has achieved this.
- The "Bush Doctrine"—Notion of pre-emptive strikes against potential enemies. Used against Iraq in 2003 and on a smaller scale against Yemen in 2002.
- Regime change—Phrase that means a U.S.-sponsored toppling of a current government to be replaced by an entirely new constitutional set up.
- "Compassionate conservatism"—Bush campaigned that he could work well with the Democrats and would be strictly bipartisan—this never occurred. Other trappings include: speaking Spanish, embracing minority membership in the party, and promoting the "faith-based" initiatives, which allow federal money to be used by private religious organizations.
- Homeland Security Department—Newest Cabinet department, created in the wake of the 9/11 attacks. The department takes agencies like the FBI, CIA, etc., out of other Cabinet departments and creates a more coordinated approach to internal security.
- Unilateral—A foreign policy approach in which the U.S. acts as it sees fit without consideration for the views of traditional allies or of the United Nations Security Council. The opposite, more inclusive approach is known as multilateral.
- United Nations Resolution 1441—The Bush Administration interpreted this resolution to legitimize war against Iraq, while

most other states on the Security Council—most notably Germany, Russia, and France—loudly opposed this view. The resolution dealt with Iraqi cooperation over a UN search for "weapons of mass destruction."

- Patriot Act—A law passed in the aftermath of 9/11 that basically gives extra powers to intelligence and law enforcement officers in the effort to combat terrorism. Examples include the interception of mail, phone tapping, e-mail surveillance, and so on. The law has proven to be controversial.

- Halliburton—Oil services company that has secured more than $2.2 billion in government contracts under the Bush administration in defense-related business. Prior to becoming Bush's Vice President, Dick Cheney was Halliburton's CEO, leading many to perceive a possible conflict of interest in some of the administration's involvements.

- Camp X-Ray—Detention camp at the U.S. naval base in Guantanamo Bay, Cuba. Detainees have been held here since shortly after 9/11, many without being charged with any crime. Questions have arisen as to the constitutionality of Camp X-Ray and some foreign observers have claimed that it violates the Geneva Convention on the treatment of "prisoners of war." The administration has denied that the detainees meet the definition of "prisoner of war"; nor, it says, are they covered by the U.S. Constitution.

The key members of the administration are:

- Richard Cheney: Vice President
- Condoleezza Rice: Secretary of State
- Donald Rumsfeld: Secretary of Defense
- Gordon England: Acting Deputy Secretary of Defense
- Stephen Hadley: National Security Advisor
- Alberto Gonzales: Attorney General

DRILL

THE GEORGE W. BUSH ADMINISTRATION

DIRECTIONS: Carefully read and answer each of the following questions, which are based on the information that you have just read.

114. The result of the 2000 presidential election was ultimately decided by

   (A) Florida's voters

   (B) the three televised Bush-Gore debates

(C)   the economy

(D)   the United States Supreme Court

(E)   Florida Secretary of State Katherine Harris

115. In which region of the country did Bush sweep Gore and take all of the available electoral college votes in 2000?

(A)   The populous Northeast   (D)   Pacific Northwest

(B)   Southwest   (E)   Midwest

(C)   The Southeast

116. "Fast track" deals with a President's ability to

(A)   appoint federal judges in shorter time periods

(B)   wage war without gaining congressional support

(C)   dictate the terms of a trade package with a foreign state

(D)   make executive agreements with foreign states as opposed to legislative agreements

(E)   keep information concealed in the name of national security

117. United Nations Resolution 1441 and the U.S.-led invasion of Iraq were both predicated on the notion that Iraq was harboring

(A)   known Al Qaeda members

(B)   terrorist cells sponsored by Saddam Hussein

(C)   weapons of mass destruction

(D)   large amounts of lucrative petroleum

(E)   thoughts of re-invading Kuwait

118. Which of the following has been cited by some as a violation of the Geneva Convention on the rights of prisoners of war?

(A)   Halliburton government contracts

(B)   UN Resolution 1441

(C)   The Bush Doctrine

(D)   The Patriot Act

(E)   Camp X-Ray

119. Traditional European allies of the U.S., excluding Britain, have opposed all of the following under the Bush administration EXCEPT

    (A) multilateralism

    (B) Camp X-Ray

    (C) the Bush Doctrine

    (D) the Iraq War

    (E) withdrawal from the ABM Treaty and Kyoto Accords

120. Which of the following has NOT been a key member of the George W. Bush administration?

    (A) Dick Cheney   (D) Donald Rumsfeld

    (B) John Snow   (E) Alberto Gonzales

    (C) Condoleezza Rice

UNITED STATES GOVERNMENT & POLITICS REVIEW

ANSWER KEY

1.	(D)	31.	(A)	61.	(E)	91.	(A)
2.	(E)	32.	(C)	62.	(B)	92.	(D)
3.	(C)	33.	(A)	63.	(A)	93.	(B)
4.	(C)	34.	(D)	64.	(A)	94.	(D)
5.	(B)	35.	(D)	65.	(D)	95.	(A)
6.	(D)	36.	(B)	66.	(A)	96.	(B)
7.	(B)	37.	(B)	67.	(C)	97.	(C)
8.	(A)	38.	(E)	68.	(B)	98.	(B)
9.	(C)	39.	(B)	69.	(D)	99.	(E)
10.	(B)	40.	(C)	70.	(A)	100.	(D)
11.	(E)	41.	(D)	71.	(A)	101.	(B)
12.	(B)	42.	(E)	72.	(C)	102.	(C)
13.	(C)	43.	(A)	73.	(C)	103.	(B)
14.	(E)	44.	(D)	74.	(B)	104.	(B)
15.	(B)	45.	(E)	75.	(D)	105.	(E)
16.	(D)	46.	(B)	76.	(E)	106.	(D)
17.	(B)	47.	(C)	77.	(B)	107.	(C)
18.	(A)	48.	(D)	78.	(D)	108.	(B)
19.	(D)	49.	(C)	79.	(A)	109.	(C)
20.	(C)	50.	(A)	80.	(C)	110.	(A)
21.	(A)	51.	(C)	81.	(C)	111.	(B)
22.	(B)	52.	(D)	82.	(A)	112.	(C)
23.	(E)	53.	(C)	83.	(E)	113.	(C)
24.	(D)	54.	(B)	84.	(C)	114.	(D)
25.	(C)	55.	(C)	85.	(D)	115.	(C)
26.	(E)	56.	(D)	86.	(C)	116.	(C)
27.	(B)	57.	(A)	87.	(D)	117.	(C)
28.	(C)	58.	(E)	88.	(B)	118.	(E)
29.	(C)	59.	(C)	89.	(C)	119.	(A)
30.	(D)	60.	(A)	90.	(D)	120.	(B)

CHAPTER 3
Comparative Government & Politics Review

COMPARATIVE GOVERNMENT & POLITICS REVIEW

A word of advice to the student in a Comparative Government & Politics course: Avoid the temptation to simply learn facts in a void. For instance, whatever you learn about legitimacy, voter turnout, or party system in Britain must be "brought along" for comparison with systems you find in other case study countries, such as Iran or Russia. Look for similarities, differences, and cause-and-effect patterns as you enhance your knowledge base about these countries.

The review sections, drill exercises, and practice tests that follow are geared to better position a student enrolled in the AP Comparative Government & Politics course for success on the AP exam.

| Comparative Government & Politics Review |

COMPARATIVE POLITICAL LITERACY

This chapter will lay a foundation for the concepts necessary to understand the comparisons made in subsequent case study (country) units. While not meant to be comprehensive, this unit provides context to the subsequent material.

A good starting point is to distinguish between the terms "state" and "nation." "State" used in its international sense is synonymous with "country." For a state to exist, the following four conditions must be met: permanent population; defined territory; organized government; and sovereignty. The last of these is the key—sovereignty is roughly defined as having ultimate political authority within one's own soil. The other three qualifications for statehood are readily met by lesser political units like cities, Canadian provinces, regions, etc. For instance, the city of Boston obviously has territory, population, and government, but isn't a state because it lacks the ultimate authority to declare war, establish immigration quotas, or coin money. These are powers retained by the United States government because it holds sovereign power.

Currently, roughly 200 states exist globally. This number is the highest in history. The break-up of the Soviet Union and other former communist Eastern European states like Yugoslavia have upped this total since the 1990s.

A "nation," on the other hand, is a cultural rather than political grouping. A nation shares a common language and religion, generally. Other shared cultural traits of a nation include fashion and clothing, cuisine and diet, and leisure interests, such as popular music and sports.

Thousands of nations exist globally. A "stateless-nation" defines any culture than actively desires statehood but lacks it. Notable examples include Palestine, the Quebecois in Canada, Kurds in the Middle East, and Chechnya.

Political scientists often group states by various labels. An outmoded, and often misunderstood, mode of labeling involved the terms "First and Third Worlds," and the relatively less used "Second World." These terms were invented during the height of the Cold War. The basic definitions of these labels stand as follows:

- First World: Industrial democracies (i.e., "The free world"—Western Europe, Japan, Canada, and the United States)

- Second World: Industrialized but not democratic. (i.e., "The communist bloc"—basically the Soviet Union and its Eastern European satellite states like Poland, East Germany, Czechoslovakia, etc.)
- Third World: Everything else! This grouping made the least sense of all, grouping a widely disparate group of states together under a throw-together heading. Relatively prosperous and stable states like Argentina or South Korea were equated with very impoverished and unstable states like Haiti or Ethiopia.

These groupings are meaningless given their overly generic scope and the end of the Cold War. In their place has come a new set of more focused labels, which has replaced the overly broad Third World and broken it down into more accurate and meaningful groupings.

Liberal Democracies

Liberal democracies is the updated label for the former First World. A synonym for liberal democracies one often hears is the "developed world." These are the states that have it made, so to speak, globally. They are wealthy states that carry global clout. A liberal democracy will hold most, if not all, of these qualities: global influence via restrictive group memberships (see the UN Security Council; NATO; the European Union; and the "nuclear club," among others); high quality of life indicators (long life expectancy, low infant mortality, high per capita GDP, etc.); democratic regimes where majority rule is restrained by minority rights; a liberal tradition of respective individual rights and private property; and an economy that is largely dependent upon the service sector (the portion of the economy that produces an intangible product, such as insurance, banking, e-commerce, entertainment, and so on). The other two sectors of the economy are industrial—tangible goods like a desk, a truck, or a refrigerator—and agricultural, which includes any commodity produced from the ground along with animal livestock.

While political scientists often argue about which states fit into which category, it is universally agreed that Japan, Canada, the United States, and the countries of Western Europe are liberal democracies. A strong case can also be made for Australia and New Zealand.

Communist/Post-Communist States

The former Second World has morphed into the Communist/Post-Communist, or C/PC, states. These states are largely found in Eastern Europe—the former Soviet Republics plus the old "Iron Curtain." Current communist regimes in such disparate locales as Cuba, Laos, North Korea,

Vietnam, and China may also be placed under this heading. In general, these states are making a transition from a command economy (state-planned production/communism) to a market economy (consumer-driven production/capitalism). However, communist political parties still tend to matter in these states, generally in a minority, critical watch-dog role. The "emerging stars" from this group, countries with increasing economic status and political clout, are Poland, Hungary, and the Czech Republic. Each has been admitted to NATO and the European Union in recent years.

The Third World

The Third World label has been broken into several smaller, more homogenous, groupings. These labels include Newly Industrialized Countries, Less Developed Countries, Islamic States, and others. Collectively, however, the countries in these groups are known as "developing countries." The Newly Industrialized Countries, or NICs, are the emerging stars of the developing world. As their name implies, NICs have reached a point of industrial production where they are exporting finished goods like calculators, DVD players, cars, or refrigerators as opposed to resource commodities such as oil, coffee, sugar, or bananas. NICs also feature political stability though not necessarily democracy, and have a solid infrastructure base. NICs wield regional influence and a growing service sector economy. Examples of NICs include Mexico, India, South Africa, the "ABC" countries of South America-Argentina, Brazil, and Chile, as well as the so-called "Tigers of Asia," led by South Korea, Singapore, and Taiwan.

Less Developed Countries (LDCs), befitting their name, are a step below the NICs in terms of economic development. LDCs have long-term potential for economic and political advancement, but this advancement is blocked by barriers, which usually involve significant cleavages, either ethnic, religious, or both, within the state. LDCs are overly dependent on a single commodity or two, such as oil or coffee. Political instability reigns and the infrastructure is poor, discouraging foreign commercial investment. Examples of LDCs include Nigeria, Colombia, and the Philippines.

The Islamic States include some 26 countries in the Middle East, North Africa, and southern Asia in which Islam and specifically the Qur'an serves as the guide for government, through a comprehensive body of law called *shari'a* and the general combination of church and state. Although these states are far from homogeneous in the interpretation and application of Islam to government, each attempts to do so. Examples of Islamic States include Iran, Egypt, Morocco, Jordan, and Pakistan.

These groupings, while not inclusive of all global states, cover the "case study" countries and provide a basis for comparison beyond the vagaries of the former "Three Worlds."

It is assumed that a student attempting to earn college credit in the field will have fundamental knowledge including the different means by which a state may divide its governmental power with sub-state government entities. The three basic options are:

Unitary—All real power is held at the national level. Sub-state governments do exist (e.g., municipalities, regions, etc.) but to administer the laws of the state government, not to make their own laws. Unitary government generally occurs in smaller geographical states with more homogenous populations where regional differences are small. Most Western European states have unitary governments.

Federal—Governing power is shared between the state and sub-state entities. This allows for regional differences within a country to be legislated differently. However, when the state and sub-state powers clash, the country's legal authority will be honored. Federal systems make the most sense in large geographical states that tend to more cleavages and a more heterogeneous population. Examples include India, Russia, Mexico, Brazil, Canada, Nigeria, and the United States. China, a huge geographical state, is unitary rather than federal because it has an authoritarian government led by the Chinese Communist Party; unitary rule bolsters its ability to rule China as it sees fit.

Confederation—The state government actually holds almost no powers here and the sub-state governments wield extensive legislative control. Thus, this system is doomed. The European Union is partially a confederation, with elements of federalism. Generally, confederacies break up into their component parts, creating a group of smaller sovereign states. The state government is usually given certain military and monetary powers only, and even this isn't assured. Examples of failed confederations include the United States from 1781–1787 under the Articles of Confederation and the Commonwealth of Independent States (CIS), and the former Soviet republics, from 1991–1993. Confederations are simply so weak as to be unworkable.

In terms of organizing an executive branch within a democracy, there are two main options from which a state may choose: a presidential or parliamentary system. American students are, of course, more familiar with the presidential system. Some hallmarks of this system include separation of powers, elections in which candidates directly vie for the presidency and a fixed election cycle—that is a definite and known date for the next election to occur.

(Remember, not all presidential systems are alike and, in fact, most of them are much stronger—that is, give the President much greater power with fewer checks—than does the American version of this system. When studying the Russian Federation or Nigeria, for example, this point will become clearer.)

Parliamentary Systems

A parliamentary system is vastly different. The executive leader in such a system is generally called Prime Minister, or in a French-speaking country, the premier. A parliamentary system involves a fusion of powers. Specifically, NO separate election is held in a parliamentary state to choose an executive. In Britain, for instance, Tony Blair was re-elected Prime Minister in 2005 but his name never appeared on a ballot running for "Prime Minister." Instead, the general election for the House of Commons decided who would then become the country's executive leader. After the results were tallied, all the country's parliamentary districts were known, and it was clear that Blair would remain Prime Minister because his party, New Labour, retained a majority of all the seats available in the House of Commons. Had the rival party, the Conservatives, won a majority of the seats in the parliament, then their leader, Michael Howard, would have become Britain's Prime Minister.

So, in any parliamentary state, whether it is Britain, Canada, or India among others, the Prime Minister is also an elected member of the country's legislature. Blair represents a northern English district called Sedgefield, for example. Furthermore, the members of the cabinet will also be members of the majority party who have been elected to represent legislative districts within parliament. The cabinet would, of course, be chosen by the Prime Minister following a general election. Thus, the executive and legislative branches operate in concert, or with fused powers, preventing the "gridlock" Americans are used to with separated chambers of government. Because the Prime Minister's party holds a majority in the legislative branch, *all* of a Prime Minister's legislative proposals will normally be passed into law. This makes parties and their manifestoes (what Americans call "platforms") much more important than the personalities of individual candidates.

A parliamentary system is also a much more flexible option than its presidential counterpart in that a country's leader can more easily be changed. Elections for example, are not set on fixed dates but rather, must generally be held within a five-year period of the previous election. This allows a Prime Minister great leverage in deciding when to call for elections, based on such factors as party popularity, the state of the economy, or weaknesses apparent in main rival parties. Having been last elected in June 2001, New Labour need not have called for an election until summer 2006, but opted for an election a year earlier believing it could defeat the Conservative at that time.

Additionally, the party holding a majority in parliament may change leaders in the middle of a parliamentary system from within. This happened to Margaret Thatcher in late 1990 as her own party, the Conservatives, decided that she was a liability toward future electoral success, and voted her out as party leader. Thus, John Major became the new Conservative Party leader, and by definition, because his party held a majority of seats in the House of Commons, he also became Britain's Prime Minister.

When one speaks of a "dual executive" or a "mixed system" as in Russia or France, it is actually a presidential system that also holds the weaker position of a "Prime Minister."

Another fundamental point of knowledge is the different ways that states may elect their legislative bodies. There are two main options here, with a third choice being a combination of the two systems. In the single member district plurality (SMDP) system, sometimes called "First Past the Post," a country is simply broken down into districts of roughly equal population. Parties run a single candidate in each district and the candidate gaining the most votes—a plurality—represents the district politically. The critique against SMDP is that it is quite disrepresentative of the electorate as a whole. Take a congressional district in the United States; say that the GOP candidate gains 47 percent of the vote, the Democratic candidate gains 46 percent, and minor party candidates split the remaining seven percent—an entirely plausible scenario in American politics. What results of course is that the GOP candidate gains 100 percent of the congressional seat, even though a majority of all votes, some 53 percent, voted *against* that candidate. A point in favor of the SMDP system is that it promotes majority government. Given the winner-take-all aspect of voting in each district, SMDP promotes a two-party system, as in the United States and Britain. Voters are dissuaded from voting for minor parties fearing their vote will be wasted since one of the two "biggies" is almost assured of gaining a plurality. This then leads one of the two major parties to hold a numerical majority of seats in the national legislature. A majority of seats leads the party to an absolute ability to pass legislation. Hence, proponents see SMDP as promoting more efficient government.

Proportional Representation

An alternative method for electing a country's legislative body is proportional representation, or PR. In this system, the country is not broken down into equally populated districts, and individual candidates are not voted upon. Instead, voters merely choose a party with their vote. Votes are tallied country wide, and the percentage won by a party translates into the percentage of seats they have earned in the legislature. For example, in a PR system if the Green Party was to win 11 percent of the vote, it would get 11 percent of the seats in the legislature. This system is much more representative of the electorate's wishes, but it leads to a plethora of parties holding seats in the legislature and thus no single party holding a majority by itself. This necessitates coalition government, or a combination of like-minded parties who combine to form a majority. Coalitions are often fragile and the smaller parties can sometimes wield undue influence or even break up a coalition. These factors are the arguments against a PR system.

Economic systems are intertwined with approaches to governing. States choose one of three basic variants for an economic model: communism, socialism, or capitalism. Marxism attempted to give the workers all power in both government and industry. In practice however, communism didn't work this way. Instead of the workers holding all the power, the Communist Party held all the ruling power, owned and ran the businesses, controlled all property, oversaw the media, and stifled dissent brutally. Thus, Marxism can be considered the ideal that was sought and communism the reality that evolved instead. In fairness to Karl Marx, the places where communism was attempted—Russia, China, Vietnam, Cuba, North Korea, Laos, etc.—were the antithesis of the highly developed capitalist states that Marx said were necessary for a successful communist revolt. To critique Marx, on the other hand, his ideas are simply unworkable given human nature and political reality, no matter where they are attempted. He spoke of needs, not wants, and seemed to assume that adherents of communism would be as selflessly devoted to the betterment of the working class as he himself was.

Marx's ideal of "From each according to ability; to each according to need" was never realized. Wages were roughly equal for most Soviet citizens regardless of family size. Some occupations—scientists, for example—were indeed paid better than others. And "perks" such as an apartment, car, or travel abroad were reserved for athletes, nuclear physicists, and others who publicly "glorified" the state. What did develop was a command economy where all production, from toothbrushes to ballistic missiles, was set by the state rather than by consumer demand. The command economy, synonymous with twentieth century communism, resulted in frequent product shortages on the one hand or massive surpluses on the other.

Socialism

Socialism, in the context we are using, is not a synonym for Marxism. Instead, it is an increased level of economic management from the state, which still allows for most businesses to be privately held. Socialism, as found in the states of Western Europe, calls for the nationalization (government monopoly) of certain key industries that are not to be run for a profit, but rather for the good of the citizens. Examples often include rail and air transportation, steel production, medical care, and communication such as telephone service. Parties in socialist states vie to deliver these services best to the voters. Thus, proponents of a socialist system contend that it provides a greater degree of democratic power to voters by giving them a direct say in plotting their country's economic course. Of course, one gets what one pays for. If a socialist state is to provide good services in these areas, taxation is generally relatively high.

Capitalism

Capitalism features a market economy, meaning the demand of consumers drives production. Risk is a main feature; financial reward can come from money invested, but investments often fail as new business ventures typically go under. Competition among businesses generally propels higher quality and lower prices.

Legitimacy is the notion that a government's rule is just and that it has the right to exist. Legitimacy is very high in the United States, Britain, and Canada, among others. Note that while many Americans may strongly desire to oust a Bill Clinton or George W. Bush from office, they do not wish to oust the Constitution and replace it with a new system. Thus, legitimacy is high. Among our case studies, Nigeria has the lowest legitimacy, which translates into the country having had a number of different constitutions in the past 40 years.

Efficacy is the belief that political action, whether by voting, writing to an elected official, or marching in the streets, matters and may influence policy. Efficacy is very low in the United States, as evidenced by the anemic turnout in federal elections for the President and even more so for Congress.

Finally, an internationally politically literate person will be familiar with NGOs, or non-governmental organizations. Some high profile examples of NGOs include Amnesty International, Greenpeace, Doctors Without Borders, and the International Red Cross. These groups are not funded by any particular government, but by private donations, mainly from citizens in the wealthy liberal democracies. However, these groups do most of their work in the more impoverished developing world, where their services are needed.

DRILL

COMPARATIVE POLITICAL LITERACY

DIRECTIONS: Carefully read and answer each of the following questions, which are based on the information that you have just read.

1. In international politics, the term "legitimacy" refers to

    (A) the belief of people that their government has the right to rule

    (B) a country's right to govern itself without outside interference

    (C) the trading of diplomats and staging of relations with other countries

    (D)   membership in international bodies such as the United Nations

    (E)   the feeling that an individual's actions make a political difference

2.   Which of the following is NOT an example of a stateless nation?

    (A)   Czechs and Slovaks

    (B)   Palestinians

    (C)   Kurds in Turkey and Iraq

    (D)   Chechens

    (E)   Tribes like the Cherokee and Sioux in the United States

3.   Low legitimacy is best exemplified by

    (A)   a party in power losing a national election

    (B)   concurring pro and anti-government rallies taking place in a national capital

    (C)   an ongoing social cleavage over class or religious differences

    (D)   increasing and recurring amendments to a government's constitution

    (E)   decreasing voter turnout in national elections

4.   A social cleavage—a significant split within a state—is LEAST likely to occur among

    (A)   various religious groups; i.e., Catholics and Protestants or Christians and Muslims

    (B)   urban and rural groups; i.e., Paris versus outlying regions of France

    (C)   genders; i.e., men versus women

    (D)   social classes; middle class and working class in Britain, "untouchables" and other castes in India, and so on

    (E)   different nations within a state that have separate histories and cultures; e.g. Quebec and Ontario in Canada

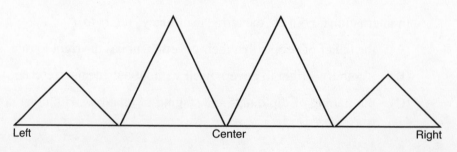

5.   A moderate conservative would be placed on the chart at which point?

   (A)   Right

   (B)   Left

   (C)   Center

   (D)   Between Left and Center

   (E)   Between Right and Center

6.   A person who favors increased individual rights at the expense of a strong state would be placed at which point?

   (A)   Right   (D)   Nowhere on this chart

   (B)   Left   (E)   Between right and center

   (C)   Center

7.   Whether or not a state utilizes a presidential or parliamentary system decides which of the following issues?

   (A)   Where the center of executive power lies

   (B)   How the power is divided between national and subnational governments

   (C)   Whether or not a state has a two-party or multi-party system

   (D)   How a state's legislature will be elected—proportional representation or single-member district plurality

   (E)   Whether or not coalition government will be necessary

8.   A parliamentary system—in which members are elected to seats based on the proportion of votes their party wins in a district—encourages

   (A)   a strict two-party system as in Britain and the United States

   (B)   minor parties to wield consider influence

   (C)   a cohesive legislative body

   (D)   minor parties to be absorbed by the major parties

   (E)   voter apathy

9.   Geography would likely affect all of the following EXCEPT

   (A)   whether or not a state has unitary or federal framework of government

   (B)   whether a state employs a presidential or parliamentary executive

(C)   whether or not a variety of cleavages exist within a state

(D)   what amount of a state's population is involved in agricultural production

(E)   the total size of a country's population

10.   A state is definitely a liberal democracy if it

(A)   holds a permanent seat on the UN Security Council, a la China or Russia

(B)   is the most economically prosperous state in its region, such as Costa Rica in Central America or Israel in the Middle East

(C)   holds a strong infrastructure and has high legitimacy

(D)   hosts major global events such as soccer's World Cup or the Olympic Games

(E)   wields global influence and has high quality of life indicators

11.   Which is NOT a necessary characteristic of a state, as the term is used in international politics?

(A)   It has a permanent population.

(B)   It exercises ultimate decision-making authority within its own territory.

(C)   It contains definite, recognized boundaries.

(D)   It is politically organized via either a unitary, federal, or confederate national government.

(E)   It has defensive military capabilities to protect its sovereignty.

12.   Which statement is NOT true of unitary governments?

(A)   A unitary government makes the most sense in a culturally homogeneous state.

(B)   In a unitary system, no subnational governments exist whatsoever.

(C)   All powers held by the government are concentrated in the central, or federal, government.

(D)   Although a unitary form of government need not be authoritarian, it would make sense from an authoritarian communist state to have a unitary rather than federal government.

(E)   Smaller geographical states are often unitary in structure.

13. The form of government that grants the most power to subnational components of the state (e.g., provinces in Canada, Russian Regions, U.S. states, cities in Mexico) is a

   (A) totalitarian system   (D) confederate system

   (B) unitary system   (E) laissez-faire system

   (C) federalist system

14. A capitalist economic system is based upon

   (A) individual investment, private ownership, profit, and competition

   (B) a strict, absolute laissez-faire approach by the government

   (C) the nationalization of certain key industries, while other industries are privately owned

   (D) the argument of equal conditions for all citizens

   (E) public ownership of all businesses

15. A federal system makes the most sense in which of the following states?

   (A) A large geographic state with a democratic government and a heterogeneous population.

   (B) A large geographic state with a communist government and a largely homogeneous population.

   (C) A small geographic state with a homogeneous population.

   (D) A capitalist state with a presidential system.

   (E) A state in which the subnational governments desire to retain the greatest possible autonomy.

16. In this form of government, the Prime Minister and Cabinet are the leaders of the legislative branch of government, as well as serving as the country's executive leaders.

   (A) Democracy

   (B) Parliamentary system

   (C) System of checks and balances

   (D) Presidential system

   (E) Unitary system

17. Someone who promotes a socialist economy would cite all of the following EXCEPT

    (A) higher taxes lead to better services

    (B) a strict market economy accentuates and increases economic gaps in a society

    (C) a "cradle to grave" safety net of social services is more desirable than Social Darwinism

    (D) the "invisible hand" ensures fairness and competition in all sectors of society

    (E) political parties will manage key economic sectors to the benefit of the larger public as opposed to a select group of shareholders

18. In which of the following groups of states would both infrastructure and per capita GDP likely be the lowest?

    (A) Liberal democracy

    (B) C/PC state

    (C) NIC

    (D) LDC

    (E) Islamic state

Comparative Government & Politics Review

THE UNITED KINGDOM

Britain remains the only case study of a liberal democracy in the AP's line-up for this course. Let's start with its name: *Britain* (Great Britain if you're more formal) or the *UK* are accurate synonyms for the United Kingdom. *England* is not a synonym for the country but rather describes the most populous and wealthy southern portion of the state. Three other regions that constitute the UK are Wales and Scotland on the British Isle and Northern Ireland, or Ulster, the six northernmost counties on the Irish Isle.

Politically, Britain is a study in evolution and not revolution. The core of British constitutional law has lasted for some eight centuries and is unwritten. (A note to the Comparative Government student: this is a political science course, not a history survey. So you need enough historical knowledge to provide context and understanding and no more for each case study. Don't confuse the course with AP European History or World History. The focus of the course is much more geared to current events and changes than to analyzing the importance of various eighteenth-century monarchs.) Britain serves as a model from which to study other parliamentary systems and is an example of a government with extremely high legitimacy.

The British system has traditionally been split between dignified and efficient institutions of government. The dignified elements are unelected and wield comparatively little actual political power. They include the House of Lords and the monarchy. The most important role played currently by these institutions is to provide stability, pride, and continuity. Both institutions are generally respected by the British populace, especially Queen Elizabeth II, hence they remain. The House of Lords is an unelected chamber, the upper house of Parliament. It cannot block legislation, but it can delay it, giving greater public attention to a particular bill. It's other political powers include the right to initiate bills and serving as Britain's highest court of appeals, a role currently called into question by the European Union's Court of Justice.

The efficient elements of government include the House of Commons and cabinet, led by the Prime Minister. They are elected and hold almost all of the UK's actual political power. As a parliamentary system, Britain contains a fusion of power. The Prime Minister is both an elected member of Parliament (representing an individual district, in Tony Blair's case, this is Sedgefield in the north of England) and the country's executive head of government. Additionally, the Prime Minister will be the leader of the majority party in parliament. And since party discipline in Britain is *strictly* enforced, this entails a tremendous benefit; all legislation that the Prime Minister wants passed almost always will be.

Because of its "first-past-the-post" system, as the Brits like to call SMDP, the country is a two-party system. While various regional parties exist, such as the Scottish National Party or Sinn Fein, the two parties that dominate Parliament and can realistically hope to govern Britain are the Conservative Party on the right and New Labour on the left. The Liberal Democrats have emerged during the last twenty years as Britain's strongest "minor" party, and it is now further to the left than New Labour. The shadow cabinet—the leadership of the major party out of power—exists to watch and criticize the government, offering their alternative program should they get elected to govern the next Parliament. This function is most evident during "Prime Minister's Questions," a weekly period in which the government is held accountable for its actions by the shadow leader and backbenchers from all parties. *Backbencher* is the generic term for any MP (Member of Parliament) who does not hold a cabinet position.

The party holding a majority in the House of Commons must call elections within a five-year period of taking office. Ideally, the government will call an election in their fourth year of holding power. This will occur if polling numbers reveal that public opinion is favorable to the governing party. If the Prime Minister's party waits the full five years before calling an election, this reveals that they are likely to lose and hence have delayed the election as long possible. By-elections are a good barometer as to how the public views the government. A by-election occurs as a special one-off election to fill a vacancy in a district between general elections because of death or resignation. If the governing party is losing seats in these elections, this is an encouraging sign for the opposition party.

Party Discipline

Party discipline is strictly maintained by a variety of methods by both New Labour and the Tories, as the Conservatives are commonly known. For backbenchers, the lure of a safe seat is strong inducement not to cross party leadership. A safe seat is a district from which a party generally wins. An MP following the party line on votes in the House of Commons will be run in a safe seat at the next general election. For cabinet members, collective responsibility exists, which means that the cabinet may passionately disagree amongst itself over a proposed policy, or even with the Prime Minister. However, once the policy is settled upon and announced, the entire cabinet, even those in disagreement, are to publicly promote the policy. The "stick" held by the Prime Minister is the annual cabinet reshuffle, in which loyal members are rewarded and promoted to more prestigious posts, while members not practicing collective responsibility in an enthusiastic fashion are demoted or even returned to the backbenches. Within the cabinet (or shadow cabinet), the three most prestigious posts and potential stepping stones to party leadership are the ministry of defence, foreign minister, and the chancellor of the exchequer, a position controlling the treasury and budget.

A couple of points to note regarding party discipline and the political spectrum in Britain. First, while Americans are not used to this level of discipline among elected officials, the British see it as only logical. Why would an MP join and run as a member of the Labour Party if he or she did not want to support its policies? If an MP finds that he or she is crossing the party on several votes, the reasoning goes, that MP should leave the party and join one whose ideology fits better. It only makes sense to the British. In this system a party manifesto (collection of beliefs) is more important than an individual MP's personality. Furthermore, the British political system does not require MPs to live in the district they represent. Again, this strengthens the expectation of voters for a candidate to represent his party's beliefs while diminishing the importance of the individual candidate's views.

Infrequently, however, a "free vote" is offered by the government. This is a vote on a bill in which party discipline is not to be enforced and occurs on "matters of conscience," such as votes on the age of consent for homosexuals or the proposed ban on fox hunting in the countryside, both of which have been offered as free votes under Tony Blair's reign as Prime Minister.

In Britain, and in Western Europe as a whole, the terms "right" and "left" have a different connotation than they do in the United States. A Republican in the U.S. should not assume that a Conservative Party member will hold similar views because both support major parties on the right. In Western Europe, right and left mainly deal with management of the economy and, to a lesser extent, the military. Social issues are not an area of concern and hold little debate or political relevance. For example, capital punishment was banned in the UK in 1966 and there is no effort by the Tories to revive it. Similarly, the legality of abortion is not an inflammatory issue, nor is gun control, which is seen as a logical way to minimize gun crime throughout Europe. Homosexuality is also a less divisive issue, with openly gay politicians commonly holding cabinet positions in Europe.

KEY LEADERS

Margaret Thatcher

Whether loved or hated—and she was much of both—Margaret Thatcher is a figure who has shaped the British political debate for much of the past thirty years. Mrs. Thatcher summarized the period from the end of World War II to 1979 as the "British Disease." By this, she meant that Britain had become overly socialist, uncompetitive, unproductive, and basically held ransom by ever-strengthening labor unions. She not only blamed the Labour Party for this, but held her own Conservative Party in contempt for attempting to play Labour's game. Thatcher's legacy is that she shifted the Tories sternly back to the right on both economic and social policies.

A divisive figure, Thatcher held office from 1979–1990. She never lost a general election, but lost favor within her own party after eleven tumultuous years of rule. When speaking of "Thatcherism," several facets of her time as Prime Minister are included. First, it is considered that Mrs. Thatcher "broke" the unions with her winning battle over the striking coal miners in 1984–85. Also, privatization, or the selling off of nationalized industry, was a key component of Thatcherism. British Petroleum, British Steel, Rolls Royce, British Airways, British Rail, municipal water supplies, and scores more were privatized under both Thatcher and her successor, John Major. Council homes, which were rented under government subsidy, were sold off by the tens of thousands. Mrs. Thatcher's "my way or the highway" style in both manner and oratory added to controversial decisions such as the Falkland Islands war versus Argentina in 1982. Her legacy, like that of most politicians, is mixed. Inflation went down, as did taxation. However, homelessness and unemployment both increased during her tenure.

John Major

Having worn out her welcome within the Conservative Party by 1990, Thatcher failed to gain enough support in a party leadership vote among Tory MPs to retain the Prime Minister's seat. John Major, a relatively inexperienced cabinet member, assumed a shaky throne. The Tories continued to divide under his leadership, essentially on the issue of the EU, especially regarding the single currency.

Major's position on the issue was moderate and indeed the same as Tony Blair's in that he promised a referendum to the British voters on the single currency before the country would ever adopt it. For the "euroskeptics" in his own party's backbenches, this was not good enough. Despising most aspects of the European Union, the euroskeptics demanded a statement denying that Britain would ever join a single currency. Although Major quieted these critics in 1995 with a surprise resignation as party leader and a subsequent vindication in being retained by the Conservative MPs, the insurrection within the Tory Party never totally died. Divided by such issues as the Mad Cow beef scare, "sleaze" scandals regarding sex and bribery, and a general feeling that the party had simply governed for too long and was bereft of new ideas, the Conservatives limped into the 1997 general election and were soundly thrashed by New Labour under the leadership of Tony Blair.

Tony Blair

The student should use the designation "New Labour" when describing the more moderate, pragmatic party under Tony Blair's stewardship. The "Third Way" that Blair speaks of is a middle road between the more extreme Thatcherism and Labour's previous socialist beliefs. A key step taken under Blair's leadership was the removal of the party's Article IV, which claimed Labour to be fundamentally a socialist party.

In Westminster, New Labour has offered several noteworthy changes to British constitutional law. For one, the referendum—a little needed or used device traditionally in the UK because of the regime's high legitimacy—has been either used or offered on several occasions, including such issues as devolution for Scotland and Wales; the Good Friday Peace Agreement in Northern Ireland; British acceptance of the EU Constitution; and eventually perhaps, on the acceptance of the euro as the British currency.

A main reform initiative has been devolution, or the transfer of some political decision-making away from the House of Commons to Scotland, Wales, Northern Ireland, and London. In addition, Britain's first-ever minimum wage was introduced with the "New Deal" program. Hereditary peers—aristocrats who pass their seats on to an heir—have been stripped of their voting rights in the House of Lords in favor of Life Peers, who earn their seats through meritorious service to the UK, whether through scientific, business, or artistic achievement, are now the only active members of the House of Lords. Also, the landmark Good Friday Peace Agreement was forged in 1998 between the UK and the Republic of Ireland. After successful referenda in Northern Ireland and in the Republic, the agreement was enacted. It contains the following provisions in an effort to end Ulster's decades of sectarian violence.

- Ireland relinquished its constitutional claim to Ulster.
- Northern Ireland was to receive its own elected assembly to legislate local matters.
- Prisoners for both the Orange (Protestant) and IRA (Catholic) causes were to gain release.
- The para-military organizations on both the Orange and IRA sides were to "decommission," or hand over, their weapons to the government.

The controversial agreement has not been totally followed by the parties involved—especially in regard to decommissioning—and thus the Northern Ireland assembly has been suspended several times under the New Labour government.

PATHS TO POWER

The term "political elites" indicates those who have access to political positions in the upper bureaucracy, parliament, the cabinet, and so on. A political elite is not limited to the elected head of state, and all countries have political elites. (Some misguided American students have indicated in past AP essay exams that political elites exist only in "bad places.") The term is not derogatory, it is a fact of political life in all countries. With each case study, we will close our examination with a look at how one may enhance one's chances at achieving political influence, success, and power.

In Britain, it is traditional to attend "public school" as a step toward a political career. *Public school* is the British label for what Americans would call a private boarding school. The name draws from the fact that these schools often prepare students for a life of public service to Britain via political office. From there, the accepted path to political heights is a university stint at one of two schools, Oxford or Cambridge, the two most prestigious universities in the UK. It certainly helps to be from the middle class rather than the working class to have the lineage, money, and access to attain the education described. Again, "middle class" has a different connotation in Britain than it does in the U.S., where class status matters much less. Middle class to the British implies a lineage of education, good public standing and "old money." A famous football star like David Beckham remains working class no matter how many millions of pounds he earns because the distinction is not based on money alone as it would be in the U.S., but on family history and previous position in society.

Aside from being middle class, it helps to be English and indeed, from London, as opposed to Welsh , Scottish, or from Ulster. The vast majority of the UK's population lives in and around London and thus, the mainstay of British political influence is found there as well.

Additionally, the British civil service also affords the opportunity for political influence. The civil service is based on merit and its personnel does not change with electoral changes in the British general elections. Thus, the bureaucracy tends to be a source of stability and or professional expertise as opposed to one of mere political support and patronage. Remember, however, that because cabinet positions are determined largely by party discipline and collective responsibility, the ministers themselves are not expert by training in their assigned departments, which again enhances the importance of the civil service beneath them.

DRILL

THE UNITED KINGDOM

DIRECTIONS: Carefully read and answer each of the following questions, which are based on the information that you have just read.

19. A majority party in the House of Commons is most likely to call for national elections

   (A) when the public displays a readiness for a national election

   (B) immediately following an unexpected party leadership vote by the majority party

   (C) after a cabinet shake-up

   (D) in response to a backbenchers' revolt

   (E) after a series of five by-election votes, in which the majority retained three seats it previously held and gained one from the opposition

20. If one leans moderately to the left politically in the United States he or she will likely support the programs and policies of the Democratic Party. A politician who leans more than moderately to the left in contemporary Britain is most likely to support the programs and policies of which party?

   (A) Scottish National Party   (D) Liberal Democrats

   (B) Conservative   (E) Sinn Fein

   (C) Labour

21. In the United States, elections in the House of Representatives are held every two years and elections in the United States Senate are held on a staggered six-year basis. In contrast, British parliamentary elections are held

   (A) every five years

   (B) every four years

   (C) whenever the public calls for them by petition

   (D) whenever the majority party decides to hold them

   (E) whenever the majority party decides to hold them within a five-year limit

22. As a result of parliamentary acts, the main political power of the House of Lords is to

    (A) delay legislation from passage for up to one year

    (B) introduce legislation

    (C) ratify bills passed in the House of Commons

    (D) serve as Britain's highest court of appeals

    (E) award notable individual achievements with life peerages

23. Margaret Thatcher's reaction to socialism included all of the following EXCEPT

    (A) reducing inflation by restricting the money supply

    (B) stimulating private sector growth by lowering direct taxes and interest rates

    (C) reduction of trade union power

    (D) re-emphasis on free enterprise and entrepreneurship

    (E) reducing Britain's national debt by cutting defense spending by 1/3

24. The British have succeeded in maintaining a stable democratic government over the past 300 years primarily because of the

    (A) civilian political control over the British military

    (B) existence of a national church devoted to reform and modernization

    (C) relative wealth of average British citizens compared with their continental (European) counterparts

    (D) absence of significant social cleavages within the population

    (E) ability of governing groups to adapt political structures to accommodate change

25. Which of the following statements best explains the general view of the British electorate toward the European Union?

    (A) It views the EU as necessary for Britain's economic future, but fears a loss of British sovereignty.

    (B) It views the EU as necessary for Britain's military security, but fears that Germany and France will dominate the union at Britain's expense.

(C) It views the EU as necessary for Europe's health in the global economic market, but fears that EU rules will result in an unwanted influx of immigration to the United Kingdom.

(D) It wants Britain out of the European Union as quickly as possible.

(E) It wants Britain more fully integrated into the EU, accepting its single currency and social chapter rulings.

26. Which of the following British political associations is NOT correct?

(A) An MP, as opposed to a "peer"—serves in the House of Commons

(B) Cabinet reshuffle—a reflection of collective responsibility

(C) 'First past the post'—British synonym for the SMDP election scheme

(D) Speaker of the house—helps form government policy

(E) Chancellor of the exchequer—similar to secretary of the treasury in the United States, only more powerful, with some powers also associated with the U.S. Federal Reserve Chair

27. Contemporary British society can be classified as all of the following EXCEPT

(A) post-industrial, with a mixed economy emphasizing high-tech services

(B) maintaining a semi-rigid class consciousness

(C) being religiously diverse: Anglican, Presbyterian, Catholic in different regions

(D) maintaining a "cradle to grave" welfare state

(E) politically homogeneous on economic issues, but not on social issues

28. In the United Kingdom during the period from 1945–1979,

(A) the Labour Party solely held governing power

(B) socialism and the welfare state became more entrenched in the British political culture

(C) Labour replaced the Liberal Party as the leading British party on the left

(D) Britain became more industrially competitive worldwide as it abandoned its former colonial empire

(E)   the Conservative Party dictated the political agenda that Labour followed

29.   The shadow cabinet's main role is to

(A)   howl with derision at the Government front benches during the weekly Prime Minister's Questions period

(B)   sever the collective responsibility held by the Prime Minister's cabinet

(C)   call for general elections at the earliest possible date

(D)   serve as a public watchdog and critic of the government

(E)   criticize the majority party's manifesto

30.   The following statement is quoted from Margaret Thatcher:
"The Old Testament prophets do not say 'Brothers I want a consensus.' They said, 'This is my faith, this is what I passionately believe. If you believe too, then come with me.'"
Which of the following views about the British political is reflected in the quote above?

(A)   Although Great Britain was plagued by disputes between the left and the right, Thatcher would be the voice of the center.

(B)   The left and right should forego past squabbles to economically reinvigorate the nation.

(C)   Judeo–Christian values on such issues as abortion, homosexuality, divorce, and the death penalty should guide the government's policy-making.

(D)   The United Kingdom's problems could be solved by strong leadership with a clear vision for the nation.

(E)   The decline of class distinctions was leading to an unhealthy emphasis on decision-making based on consensus in the cabinet.

31.   Careers for elites in parliament, the cabinet, the civil service, top business leaders, high ranking military officials, and the leadership of the Anglican Church are most available to which groups within the United Kingdom?

I.   Residents of London and the south of England

II.   "Ox-bridge" alumni

III.   public school graduates

IV.   educated, white wealthy males

V.   the middle class

(A)   I, II, III, IV and V   (D)   IV and V only

(B)   II, III, and IV   (E)   II only

(C)   I only

32.   Which of the following statements regarding class politics in Britain is true?

(A)   Of all the cleavages within the British political system, the working class/middle class split promotes the most violence throughout the country.

(B)   New political issues, such as the minimum wage and foreign asylum-seekers, have reinforced class divisions.

(C)   Manual workers in general have been disappointed by the views of "New Labour" and have largely defected to the Conservative Party.

(D)   While the Thatcher years saw class nearly disappear as an issue in England, it remains a strong cleavage in Scotland and Wales.

(E)   The Labour Party tries to politicize most issues on a class basis because the percentage of Britons who consider themselves "working class" continues to increase.

33.   The Labour government under Tony Blair has made all of the following reforms since 1997 EXCEPT

(A)   imposing a minimum wage on British businesses

(B)   separating the Church of England (Anglican Church) from official participation in government

(C)   moving to eliminate hereditary peers from the House of Lords

(D)   allowing certain regions and cities to exert more legislative autonomy throughout the United Kingdom

(E)   proposing a referendum before taking an official stance on the single European currency

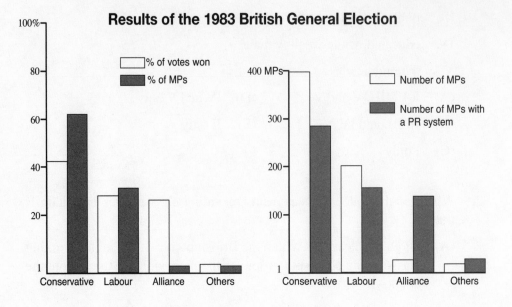

Results of the 1983 British General Election

34. The chart above suggests that

   I.   Britain employs proportional representation

   II. the Alliance (Social-Liberal Democrats) must have finished a strong
        second in many parliamentary districts

   III. the single member district plurality system favored the Conservative
        Party more than either Labour or the Alliance

   IV. if Britain had employed a PR system in 1983, the leftist parties
        could have formed a coalition government to rule as a "majority"

   (A) II and III only   (D) III only

   (B) III and IV only   (E) II, III, and IV

   (C) I and III only

Comparative Government & Politics Review

THE EUROPEAN UNION

The European Union has steadily grown in both scope and number of member states since its inception in 1957 with the Treaty of Rome. This treaty created a common market in regard to coal and steel tariffs and production levels. The "original six" who signed this treaty were (West) Germany, Italy, France and the "Low Countries"—Belgium, Luxembourg, and the Netherlands. This original incarnation was known as the European Economic Community, or EEC.

During the 1970s, the European Community, as it became known, added Britain, Ireland, and Denmark. In the '80s, Greece, Portugal, and Spain joined, and by 1995 Finland, Austria, and Sweden had become members of what was now known as the European Union, placing the union at fifteen member states where it would remain for roughly a decade. The European Union remains foremost an economic benefit to its member states, providing "free trade" (i.e., no tariffs on most goods) among EU members. However, this comes with a price of sorts—a loss of national sovereignty to the EU on subsidies and production levels on certain goods.

The Maastricht Treaty (1991) created a single monetary policy for the European Union. Eleven of the fifteen member states adopted the *euro* as their currency beginning in 2002. Britain, Sweden, Denmark, and Greece did not adopt the currency on the initial wave.

The Treaty of Nice (2001) called for the expansion of the EU to as many as thirteen new states within a decade. Indeed, the EU formally added ten new members, mainly from the former communist bloc of Eastern Europe, in May 2004. These new member states, commonly referred to within the EU as "ascension states," include the Czech Republic, Hungary, Poland, Slovakia, Slovenia, Lithuania, Latvia, Estonia, Malta, and Cyprus. (Turkey has recently been approved for negotiations to join the EU.) These new members are sometimes referred to as "poorer cousins" of the EU and they will not receive full membership benefits for some time. For instance, none are immediately eligible to join the single currency and their voting shares in the European Parliament will be proportionally lower than the more senior member states.

Here are some other important terms to know:

Convergence criteria—The steps an EU member must satisfy in order to be eligible to join the single currency. This includes both debt and deficit levels, interest, and currency exchange rates. On the first wave of adoption, these criteria kept Greece from joining the single currency.

Stability pact—To avoid the threat of punitive action from the EU, including fines, member states using the single currency are to meet the following guidelines:

- Annual budget deficit must not exceed 3 percent of total GDP
- Annual inflation rate also must not exceed 3 percent

Interestingly, both Germany and France, the presumed leaders of the EU, have violated this pact without punishment in recent years.

Common Agricultural Policy (CAP)—This is designed to make subsidies between member states equal. A subsidy is a guaranteed payment from a government to a producer, usually farmers, for a certain commodity. Thus, it is the artificial raising of prices. France has fought hardest against the implementation of the CAP.

European Parliament—Fairly weak legislative arm of the EU. In the past, seats were allocated mainly on the basis of population per state (à la the U.S. House of Representatives), but that formula is being changed with the ascension of the Eastern European states to favor the established members of the newcomers, regardless of population totals. The 2004 European parliamentary elections drew record low turnouts, even with the hoopla surrounding the admission of the new member states just a month earlier. (The designation *MEP* equals a member of the European Parliament.) Because this body seems relative meaningless and remote to many citizens, those who do vote for their MEP are more likely to cast a protest vote in regard to the performance of their country's current government than a studied vote on who might serve the voter best in Brussels (Belgium), which is the headquarters of most EU organizations.

Fundamental Charter of Rights—Basic individual rights according to the EU. Includes provisions that ban capital punishment, guarantee health care for all and mandate equal pay for equal work among the genders.

European Court of Justice—Judicial arm of the EU holding the power of judicial review over decisions made by courts in member states (i.e., House of Lords as Britain's highest court of appeal). Thus, the ECJ holds considerable ability to limit member sovereignty via its rulings. Each EU member state places a judge on the ECJ.

EU Constitution—This would include all previous EU treaties discussed above, as well as establishing a stronger EU presidency and a more coordinated EU foreign policy. Britain, among other states, again seems reluctant to cede more sovereignty to the EU under this constitution, and Tony Blair has reluctantly allowed for a referendum to be held on its passage. Other states may do the same; it remains to be seen if this constitution is thus doomed to rejection.

DRILL

THE EUROPEAN UNION

DIRECTIONS: Carefully read and answer each of the following questions, which are based on the information that you have just read.

35. The two countries that have held the most sway in setting EU policies are

(A) Britain and Spain   (D) Germany and France

(B) Italy and Germany   (E) Britain and Germany

(C) France and Belgium

36. The Stability Pact is designed to limit

(A) eligibility for the single currency

(B) subsidy levels

(C) spending and inflation

(D) future EU membership

(E) tariff levels

37. The Treaty of Rome established a common market on

(A) coal and steel

(B) automobile production

(C) agriculture

(D) military production

(E) banking and insurance policies and procedures

38. The European Union most strictly infringes upon member state's sovereignty in regard to

(A) culture, including sports and tourism

(B) immigration policies

(C) foreign policy

(D) military production

(E) economic policies

39. Which of the following countries is a member of the European Union?

    (A) Norway   (D) Monaco

    (B) Hungary   (E) Turkey

    (C) Switzerland

40. The proposed European Union Constitution would create a significantly stronger EU

    (A) presidency   (D) currency

    (B) parliament   (E) military

    (C) court system

41. Voters in EU member states seem to view elections for the European Parliament as

    (A) important and politically meaningful

    (B) a referendum on their state's current governing party

    (C) a way to curb further EU integration

    (D) completely irrelevant

    (E) a way to promote further European integration

Comparative Government & Politics Review

RUSSIAN FEDERATION

Within the Russian unit, much intra-comparison will occur between the current Russian Federation and the former Soviet Union. Students should be careful when writing or saying the word "Russia" that they mean the state that has existed since 1991. When referring to the communist state that existed from the Bolshevik Revolution in 1917, one should say or write "Soviet Union" or "USSR." When referring to the pre-Soviet period, one should say or write "Czarist Russia." The Czar (Russian for *Caesar*) was the absolute monarch that ruled Russia without check until Nicholas II was killed by the Bolsheviks, or Russian communists.

Knowledge of the Soviet Union is important as a stepping stone to understanding the evolution of the current Russian Federation. Rather than focus on all the general secretaries from Lenin forward, we will concentrate on two: the man who most greatly shaped the Soviet system—Stalin—and the one who ended the Soviet Union by misadventure—Gorbachev.

Born from the carnage and chaos of the five-year Bolshevik Revolution (1917–1922) the Soviet Union was not an ideal staging ground for a communist experiment. Karl Marx had claimed that only the most industrial of states with a long-exploited proletariat could hope to stage a successful communist uprising. Vladimir Lenin attempted to revise this process by instigating the revolution via a small committed band of communists known as the "vanguard." For Russia to develop a proletariat (industrial working class) might take centuries, as Lenin well knew. So he jump-started the process with the Bolshevik Revolution, eventually defeating czarist and other opposition forces, leading the Communist Party to power, and creating the Soviet Union.

Lenin's unexpectedly early death in 1924 left a power void and much infighting within the CPSU (Communist Party of the Soviet Union). The general secretary, Josef Stalin, used treachery and guile, as he would for the next quarter century, to consolidate his power. From Stalin on, the position of "General Secretary of the CPSU" became synonymous with the leader of the USSR. (Both Lenin and Stalin were made-up names. *Lenin* is a river in Russia and *Stalin* means "man of steel.")

Stalin's rule had the most impact on what the Soviet Union would become, most of it negative. The five-year plans embarked the USSR on a massive crash-course toward industrialization. The country did industrialize but at great human cost. Collectivization of agriculture was meant to free up labor to be moved to the cities. One group of wealthy peasants, the *kulaks*, were simply murdered as a class of people because Stalin believed they could not be co-opted into collective farming for the state. The shift in agricultural production also led the Great Famine, in which ten million people, mostly in the Ukraine, are believed to have starved to death.

Stalin's infamous *gulags* killed an estimated 20 million Soviet citizens, a far larger number than Hitler could claim in the ghastly Nazi concentration camps. The *gulags* served as prisons, forced labor camps, and ultimately death chambers. These grim prisons served as the final destination for Stalin's imagined rivals for power within the CPSU. If it was dangerous to be Stalin's enemy, it was equally perilous to be close to him, as many former associates discovered too late. The killing of thousands of top CPSU officials, including heroes of the Bolshevik Revolution, former comrades of Lenin, and top Red Army leaders, is known as the Great Purge.

Gosplan gained great political influence under the five-year plans. This agency served as the central economic planning organ for the CPSU, setting production levels in all areas of production. A system of fraud and cynicism also emerged here. The quotas set by *Gosplan* under Stalin were often impossibly high to reach, or certainly impossible to reach with quality production. But Soviet managers realized that to speak this truth would lead to their deaths in the *gulags,* so they simply faked their figures, said the right things, and stayed alive.

Upon Stalin's death in 1953, Nikita Khrushchev succeeded him as CPSU general secretary. Three years later at a party congress, Khrushchev criticized Stalin for his "crimes," including the terror of the *gulags* and the "cult of personality" Stalin had encouraged, in which he [Stalin] was presented as all-knowing and infallible in Soviet literature, art, and other forms of propaganda.

The *nomanklatura* developed as the key to advancement in the Soviet system. It was a list of names to be considered by the party for any important post, from a position in the bureaucracy, or *apparatchi*, to a gymnastics coach or university professor.

KEY LEADERS

Mikhail Gorbachev

By 1985, the Soviet system had stagnated. No longer was even the pretense of a worker's paradise attempted. Three little-loved general secretaries had come and gone via ill health an old age in three years. Enter Mikhail Gorbachev, who would shake the Soviet system to its foundation, a foundation that ultimately could not survive his reforms.

Gorbachev is an intriguing leader who lacked the vision, the skill, or both to implement his reforms. He desired to make the CPSU a more popular and responsive party, thus ensuring that it would keep its political monopoly. He also wanted the Soviet Union to become economically stronger. In the end, Gorbachev inadvertently killed both his beloved party and the USSR.

The key reform was *perestroika,* or the reform of Soviet industry. Gorbachev wished to change the travesty that went with *gosplan's* central economic planning. Not only were production figures falsely reported, but quality was often sub-par on the goods that were produced. Few Soviets desired to own a Russian-made television, refrigerator, or car, for example. Certainly no foreign countries desired to import these shoddily made products. Also, central planning continued to lead to chronic overages and shortages of various products. The Soviet economy was competent in producing military arms like tanks and rocket launchers, but Gorbachev realized that an economy could not be based on this. How many average people purchase a tank or a rocket launcher? Instead, the "soft goods"—consumer items, like toasters and televisions—were a key toward revitalizing the Soviet economy.

Perestroika involved rethinking Soviet production. It granted more power to managers. In the effort to produce quality goods, managers would set reasonable quotas and workers would now be accountable for quality. These same workers had long been used to high rates of absenteeism and drinking on the job, and so predictably chafed at the notion of being held accountable. Managers, too, preferred the old system of "lie and pretend" to actual responsibility. Soviet citizens didn't see a marked change in supply or quality of products quickly enough to win them over.

A second reform that ran amok was democratization. Gorbachev envisioned this as a way to revitalize his party and make it more responsive and accountable to the Soviet people. He desired campaigns and unrigged elections for the first time in the USSR. However, these campaigns and elections were to be between CPSU candidates only. The party would maintain its monopoly on power yet become more efficient and popular, or so Gorbachev thought. In actuality, the public began calling for "true" elections including non-communist candidates, such as Boris Yeltsin. By the summer of 1991, Yeltsin had won a landslide victory for the presidency of the Russian Soviet Republic. Meanwhile Gorbachev, who had never been elected to anything, began to cede political power to Yeltsin almost immediately. Gorbachev was increasingly a lame duck, a leader in name only.

Glasnost was a third reform that turned against Gorbachev in the end. The word means openness and was designed to be a selective relaxation of Soviet expression and policies. *Pravda* and other leading newspapers were encouraged to report international events accurately for the first time in Soviet history. Additionally, criticism of Stalin and Brezhnev was encouraged, as was discussion of Khrushchev's attempted reforms. Off limits was criticism of Gorbachev or the Communist Party. However, having tasted some freedom of expression, the Soviet media and citizenry pushed the gates open and condemned Gorbachev for the failures of *perestroika* and for not permitting full-fledged elections.

By August, 1991 a small group of hard-liners within the military and CPSU, attempted to remove Gorbachev from power and remove the Soviet Union to its former authoritarian past. The move by various republics such as Latvia, Lithuania, and Estonia to become independent was apparently the final straw. Held captive in his *dacha,* or summer vacation house near the Caspian Sea, Gorbachev remained helpless as events unfurled. However, the public failed to support the coup and Boris Yeltsin's historic ride into Moscow aboard a tank and his subsequent speech consolidated his power within Russia.

Boris Yeltsin

By Christmas Day 1991, Gorbachev was left without a country to rule as the republics—Ukraine, Belarus, Georgia, et al.—of the former USSR declared sovereignty one by one. On that date, Gorbachev signed the Soviet Union out of existence and himself out of political office. Boris Yeltsin remained President of the renamed Russian Federation. Yeltsin's reign was at least as turbulent as Gorbachev's had been. A short-lived Commonwealth of Independent States (CIS) was formed between the former republics of the Soviet Union, but this commonwealth soon faded into oblivion.

By 1993, Yeltsin offered a new constitution to the Russian people, one that would hold strong presidential powers yet maintained—in theory—checks and balances. The President was allowed to rule by decree under national emergency, dissolve the Duma if he wished, call for new general elections, and call for referendums if he wished to circumvent the Duma altogether. The constitution was narrowly approved by the Russian electorate. Meanwhile, Yeltsin turned Russian tanks on members of the parliament during the "White House coup," so named for the building the Russian Duma meets in. These members of parliament—many of them Communists—had been elected late in the Soviet era, under Gorbachev's reign. They resented what they viewed as Yeltsin's "grab for power." The parliamentary elections of 1993 swept an anti-reform state into power.

Yeltsin's popularity continued to dip when he enacted "shock therapy," an immediate leap to a market economy without a "safety net" transitional period. This painful therapy would lead to more rapid economic gain, Yeltsin claimed.

THE RUSSIAN ECONOMY

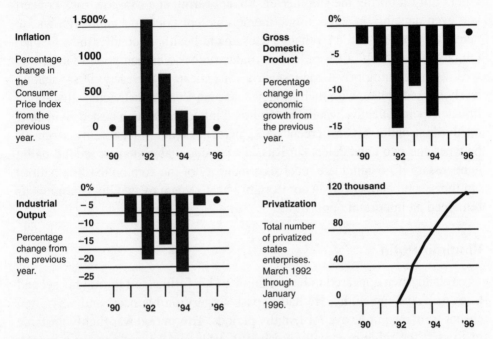

All indexes and percentage changes are "real," or adjusted for inflation.

• Data not available for year.

Sources: "Russian Economic Trends." Russian European Center for Economic Performance; Russian State Committee for Statistics; PlanEcon

All pain and no gain is what most Russians experienced as hyper-inflation resulted during the mid-1990s. Hyper-inflation describes annual inflation rates of more than 100 percent. Also, organized crime became an increasing fact of life in Moscow and St. Petersburg, as Leningrad had been renamed after the collapse of the USSR.

In Duma elections in 1993 and 1995, conservative opposition forces to Yeltsin, the xenophobic Liberal Democrats and rejuvenated Communist Party (CPRF), won the most seats, illustrating both Yeltsin's unpopularity and his difficulty in getting reform legislation passed. The Duma serves for a maximum of four years and 225 of its deputies are elected by SMDP, while the remaining 225 seats are chosen by PR. Thus, Russian voters choose one candidate to represent their district and then vote for a party to hold another seat under PR. The cut-off for a Russian party to gain any PR seats is to hit 5 percent of the total PR vote.

In 1996, Yeltsin was up for re-election and was decidedly the underdog to the Communist Party candidate, Gennady Zyuganov. Yeltsin consistently trailed in public opinion polls by double figures. However, a combination of factors served to lead Yeltsin to a stunning comeback victory on the second ballot.

First, Yeltsin was an unrelenting campaigner and he went after the Russian voters full tilt during the summer of '96, appearing at a Moscow rock concert and even dancing on stage in one memorable episode. This campaign was to take a tremendous toll on Yeltsin's subsequent health. Secondly, the so-called Oligarchs—a group of seven leading industrialists who had gotten fabulously wealthy by gaining privatized industries dirt cheap in the early '90s—shamelessly backed Yeltsin with their money, fearing a Communist victory that might threaten their collective wealth and political influence. Yeltsin bested Zyuganov on the first ballot by 35 percent to 32 percent of the vote, forcing a run-off between the two candidates. (In Russia's presidential system, a second ballot is necessary if no candidate receives a majority of the vote on the first ballot.) On the second ballot, Yeltsin comfortably beat Zyuganov, yet the Communists remained an important opposition.

Vladimir Putin

Yeltsin often appeared to be a shadow of his former self during his second term, stiff and unhealthy. He had bypass surgery on his heart and was often absent from the public eye for lengthy periods. This period was highly unstable in Russia: the ruble eventually crashed in 1998 and Yeltsin applied a merry-go-round mentality to his prime ministers, firing and replacing them every few months. Into this reality stepped seemingly another little-known and seemingly forgettable Prime Minister, a former KGB operative named Vladimir Putin.

Putin was the antithesis of Yeltsin in many ways. Several decades younger, Putin held a black-belt in judo. He was the strong leader that Russians admire; a man of few words but decisive action. This first became apparent in the summer of 1999 when a Moscow apartment blast was blamed on Chechen terrorists. The first Chechen War had ended three years earlier in a stalemate, but Putin seized this incident to again unleash the Russian military on Chechnya. This initial popularity launched Putin to the presidency when Yeltsin unexpectedly resigned On December 31, 1999. Also, in Duma elections that December, the Unity Party—a pro-Putin party—did well, tying the Communists for a plurality in the Duma.

In March 2000, Putin was elected President on the first ballot with 51 percent of the vote. Zyuganov finished a distant second with 31 percent. Putin spoke of a "tyranny of law" upon entering office, indicating a crackdown on both organized crime and on the powerful Oligarchs. Like Yeltsin, who was supported by the "Our Home is Russia" party, Putin himself has not officially joined any organized political party.

The Russian economy slowly rebounded during Putin's first time, largely because global oil price rose steadily. The political situation became more stable and predictable, but far from perfect. Violent crime, including the murder of some ten Duma members over a decade, remained a key social problem. The Second Chechen War waged on in a hopeless quagmire, as Moscow refused to let go of the Islamic region, fearing the precedent this would set and heedful of the petroleum reserves held in Chechnya. A suicide bombing at a Moscow rock concert in 2003 followed the tragic Moscow theatre standoff a year earlier. Still, blame for Chechnya was generally deflected away from Putin.

The Oligarchs were neutralized as a potential political enemy by exile or prison. Two went to London to avoid prison, where one, Roman Abramovich, bought the Chelsea football club. Another, Mikhail Khodorkovsky, considered to be the wealthiest man in Russia as the owner of Yukos Oil, was sent to prison for allegedly not paying taxes. More likely it was for his outspoken criticism of Putin's policies.

In 2003, United Russia, as the pro-Putin movement was now known, handily won the Duma elections, buoyed by financial support and a supportive media. By 2004, no independent television stations remained in Russia. With a state-controlled media, Putin was able to silence potential critics as he headed more toward a "coronation" than a re-election. (In the 2004 election in which the main rival candidates refused to participate because of Putin's perceived unfair advantages, Putin was to win on the first ballot with more than 70 percent of the vote.)

As a further means to strengthen United Russia's power, Putin has proposed having the Duma entirely elected by a PR formula, knocking out all SMDP seats. With United Russia's money and media control, this would likely enhance its ability to gain seats in the parliament, thus enhancing Putin's own power. Furthermore, there are signs that Russia's constitution may be amended to allow a president to hold more than two terms in office, which could allow Putin to again stand for the presidency in 2008.

Candidate	Party	Votes	%
Vladimir Putin	None	48,931,376	71.2
Nikolai Kharitonov	Communist	9,440,860	13.7
Sergei Glazyev	Motherland	2,826,641	4.1
Irina Khakamada	None	2,644,644	3.8
Oleg Malyshkin	LDPR	1,394,070	2.0
Sergei Mironov	None	518,893	0.8
Against all		2,319,056	3.5
TOTAL		66,307,156	

DRILL

THE FORMER SOVIET UNION & THE RUSSIAN FEDERATION

DIRECTIONS: Carefully read and answer each of the following questions, which are based on the information that you have just read.

42. All of the following were true of the Soviet Communist Party EXCEPT

    (A) no other political parties were allowed to exist in the Soviet Union

    (B) a majority of citizens in the Soviet Union were members of the CPSU

    (C) the politburo was an elite decision-making body

    (D) it proved to be a slow, inefficient, stifling bureaucracy

    (E) it favored the interests of the Russian Soviet Socialist Republic over that of the other fourteen Soviet republics

43. Which was NOT a policy that Mikhail Gorbachev favored?

    (A) Less central economic planning.

    (B) Unlimited freedom of expression by Soviet citizens.

    (C) Greater emphasis on consumer goods production.

    (D) Dissolution of the "Iron Curtain" of Eastern European Soviet satellite states.

    (E) Competitive elections between Communist Party candidates.

44. From 1993–2003, members of the Duma were elected by

    (A) SMDP, like both Britain's House of Commons and France's National Assembly

    (B) proportional representation

    (C) members of the Federation Council

    (D) a half-SMDP and half-PR formula

    (E) an electoral college, similar to the method used in electing France's Senate

45. Which party is currently most "pro-Kremlin"?

    (A) United Russia   (D) Liberal Democrats

    (B) Fatherland-All Russia   (E) Yabloko

    (C) the Communists

46. Throughout the Soviet era, 1917–1991, the greatest political power was wielded by

    (A) the politburo   (D) the Red Army commanders

    (B) the Supreme Soviet   (E) the general secretary of the CPSU

    (C) *gosplan*

47. Today, most Russians consider Mikhail Gorbachev to be

    (A) a political savior capable of rescuing the Russian Federation from destruction if he would re-enter political life.

    (B) an irrelevant bungler whose experiments unwittingly and mistakenly brought an end to the Soviet empire.

    (C) a brave political innovator revered for bringing the end of the CPSU, but now considered too old to hold office.

    (D) a much more effective leader than do political analysts in France and Britain.

    (E) a communist stooge.

48. The greatest barrier to continuing capitalist and democratic reform in the Russian Federation under Boris Yeltsin was

    (A) the Chechen civil war

    (B) the lack of strength of reform-oriented parties in the Duma

    (C) the opposition to reform by the Red Army

    (D) ongoing and widely reported criticism of his programs by Mikhail Gorbachev

    (E) the electoral successes of communist parties in neighboring Hungary and Poland

49. Mikhail Gorbachev's reforms were initially designed to

    (A) rid the Soviet communist government of its Stalinist characteristics

(B)   introduce a market economy to the Soviet Union

(C)   dissolve the Soviet army

(D)   end *glasnost* and *perestroika*

(E)   support the USSR's slipping position in the Cold War

50.   Which term associated with Soviet politics is NOT correctly defined?

(A)   *glasnost*—increasing truthfulness in the media

(B)   *nomenklatura*—a privileged list of candidates to fill CPSU positions

(C)   *perestroika*—restructuring of the Soviet military

(D)   *apparatchiki*—members of the inefficient Soviet bureaucracy

(E)   *kulaks*—wealthy private farmers largely killed off during Stalin's collectivization drive

51.   *Gosplan*

    I.   planned production and controlled industry in the Soviet era

   II.   was Gorbachev's first attempted major reform

  III.   illustrated the initial resistance of peasants to collective farming

  IV.   was often short-sighted and inflexible

(A)   I and IV   (D)   I and III

(B)   II and IV   (E)   III and IV

(C)   III only

52.   The attempted August 1991 coup occurred because

(A)   Boris Yeltsin's supporters believed Gorbachev was dragging his feet on promised reforms

(B)   Mikhail Gorbachev reverted to hard-line Communist policies

(C)   unemployment, prices, and crime were all on the rise in Moscow

(D)   some of Gorbachev's top advisors wanted the CPSU to retain sole political authority

(E)   the Russian people had simply grown tired of communism

53. Which of the following is NOT a "successor state" to the Soviet Union?

    (A) Ukraine   (D) Siberia

    (B) Kazakhstan   (E) Lithuania

    (C) Belarus

54. All of the following are true of Vladimir Putin EXCEPT that he

    (A) was a high-ranking KGB agent

    (B) seems to be a decisive and firm leader

    (C) reignited the Chechen War

    (D) intensified Yeltsin's liberal reforms

    (E) doesn't actually have "steel eyes and iron hands," as some authors have claimed

55. Which Russian leader attacked the "White House" with the tanks and artillery?

    (A) Gorbachev   (D) Khrushchev

    (B) Putin   (E) Yeltsin

    (C) Stalin

56. This CPRF leader has finished second in both presidential elections held in the Russian Federation in 1996 and 2000. In 2004, he refused to run, although his party once again finished a distant second. Who has been described?

    (A) Zyuganov   (D) Luzkhov

    (B) Zhirinovski   (E) Primikov

    (C) Yavlinski

PEOPLE'S REPUBLIC OF CHINA

A second Communist/Post-Communist case study is China. Logically, most Chinese comparisons will occur between it and Russia (and thus the former Soviet Union), the other C/PC state involved in the course.

Imperial dynasties ruled China to 1911. A "mandate of heaven" was the belief by the populace that the gods favored the maintenance of the current dynasty. If crops were good, wars were won and plagues were avoided, then the emperor maintained the gods' favor and thus held a mandate of heaven. This notion of legitimacy still remains today, especially with China's vast rural peasant population. It is interesting to note that the mandate of heaven is rather the opposite of the "divine right" theory held by European monarchs, whereby it was held that God granted the throne to the ruler and it was therefore heresy to question, let alone remove, a ruler. The mandate of heaven left legitimacy in the hands of the ruled.

China is a vast land mass with more than 1.3 billion people. Nearly one in five people on Earth today lives in China. This vast population is also relatively homogenous with some 91 percent being Han Chinese. The language commonly referred to as "Chinese" is actually Mandarin. China's capital city is Beijing in the north, but its most populous city is Shanghai in the south.

The Chinese Communist Party (CCP) culminated more than two decades of fighting with victory over the Nationalist (KMT) forces of Chiang Kai-shek in 1949, creating the People's Republic of China. Led by Mao Zedong, the CCP instituted a policy known as the mass line to achieve this success, overcoming great obstacles. The mass line was an attempt to make Marxism "work" in a non-industrial, peasant country. With it, Mao declared that the party must serve the immediate needs of the peasantry, rather than spout Marxist dogma to the struggling farmers. Thus, during the civil war the CCP helped peasants harvest crops, build dams, repair fences, and meet other tangible needs. Understandably, this endeared the CCP's cause to the peasants, who often allied with the communists in fighting the Nationalist forces. The People's Liberation Army (PLA) thus was able to defeat the KMT, who were forced to flee to Taiwan and set up a separate country, the Republic of China. Both the PRC and the ROC claim to represent the "real" China.

The mass line has remained an integral concept for the CCP in holding its mandate of heaven because the peasantry still comprises a majority of the Chinese population. This philosophy has been updated by various CCP leaders and remains an effective tool for maintaining peasant support.

KEY LEADERS

Mao Zedong

Mao Zedong ruled the People's Republic from its inception until his death some 27 years later in 1976. Mao believed in revolution and feared the stagnation of his beloved People's Republic. His policies back up this philosophy. In 1957, against his top advisors' wishes, the CCP embarked upon the "Hundred Flowers" program, which gained its name from Mao's contention that "gentle, refreshing" criticism of the party could be constructive and keep the party vital. A hundred different schools of thought should bloom, according to Chairman Mao. The Hundred Flowers campaign was short-lived when the criticism proved to be neither gentle nor refreshing to Mao and his government. It was more like a torrential storm. Pulling the plug on free expression, the CCP unleashed a sort of revenge program known as the "anti-rightist" campaign of 1958 in which many of those critical of the CCP were imprisoned or even killed.

Next, Mao turned his revolutionary zeal toward the rapid industrialization of China. The Great Leap Forward, begun in 1958, was designed to catch China up with the West industrially in a mere 15 years of concerted effort using China's massive human resources. The program was abandoned after only two years of operation and resulted in widespread misery throughout China. The attempt to create "backyard steel" resulted in widespread erosion and flooding as, lacking coal, thousands of trees were sacrificed in the effort to smelt iron ore. The peasantry generally disliked the communal farming efforts and the lack of privacy and individuality they were afforded, calling each other "blue ants" after the uniforms they wore. In 1961–62 China suffered a catastrophic

*A cultural note on Chinese names: the name that appears first is the family name, or "last" name, as Americans would say. Thus, with Yao Ming, the NBA star, "Yao" rightly appears on the back of his jersey as his family name. Most family names in Chinese are one syllable and relatively easy to say and spell. The second name listed, the person's familiar (or first) name, is often longer. When writing or speaking, the student need only use the family name, such as Mao, Deng, or Hu.

famine because of the crop shortages that emerged from the Great Leap and its emphasis on industry.

The Cultural Revolution would be the monument to "permanent revolution" that would last a decade and only end with Mao's death. From 1966–1976, the CCP turned on itself and in the process, robbed China of a generation of leadership and advancement. Mao unleashed enthusiastic high school and college students known as Red Guards to "uncover" repugnant elements of the Party, such as the dreaded "capitalist roaders" to be sent down to the countryside with the peasantry for a re-orientation toward zealous communism. This re-orientation often involved beating and sometimes death.

Other forms the Cultural Revolution took included the destruction of the "Four Olds"—traditional customs, beliefs, etc.—by the Red Guard. Thus, priceless works of art, myriad literature, and ancient buildings were obliterated. "Struggle sessions" occurred whereby the Guards publicly questioned the loyalty and/or Maoist credentials of authority figures such as CCP cadre (bureaucrats), school teachers, parents, or any other authority figure they might have a grudge against and wished to publicly humiliate.

Deng Xiaoping

This enduring nightmare didn't automatically end when Mao died. Deng Xiaoping (pronounced "Dung Shou-ping"), himself labeled a "capitalist roader" and twice sent down to the countryside during the Cultural Revolution, re-emerged and battled the ominously named "Gang of Four" for post-Mao control of the CCP and the PRC. The Gang was led by Mao's notorious wife, Jiang Qing, and it professed to continue all Maoist policies without question.

Deng convinced the PLA leadership that he was the better bet for a stable and prosperous Chinese future, and by 1978, he held the reigns of power, arresting, trying, and convicting the Gang of Four. Deng began carefully implementing what he called "socialism with Chinese characteristics," i.e. capitalism, with his "Four Modernizations" program. China had been badly damaged the decade of chaos preceding Mao's death and no one realized this better than Deng. The four areas he chose to target were industry, agriculture, education, and the military.

To "buffer" Hong Kong's potential influence on the mainland, Special Economic Zones (SEZ) were created in the south bordering the coastal city. In these zones, foreign investment and capitalism would not only be allowed, but encouraged. The advantages to a Reebok, Sony, or General Motors were obvious: a foothold in the world's most populous market, a cheap and large labor pool, cheaper taxes, and more lax environmental policies. Thus, the SEZs became capitalist boomtowns, and currently all Chinese cities now basically operate in such fashion. The experiment that was supposed to isolate Hong Kong has instead swallowed all of China outside the rural villages.

Deng was cagey enough to know that he needed China's vast peasantry on his side. He utilized the mass line by instituting the "responsibility system," which told the peasants that once they met the state quota for a certain crop (often wheat), they were free to grow whatever they chose and sell it for whatever the market would bear. With this incentive, the Chinese countryside became more efficient and more prosperous than ever. Where Mao relied on revolutionary zeal, Deng turned to personal motivation. His famous quote—"It doesn't matter if a cat is black or white; if it catches mice it is a good cat"—indicated that if capitalism helped the CCP and China, then so be it.

In education, a "red versus expert" debate had long existed in the People's Republic. Mao had believed that party positions should be held for the most committed communists—the "red" side of the debate. Deng believed that specialized expertise in engineering, economic planning, or technology was more important than party zeal. Additionally, Deng believed that finite educational resources should not be spread equally to all Chinese, but should be focused to a greater extent on the most capable.

To any "paramount leader," the PLA is the key organ toward maintaining a mandate of heaven. Thus, Deng upgraded the technology and weaponry of the PLA. The changes of the Four Modernizations combined to chip away at the "iron rice bowl," which described the CCP's promise of life-long security through employment, housing, and basic medical care.

The end of Deng's reign was marked by the Tiananmen Square massacre in June 1989. A month and a half earlier, many Beijing-area university students had gathered for the funeral of a moderate reformer named Hu Yaobang. From this meeting, a fledgling democracy movement blossomed and was allowed to continue. A split within the top echelon of the CCP occurred over whether to oppose the student movement or coopt the leaders into the CCP. The hard-liners won out, and on June 4, the PLA was called in to clean out the square. Approximately 1,400 deaths occurred on the avenues along the way to Tiananmen Square; student leaders were then jailed or exiled.

Interesting parallels can be drawn between the Tiananmen Square demonstrations and that of Democracy Wall ten years earlier. A young dissident named Wei Jiangsheng had established the wall in Beijing with large character posters calling for a "Fifth Modernization" in accords with Deng's economic reforms. The Fifth Modernization was to be democracy. Deng and the CCP allowed Democracy Wall to exist for several months before taking over the area and arresting Wei. He spent the next 15 years in prison before being exiled to North America.

Jiang Zemin

As Deng became infirm, Jiang Zemin emerged as the succeeding paramount leader. A former mayor of Shanghai, Jiang sided with the hard-liners during the Tiananmen crisis. His management of the economy largely mirrored Deng's, as the SEZ experiment spread across China and the "iron rice bowl" was basically discarded. The CCP's human rights record has not altered dramatically. The policy of re-education through labor is still widely employed by the Chinese judicial system. The accused is considered guilty without trial, offered no appeal, and sentenced to imprisoned labor in the countryside. Also, the *hukou*, internal passports or documents that control residence and freedom of movement within China, remained enforced. Nevertheless, Jiang was able to guide China to its long-sought entrance into the World Trade Organization and land the 2008 Olympic Games for Beijing. Additionally, Jiang oversaw the "one country/two systems" policy as Hong Kong and Macao rejoined the People's Republic. Hong Kong's return from Britain in 1997 received greater publicity, but Macao, a coastal city and gambling Mecca, was also returned from Portugal in 1999. The "one country/two systems" approach allowed these areas to keep their local economies and governments for the next fifty years. Taiwan steadfastly resists joining the People's Republic under these same terms, and has recently begun openly discussing a declaration of independence.

The one child policy, enacted early in Deng's administration, was a response to the problems caused by China's huge and growing population. The policy limited families to a single child without taxation penalties. By Jiang's reign the policy was seemingly relaxed because of the public outcry against female infanticide—the abandonment of female babies—that had occurred in response to the policy. Males were more valued for several reasons, including Confucian traditions and marital realities. At the point of marriage, the bride's family pays a dowry of land or property to the groom's family. Subsequently, the bride moves in with her husband's family and takes care of his parents, not her own, as they age. Little wonder that a Chinese saying has been, "having a daughter makes another man rich." These factors added to the one child policy no doubt contributed to female infanticide in the countryside. This in turn has led to the current imbalance among males and females of marriageable age. An estimated seven million Chinese males will not be able to marry due to this imbalance. An interesting side effect to the one-child policy has been a generation of only children found in Chinese urban centers such as Shanghai and Beijing. The "little emperor's syndrome" describes these generally spoiled children, who have been doted upon by their parents both economically and emotionally.

Among the groups that tested Jiang's rule were the Falun Gong and the Tibetan Buddhists. The Falun Gong shocked the CCP in 1999 when some ten thousand strong appeared white-robed in Tiananmen Square for some synchronized stretching and chanting. The party was apparently alarmed that the group could organize such a show without CCP knowledge. In time, the party labeled the Falun Gong "a dangerous cult" and banned them from legally existing. Some members have been jailed, some immolated themselves publicly as a protest, while other leaders fled in exile to lead the group via the internet. The internet itself, like the Falun Gong, is seen as a "poisonous weed," or negative influence, by the CCP. Internet access is an area of increasing concern to the current regimes in China and Iran, among our case study states. In Tibet, in fact, a special ID card has just been issued to allow Internet access so that the CCP can better monitor such activities.

Tibet remains a worrisome region for the Chinese Communist leadership. The region in China's arid and remote southwest desires sovereignty. The nomadic Tibetans are a separate nation from the Han Chinese and desire their own state. Since an attempted uprising in Tibet in 1959, the region has felt a heavy PLA presence. Its exiled spiritual leader, the Dalai Lama, has received the Nobel Peace Prize and globally lobbies for Tibetan independence. The CCP rejects this option for the precedent it would set, including a perceived loss of authority over China.

In 2002, the CCP engaged in an historic transition of leadership. Typically, leadership changes in an authoritarian regime occur only at death or incapacity, as had happened with Mao and Deng. Jiang Zemin, then 76, had been influenced by younger leaders he dealt with, such as Tony Blair and Vladimir Putin. Jiang stated that China needed younger, more vigorous leadership and that transitions within the CCP should be more planned and transparent. At the party congress meeting that year, it was announced that Hu Jintao would assume the CCP's leadership mantle. Hu's "fourth generation" (Mao, Deng, and Jiang preceding him) of leadership was challenged by the SARS health crisis in his first year. SARS—severe acute respiratory syndrome—had apparently originated in Hong Kong and became a world health scare, as it was both extremely contagious and lethal. After first denying access to World Health Organization officials, Hu managed the crisis by declaring curfews in afflicted areas and mandating the wearing of nose and mouth masks. Hu fired the mayor of Beijing and his minister of health as the crisis lingered. The Rolling Stones, who had long sought to tour in China given its lucrative potential market, finally won that right in 2003, but canceled the tour at the height of the SARS scare.

KEY FACTS: THE CCP

- Parallel Hierarchies—This is a concept that attempts to ensure CCP power. It states that for every government position, a corresponding CCP position will exist to "shadow" it.

- National People's Congress—In theory, this is the legislative branch of the federal government. Formerly, it was merely a rubber stamp for policies decided by the standing committee of the CCP. Increasingly, it actually does debate, if not overtly contest, CCP policies.
- Village Democracy—Once again, the mass line in action. Village elections have been the law in China since 1998. Villagers elect their own village representative, who in turn ideally will promote greater profit among local crops, help peasants understand and implement the latest CCP directives and so on.

Will this "grass roots" democracy spread upward? That's the question.

- Paramount Leader—You have seen this term used to describe the political leader of the CCP because, unlike in the Soviet Union, this person is not necessarily the general secretary of the party. Deng, for example, held no formal titles at one point, but he was clearly calling the shots for the CCP. So the generic title "paramount leader" indicates the true political head of the CCP.
- Is Hu Jintao actually China's paramount leader? The answer seems a clear and resounding "yes" by late 2005. Jiang Zemin has long since relinquished all of his political and military titles and Hu is firmly in charge of the CCP heading China's "fourth generation" of leadership.

DRILL

THE PEOPLE'S REPUBLIC OF CHINA

DIRECTIONS: Carefully read and answer each of the following questions, which are based on the information that you have just read.

57. Compared to the Duma of the Russian Federation, the National People's Congress of China

   (A) has roughly the same legislative power and checks on the executive

   (B) has more legislative power, but has no real checks on the power of the executive

   (C) is more autonomous and free from interference by executive leaders

   (D) has greater support and legitimacy from the Chinese people

(E)   has no real legislative power; it can merely discuss actions already taken by the CCP

58.   One *difference* between the politics of China and the politics of the former Soviet Union is that in the former Soviet Union

(A)   women held positions of high political authority

(B)   the army played a more substantial role in politics

(C)   ethnic and nationality divisions were more significant in politics

(D)   greater efforts were made to promote political involvement through mass mobilization

(E)   the Communist Party apparatus had significantly more power in the political system

59.   Maoism differs from Marxist-Leninist ideology because of Maoist emphasis on

(A)   the role of the peasantry in revolutionary change

(B)   the role of the Communist Party in leading the revolution

(C)   classical Chinese political thought as a key source of revolutionary ideology

(D)   reliance on assistance from foreign communist movements

(E)   nonviolent means to bring about social and political change

60.   Compared to the Russian Federation, the People's Republic of China has

(A)   fewer and more widely dispersed ethnic minority groups

(B)   greater and more concentrated ethnic minority groups within its borders

(C)   a similar number of ethnic minorities to deal with as an internal concern

(D)   more militant and dissident ethnic minority groups to contend with

(E)   a virtually totally homogeneous population

61. A problem China faces to a greater extent than the Russian Federation is

   (A)   controlling political opposition

   (B)   curtailing capitalist economic movements

   (C)   controlling the black market

   (D)   limiting population growth

   (E)   collecting taxes owed by businesses

62. Bureaucracies in communist systems such as China and the Soviet Union have tended to

   (A)   hinder reform

   (B)   be dominated by interest groups such as labor unions

   (C)   implement all policies effectively and obediently

   (D)   be composed solely of party members

   (E)   avoid interagency competition for resources

63. Mao's "Hundred Flowers" campaign of 1957 resembles Mikhail Gorbachev's *glasnost* program of the 1980s in all of the following ways EXCEPT

   (A)   both programs were intended to improve, not destroy, the respective communist parties in China and the Soviet Union

   (B)   both programs met with disapproval from the bureaucracy in each country

   (C)   criticism of both the CCP in China and CPSU in the Soviet Union was greater than had been expected

   (D)   as a result of these campaigns, the media in both China and the Soviet Union became more reliable, respected, and more free to report upon international events without internal party censorship

   (E)   both Mao and Gorbachev lacked the vision to see where these programs would lead

64. China and the former Soviet Union are similar in all of the following ways EXCEPT

   (A)   communism has been a dominant political influence in both countries in the twentieth century

(B)   workers have dominated the Communist Party in both countries

(C)   both countries experienced relatively bloody revolutions in order to instill communist governments

(D)   leaders in both countries resorted to "cult of personality" tactics in order to consolidate national power

(E)   the pre-revolutionary economies of both countries were largely agricultural and non-industrial in character

65.   A similarity between Russian and Chinese political culture before communism came to either country is that in both

(A)   peasants had traditionally been a political agent for change

(B)   Confucianism strongly influenced political thought

(C)   democratic institutions were strong

(D)   authoritarian rule was historically accepted

(E)   societies were completely closed to outside civilizations

66.   A principal difference between reform in China and in the Soviet Union between 1980 and 1990 was that

(A)   economic reform was more successful in China than in the Soviet Union

(B)   the Chinese Communist Party was more open to multi-party competition than was the CPSU

(C)   nationalist movements were more important in China than in the Soviet Union

(D)   Soviet reformers were more successful in establishing and comprehensive commercial relations with Western industrialized countries than were Chinese reformers

(E)   Soviet reformers were more hostile to Western philosophies and practices than were Chinese reformers

67.   The movement for reform in both the Soviet Union and China in the 1980s included which of the following?

(A)   Increasing Communist Party involvement in local economic management

(B)   Emphasizing ideology over pragmatism

(C)   Emphasizing the role of the military in domestic politics

(D)   Establishing competitive, multi-party elections

(E)   Reducing, restructuring, and restaffing government and party bureaucracies

68.   Judging by his political philosophy, Deng Xiaoping most likely looked at which of the following Soviet actions favorably?

(A)   Khrushchev's exposé of Stalin's excesses

(B)   The purges staged by Stalin and his "cult of personality"

(C)   *Perestroika*

(D)   *Glasnost*

(E)   *Demokratatzia*

69.   To maintain his mandate of heaven, Hu Jintao should be most concerned with

(A)   political meddling from Jiang Zemin

(B)   staging the 2008 Olympic Games successfully

(C)   curtailing the power held by the PLA

(D)   continuing China's rapid economic growth

(E)   Hong Kong, Macao, and Taiwan

Comparative Government & Politics Review

MEXICO

As a Newly Industrialized Country, or NIC, Mexico is an emerging global star. Its proximity to the United States has been both a blessing and a curse and is an integral part of this case study. Bordering a wealthy liberal democracy certainly holds some advantages.

Socially, Mexico is also blessed by relative homogeneity. More than 90 percent of the population is Roman Catholic, speaks Spanish, and has Iberian ancestry—Creoles have only Iberian blood and Mestizos are a mixture of Iberian and indigenous natives. Traditionally, Mexico has been a society of male domination, or machismo. This fact is changing as women demand more legal and political rights.

Mexico's Revolution began in 1910 in the name of land redistribution to the impoverished campesinos, or peasants, along with an end to the caudillo rule of Porfirio Diaz and greater democratization. By 1917, the Revolution had ousted Diaz and resulted in a new constitution, one that has lasted to this date and ranks among the longest serving constitutions on the planet. Democracy was established, although not fully realized for decades, and the campesinos were granted communal farms called ejidos, yet these farms were often placed on infertile land. In an attempt to prevent a new dictatorship à la the "porfiriato," the Mexican constitution limits a President to a single six-year term known as the "sexenio." Additionally, Mexican politicians may not be re-elected to the same federal or local office immediately upon serving a term. A federal system was set up that, in theory, would entail a separation of powers between the three branches of government and a system of checks and balances. In actuality, Mexico would be run as a unitary one-party state with almost no checks on a very powerful President for the next seven decades.

The PRI

By the late 1920s a political party had emerged that would dominate Mexico for the rest of the twentieth century. The PRI, which in English translates into the Institutional Revolutionary Party, used a variety of techniques to consolidate and maintain their power. Ideologically, the "pendulum theory" allowed the PRI to sway from left to right to fit the current mood of the Mexican electorate. Also corporatism allowed the party's bureaucracy to pull in key sectors of Mexican society, including the campesinos, labor and business leaders, thus guarantee-ing the considerable votes held by members of these sectors in return for access and influence within the party. The party's name and its legal monopoly on red, green, and white—the same as Mexico's flag—added to its aura of patriotism. The additional use of dubious electoral practices—generally padding victory results rather than outright stealing of elections—only added to the PRI's politi-cal strength.

Other strategies used by the PRI to perpetuate their rule included the dedazo, which roughly means "pointing the finger at," and involved the outgoing Presi-dent hand-picking his successor without any primaries or party conventions. This was a very closed procedure that made it likely that the outgoing President would choose a similarly-minded successor. Also, the party kept tight control on the Mexican media, shutting down and controlling any critical newspaper, radio, or television outlets. A very powerful executive system also allowed the President to basically run Mexico as a unitary and parliamentary system in practice, even though its constitution claimed it was neither of these. In other words, a fusion of power existed whereby few if any checks of power could be placed on the PRI and its leadership.

If these methods failed to garner power, the PRI was not above using strate-gic benevolence—the granting of government favors to constituencies of voters. This might include a sewage project in a barrio neighborhood in Mexico City, or bags of groceries, emblazoned with the party's seal, handed out from the back of a flatbed truck on election eve.

The rival party to the PRI was the PAN, or National Action Party. A right-of-center party associated with commercial interests, law and order, and the Catholic Church, the PAN was traditionally seen as the party of the wealthy and the north. In 1976, the PAN sagely refused to participate in the election process at all, noting how the system was fixed to perpetuate the PRI's dominance. The PRI was forced to begin reform of the system that was to continue for the next two decades, for the PRI dreaded the appear-ance that Mexico was actually a one-party authoritarian state and would go to extremes to keep up the appearance of at least "semi-democracy." What resulted initially was a pledge to add PR seats to the Chamber of Deputies which could not be won by the PRI, thus increasing the count held by the PAN and other minor parties. At first, 100 PR seats were added and a decade later, another hundred.

Thus, a pattern was begun whereby the PAN chipped away at the PRI's political stranglehold. In 1989, the PAN won their governor's seat. For the next decade, the PAN enjoyed more success—all in the north—winning mayoral seats in all the big cities such as Tijuana, Juarez, and Monterrey, and holding six state governor seats.

Meanwhile, a new threat from the left had also emerged to challenge the PRI. The PRD, or Democratic Party of the Revolution, was formed in the late '80s by disaffected PRI deputies, led by Cuautémoc Cárdenas, the grandson of the "father of the PRI," Lázaro Cárdenas. The elder Cárdenas had been President from 1934–1940 and had instilled corporatism and nationalized PEMEX, the Mexican oil monopoly, during his sexenio. The PRD has proven especially strong in Mexico City and has held the mayor's post there since 1997. As the 2006 Mexican election looms, Mexico City Mayor Lopez Obrador stands as the early favorite to become President.

KEY LEADERS

Carlos Salinas

Carlos Salinas served as President from 1988–1994. Although his victory in 1988 was widely disputed in Mexico—the computer system "crashed" on election day with Cardenas ahead of Salinas; the next day, when the computers were "fixed," Salinas held 51 percent of the vote and Cardenas only 31 percent—Salinas was initially seen as a positive, modernizing force for Mexico. He signed the North American Free Trade Agreement [NAFTA] with Canada and the United States, reducing tariffs and eliminating quotas between the three countries. Salinas promised Mexico a "First World" status and proceeded to privatize the Mexican telephone service, the national airline, copper mines, banks, and even highway construction. Short-lived economic gains glossed over shady deals and insider trading that created wealthy cronies of Salinas. By the end of his *sexenio*, Salinas saw the peso crash dramatically. This rendered the savings of many Mexican families worthless.

Additionally, January 1, 1994, saw Mexico shaken by a violent uprising in the southern state of Chiapas. Poor indigenous campesinos revolted against local and federal authorities to display their anger at NAFTA and its perceived economic aid only for Mexico's already wealthier north. The Zapatistas, as these bandanna-covered rebels called themselves, were to battle the next two Mexican administrations as well, led by their enigmatic spokesman Subcommander Marcos.

The PRI itself seemed to implode at the end of Salinas' term. The dedazo choice to follow Salinas, Donaldo Luis Colosio, a charismatic populist, was assassinated in Tijuana in early 1994. Then, the PRI's secretary-general was murdered in Mexico City. Salinas' brother Raul was later charged with this murder, over allegations of laundered drug money and secret Swiss bank accounts. Carlos Salinas was now so vilified that he could not live in Mexico and instead exiled himself in Ireland.

Ernesto Zedillo

In the wake of Colosio's killing, Ernesto Zedillo became "the accidental President" in 1994. Although little loved, Zedillo managed to rebuild the Mexican economy via massive loans from the United States in the mid-1990s. Zedillo's main legacy will likely be opening up the PRI from the control of the old guard, called "los dinos" in favor of the technocrats, or *tecnicos*, who would now manage the party. Two main changes initiated by Zedillo were the installation of IFE (pronounced ee-fay in Spanish) to oversee Mexican elections and the ending of the *dedazo* in favor of a PRI primary. IFE, a federal election commission not tied to any party, issued voter ID cards, increased polling observation, computerized vote tabulations, and enforced party spending limits during campaigns. Its effect on Mexican politicians since 1997 has been apparent, with PRI losing first the Chamber of Deputies and subsequently the presidency.

Vicente Fox

The PAN's lonely decades of opposition to the PRI paid off in shining glory in July 2000 when Vicente Fox was elected President. A successful northern state governor, Fox had previously been president of Coca-Cola in Mexico. Ultimately, Fox has turned out to be a better campaigner than President, but to be fair, perhaps expectations at this historic exchange of power were simply too high.

Fox was negotiating with the United States and President George W. Bush over relaxed immigration standards for Mexicans illegally in the U.S. and a future system of temporary workers' visas when the September 11, 2001, terror attacks occurred in the U.S. Concerns over security thwarted those talks. Immigration to the United States is a touchy issue for Mexico. The money sent back from immigrants—legal and illegal—amounts to about one-fourth of the total Mexican economy. However, the migration northward costs Mexico some of its best minds, the "brain drain." Also, with the cat-and-mouse game between illegal immigrants and the INS (U.S. Immigration and Naturalization Service), more and more deaths occur at or near the border. In recent years, groups of fleeing immigrants have suffocated in truck beds and sealed freight cars attempting the journey. The motive for the journey is simple: the per capita GDP is about four times higher in the U.S. than in Mexico. The Canadian border remains unguarded and relatively few Canadians ever immigrate southward. Why? Because the Canadian standard of living is on the same par as the United States'. Most Mexicans who migrate north do so with only a temporary stay in mind, and the money they earn is largely sent home to their families left behind.

Fox has also been unable to end the uprising in Chiapas. His proposed "Pueblo to Panama" plan (PPP) was rejected by the Zapatistas as a shallow plan to bring light services like McDonald's fast-food eateries to the area rather than dealing with the root causes of the region's poverty.

The PAN President has been unable to work with the PRI and PRD to get substantial legislation passed. In the 2003 mid-term elections, those parties, especially the PRD, made gains at the expense of the faltering PAN. Fox's last big attempt at leaving a positive legacy hinges on making the Mexican judicial system more transparent and fair. He is proposing that only publicly made confessions before a judge be allowed to minimize police beatings and that all criminal trials be held publicly, among other proposals.

KEY FACTS: MEXICAN POLITICS

Among the many things in flux about Mexican politics is the old maxim, "It's not what you know, but who you know, that matters." The Mexican system has been heavily based on "clientalism," or connections. This most clearly manifests in *camarillas*, which are political cliques, of sorts, like a ladder that one climbs to get to a higher level. Camarillas are overlapping groups—a single politician may belong to several different ones, and must head their own camarilla if they are to be serious "political players." A more precise definition may be "a group of like-minded politicians united to further their own cause(s)."

NAFTA and increasing Mexican trade have called *maquiladoras* to attention. A maquiladora is a high-tech factory located in Mexico's wealthier north, near the U.S. border. The attraction of the maquiladora is twofold for U.S. or Canadian firms. First, Mexico has a cheaper labor market to keep production costs lower and potential profits higher. Also, the location near the southern U.S. border minimizes transportation costs.

In the Mexican congress, Senate terms are for six years. Each Mexican state holds four seats in the Senate, for 128 total seats. Terms in the Chamber of Deputies are for three years.

A note on Mexican names: When reading, a student will sometimes see Salinas's name written as "Carlos Salinas de Gortari," for example, or Zedillo's name as "Ernesto Zedillo Ponce de Leon." The "added portion" of the name [de Gortari] indicates the mother's maiden name.

DRILL

MEXICO

DIRECTIONS: Carefully read and answer each of the following questions which are based on the information which you have just read.

70.   A *caudillo* is a leader who provides

    (A)   stability, but not individual freedoms

    (B)   economic advancement at the cost of individuality

(C)   democracy, but not stability

(D)   military protection at the cost of economic advancement

(E)   little for the people and takes resource wealth for himself

71.   Vicente Fox's ultimate legacy may be

(A)   instituting IFE

(B)   defeating the PRI

(C)   privatizing PEMEX

(D)   forming the PRD

(E)   ending the violence in Chiapas

72.   The use of the *sexenio* in Mexican politics was designed to avoid rule by

(A)   corporatism   (D)   the *dedazo*

(B)   *caudillo*   (E)   la *mordida*

(C)   *camarillas*

73.   The PRI traditionally used which strategy to grant an official position within the party to labor, business, and the campesinos, and thus keep them beholden to the party?

(A)   the pendulum theory   (D)   the *dedazo*

(B)   "electoral alchemy"   (E)   corporatism

(C)   incremental political reform

74.   Key reforms in opening up the Mexican electoral system included all of the following EXCEPT

(A)   doubling the size of the Senate from two members per state to four members per state

(B)   ending the use of the *dedazo* in favor of a national party primary

(C)   introducing 200 proportional representation seats to the Chamber of Deputies

(D)   granting the IFE widespread independent monitoring powers over campaigns and elections

(E)   discontinuing the use of the *camarilla* political networks

75. Mexico faced an uncharacteristically unstable year in 1994. Which of the following events did NOT occur during that turbulent year?

    (A) The peso crashed and many Mexicans lost their accumulated savings.

    (B) Raul Salinas, the President's brother, was charged with killing a top PRI official.

    (C) The presumed incoming President was assassinated while campaigning in Tijuana.

    (D) The U.S. Congress placed trade sanctions on Mexico following its annual drug certification process.

    (E) NAFTA was initiated, spurring an armed uprising in Chiapas.

76. Mexico is considered to be an NIC, or Newly Industrialized Country, because it

    (A) exports items such as petroleum and Corona beer for consumption to liberal democracies

    (B) has an economy based extensively on tourism from Cancun, Tijuana, and Puerto Vallarta

    (C) has the infrastructure for export-led growth from its *maquiladoras*

    (D) lacks any social cleavages that might lead to political turmoil or instability

    (E) has hosted both the Summer Olympics and the World Cup

77. The electoral system used to fill Mexico's Chamber of Deputies is most similar to that used by the

    (A) British House of Commons

    (B) British House of Lords

    (C) Russian Duma

    (D) Russian Federation Council

    (E) Chinese National People's Congress

| Comparative Government & Politics Review |

NIGERIA

Nigeria is a fascinating case study for so many reasons. It is the most populous country in Africa, with a wealth of human talent and a broad resource base, including oil. As such, it has always been considered the potential African "Super-state." Yet it remains mired in poverty, corruption, and instability. A study in state-building, Nigeria has yet to unify its 300-plus nations into one "Nigeria." Because of this disunity, the military has played a key role in Nigeria's post-independent history.

A former British colony, Nigeria was unprepared for its relatively sudden independence in 1960. Since then, nearly fifty years of political experimentation have ensued in the effort to build a viable state. A problem confronting Nigeria is the lack of political integration, or the notion that the citizens of a state will primarily identify themselves with the state, as opposed to their ethnicity or religion. This has failed to happen yet in Nigeria, where citizens are much more likely to use terms like "Yoruba" or "Christian" to identify themselves rather than "Nigerian." That the country has attempted eight different national anthems in its short life span is one indicator of the difficulty of state building in Nigeria. About the only time a large wave of "Nigerianism" sweeps the populace is during a major football ([soccer]) tournament such as the African Nations Cup or World Cup when the beloved Super Eagles—Nigeria's national team—is playing.

Patterns of European colonization help explain the tension and violence seen within Nigeria and other African states. The boundaries drawn by the British for Nigeria illogically grouped a vast number of ethnic groups and belief systems that neither liked nor trusted one another. Thus, various nationalities compete rather than cooperate, to the detriment of Nigeria as a whole. The main cleavage is ethnic, and the three largest groups are the Hausa-Fulani in the north, the Yoruba in the southwest, and the Ibo in the southeast. Together these three nations comprise about two-thirds of Nigeria's population, yet it is important to remember that hundreds of other ethnicities exist with their own agendas throughout the country. Other splits fracture Nigeria, as well. Religion is such a contentious issue that it drove the 2002 Miss World beauty contest from Nigeria when a Christian reporter wrote comments that Muslims took as blasphemous. Days of rioting and killing ensued. Nigeria's north is predominantly Muslim, while the south is mainly Christian. A minority of Nigerians are animists, practicing traditional polytheistic beliefs that tie the gods into the natural environment. A third cleavage is economic. The north is largely a dry, impoverished agricultural region, whereas the south has the coasts, oil production, a variety of crops, and the largest city, Lagos.

Nigeria's First Republic was launched in 1960 with great optimism. The country borrowed a parliamentary system from Britain and used a federal framework of government to logically account for the wide variety of nations. However, the promise of independence had faded into chaos by 1966, when the civilian government was suspended in favor of military rule. Several conditions promoted this chaos. First, "the dash," which was the accepted practice of political corruption, had grown rampant. Second, the members of nations who held political office attempted to govern in the best interest of their own ethnicity rather than in the best interest of Nigeria as a whole. This practice is known as "chop politics" and both it and "the dash" remain concerns today. Finally, the government attempted to take a census to determine seat allocation in parliament throughout the country. Predictably, this exploded into violence as almost every group attempted to rig the population count in order to gain political power. A census still remains a touchy prospect in modern-day Nigeria. Obviously, this is not the easiest of places to govern.

The military stepped in to rule in 1966 and would refuse to go "back to the barracks" for some thirteen years. However, military rule was generally welcomed at the end of the First Republic as bringing stability to the political and social upheaval that previously prevailed. The coup that displaced the ineffective civilian government was led by an Ibo officer, Aguiyi Ironsi. He made a tragic mistake in announcing that Nigeria would be run as a unitary system under his military rule. Fears of an Ibo-dominated system spread across Nigeria and a violent backlash against the Ibo people occurred. Even after Ironsi rescinded the ill-conceived idea, the killing of Ibos did not cease, resulting ultimately in Ironsi's own death during a counter-coup.

Ibos decided at this point, 1967, to secede from Nigeria, forming their own short-lived state of Biafra. The remaining Nigerian nations fought against this effort in a brutal three-year civil war. Largely by blockading and starving Biafra, Nigeria was able to reclaim the Ibo region in 1970. The rancor from this bitter war has yet to completely disappear.

By 1979, General Olesegun Obasanjo was to become the first military leader to return to the barracks. The Second Republic was based on the U.S. presidential system, with a bicameral Congress and a federal system. Shehu Shagari, a northern Hausa-Fulani, was elected President. Things looked bright as Nigeria had joined OPEC and anticipated oil windfalls in a global atmosphere of high petroleum prices. The country borrowed heavily from lending organizations to finance much-needed infrastructure improvements. Nigeria appeared poised to realize its vast potential.

However, by 1982 world oil prices had crashed, and Nigeria was left with a substantial debt that is still a problem. With the economy sour, Shagari found himself with an administration as racked by the dash and chop politics as the First Republic. In 1983, Shagari was re-elected, but the election was beset by allegations of widespread voter fraud. As violence spread among rival Nigerian nations, the military again took control of the government. This time, various generals would stay in power for sixteen years.

KEY LEADERS

Ibrahim Babangida

The most interesting and ambitious of these military rulers was Ibrahim Babangida (1985–93), who was determined that Nigeria learn from its previous errors before attempting a third round of civilian rule. His rule was initially popular, both at home and abroad, as he attempted to analyze why past civilian regimes had failed. His conclusions resulted in the Third Republic, which held many unique features:

- The capital was moved from coastal Lagos to Abuja in the middle-belt, a more neutral ethnic location.
- A new census was to be taken.
- Only two political parties could exist. This would necessitate the building of cross-ethnic coalitions.
- "Zoning" would be enforced on tickets. That is, a party must run two members of different ethnic groups on a ticket, say, for governor and lieutenant governor of a locality.
- All politicians who had previously held office in either the First or Second Republics were barred from doing so under the new constitution.
- Nigeria's "states" (localities) were to be redrawn to further split and mix various ethnicities. The number of states was to be increased from 21 to 30.

Much of this interesting, if controversial, package of ideas came to fruition. The capital was moved from Africa's most populous city to the dusty Middle Belt; a census was taken, but it was plagued by violence and charges of under-counting as usual. Two parties were formed and zoning was practiced in an effort to build compromise and coalitions, two concepts sorely lacking in the political history of various West African nations. Traditionally, the ethnicities had viewed their dealing with one another as a "zero-sum" game. That is, one either wins or loses, 100 percent or nothing, in any relationship. Babangida was attempting to alter this mentality, by promoting consensus, compromise and cooperation, each of which, he realized, was necessary to foster a true democracy. Previous politicians from the First and Second Republics were banned, thus losing valuable experience in an effort to avoid a recurrence of the dash-and-chop politics that could again doom the legitimacy of a civilian government.

Local elections were successfully held in 1992, and in June 1993, the two sanctioned parties squared off in a presidential election. Mashood Abiola apparently won the election, but Babangida annulled the results the following day, citing electoral fraud. Babangida seemed unable to let go of the brass ring of power, and subsequent evidence revealed that he and his top aides or "lootocrats," as they came to be called, had become obscenely wealthy, lining their own pockets with Nigeria's oil profits as well as through other shady activities. Riots occurred in Lagos and elsewhere in defiance of the annulment, and the military realized Babangida now had to go.

Sani Abacha

After some intrigue, the shuffle for power fell to yet another northerner (Hausa-Fulani), General Sani Abacha. His five-year rule turned out to be Nigeria's nightmare and the darkest period the country has yet faced. Unlike Babangida, who at least had some positive qualities to balance his personal shortcomings, Abacha's record was one of unrelenting darkness. Abiola was jailed in 1994 for claiming he was Nigeria's rightfully elected ruler. He died in prison four years later. Abiola's wife was murdered on the streets of Lagos in 1997 as she attempted to keep her husband's political voice alive. The murder was never solved but was widely believed to be tied to Abacha.

Former ruler Olesegun Obasanjo was jailed for allegedly plotting a coup. Observers believed it was because of Obasanjo's popularity and the hope he exemplified to Nigeria's electorate of returning military power to civilians. Nobel literature laureate Wole Soyinka was driven into exile teaching in the United States, where he wrote *The Open Sore of a Continent*, decrying the pitiful state of Nigeria under Abacha. Soyinka is a dramatic example of a serious problem in Nigeria: the "brain drain." The brain drain describes the exodus of talented and capable people from a country where opportunity is limited. Talented Nigerians are found by the thousands in Toronto, London, and New York. For Nigeria to retain this pool of talent, the per capita GDP and general standard of living must rise, while the ethnic violence, chop politics, and corruption subside. During Abacha's reign of terror, the brain drain was at epidemic proportions.

Abacha's most serious human rights offense was the execution of writer Ken Saro-Wiwa and nine other members of his Ogoni tribe. The Ogoni, led by Saro-Wiwa, were protesting the damage done by oil drilling and production to traditional Ogoni farming lands. Acid rain from the incessant drilling and pipeline leakage in the area had ruined substantial area of farmland. In demanding compensation, Saro-Wiwa was threatening one of Abacha's primary cash cows—Shell Oil. The result was a trumped-up murder charge against the Ogoni defendants for allegedly killing government agents. A kangaroo trial followed and the Ogoni were sentenced to die by hanging. Shell remained mute during this process and faced global condemnation and boycotts, especially in Europe, for their part in this atrocity. It is said that it took several attempts at hanging Saro-Wiwa to kill him and that on one attempt his rope broke, causing him to fall to the ground. He reportedly said, "What kind of country is this?!" The very question Nigerians are still groping to answer.

As Nigeria's Super Eagles headed to 1998's World Cup in France, the country received a surprising jolt with the death of General Abacha. The reign of terror had finally ended. Obasanjo was freed from prison and within a year, the Fourth Republic constitution had been hastily completed. In 1999, the former general and ruler, Obasanjo, was elected as civilian President. A Yoruba and born-again Christian, Obasanjo was to have little success in achieving political integration among Nigeria's vast ethnic and religious groups.

By 2000, twelve mainly Muslim northern states had adopted *shari'a* law, a fundamentalist Islamic law code based on the literal word of the *Qur'an*. This proved divisive to the Christian minorities, such as Yoruba and Ibo, living in the north. While the world press fixated on the odd sensational verdict under the *shari'a* code, such as a stoning sentence for adultery, the everyday reality of the code was more off-putting for non-Muslims living under it. Pubs were banned as was gambling, such as the lottery. Though Obasanjo is opposed to *shari'a* law, he is powerless to stop it in the north under Nigeria's federal system.

Life has scarcely gotten better for Nigerians under this civilian reign. Infrastructure remains largely undeveloped with perpetual traffic jams, or "go-slows" as they're called locally, stifling Lagos. Power outages also remain such a common occurrence that Nigeria's power monopoly, NEPA, has been nicknamed to stand for "Never Electric Power Always."

Bakassi Boys

Ethnic militias have formed throughout the country to settle scores in a vigilante manner. Among the most notorious of these roaming groups of unemployed youth are the Bakassi Boys, an Ibo militia. Perhaps only in Nigeria could the Miss World contest lead to religious violence as it did in late 2002, when an ill-advised journalist stupidly commented that the Muslim prophet Mohammed would have been proud to wed any one of the contesting beauties. Muslims took the comment as blasphemy and went on a killing spree against local Christians, leading to the relocation of the contest from Abuja to London.

Recurring oil strikes have also plagued the Nigerian economy in recent years. The dash has remained so endemic that "419" schemes, a sophisticated con scheme generally perpetrated via the Internet, have gained Nigeria global notoriety. Against this volatile backdrop, Obasanjo and his People's Democratic Party (PDP) stood for re-election in 2003. He was opposed for the presidency by another former general, Muhammadu Buhari, a Hausa-Fulani northerner and a Muslim who headed the All-Nigeria People's Party (ANPP).

Obasanjo was credited with more than 60 percent of the vote while the PDP won 27 of 36 state governors' seats and also took the vast majority of all seats in the Nigerian federal congress. In an election marred by sporadic violence, especially in the oil-rich southern delta region, the PDP was charged with widespread electoral fraud by the ANPP.

For the scheduled 2007 presidential race, former ruler Ibrahim Babangida may once again attain power. With name recognition, financial backing, and the confidence of the military leadership that a former general would hold, Babangida's return "path to power" could be rather similar to that followed by Obasanjo. Indeed, Babangida is attempting to garner cross-ethnic support from Ibo, Hausa, and Yoruba peoples via the "Nigerian Project," a movement of influential Nigerian political and business leaders.

Between its many different civilian and military government models since 1960, Nigeria serves as a model of regime instability and anemic legitimacy. Governing this diverse and volatile land is a challenge yet to be met.

PROMOTING A 2-PARTY SYSTEM

Nigeria's 1999 constitution has an interesting feature designed to promote cross-ethnic support for any successful presidential candidate. To win, a candidate must achieve two things:

1) Receive a majority, not just a plurality, of the total Nigerian votes cast. If this does not occur, a second ballot, or run-off, between the top two candidates will occur.
2) The winning candidate must receive one-quarter of the popular minimum in at least two-thirds (or 24) of Nigeria's states.

Thus, the candidate cannot merely come from a populous ethnicity like the Yoruba or Hausa-Fulani and gain no outside support and still win the presidency. This system tends to promote a two-party system, which in Nigeria's case may be a very good idea for fostering coalitions and compromise between the ethnicities.

```
                    DRILL

                    NIGERIA
```

DIRECTIONS: Carefully read and answer each of the following questions, which are based on the information that you have just read.

78. The current Nigerian constitution promotes

   (A) coalition government   (D) a parliamentary system

   (B) a two-party system   (E) economic diversity

   (C) a socialist economy

79. A main difference between the military in Nigeria and in China is that

   (A) the People's Liberation Army in China is a much smaller force

   (B) the Chinese military is an organ of the CCP while the Nigerian army remains apolitical

   (C) members of the Nigerian military are less educated and receive poor military training

   (D) Nigeria's army trains mainly for external conflicts with neighboring African states, while the People's Liberation Army mainly serves as an internal security force

   (E) the PLA exists within the structure of a higher political party, while the Nigerian military does not answer to any political party

80. Nigeria's ethnic and religious situation is

   (A) similar to Mexico's—nearly a homogeneous tribal population with 95 percent professing to be Muslims

   (B) similar to Britain's in that a vast majority of the nation consider themselves to be "Nigerians," while an increasingly unwelcome number of Asian and Arab immigrants come to work in the oil industry, leading to the formation of a "Nigerians First" political front among military leaders

   (C) strictly controlled by the military in terms of religious freedom, press censorship, and population growth

   (D) uniquely diverse, with a concentration of Muslims in the Hausa-Fulani North region and with mainly Christians in the Yoruba and Ibo South

(E) similar to that of Russia, with a majority Ibo Muslim population in the North socially, economically, and politically dominating non-Muslim Yoruba and Hausa-Fulani groups in the South

81. All of the following Mexico-Nigerian comparisons stand up to scrutiny EXCEPT

(A) both countries' constitutions have been influenced by the United States

(B) oil has been a mixed blessing economically—and sometimes a curse—for each

(C) police corruption—*la mordida* and the dash—is a problem in both states

(D) although both states have a federal structure, this leads to more controversy among different groups in Nigeria than in Mexico

(E) foreign economic investment is much more likely for Mexico than for Nigeria

82. Mexico and Nigeria are MOST similar in that they are both

(A) so-called developing states

(B) ridden with preventable diseases

(C) members of OPEC

(D) opposed to free trade and globalism

(E) former European colonies with similar traditions and problems

83. The Nigerian civil war (1967–1970) was fought

(A) to end British colonial rule

(B) to end the succession of military governments and return to a republic

(C) to avoid a Yoruba rule of Nigeria

(D) because the Ibo people wished to create their own sovereign state

(E) because Biafra wanted to control the vast delta oil wealth

84. All of the following occurred under the military leadership of Ibrahim Babangida (1985–1993) EXCEPT

   (A) military corruption was widespread headed by the so-called looto-crats

   (B) two official political parties were allowed only in an attempt to bolster inter-tribal unity

   (C) a new national capital was eagerly embraced and a new census was successfully completed

   (D) Nigerians with previous political experience were banned from holding further local or national elected office

   (E) political parties were required to run different ethnicities on their tickets together

85. Regime instability refers to

   (A) the constant changing of prime ministers and cabinets in a democratic parliamentary system

   (B) recurring change to a country's entire political framework

   (C) the volatile patterns of voting exhibited in France during the Fifth Republic

   (D) the lack of legitimacy held by a government's bureaucracy

   (E) military leadership within a country

86. In Nigeria's history as a state since 1960, the most positive role played by the military has been

   (A) its victory in the 1967–1970 Nigerian civil war

   (B) training its officers for roles of national political leadership

   (C) providing stability and order to society at times when it was on the brink of chaos

   (D) intimidating Nigeria's sub-Saharan neighbors from engaging in military conflict

   (E) its cautious attitude toward initiating the Third Republic

Comparative Government & Politics Review

ISLAMIC REPUBLIC OF IRAN

Iran provides the student the opportunity to analyze the politics and culture of an Islamic state. Islamic states are generally located in the Middle East or North Africa and are usually governed as theocracies or monarchies, guided by Islamic beliefs often including Shari'a law.

The watershed event in recent Iranian history was the 1978–79 revolution that resulted in the overthrow of the hated Shah (Persian for *King*) of Iran, Reza Pahlavi. Long associated with torture and other human rights abuses, the Shah held fabulous oil wealth while the vast majority of all Iranians were mired in destitute poverty. Moreover, the United States enthusiastically supported the Shah's rule because of his anti-communist credentials during the Cold War. Thus, anti-American sentiment simmered under the Shah.

The Shah's close relationship with the United States also infuriated the *mullahs*, or top Muslim clerics. They saw an increasing acceptance of alcohol, sex, and other permissive western influences as an affront to Islam. One of the Shah's leading critics, the Ayatollah Khomeini, was exiled from Iran in 1964. Meanwhile, Iran went into debt as the Shah spent lavishly and the public grew ever poorer. By 1978, Tehran was awash in demonstrations supporting the Shah's demise. Khomeini then returned from Paris and led the Islamic Revolution to fruition, adopting a new conservative religious constitution in 1979.

What resulted afterward was a theocracy, or rule by religious leaders. Until his death in 1989, the Ayatollah Khomeini served as Iran's authoritarian clerical ruler. *Ayatollah* is a title, not a name, that indicates a top Shi'a religious leader. Shi'a is one of the two main branches of Islam. Sunni is the other main branch and the larger of the two globally. However, the Shi'a dominate in Iran. Khomeini is best remembered globally for his extremist policies—the holding of American hostages for more than 400 days and the death threat, or *fatwa*, declared against the author Salman Rushdie for his supposed blasphemy against Islam in his book *The Satanic Verses*. He also waged an eight-year war against his hated neighbor, Saddam Hussein and Iraq, which at that time was supported by U.S. weapons and financial aid.

Since 1989, Iran's elected institutions have played a more important, but still subservient role, compared to the Muslim clerics, who have veto power in Iranian politics. Currently, a battle between more conservative Islamic forces and more moderate reformers is ongoing.

The *Faqih*, or supreme religious leader, still holds the greatest political say in the system, more so than the country's elected President. Currently, the Faqih is Ali Hoseini-Khamenei. His powers include the declaration of war, control of Iran's judiciary, its security police, media, and intelligence agencies.

The *Faqih* is chosen by an "Assembly of Experts." This 86-member body is composed of *mullahs* who are elected for eight-year terms. The *Faqih* must be a male and will likely be an Ayatollah. Beneath the *Faqih*, the most powerful position is President. A President may serve two four-year terms. Mohammed Khatami, a moderate reformer, finished his second term on August 2, 2005. Iran elected a new President, Mahmoud Ahmadinejad (the mayor of Tehran) after two rounds of voting in June of 2005. Ahmadinejad is considered a conservative and his election may halt Iran's recent trends toward reform.

Iranian Government

The legislative branch is unicameral, made up of the single house called the Majlis, or parliament. Its 290 members are elected by an SMDP format for four-year terms. Candidates run as individuals, as political parties are not allowed under the current constitution. The Majlis is heavily checked by the "Council of Guardians." The Council, which is comprised of twelve mullahs chosen by the Faqih and Iran's Supreme Court, is a conservative body that reinforces the power of the Islamic fundamentalists in the Iranian political system in several ways. First, the Council of Guardians decides who may or may not run for a seat in the Majlis. Reformist candidates were often blocked from running in the 2004 election. Secondly, the Council may block any bill passed by the Majlis without explanation. Many reformers in Iran were disappointed that President Khatami did not resign in protest of the compromised elections for the Majlis, as he had threatened to do.

Iran has been controversial in recent years for its flirtation with atomic power. The Iranian government has claimed it is merely attempting to harness nuclear energy capabilities, while Iran's critics, notably the U.S. under President George W. Bush, have charged that the Iranians are attempting to develop nuclear weapons in violation of the Non-Proliferation Treaty. In 2002, Bush called Iran part of an "Axis of Evil" with Iraq and North Korea, which predictably fueled anti-American rhetoric in Iran.

Economically, Iran is, like Nigeria, an OPEC member overly dependent on its oil exports. Khatami has attempted to diversify Iran's economy and strengthen the service sector. A word about OPEC: it is an acronym for the Organization of Petroleum Exporting Countries and is a cartel of eleven oil-producing states. A cartel attempts to control the price of a certain commodity by limiting its production. The eleven OPEC states produce 40 percent of the world's oil. Most of the member states are found in the Middle East and North Africa. The exceptions are Indonesia, Nigeria, and Venezuela. The OPEC members meet twice yearly to determine production levels. Factors such as the global economy, war in oil producing states (à la Iraq), global climate, and oil consumption all factor into the levels of production OPEC sets.

Culturally, Farsi (Persian) is the country's dominant language. Remember, Arab and Muslim are not synonyms. An Arab is someone who speaks Arabic as his or her primary language. So Arabs can (and do) live from Michigan to Morocco, but they are not necessarily Muslims and can be Christians or Jews as well. So primarily, Iran is not an Arab country.

Women are allowed to vote and, moreover, were a key to Khatami's initial election in 1997. Some women now hold office in the Majlis. However, traditional conservative pressure also forces many women to wear the *chador,* the head-to-toe black cover, whenever they appear in public. Younger women are more resistant to the *chador*, but may wear it publicly to avoid trouble. Younger and more moderate women appear in public wearing not the chador, but the head scarf only, called the hijab, to cover their hair.

Iran is a young and growing country, with some 40 percent of the population born after the Revolution. Unlike in China, families are encouraged by the conservative government to have numerous children. The capital, Tehran, is a teeming metropolis of some 14 million people. A lack of economic development has left many of Iran's younger generation unemployed, underemployed, and rather cynical about their *mullah*-led government. (For the millions of Iranians under 25, the Revolution occurred before they were born and is somewhat a remote event rather than a passionate memory.) This lack of legitimacy could ultimately aid the cause of the moderate political reformers. Time will tell.

However, in the presidential election of 2005, reform took a back seat to the economic concerns of the electorate. Tehran's mayor, a decided underdog in the race, ran a maverick campaign focusing on creating jobs for the generation now in their teens and twenties, and won a surprise victory on the second ballot. (As in Nigeria and Russia, the President must receive a majority and not just a plurality of all votes cast.)

Mahmoud Ahmadinejad thus begins his term as President with several challenges to overcome. To create the promised job growth, Iran will need western investments and, ideally, improved relations with the United States. Yet, Iran remains committed to a program of nuclear technology development, which carries threats of economic sanctions from the U.S., EU, and potentially the United Nations Security Council. Iran had notified the Nuclear Non-Proliferation Treaty in 1970, a Cold War-era agreement attempting to limit the spread of nuclear capabilities that critics claim Iran is violating with its current nuclear pursuits. Iran claims the move is purely defensive and is warranted since its neighbor and potential enemy Israel (who never signed the NPT) has nuclear weaponry.

To end this standoff between the West and Iran, a "grand bargain" is often spoken of in Tehran. This bargain may include such inducements as admitting Iran into the World Trade Organization in exchange for the curtailment of the country's nuclear program.

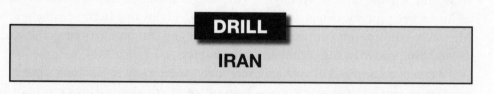

DRILL

IRAN

DIRECTIONS: Carefully read and answer each of the following questions, which are based on the information that you have just read.

87. Iran's government is best described as a

    (A) theocracy   (D) fascist state

    (B) monarchy   (E) parliamentary system

    (C) democracy

88. To a reform-minded President, the key political ally for reform to take place would be the

    (A) Majlis   (D) Faqih

    (B) Assembly of Experts   (E) media

    (C) Council of Guardians

89. Iran's government has recently caused controversy globally for its

    (A) public support of Saddam Hussein in Iraq

    (B) possible development of nuclear weapons

    (C) suppression of women's rights

    (D) support of the Palestinian movement in Israel

    (E) use of capital punishment in accord with Shari'a law

90. OPEC is most similar to the European Union and NAFTA in that all three

    (A) deal with energy issues primarily

    (B) are joint defensive alliances

(C)   strongly promote democracy and the rule of law

(D)   promote global trade

(E)   limit sovereignty of member states in the name greater economic gain

91.   The legitimacy of newly-elected President Mahmoud Ahmadinejad depends most greatly upon

(A)   global oil prices

(B)   negotiations with the EU over Iran's nuclear program

(C)   economic growth and job creation within Iran

(D)   developing a leadership role among leaders in the Middle East

(E)   his assuming a greater religious role within Islam

92.   Iran and Nigeria hold which of the following in common?

   I.   An oil-dominated economy

   II.   A large Muslim population

   III.   OPEC membership

   IV.   Theocratic government

(A)   All of the above   (D)   II and III only

(B)   I, II, and III   (E)   IV only

(C)   I and IV only

93.   Iran's younger generation seems likely to

(A)   keep the Revolution's memory alive

(B)   promote theocracy over democracy

(C)   hold conservative rather than moderate political views

(D)   hold moderate rather than conservative political views

(E)   be enthusiastic and involved rather than cynical and withdrawn from politics

COMPARATIVE GOVERNMENT AND POLITICS

ANSWER KEY

1. (A)	25. (A)	49. (A)	73. (E)
2. (A)	26. (D)	50. (C)	74. (E)
3. (D)	27. (E)	51. (A)	75. (D)
4. (C)	28. (B)	52. (D)	76. (C)
5. (E)	29. (D)	53. (D)	77. (C)
6. (B)	30. (D)	54. (D)	78. (B)
7. (A)	31. (A)	55. (E)	79. (E)
8. (B)	32. (B)	56. (A)	80. (D)
9. (B)	33. (B)	57. (E)	81. (E)
10. (E)	34. (A)	58. (C)	82. (A)
11. (E)	35. (D)	59. (A)	83. (D)
12. (B)	36. (C)	60. (A)	84. (C)
13. (D)	37. (A)	61. (D)	85. (B)
14. (A)	38. (E)	62. (A)	86. (C)
15. (A)	39. (B)	63. (D)	87. (A)
16. (B)	40. (A)	64. (B)	88. (D)
17. (D)	41. (B)	65. (D)	89. (B)
18. (D)	42. (B)	66. (A)	90. (E)
19. (E)	43. (B)	67. (E)	91. (C)
20. (D)	44. (D)	68. (C)	92. (B)
21. (E)	45. (A)	69. (D)	93. (D)
22. (A)	46. (E)	70. (A)	
23. (E)	47. (B)	71. (B)	
24. (E)	48. (B)	72. (B)	

PRACTICE TEST 1
AP United States Government & Politics

AP UNITED STATES GOVERNMENT & POLITICS

PRACTICE TEST 1

SECTION I

TIME: **45 Minutes**
       60 Multiple-Choice Questions
       50% of Total Grade

(Answer sheets appear in the back of this book.)

DIRECTIONS: Read the following questions and incomplete sentences. Each is followed by five answer choices. Choose the one answer choice that either answers the question or completes the sentence. Make sure to use the ovals numbered 1 through 60 when marking your answer sheet.

Question 1 refers to the cartoon below.

Reprinted by permission of the Christian Science Monitor.

1. Which of the following is implied by the political cartoon on the previous page?

    (A) The United States did not adequately plan for Iraqi sovereignty.

    (B) The United States was ill-advised to invade Iraq.

    (C) Iraq can never handle sovereignty.

    (D) Saddam Hussein, while ruthless, was able to keep a lid on Iraq's inherent divisions.

    (E) Iraq now has freedom thanks to the American-led invasion.

2. Which of the following is NOT an example of an informal amendment to the United States Constitution?

    (A) Plea bargains are commonly used by prosecutors to aid police investigations and reduce overcrowded correctional facilities.

    (B) A "wall of separation" should exist between religion and government.

    (C) Bail should fit the seriousness of the crime.

    (D) A President takes advice from a cabinet.

    (E) The electoral college is a "winner-take-all" system in each of the 50 states.

3. If the House of Representatives and the Senate pass similar, but not identical, versions of a bill, what results?

    (A) The bill becomes law with the all of the various stipulations added by each house of Congress.

    (B) The bill is killed.

    (C) A Conference Committee is called between the houses to fashion a single compromised bill.

    (D) The bill is sent to the Supreme Court for judicial review.

    (E) The President decides which version to sign and which to veto.

4. The voting group that has grown most significantly in the past fifteen years is

    (A) labor union members   (D) Hispanics

    (B) 18-25 year olds   (E) the physically disabled

    (C) working women

5. Minor, or third parties, hold the greatest hope for electoral success in which of the following races?

    (A)   State governor's race   (D)   City-county council seat

    (B)   Mayor of a large city   (E)   Presidential election

    (C)   U.S. House of Representatives

6. Pork-barrel legislation is designed to benefit

    (A)   the President   (D)   Democrats only

    (B)   rural areas only   (E)   a legislator's constituents

    (C)   fiscal responsibility

7. Under the administration of George W. Bush, federal spending has risen most markedly in the area of

    (A)   drug enforcement   (D)   social welfare

    (B)   the military   (E)   foreign aid

    (C)   civil rights

8. Which of the following would be most effective in reducing pork-barrel legislation?

    (A)   The elimination of "soft money" financial contributions.

    (B)   Term limitations on members of the House or Representatives and the Senate.

    (C)   A constitutional amendment requiring a balanced budget.

    (D)   Granting the President line-item veto power.

    (E)   Redistricting congressional districts more thoroughly and more often.

9. To be named a committee chair, a member of Congress must fit which of the following criteria?

    I.   Be in the majority party of their chamber.

    II.   Be in the President's party.

    III. Have total congressional seniority over all other committee members.

    IV.   Have committee seniority over all the other "chair eligible" members of their party.

V.   not chair any other type of committee.

(A)   I, IV, and V   (D)   I and V only

(B)   II, III, and IV   (E)   IV and V only

(C)   I only

10.   Which of the following statements concerning presidential campaigns from 1992 to 2004 is most accurate?

(A)   Voter turnout has dropped markedly during this period.

(B)   The role of television in influencing public choice has waned.

(C)   Campaigns have lengthened in duration and increased significantly in cost.

(D)   Independent voting has played a less important role.

(E)   Public debates have greatly intensified voter interest in the process.

11.   A large bureaucracy, such as the 38,000 employees of the Department of Health and Human Services, tends to promote which of the following scenarios?

(A)   Efficient and timely constituent services

(B)   Lowered tax rates

(C)   Department in-fighting over available resources

(D)   Reduced regulation of affected industries

(E)   Fewer forms and paperwork for constituents served by the department

12.   The term "Solid South" has changed in meaning since 1980 in that

(A)   prior to that time the region was strongly Democratic, and since then it has become strongly Republican

(B)   prior to that time the region was strongly Republican, and since then it has become strongly Democratic

(C)   before then, the region was more socially liberal and since then, the region has become increasingly conservative on social issues

(D)   the majority of all Black support for the Democratic Party came from the South, but a large northward migration of African Americans in the last two decades has reversed this trend

(E) the Ku Klux Klan and local militias have waned in their political influence since the 1970s

13. Within the Supreme Court, the "rule of four" describes the number of justices needed to

(A) overturn previous case precedent

(B) confirm a prospective chief justice

(C) end the oral arguments of a given case

(D) agree to a change in the numeric composition of the Supreme Court

(E) accept a case for judicial review

14. Congress has long ago voted itself the privilege of free postage to "keep the folks back home informed." This practice is known as

(A) logrolling   (D) mark-up

(B) franking   (E) gerrymandering

(C) case work

15. Which statement most accurately describes the legal status of marriage licenses, birth certificates, a final will and testament, and other "basic legal documents"?

(A) From state to state, these documents become invalid and must be renewed.

(B) These documents are legally respected throughout the USA by the Constitution's "Privileges & Immunities" clause.

(C) States may tax these documents to declare them legally valid.

(D) These documents are legally respected throughout the U.S. by the Constitution's "Full Faith & Credit" clause.

(E) States may reasonably discriminate against out-of-state residents regarding these legal documents.

16. The foreign policy approach of the (George W.) Bush administration from 2001–2005 could most accurately be described globally as

(A) consensual and cautious

(B) Congressionally led and unifying

(C)   unilateral and antagonistic

(D)   multilateral and ambitious

(E)   bilateral and belligerent

17.   Which of the following is true of the First Amendment's right of assembly?

(A)   The right is unqualified.

(B)   All peaceful assembly is constitutionally protected.

(C)   The assembly is only protected if it is to petition a grievance to the government.

(D)   Time and place restrictions may regulate such assembly.

(E)   Assembly is never restricted during times of "national emergency."

18.   Which two states, although they hold very few electoral college votes, hold an extremely important influence over the process of choosing the American President?

(A)   New York and California

(B)   South Carolina and New Mexico

(C)   Wisconsin and Vermont

(D)   Florida and Texas

(E)   Iowa and New Hampshire

19.   Under the Articles of Confederation, the federal government lacked all of the following EXCEPT

(A)   the ability to declare war   (D)   the ability to raise an army

(B)   a judicial branch   (E)   an executive branch

(C)   the power to tax

20.   Which of the following is true of an *ex post facto* law?

(A)   They can apply to neither civil nor criminal laws.

(B)   A law may not be passed after the fact if it will permit amnesty or other leniency towards a previous criminal act.

(C)   They may apply to both civil and criminal laws.

(D) They may be applied to civil but not criminal law.

(E) An *ex post facto* law is not constitutional because it violates the principle of "no double jeopardy."

21. To formally amend the Constitution, which of the following are necessary?

I.   Bi-partisan support for the proposed idea

II.   Sectional support for the proposed idea

III. The President's support for the proposed idea

IV.   The support of the Supreme Court

V.   The support of 3/4 of all state legislatures

(A) III and V only   (D) V only

(B) II, III, IV, and V   (E) I and V only

(C) I, III, and IV

22. Which statement is NOT true of the electoral college?

(A) It tends to exaggerate margins of presidential victory.

(B) Only once, in the election of 1824, has the House of Representatives officially decided a presidential election, according to the terms of the Constitution.

(C) It promotes campaigning in uncompetitive but highly populous states over candidate visits to moderately populous states that are highly competitive in a given election.

(D) Prior to the 2000 election, it had been more than a century since a popular vote winner lost the presidency due to the electoral college.

(E) Since its creation, the electoral college has since been shaped by both formal and informal amendment.

23. Which two states have altered the "winner take all" aspect of the electoral college, breaking their popular vote total down to reflect the plurality winner within individual congressional districts?

(A) Vermont and Utah   (D) Delaware and Kentucky

(B) Nebraska and Maine   (E) North Dakota and Arizona

(C) Oregon and Wisconsin

24. The economy under George W. Bush from 2001–2005 has been most positive for American consumers in which of the following regards?

    (A) Home mortgage interest rates

    (B) The stock market

    (C) Consumer confidence in corporate America

    (D) E-commerce

    (E) Creation of manufacturing jobs

25. Which of the following Constitutional amendments does NOT attempt to increase suffrage by defining it more specifically for localities?

    (A) Fifteenth Amendment

    (B) Twenty-Sixth Amendment

    (C) Twelfth Amendment

    (D) Nineteenth Amendment

    (E) Twenty-Fourth Amendment

26. Which of the following is an important informal check on presidential power?

    (A) The federal court system   (D) The electoral college

    (B) The media   (E) The United States Senate

    (C) The two-term limit

27. Which of the following is LESS likely to consume the time of a member of the House of Representatives than of a Senator?

    (A) Committee and subcommittee hearings

    (B) Dealing with PACs and lobbyists

    (C) Using the franking privilege

    (D) Case work

    (E) Scheduling time for the media

28. The boundaries of United States congressional districts are usually determined by

    (A) the Federal Election Commission [FEC]

    (B) state legislatures

(C)   the United States Senate

(D)   the majority party in the House of Representatives

(E)   the director of the United States Census Bureau

29.   "Soft money" is the term used for campaign donations that are

(A)   raised through high-priced dinners involving big-name party figures

(B)   solicited through the Internet via individual candidate websites

(C)   gained by using the franking privilege

(D)   unlimited in amount, hard to trace, and hard to follow in terms of how a major party uses the funding

(E)   placed on individuals within campaign finance law restrictions

30.   A "cannot voter" has been defined as a person, otherwise eligible to vote, but who cannot register to do so either because of their religious beliefs or their legal status. Which group below constitutes the largest and fastest growing group of "cannot voters"?

(A)   The incarcerated or paroled

(B)   Mentally disabled

(C)   Jehovah's Witnesses

(D)   The homeless

(E)   Seventeen-year-olds

The Federal Government Dollar (Fiscal Year 2002 Estimate)

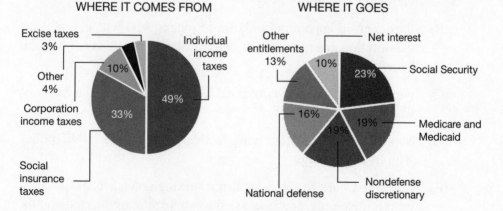

WHERE IT COMES FROM

Excise taxes 3%
Other 4%
Corporation income taxes
Social insurance taxes
10%
33%
Individual income taxes
49%

WHERE IT GOES

Other entitlements 13%
Net interest
10%
23% — Social Security
16%
19% — Medicare and Medicaid
19%
National defense
Nondefense discretionary

Source: Budget of the United States Government, Fiscal Year 2002: A Citizen's Guide to the Federal Budget (Washington, D.C.: U.S. Government Printing Office, 2001), 5,9.

31. Which of the following statements is supported by the graphs above?

    (A) In fiscal year 2002, the United States had a balanced budget.

    (B) Medical costs are a main target of federal budget spending.

    (C) Corporate America funds more government services than do individual Americans.

    (D) The United States engaged in deficit spending in fiscal year 2002.

    (E) The existing national debt of more than $5 trillion has no bearing on the budget for an individual year like 2002.

32. The candidacy of Howard Dean for President in 2004 will likely have the longest lasting political impact because of his

    (A) staunch opposition to the Iraq War and to Bush foreign policy

    (B) attempt to gain the presidency despite having governed in a very sparsely populated state

    (C) use of the Internet to raise a large amount of campaign funding

    (D) proposal of unified national voting system and the scrapping of the electoral college

    (E) infamous scream following an early defeat in a crucial caucus

33. The concept of judicial activism involves the

    (A) Senate, in blocking court appointees that hold opposing political views to the majority party

    (B) President, in appointing only those judges who will interpret the Constitution in a manner that supports the President's core political beliefs

    (C) public, in picketing controversial decisions made by the Supreme Court

    (D) Supreme Court, in attempting to shape and initiate public policy with its case rulings

    (E) Supreme Court, in refraining from striking down acts of Congress or executive programs because those branches are elected and the Supreme Court is not

34. The government's right to take private land—with compensation—for public use is known as

    (A)   eminent domain   (D)   quid pro quo

    (B)   extradition   (E)   prior restraint

    (C)   statute of limitations

35. A judge would be most likely to issue an injunction in which of the following strikes?

    (A)   Coal miners   (D)   State police

    (B)   Flight attendants   (E)   Newspaper printers union

    (C)   Auto workers

36. The Department of Homeland Security became a cabinet department in the wake of 9/11 mainly to

    (A)   hunt down and eradicate potential terrorist threats, such as Al-Qaeda

    (B)   coordinate cooperation and communication between various federal intelligence agencies

    (C)   enforce the Patriot Act and promote patriotism

    (D)   train airport personnel to ensure greater airline security

    (E)   investigate why the 9/11 attacks had been able to occur on American soil

37. Given the fact that a "gender gap" exists in American politics, it would be more likely for a woman rather than a man in this country to say all of the following EXCEPT:

    (A)   "I am pro-choice on abortion."

    (B)   "Equal pay for equal work is a valid concept."

    (C)   "I strongly believe in the death penalty."

    (D)   "Government-provided daycare is a good idea."

    (E)   "The environment should come before profit margin."

38. Which pair of states represent the fastest population growth areas in the United States since 1995?

    (A)   North Carolina and Tennessee

    (B)   New York and New Jersey

    (C)   Vermont and New Hampshire

    (D)   California and Oregon

    (E)   Arizona and Nevada

39.   A federal census could change all of the following EXCEPT the

    (A)   amount of federal aid a state receives

    (B)   total number of seats available in the House of Representatives and Senate

    (C)   total number of Representatives a state holds in the U.S. Congress

    (D)   shape of congressional boundaries within the various states

    (E)   amount of electoral college votes that the various states receive

40.   Which of the following would occur first in the Congressional law-making process?

    (A) Mark-up session

    (B) Final committee decision on bill

    (C) "Pork-barrel" amendments

    (D) Conference committee

    (E) Logrolling

41.   Double jeopardy, the portion of the Fifth Amendment that mentions "no person shall be put twice in jeopardy for the same offense," was meant to accomplish which of the following?

    (A)   It avoids the need for a criminal jury to reach unanimous verdicts.

    (B)   It prohibits the accused from being tried in both civil and criminal courts, as in the case of O.J. Simpson.

    (C)   It prevents the police and prosecutors from introducing new evidence after an acquittal has been granted.

    (D)   It prevents criminals from seeking an appeal to an earlier conviction.

    (E)   It created the concept of the "mistrial" and the "hung jury."

42. Which of the following is NOT one of the four original cabinet positions?

    (A) Attorney General   (D) Secretary of State

    (B) Postmaster General   (E) Secretary of the Treasury

    (C) Secretary of War

43. Which of the following actions by George W. Bush tended to unite rather than divide the American populace?

    (A) The call for a constitutional amendment banning gay marriage.

    (B) His call for a renewal of the Patriot Act in 2004.

    (C) The conduct of American foreign policy.

    (D) His conduct in the weeks following the September 11th attacks

    (E) His handling of the economy.

44. Which group more typically votes Democratic than Republican?

    (A) Suburban residents   (D) White-collar workers

    (B) The self-employed   (E) Jews

    (C) Protestants

45. Bill Clinton did not campaign heavily for Al Gore in the 2000 election because

    (A) the Gore camp was wary of the moral backlash that might cost them votes

    (B) Clinton was totally involved as his wife's campaign manager in her bid to gain a United States Senate seat in New York

    (C) Clinton and Gore were never ideologically aligned

    (D) the two men were ideologically aligned but did get along personally

    (E) Clinton felt abandoned by Gore during his impeachment trial

46. Which statement below is accurate concerning major party membership in the past fifty years as a proportion of the total electorate?

    (A) Both major parties have gained public membership.

    (B) Both major parties have significantly lost public membership.

(C) The Democrats have gained public membership while the Republicans membership has declined.

(D) The Republicans have gained public membership while the Democratic membership has declined.

(E) Major party membership has remained static for the past fifty years.

47. Which of the following states does NOT hold one of the top five electoral college vote totals?

(A) Florida   (D) New York

(B) Texas   (E) California

(C) Virginia

48. States may reasonably discriminate against out-of-state residents in which of the following ways?

(A) Voiding marriage license issued out of state

(B) Setting slower interstate speed limits for cars holding out-of-state license plates

(C) Charging higher public college tuition fees for out-of-state students

(D) Limiting abortion access for people from out of state

(E) Refusing property ownership

49. As a result of the 2000 election, the United States Senate was evenly split between 50 Republicans and 50 Democrats. Given this reality, which statement concerning control of committee chairs below is accurate?

(A) The two parties split control of the 18 Senate committee chairs.

(B) The Democrats controlled all the committees as a result of a coin flip.

(C) Each committee was simply chaired by the most senior member regardless of party affiliation.

(D) The Democrats controlled all 18 committee chairs because their party held the tie breaker—the vice presidency

(E) The Republicans controlled all 18 committee chairs because their party held the tie breaker—the vice presidency

50. The greatest economic power held by the Federal Reserve is to

    (A) print currency

    (B) set the prime interest rate

    (C) purchase precious medals

    (D) name the Secretary of the Treasury

    (E) approve foreign trade agreements

51. The type of political campaign propaganda utilized in most negative attack ads is

    (A) testimonial   (D) glittering generality

    (B) bandwagon   (E) transfer

    (C) card-stacking

52. In President Bush's 2002 State of the Union address, he labeled which of the following as constituting an "axis of evil"?

    (A) Libya, Saudi Arabia, and Tunisia

    (B) Iran, Iraq, and North Korea

    (C) France, Germany, and China

    (D) Russia, Iraq, and Cuba

    (E) Colombia, Libya, and Zimbabwe

53. All of the following are powers held by the Senate and not the House of Representatives EXCEPT

    (A) the filibuster

    (B) confirming Supreme Court appointees

    (C) trying federal impeachment cases

    (D) initiating all legislation

    (E) ratifying treaties

54. A legislative issue decided by a popular vote is known as

    (A) an initiative   (D) an injunction

    (B) a referendum   (E) mediation

    (C) a recall

55. The recall of California Governor Gray Davis centered on what issues?

    (A) Scandals within the administration

    (B) Potential voting fraud allegations in the 2002 election

    (C) Lax immigration policies

    (D) Teacher shortages and state-wide employee strikes

    (E) State budget deficits and recurring energy shortages

56. To say that the presidential primary season is now "front loaded" means that

    (A) only successful candidates attract funding from party loyalists

    (B) very few candidates now enter the early caucuses and primaries

    (C) only the most populous states determine who the parties' nominees will be

    (D) the vast majority of the contests occur early in the process

    (E) the final few primaries hold a vast importance

57. The Twenty-Seventh, or most recent, Constitutional amendment concerns itself with

    (A) equal pay for equal work

    (B) gay marriage

    (C) congressional pay raises

    (D) term limits for Congress

    (E) a mandated balanced federal budget

58. What happens to the vast majority of bills introduced into the House of Representatives and Senate?

    (A) They die in committee or subcommittee.

    (B) They are defeated due to the lack of a quorum in either chamber.

    (C) They are defeated on the floor of the Senate.

(D)   They require a conference committee.

(E)   They are passed into law and signed by the President.

59.   Critics often refer to affirmative action as

(A)   reverse discrimination

(B)   welfare dependency

(C)   expensive and unrealistic

(D)   a "glass ceiling"

(E)   a temporary solution to a permanent problem

60.   Which of the following is NOT true of the 2000 presidential election?

(A)   The losing vice presidential candidate retained a seat in the United States Senate.

(B)   Al Gore received a greater share of the popular vote than did George W. Bush.

(C)   Both candidates handily won their home states.

(D)   The United States Supreme Court ordered Florida recounts of votes to cease.

(E)   Neither candidate came across particularly well in pre-election televised debates.

STOP
This is the end of Section I.
If time still remains, you may check your work only in this section.
Do not begin Section II until instructed to do so.

SECTION II

TIME: 100 Minutes
4 Free-Response Questions
50% of Total Grade

DIRECTIONS: Write an essay based on each of the following four questions. Be sure to pace yourself by allotting about one-fourth of your time, or 25 minutes, for each question. Where appropriate, use substantive examples in your answers. Your essays should be numbered to correspond with the questions to which you are responding.

1. It has been said that "a third party is like a bee; once it stings, it dies." Address this quote regarding the following:

    a) Discuss any two "third party" movements that have made a significant impact upon American politics.

    b) Why did these movements gain notable support?

    c) Why did these movements ultimately decline or disappear?

2. What is the relationship between the executive and legislative branches of government in the making of foreign policy? In explaining this relationship, identify some of the specific issues that have arisen in recent years over the respective powers of the two branches.

3. The presidential election of 2000 was controversial for several reasons. Address any two of the points below as they relate to the election of 2000:
    *   a federal approach to national elections
    *   the electoral college
    *   the recounting process
    *   the U.S. Supreme Court

4.   Campaign finance has been a contentious political issue in recent years. Address the following points in clarifying the issues involved:

a)   How would publicly financed campaigns differ from the current system?

b)   How would publicly funded campaigns alter the campaigning process?

c)   Why might incumbent candidates oppose this change?

END OF EXAMINATION

UNITED STATES GOVERNMENT & POLITICS

PRACTICE TEST 1

ANSWER KEY

1.	(A)	16.	(C)	31.	(B)	46.	(B)
2.	(C)	17.	(D)	32.	(C)	47.	(C)
3.	(C)	18.	(E)	33.	(D)	48.	(C)
4.	(D)	19.	(A)	34.	(A)	49.	(E)
5.	(D)	20.	(D)	35.	(D)	50.	(B)
6.	(E)	21.	(E)	36.	(B)	51.	(C)
7.	(B)	22.	(C)	37.	(C)	52.	(B)
8.	(D)	23.	(B)	38.	(E)	53.	(D)
9.	(A)	24.	(A)	39.	(B)	54.	(B)
10.	(C)	25.	(C)	40.	(A)	55.	(E)
11.	(C)	26.	(B)	41.	(C)	56.	(D)
12.	(A)	27.	(E)	42.	(B)	57.	(C)
13.	(E)	28.	(B)	43.	(D)	58.	(A)
14.	(B)	29.	(D)	44.	(E)	59.	(A)
15.	(D)	30.	(A)	45.	(A)	60.	(C)

DETAILED EXPLANATIONS
OF ANSWERS

TEST 1

SECTION I

1. **(A)**

The cartoon shows an Iraq in rubble being returned by Uncle Sam to the Iraqis themselves. A common criticism of the Iraqi War aimed at the Bush administration has been a lack of coherent planning or understanding of the internal Iraqi opposition to the occupation of Iraq. The Bush administration returned "sovereignty" to Iraq on June 30, 2004, or about 15 months after the initial invasion of the country.

2. **(C)**

Informal amendments are understood and are widely accepted components of U.S. Constitutional law, yet they are unwritten changes to the formal Constitution. Thus, (C) is the correct answer in this "NOT" question because the Eighth Amendment addresses the prohibition of "excessive bail" requirements.

3. **(C)**

Typically, the House and Senate will pass different versions of a bill on similar subject matter. If so, a Conference (or Joint) Committee is necessitated. This involves key members from affected committees and constituencies from both the House and Senate to work out a single compromised version of the bill.

4. **(D)**

As of the 2000 U.S. Census, Hispanics passed African Americans as the country's largest minority group. The other groups listed have either declined (as with union membership), remained fairly static (working women and 18- to 25-year-olds), or grown much less dramatically than has Hispanic immigration to the U.S. (as with the physically disabled).

5. **(D)**

The chances for success of minor parties or independent candidates goes up as the constituency gets smaller. In other words, the more localized the election, the better chance that the major parties can be "upset" by a surprise candidate, as factors such as television advertising, name recognition, and thus, big money play a less important role. The city-council seat would hold the smallest constituency of the examples given.

6. **(E)**

Pork involves non-essential projects and spending tacked on to bills. The sponsors of pork hope to please their own constituents with improvements, services, etc., in an effort to gain re-election. Pork is certainly not fiscally responsible (C), as it adds to budget deficits. It has been used to aid both urban and rural districts and is the domain of Congress and not the President.

7. **(B)**

Spurred largely by the "war on terrorism" following 9/11/2001 terror attacks and military intervention in Afghanistan and Iraq, military spending has climbed markedly under the Bush administration.

8. **(D)**

A line-item veto has long thought to be a cure for pork spending. It would allow a president to keep those parts of a bill believed worthy and necessary and to trim unnecessary additions. Currently, the President must sign or veto a bill in its entirety. Congress granted President Clinton a form of a line-item veto, but it was ruled unconstitutional by the Supreme Court. A constitutional amendment would be necessary to grant the President this power.

9. **(A)**

Committee chairs wield considerable power, namely the power to kill or shape bills. Thus, knowing how one achieves this position is worthwhile. Three basic rules are followed: 1) Chair will always come from the majority party in that chamber; 2) It is seniority in the committee rather than in Congress overall that matters—chair will have more committee seniority than any fellow party member; 3) A member of the House or Senate may only chair a single committee. All of these are informal amendments that the major parties themselves have devised to spread power and satisfy their own congressional membership.

10.   **(C)**

The trend of beginning campaigns sooner, and thus having to fund more television commercials, newspaper ads and personal visits, has intensified during the past four campaigns. The party *not* holding the White House especially seems to be starting its election "assault" sooner. For instance, the Democratic Party had staged a number of nationally televised cable debates by the fall of 2003, a full year before the actual election would occur.

While voter turnout remains relatively low—it was in 1992 also—it has not "dropped markedly" (A). Television has become more of a factor in the process, not less (B). Independent, or split-ticket, voting, is a rising factor of importance (D). While televised debates both during the primary and presidential season have become commonplace, the lengthening political process has not intensified voter interest, but has rather led to lessened interest in the process.

11.   **(C)**

A large bureaucracy such as the Department of Health and Human Services, with many competing programs and interests, will experience intra-department battles for scarce money available. The Secretary of HHS will ultimately decide how to allocate these financial resources.

12.   **(A)**

Following Reconstruction all the way to the election of Georgian Jimmy Carter in 1976, the Deep South consistently voted for Democrats, both nationally and locally. However, when running for re-election in 1980, Carter was thoroughly defeated in the South by Republican challenger Ronald Reagan. The South had always been more socially conservative than the North over issues such as abortion, religious toleration, civil rights, and busing (C), so this shift in voting made ideological sense.

13.   **(E)**

Four of the nine justices must agree to accept a case, or issue a *Writ of Certiorari*. Case precedent is only overturned via court rulings, which would call for a vote of five justices generally (A). The court itself does not confirm or deny chief justice appointees; rather the Senate does (B). Oral arguments are set at 30 minutes per side in any given case by informal amendment (C). Only Congress could change the numerical size of the Court from its current nine, which is highly unlikely to happen.

14.   **(B)**

Franking describes free congressional postage to constituents. Logrolling is the trading of votes between members (A). Case work is doing favors and other necessary services for constituents (C), while a "mark-up session" involves revising a bill in subcommittee or committee (D). Gerrymandering is redistricting congressional boundaries, often into illogical shapes, to gain partisan advantage for the party drawing the boundaries (E).

15.   **(D)**

Basic legal documents such as marriage licenses, birth certificates, a final will and testament, and so on, are respected from state to state according to the "Full Faith & Credit" clause of the Constitution's Article IV. States may not discriminate against these basic legal documents.

16.   **(C)**

The foreign policy of the Bush administration has been divisive and unilateral. (Unilateral means directed by U.S. interest only without regard to traditional allies.) Examples include the Iraq War in the face of UN Security Council opposition, disregard for the Kyoto Accords on global warming; and the U.S. renunciation of the ABM Treaty concerning nuclear arms. (E) might seem a tempting answer given British support for the Iraqi invasion, but Britain has not been consulted, or shown agreement with, most of the foreign policy stances described above.

17.   **(D)**

Issues such as potential traffic problems, state of national emergency, permission to be on private property, etc., may indeed limit expression that would be otherwise protected by the First Amendment.

18.   **(E)**

Iowa and New Hampshire fit the description: few electoral college votes (because neither is very populous) but a tremendous impact on the process of choosing the president via the country's first presidential caucuses in Iowa and the first primary in New Hampshire.

19.   **(A)**

Among the very few powers held by the national government under the Articles of Confederation was the ability to declare war. However, this was a rather empty power considering that the federal government could not draft troops to raise an army. That decision, like almost all others, was left up to the thirteen individual states, which ultimately made the Articles unworkable.

20. **(D)**

Ex post facto means "after the fact"—a law passed after an act has been committed. This can be done with civil law (e.g., taxation retroactive to an earlier point) but not with criminal law. In other words, if Internet fraud is not on the law codes as a crime, and a person commits Internet fraud, he or she cannot be held legally responsible if it *later* is passed into law.

21. **(E)**

The process to formally amend the Constitution involves 2/3 passage in both the House of Representatives and the Senate followed by ratification by 3/4 (or 38) of the states. The 2/3 passage would necessitate bi-partisan support since neither party alone would hold reasonably this number of seats in Congress. A presidential veto is unlikely if 2/3 passed the proposed amendment because it could be overridden and would likely have public support anyway. Sectional support alone would not help a proposed amendment make it through Congress or gain enough state-by-state support for ratification. The Supreme Court plays no role in the ratification process.

22. **(C)**

Candidates would not generally tend to visit, say, a state such as California or Texas repeatedly, even though they have very high electoral college vote totals, if the states were not competitive because this would be wasting precious campaigning time. In 2000, both Al Gore and George W. Bush visited Missouri, with its 11 electoral college votes, many times because the race there was considered a toss-up.

The "corrupt bargain" of 1824 remains the only time the House of Representatives followed the format laid out within the electoral college for choosing a president in the event all candidates fail to win an electoral college majority (B). The winner-take-all format indeed exaggerates victory margins (A). Prior to 2000, the last time that the popular vote winner had been cost the presidency by the electoral college was 1888, when Benjamin Harrison defeated Grover Cleveland (D). The 12th Amendment of the Constitution is an example of a formal change while the "winner-take-all" aspect is an example of an informal change to the electoral college (E).

23. **(B)**

Nebraska and Maine have altered the "winner-take-all" aspect of the electoral college, breaking their popular vote total down to reflect the plurality winner within each congressional district. These states also award their two remaining EC votes the old fashioned way—plurality winner statewide takes both of these votes.

24.   **(A)**

The economy was largely stagnant or worse from 2001–2005. Home mortgage interest rates hit 40-year lows during this period, however. More than three million jobs were lost (E) and corporate confidence was not high among consumers in the wake of Enron, WorldCom, Martha Stewart, and Halliburton scandals (C). Both the stock market and e-commerce were economically volatile (B) and (D).

25.   **(C)**

The Twelfth Amendment refigured the way the electoral college would work, eliminating the occurrence of the second-place EC vote winner becoming vice president. The other amendments listed increased suffrage for Blacks (Fifteenth and Twenty-fourth), women (Nineteenth), and 18-year-olds (the Twenty-sixth).

26.   **(B)**

The media are an important informal check on presidential power. The other choices listed either were formal—that is, constitutional—checks on executive power, such as the Senate or two-term limit, or unrelated, such as the electoral college.

27.   **(E)**

A member of the House of Representatives is less likely than a Senator to be interviewed by the media because the Senate is the more high-profile job with just two members per state.

28.   **(B)**

The boundaries of United States congressional districts are usually determined by the majority party within each individual state's legislature.

29.   **(D)**

"Soft money" is the term used for campaign donations that are unlimited in amount, hard to trace, and hard to follow in terms of how a major party uses the funding. Candidates often talk of reforming this system, but once in office they realistically become somewhat dependent upon soft money for their own re-election hopes.

30.   **(A)**

The incarcerated or paroled are often not eligible to register to vote—and this is especially true for parolees in Southern states. This group is the fastest growing and largest segment of "cannot voters." The homeless are more able to register in certain states that have waived permanent residence as a requirement for registration, it should be noted (D). Seventeen-year-olds don't fit the absolute definition of a "cannot voter" (E).

31.   **(B)**

On the second pie graph—expenditures—comparatively large percentages are spent on Medicare, Medicaid, and Social Security. The graph does not address total dollar amounts raised or spent by the government, so neither (A) nor (D) could be the correct answer. Corporate America funds a much lower percentage of all government revenues than do individual income tax payers (C) and the fact that "net interest" is under expenditures indicates that financing the existing national debt of more than $5 trillion is a consideration in the budget.

32.   **(C)**

Former Vermont Governor Howard Dean utilized the Internet in an innovative fashion to get a jump on his Democratic rivals in fund-raising prior to the 2004 primary season. This will undoubtedly be noted and copied by other politicians, especially on the national level.

33.   **(D)**

The concept of judicial activism involves the Supreme Court, attempts to shape and initiate public policy with its case rulings. This type of court would be more likely to strike down acts of Congress or presidential initiatives. Judicial activism has been evident in such landmark cases as *Brown vs. Board of Education* and *Roe vs. Wade*. Judicial activism is the opposite of judicial restraint.

34.   **(A)**

The government's right to take private land—with compensation—for public use is known as eminent domain. An example is the purchase of a strip of private homes for the purpose of adding an interstate exit ramp across that land.

35.   **(D)**

An injunction is a court order to end a strike. Injunctions are issued when the public safety is placed in jeopardy, so the police strike would more accurately fit this description than the other potential strikes listed.

36.   **(B)**

The Department of Homeland Security became a cabinet department in the wake of 9/11 mainly to coordinate cooperation and communication between various federal intelligence agencies, such as the FBI and CIA. Traditionally, competition and jealousy have precluded such agencies from full cooperation.

37.   **(C)**

The gender gap refers to a greater likelihood that a woman will be more liberal, and thus more likely to vote for the Democratic Party. Being for the death penalty is a more traditional, conservative, and thus Republican belief.

38.   **(E)**

Spurred by factors including retirees relocating there and growing Hispanic population, Arizona and Nevada have been the fastest-growing pair of states in the past decade. The Phoenix and Las Vegas areas especially illustrate this growth.

39.   **(B)**

A federal census by itself could not change the total number of seats available in the House of Representatives and Senate. The House of Representatives is set by law at 435 seats and is not likely to be changed. The constitution places the Senate membership at two per state and it is even less likely this number would be changed by constitutional amendment. Federal aid is often tied to proportional population compared to the U.S. as a whole (A). Population determines how many members a state will receive in the House (C) and thus, how many electoral votes they will hold (E). Following a census, states will redistrict, or redraw their congressional boundaries to make them equal in terms of population within each (D).

40.   **(A)**

A mark-up session would occur first in the Congressional law-making process, usually at the sub-committee level. A final committee decision on a bill would occur next (B). Both logrolling and pork would occur during full floor debate, or the second reading of the bill (C) and (E). A conference committee session would occur after a final vote had been taken in each house and the bill had passed each, but in different versions (D).

41.   **(C)**

Double jeopardy is often mistakenly referred to with the incomplete phrase, "No person can be tried twice for the same crime." Sure they can! Prisons are full of convicted felons who desperately desire (and only rarely get) to be tried twice for the same crime—that's called an appeal. The part of the phrase that is missing is, "if they were first acquitted." This rule is why police and prosecutors painstakingly put together a case before seeking a trial. They know they only get a single chance to convict the accused and may not introduce new evidence after the fact.

42.   **(B)**

Postmaster General has never been on official cabinet position. Remember, prior to the Cold War, "Secretary of War" was the title for what is now called Secretary of Defense (C). To this day, these four original positions are considered to be the most prestigious among the entire cabinet.

43.   **(D)**

In the wake—and shock—of the September 11th attacks, President Bush held his highest approval ratings as the country rallied and united to cope with the events. Bush enjoyed bi-partisan support in Congress, which explains the easy passage of the Patriot Act, which, in retrospect, drew criticism for the limits it places on certain individual freedoms. Thus, the renewal of the Patriot Act in subsequent years has aroused heated debate, both in and out of Congress (B). The call for a Constitutional amendment banning gay marriage in the wake of local laws in Massachusetts and San Francisco allowing it promoted disagreement between fundamental Christian groups supporting the ban and more secular liberal groups opposed to it (A). The "war on terrorism" in general and the Iraq invasion in particular have sparked heated debate across the country (C), while the Bush tax cuts have caused division over whether they should be more targeted to the middle class and less toward wealthier Americans (E).

44.   **(E)**

Jewish people tend to vote Democratic, as do Catholics, labor union members, blacks, and younger voters. The other choices listed tend to vote GOP.

45.   **(A)**

Bill Clinton presented a dilemma for the Gore campaign in a very close race: On one hand, a popular two-term president who presided over a healthy economy; on the other hand, a divisive figure, impeached, who carried the baggage of questionable personal moral behavior. The Gore campaign basically decided to go it alone, without Clinton. There was no personal or ideological rift between the two men.

46.   **(B)**

Currently, only about 47 percent of the American electorate claims membership in either major party. This is down significantly from the 1950s, when that number was closer to 75 percent. This means that independent or split-ticket voting has risen markedly in recent decades.

47.   **(C)**

Although it has a higher electoral college total than most states, Virginia is not among the five most populous states in the country.

48.   **(C)**

Under the terms of the Constitution's "Privileges & Immunities" clause in Article IV, states may reasonably discriminate against out-of-state residents. Among the examples of how this may occur include charging higher public college tuition fees for out-of-state students or higher fees for fishing and hunting licenses to out-of-state residents. The other examples given were not "reasonable" in their scope of discrimination.

49.   **(E)**

Even with a 50–50 split in the U.S. Senate in 2001, the Republicans controlled all 18 committee chair positions. Why? Because the GOP controlled the White House and thus, Vice President Cheney's tie-breaking vote would go to his own party. Interestingly, the defection of Vermont Senator Jim Jeffords (he left the GOP to become an independent) in 2002 returned control of the Senate to the Democrats.

50.   **(B)**

The greatest economic power held by the Federal Reserve is to set the prime interest rate. Alan Greenspan, whose term ended on January 31, 2006, wielded tremendous political power in his role as Federal Reserve chairman. He served under Presidents Reagan, Bush, Clinton, and Bush.

51.   **(C)**

The type of political campaign propaganda utilized in most negative attack ads is card-stacking, in which outright lies are not told, but rather "facts" are given out of context or only half of the story is told. Testimonial involves a celebrity endorsement for a candidate (A). Bandwagon attempts to create the illusion of widespread support, e.g., "Everybody else is voting for Candidate X—aren't you?!" (B) A glittering generality is a bold but vague claim, often a phrase, that virtually means nothing upon closer scrutiny (D), and transfer involves using a "symbol" like the Bible, the American flag, or a popular rock song to gain votes for a certain candidate (E).

52.   **(B)**

In President Bush's 2002 State of the Union address, he labeled Iran, Iraq, and North Korea as an "axis of evil." As with most of Bush's foreign policy rhetoric, this proved internationally unpopular and domestically divisive.

53.   **(D)**

Legislation may initiate from either house of Congress, with the exception of taxation bills, which must originate in the House of Representatives.

54.   **(B)**

A legislative issue decided by a popular vote is known as a referendum. An initiative is petition-driven effort to get a legislature to consider a certain bill (A); a recall attempts to remove a locally elected official before his/her term has expired (C); an injunction is a court order to end a work stoppage (D); and mediation involves a neutral third-party arbitrating a contract for a stalemated labor-management conflict (E).

55.   **(E)**

The recall of California Governor Gray Davis centered around several issues, including Davis's perceived lackluster personality. (Although it is interesting to note Davis had secured a second-term re-election less than a year earlier from California's fickle electorate.) Politically, the most damning issues for Davis were state budget deficits and recurring energy shortages.

56.   **(D)**

To say that the presidential primary season is now "front loaded" means that most of the primaries and caucuses now occur very early in the season—during January, February, and early March.

57.   **(C)**

The Twenty-Seventh, or most recent, Constitutional amendment concerns itself with congressional pay raises. In fact, the amendment stipulates that while Congress may vote itself any pay raise it sees fit, that raise may not take effect until the following Congress has assumed office. The logic: let the voters decide if those who voted themselves the raise deserve to get it at all.

58.   **(A)**

Committees in both houses serve as a screen and they mainly kill bills. Roughly 90 percent of all bills are killed in committees.

59.   **(A)**

Critics often refer to affirmative action as reverse discrimination, because it attempts to reserve positions in universities and government employment for women and minorities, or groups previously discriminated against in the workplace.

60.   **(C)**

Much to his chagrin, Al Gore was not able to win his home state of Tennessee. If he had, he would have won the presidency with or without Florida. Indeed, Bush swept all of the Southern states. Joseph Lieberman, the Democratic vice presidential candidate, retained his seat in the United States Senate, representing Connecticut (A). Al Gore did win the popular vote race nationwide (B). The Supreme Court voted along party lines, 5–4, to cease all ballot recounting in Florida in December 2000 (D). In the three televised debates prior to the election, Bush made several verbal gaffs while Gore was chastised for his condescending attitude toward Bush (E). Neither candidate distinguished himself from his opponent particularly well.

SECTION II

Question 1–Sample Essay that Would Achieve a Top Score

The analogy between a third party and a bee has much validity, given the history of U.S. politics. It seems that once a party "stings," it soon fades into oblivion. Two parties that did just that are George Wallace's American Independent Party of 1968 and the Populist Party of the late 19th Century.

Wallace's party was largely just a vehicle for his individual beliefs, which included firm stands on states' rights, anti-integration, and support of the Vietnam War. A generally southern conservative agenda rounded out the tenets of the party. This gained Wallace more than 30 electoral college votes, as he won several southern states in the 1968 election.

The Populist Party sprang from the gripes of plains farmers over issues such as railroad gouging and the desired minting of silver. Other groups, such as miners and some southern tenant farmers, joined their crusade. The Populist Party won governor seats in several plains states and made inroads in gaining support for their congressional and presidential candidates by the early 1890s.

Third parties that achieve any level of success have conveyed the message that neither major party is adequately addressing a specific issue, or that the major parties are ignoring the needs of an important portion of the electorate. Successful third parties find an issue, or issues, that the two major parties are neglecting, whether that be perceived opposition to busing and affirmative action or a lack of legislation to breakup railroad monopolies and increasing the prices from crop yields.

To combat these threats, the major parties adapt. The Democrats and the Republicans tend to "steal the thunder" from a third party by incorporating its ideas into their own platforms. By doing so, the major party will gain the support of the third party following.

For example, the Republicans under Ronald Reagan adopted many of Wallace's ideas, such as opposing busing and affirmative action while being tough on crime and increasing military spending, and packaged the beliefs in friendlier rhetoric. Thus, by 1980, the GOP had broken the "solid South" of its reputation as a stronghold of Democratic support.

Similarly, in 1896, Democrat William Jennings Bryan gave his famous "Cross of Gold" speech, in which he announced unqualified support for the minting of silver, assuring that the Populist Party votes would largely go his way, while also sounding the death knell of the Populist Party itself.

Question 2–Sample Essay that Would Achieve a Top Score

The development of primary elections was an outgrowth of the Populist Movement during the late 1800s. The Populists believed the dominant business interests had acquired too much influence over political parties and the nomination process. They believed that an unsavory alliance between the "plutocrats" (wealthy industrialists) and political party leaders had developed, producing a situation in which financial campaign support by the business interests was rewarded with favorable pro-business public policies.

The Populists supported policies of economic reform that were intended to improve the economic conditions of rural and urban working class Americans. However, they came to believe such economic reforms were not possible unless political reform was first accomplished. It was their view that the people's power to elect public officials had been compromised by the control over the nomination of candidates exercised by the business-party leadership alliance.

The Populists were among the first organized groups to call for "returning power to the people." In order to accomplish this objective, they championed numerous election reforms, including the right to vote for women, the direct election of United States senators, direct primary elections, and a national presidential primary. Although the Populists were unsuccessful in accomplishing these reforms in their third-party movement, most of their reforms were adopted and implemented into law by "progressive" leaders in the Democrat and Republican parties.

Two of those political reforms, direct primary and presidential primary elections, were intended to remove the party leadership's stranglehold over nominations. These reforms were intended to take the nomination out of the "smoke-filled room" and return it to the people through the ballot box. Since neither reform was enacted by Congress, each developed gradually and in a variety of forms through legislation enacted independently at the state and local level.

Direct primaries first appeared at the turn of the century in Wisconsin and Florida, and over the ensuing four decades slowly spread to the other states. In 1948, Connecticut, the last state to provide for direct primary elections, completed the process. Direct primary elections, sponsored by each party, replaced convention nominations by the party leaders with popular nominations by the voters. Thus, the term "direct" primary is meant quite literally—the winner of the party primary, nominated directly by the voters, is the party nominee.

Presidential primaries, in contrast, might be called "indirect primaries." The Populist proposal calling for each party to nominate their presidential candidate in a national presidential primary has never been implemented. Instead, individual states gradually and independently adopted legislation permitting political parties to use presidential primaries as a method for selecting delegates to attend their party's national nominating convention. The winner of a presidential primary has not won the party nomination. Instead, the presidential primary winner has won only a bloc of delegates who are more or less committed to his/her nomination at the national convention.

It should be noted that the development and expansion of the use of presidential primaries for delegate selection, which began in 1912, has not yet been completed. However, an important phase in that development was reached in 1968. Prior to that year, a majority of convention delegates were selected by the state party leaders. Since 1968, an increasing number of convention delegates have been selected in the state party presidential primaries. In 1912, Theodore Roosevelt won all 12 Republican presidential primaries held that year, but lost the nomination to William Howard Taft on the first ballot at the national convention. Although possible, it is highly unlikely that a candidate who wins more than one-half, if not all, of his party's 40-odd presidential primaries would be denied the convention nomination.

The development of primary elections and presidential primaries has neutralized the party leaders and party organizations in the nomination process. State party conventions have gone by the wayside, and the state leaders no longer select the party candidates for national, state, and local offices, nor do they select the vast majority of national convention delegates.

There can be no doubt that this weakened party role and influence has also affected the candidates and the nature of election campaigns. The route to elected office no longer requires individuals to work their way up within the party organization. Anyone can declare candidacy and seek the nomination in the party primaries. Each candidate for nomination, however, must build his/her own campaign organization, raise campaign contributions, and plan and execute the campaign. Consequently, since the party is neutral during the primaries, candidates must rely more on interest groups for campaign contributions and on the media for political communication (including news coverage and advertising).

Question 3–Sample Essay that Would Achieve a Top Score

(Note: The question only demands that two factors be analyzed, but all four will be covered in this example.)

In the presidential election of 2000, Democrat Al Gore gained more popular votes nationwide than did the eventual winner, Republican George W. Bush. This fact alone would have made the election memorable, if not exceptionally controversial, given the realities of the electoral college. But the final state to be decided—Florida—was so rife with intrigue over mistakenly marked ballots, counts, and recounts that this election was finally decided over a month after the fact by the United States Supreme Court.

The events in Florida led to an increased call for federal election standards. This could include a uniform method of voting nationally instead of the hodge-podge variety of voting methods now employed (everything from computerized touch screens to paper ballots and punch cards). Perhaps to avoid a similar controversy in the future, the U.S. might implement uniform voting standards nationwide, much like a unitary form of government. This would require a commitment of federal funding.

Although the electoral college is an easy target, it has proven remarkably adept at survival. The most realistic challenge to the current electoral college system would be the alternative currently used in Maine and Nebraska, which abolishes the "winner take all" aspect. Both states distribute their electoral college votes on a congressional district basis, awarding one electoral college vote to the winner of the popular vote in each district. The two remaining "at large" electoral college votes go the the state's overall plurality winner. The validity of this method of distributing electoral college votes was not supported by the 2000 election. If such a system had been implemented nationwide, George W. Bush's victory in the electoral college would have been greater than the 271 to 267 margin by which he won, although he would have still lost the popular vote. In other words, this alternative system does not ensure that the electoral college vote will accurately reflect the popular vote.

The recounting process in Florida became extremely contentious, holding the country's attention for more than a month following the election. Questions arose concerning the dreaded "hanging chad" and what did or did not constitute a properly marked ballot. Both Gore and Bush, and their respective teams of lawyers, converged on Florida in an attempt to win this high-stakes game. As annoying as this process was to some, the recounting process may be one of the strongest arguments for keeping the electoral college. This "localized"the recounts to areas such as Florida, New Mexico, and Iowa, where the votes were extremely close. Otherwise, a complete national recount would become necessary in an election in which neither candidate concedes defeat.

The Supreme Court's role in the outcome of the 2000 election will ultimately be judged by history for its significance far more than we are perhaps able to see today. By its typical 5 to 4 conservative/liberal split, the Court voted to stop all recounts in Florida, assuring George W. Bush's victory in the state and his electoral vote majority. With the legitimacy of the U.S. government relatively high, this decision met little resistance nationwide. There were few instances of public protest over the decision and it has been widely accepted. In fact, Democratic challenger Al Gore made what was perhaps his most eloquent speech of the entire campaign when he gracefully bowed out of the race following the Court's decision. The precedent has now been set: if a state cannot seem to come to a conclusion on an election, the Supreme Court will enforce one upon it.

Question 4–Sample Essay that Would Achieve a Top Score

Publicly financed campaigns would be funded strictly via federal revenue—that is, by taxpayers. It would allocate a level amount of money to the major parties for their candidates in races for congressional seats, the U.S. Senate, and for the presidency. This would differ significantly from the current reality, in which successful fund-raising is a key component to realistically having a chance to hold a federal office. For instance, when Elizabeth Dole dropped out of the Republican presidential primary race in 2000, she cited George W. Bush's ability to raise eight times as much money as she as a leading factor behind her decision. Publicly funded campaigns would greatly decrease the cost of gaining public office.

One obvious change from the current system to a publicly financed one would be the death of the "$1,000-a-plate political dinner." Name candidates would lose their fund-raising advantage. Another positive change would be the death of "soft money," which is money doled out by the major parties' national committees to candidates around the country. This money is often shrouded in mystery; often difficult to track its source, and difficult to know where and to whom it is funneled. Soft money perpetuates much of the negative stereotypes about politics and politicians, such as that they are "phony," "in politics only for the money," and "will say or do anything to get (re)elected."

Incumbents would likely oppose publicly financed campaigns for the same reasons they have opposed other forms of campaign finance reform: it could cost them re-election. Publicly financed campaigns would place challengers on an equal playing field in terms of finances for television ads and other forms of campaigning. For the same reason "pork" is often lambasted by outsiders but left untouched by incumbent members of Congress, they would likely not support such a radical change in campaign finance law.

PRACTICE TEST 2

AP United States
Government & Politics

AP UNITED STATES GOVERNMENT & POLITICS

PRACTICE TEST 2

SECTION I

TIME: 45 Minutes
60 Multiple-Choice Questions
50% of Total Grade

(Answer sheets appear in the back of this book.)

DIRECTIONS: Read the following questions and incomplete sentences. Each is followed by five answer choices. Choose the one answer choice that either answers the question or completes the sentence. Make sure to use the ovals numbered 1 through 60 when marking your answer sheet.

1. The Supreme Court preserved the phrase "One nation under God" in the Pledge of Allegiance in a 2004 ruling prompted by an atheist's challenge. The Constitutional question at issue here is

    (A) the separation of church and state

    (B) double jeopardy

    (C) the legal rights of minors versus the legal rights of adults

    (D) eminent domain

    (E) states' rights

2. The "establishment clause" most directly relates to

    (A) the building of an airport on municipal lands

    (B) the refusal of a Catholic hospital to accept non-Catholic patients

(C) definition of what prayer is allowed in a public school and what is not

(D) 18-year-olds who must register for the national military draft

(E) requirements that must be met before a citizen of the United States can vote

3. Which of the following statements about Democrats and Republicans is NOT true?

(A) City dwellers are more likely to call themselves Democrats than Republicans.

(B) Republicans are more likely than Democrats to label themselves "conservatives."

(C) Blacks, Jews, and Hispanics typically vote for the same major party—the Democrats.

(D) Republicans are more likely than Democrats to believe that adequate medical care should be guaranteed by the federal government.

(E) People in working-class occupations are more likely to call themselves Democrats than Republicans.

4. Which amendment in the Bill of Rights does NOT expressly protect the rights of the accused?

(A) The Third   (D) The Sixth

(B) The Fourth   (E) The Eighth

(C) The Fifth

5. A conference committee on a military equipment upgrade bill would be composed mainly of

(A) senior members only from both the House and the Senate

(B) committee chairs only from both the House and the Senate

(C) the Speaker of the House, the President Pro Tem, and other party leaders from both houses of Congress

(D) a mixture of interested members of Congress, the President, and key lobbying interests

(E) members from the Armed Services committees in both the House and the Senate, with the majority party in each house holding more seats on the conference committee

6. The primary election system of selecting presidential candidates has had which of the following effects?

(A) It has increased the importance of state party organizations.

(B) It has loosened the hold of party leaders over the nomination process.

(C) It has reduced the role of citizens in the candidate selection process.

(D) It has lowered the cost of running for office.

(E) It has led to a decline in the importance of party voter registration drives.

7. Supporters of granting the President a line-item veto would most likely argue that this power would increase a President's ability to

(A) work effectively with the opposition party

(B) control federal spending and limit "pork barrel" politics

(C) negotiate treaties with foreign heads of state

(D) avoid costly disputes with the judiciary

(E) provide effectively for national defense

8. The "solid three" conservative justices on the Supreme Court from the early 1990s through the early 2000s were

(A) O'Connor, Kennedy, and Stevens

(B) Scalia, Rehnquist, and Thomas

(C) Ginsberg, Breyer, and Souter

(D) Souter, Scalia, and Kennedy

(E) O'Connor, Thomas, and Breyer

9. All of the following factors add to public disillusionment with members of Congress in terms of their effectiveness and integrity EXCEPT

(A) pork-barrel politics

(B) logrolling

(C)   frequent use of the franking privilege

(D)   the influence of lobbyists and PACs

(E)   case work

Question 10 refers to the following statement:

"Students who voluntarily participate in school athletics have reason to expect intrusions upon normal rights and privileges, including privacy."

10.   This opinion, written by Justice Antonin Scalia in a 1995 decision, was part of which case ruling?

(A)   *TLO vs. New Jersey*

(B)   *Kuhlmeier vs. Hazelwood Schools*

(C)   *Mergens vs. Westside Schools*

(D)   *Acton vs. Vernonia School District*

(E)   *Tinker vs. Des Moines*

11.   Which of the following is true of a presidential veto of a piece of legislation?

(A)   It is rarely overridden by Congress.

(B)   About 25 percent of all bills are vetoed.

(C)   A President can veto any legislation passed with the exception of "revenue raising" (taxation) bills.

(D)   The veto process is automatically reviewed by the Supreme Court.

(E)   The President's party in Congress must concur with any presidential veto.

12.   Which statement below concerning religion is accurate?

(A)   In the United States, people have freedom of religious action, but not of religious choice.

(B)   In the United States, people have freedom of religious choice, but not religious action.

(C)   Except during extracurricular club periods, no prayer is currently permitted in public high schools.

(D)   The federal or local governments never encourage the building of churches and other places of worship.

(E)   There is no place for religion at all in American politics.

13.   All of the following are common steps to the passage of a bill by Congress EXCEPT

(A)   introduction into both the Senate and the House

(B)   referral to committees for recommendation

(C)   presidential approval of committee recommendations

(D)   House and Senate floor debate

(E)   House and Senate compromise

14.   Which of the following is an example of a "nonvoting voter"?

(A)   A convict serving a sentence in a federal prison

(B)   A person who is either too alienated or apathetic to exert the effort to vote

(C)   A person who pulls the "straight ticket" lever in the voting booth

(D)   A person who meant to register to vote but missed the deadline for doing so

(E)   A person who votes in the presidential, senatorial, and mayoral races, but does not vote in the other races listed

15.   During the presidential primary season, the party that holds the White House usually

(A)   engages in a hard-fought battle over the presidential nomination

(B)   does not enter many primary races

(C)   stands pat with the incumbent President or a hand-picked successor

(D)   aggressively attacks the opposition party

(E)   splits into minor party factions

16.   Which of the following was never among the two major American political parties?

(A)   Democrats   (D)   Republicans

(B)   Whigs   (E)   Populists

(C)   Federalists

17. Which of the following statements concerning party primaries and party national conventions is most accurate?

(A) Both tend to be divisive for the political party involved.

(B) Both tend to be unifying influences for the party involved.

(C) Primaries tend to unify a party, while the national convention often divides it.

(D) Primaries tend to divide a party, while the national convention often unites it.

(E) Neither one holds much influence on party unity in modern-day politics.

18. A useful public opinion poll requires all of the following EXCEPT

(A) a representative sample

(B) carefully constructed questions

(C) an accurate statistical analysis

(D) meticulous planning

(E) face-to-face interviewing

19. Which of the following is considered to be constitutionally protected symbolic speech?

(A) Hiding obscenities within the lyrics of a rock song

(B) A police officer's right to wear an earring on the job

(C) Wearing any legally purchased concert T-shirt to a public high school the following day

(D) Burning the American flag

(E) Going barefoot into a shopping mall or restaurant

20. All of the following conditions characterized the United States under the Articles of Confederation EXCEPT

(A) virtual sovereignty was left to the states

(B) the federal government was virtually bankrupt

(C) interstate trade and commerce was stifled

(D)   a series of attacks on courthouses in Massachusetts called attention to the demands of debtors

(E)   several states were on the verge of rebellion because of harsh new restrictions placed by the national government on interstate trade

21.   All of the following help explain why such a high percentage of incumbents are reelected to Congress EXCEPT that

(A)   their campaigns receive a greater share of federal matching funds

(B)   their staffs can help constituents deal with the government

(C)   they can win constituent support by providing pork-barrel projects for the district they represent

(D)   the franking privilege and media opportunities provide greater name recognition for incumbents

(E)   PACs are more likely to support incumbents than challengers

22.   If the United States were operating today under the Articles of Confederation instead of the Constitution, a problem like air pollution or the preservation of endangered species would most likely be handled by

(A)   the Supreme Court

(B)   the individual states

(C)   the President

(D)   the Department of Interior

(E)   Congress, acting through the Speaker of the House and the President of the Senate

23.   The First Amendment of the Constitution addresses all of the following issues EXCEPT

(A)   the ability of the people to complain to the government about its practices

(B)   the gatherings of groups in public

(C)   the circumstances under which a search and seizure can be conducted by the police

(D)   what religions may be practiced in the United States

(E)   what information magazines and television newscasts may reveal

24.   When the media speak of a candidate or officeholder putting a "spin" on a particular issue, they are referring to the politician's attempt to

    (A)   present his actions or stance on an issue in the most favorable light possible

    (B)   honestly and directly answer the questions presented by the media

    (C)   shed responsibility for past campaign promises

    (D)   blame his national party for unpopular programs back home

    (E)   avoid answering a particular question

25.   Plea bargaining has become commonplace in the American legal system for all of the following reasons EXCEPT

    (A)   the public widely supports the practice

    (B)   prosecutors see it as a way to make their caseloads workable

    (C)   many prisons are currently overcrowded

    (D)   the police and prosecutors view it as a trade-off toward more meaningful arrests and convictions

    (E)   once arrested, many suspects opt to make a deal to avoid a trial in the hopes of lessening their sentences

Questions 26–27 refer to the chart below.

Votes for Ten Recent Supreme Court Nominees

Nominee	Judiciary Committee	Senate
John Paul Stevens	17-0	98-0
Sandra Day O'Connor	18-0	99-0
Antonin Scalia	18-0	98-0
Robert Bork	5-9	42-58
Anthony Kennedy	14-0	97-0
David Souter	13-1	90-9
Clarence Thomas	7-7	52-48
Ruth Bader Ginsburg	18-0	96-3
Stephen Breyer	18-0	87-9
John Roberts	13-5	78-22

26. Which statement is supported by the chart?

    (A) A nominee must receive majority support in the Judiciary Committee to receive a confirmation hearing from the full Senate.

    (B) The vote received from the Judiciary Committee is generally a good barometer for how the nominee will fare with the entire Senate.

    (C) The unanimous votes in the Judiciary Committee can be explained by a single party holding all of the committee's seats.

    (D) Voting on a Supreme Court nominee's confirmation is a mandatory duty for U.S. senators.

    (E) Each of the men and women listed on the chart eventually served as Supreme Court justices.

27. John Paul Stevens, chosen to serve on the Supreme Court in 1975, has turned out to be more liberal than conservative in his political judgments, despite being chosen by Republican President Gerald Ford. Which statement is LEAST likely to explain why this has occurred?

    (A) The Senate in 1975 was controlled by the Democratic Party.

    (B) Stevens perhaps became more liberal and less moderate in the years after being chosen by Ford.

    (C) Ford was concerned about disrupting the harmony of a rather liberal Supreme Court in 1975.

(D) Ford himself may have been a rather moderate Republican.

(E) Stevens' lower court rulings as a federal judge had not been overly controversial.

28. In order to prove libel or slander, it is necessary for the plaintiff to prove that a statement was

(A) intentionally harmful, whether false or not, and malicious

(B) malicious, untrue, and negatively affects the plaintiff's ability to earn a living

(C) emotionally damaging and untrue

(D) obscene as defined by the you-know-it-when-you-see-it test

(E) symbolic rather than verbal

29. The case of *Near vs. Minnesota* revolved around the issue of

(A) the right of the American Nazi Party to march in a predominantly Jewish neighborhood

(B) whether or not the U.S. flag could be altered from its original form as constitutionally protected symbolic speech

(C) protecting reporters from revealing confidential sources to the courts

(D) whether or not a publication could be censored before it printed objectionable material

(E) private militia groups to arm themselves

30. The "greatest good for the greatest amount" is served by which of the following concepts?

(A) *Ex post facto* laws   (D) Extradition

(B) Prior restraint   (E) The Twenty-seventh Amendment

(C) Eminent domain

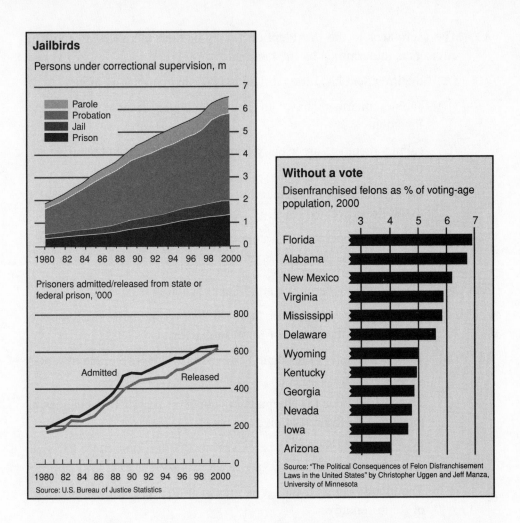

Jailbirds

Persons under correctional supervision, m

- Parole
- Probation
- Jail
- Prison

1980 82 84 86 88 90 92 94 96 98 2000

Prisoners admitted/released from state or federal prison, '000

Admitted   Released

1980 82 84 86 88 90 92 94 96 98 2000

Source: U.S. Bureau of Justice Statistics

Without a vote

Disenfranchised felons as % of voting-age population, 2000

3   4   5   6   7

Florida
Alabama
New Mexico
Virginia
Mississippi
Delaware
Wyoming
Kentucky
Georgia
Nevada
Iowa
Arizona

Source: "The Political Consequences of Felon Disfranchisement Laws in the United States" by Christopher Uggen and Jeff Manza, University of Minnesota

31. Given the information above, which of the following will NOT likely increase in the next decade?

(A) The total number of disenfranchised felons

(B) The need for more parole officers

(C) Construction of prisons and jails

(D) A need for public defenders

(E) The number of female convicts as opposed to male convicts

32. The usefulness to the President of having cabinet members as political advisers is undermined by the fact that

   (A) the President has little latitude in choosing cabinet members

   (B) cabinet members have no political support independent of the President

   (C) cabinet members are usually drawn from Congress and retain loyalties to Congress

   (D) the loyalties of cabinet members are often divided between loyalty to the President and loyalty to their own executive departments

   (E) the cabinet operates as a collective unit and individual members have no access to the President

33. Which statement concerning United States senators is NOT true?

   (A) You are more likely to see them on the evening news than you are a member of the House of Representatives.

   (B) They are usually older than members of the House of Representatives.

   (C) They do not have the campaigning concerns that their colleagues in the House of Representatives have.

   (D) In general, the Senate is perceived as a better job—more prestige and influence—than is serving in the House.

   (E) The incumbency advantage is greater in the Senate than in House of Representatives.

34. The Bush administration faced charges of combining church and state with which of the following acts?

   (A) The invasions of Afghanistan and Iraq

   (B) Faith-based initiatives

   (C) The Patriot Act

   (D) No Child Left Behind Act

   (E) Its opposition to stem-cell research

35. The most effective weapon used by the Federal Reserve in its attempt to control inflation is to

   (A) print a new design of currency

   (B) lower the prime interest rate

(C)   raise the prime interest rate

(D)   raise the tariff rate

(E)   lower the tariff rate

36.   What would be the most likely reason for a President to enter into an executive agreement with a foreign country rather than sign a treaty?

(A)   An executive agreement avoids political wrangling with the Senate since it does need to be ratified.

(B)   An agreement has more legal validity than a treaty.

(C)   A President can easily back down from an executive agreement with no recourse for the foreign country.

(D)   The 1973 Supreme Court ruling in *Miller vs. California* gave the Senate more scrutiny in the Senate ratification process.

(E)   An executive agreement requires prior Senate approval, making resulting negotiations easier for the President.

37.   All of the following are general characteristics of Democratic voters EXCEPT

(A)   blue collar employment

(B)   that they tend to be Roman Catholic

(C)   suburban residence

(D)   a desire for larger government

(E)   that they're more likely female than male

38.   Which political office has been the most consistent stepping stone for a successful candidate seeking the presidency since 1970?

(A)   United States Senator   (D)   Secretary of State

(B)   State governor   (E)   Big city mayor

(C)   Vice President

39.   When George W. Bush pulled the United States out of the Kyoto Accords, which of the following issues was involved?

(A)   Protecting the United States from further attacks in the wake of 9/11 by ending limits on the production of anti-ballistic missiles.

(B) A denial to the scientific community of further stem-cell research.

(C) Increased oil exploration in formerly protected lands in Alaska.

(D) A repudiation of global-warming limits placed on American corporations.

(E) Retaliatory steel tariffs against European competitors.

40. Which of the following is NOT typically considered a failure in most scholarly presidential rankings?

(A) Buchanan   (D) Grant

(B) Garfield   (E) Harding

(C) Carter

41. The Twenty-second Amendment, ratified in 1952,

(A) limits a President to full terms, or ten total years of service maximum

(B) defines the order of presidential succession in case of death, disability, or resignation

(C) sets the presidential inauguration date at March 4 of the year following the election

(D) sets the presidential inauguration date at January 20 of the year following the election

(E) made the electoral college a formal, rather than informal, amendment to the Constitution

42. Which of the following is NOT a common problem in conducting an accurate public opinion poll?

(A) Different phrasing of questions may give very different results.

(B) Questionnaires often are not returned when mailed to selected participants and telephone surveys often result in hang-up responses.

(C) Representative sampling is sometimes difficult or expensive to obtain.

(D) When people talk to pollsters, they tend to underestimate the amount of their political participation and knowledge.

(E) People sometimes respond to questions about issues that they know nothing about.

43. When a popular President influences voters to support candidates for other offices from the President's party, the result is called

(A) straight-ticket voting   (D) a mandate

(B) the coattail effect   (E) a landslide

(C) logrolling

44. "Mark-up sessions," in which revisions and additions are made to proposed legislation in Congress, usually occur in which setting?

(A) The majority leader's office

(B) In party caucuses

(C) On the floor of the legislative chamber

(D) In joint conference committees

(E) In committees or subcommittees

45. Which of the following is NOT an example of an informal amendment to the Constitution?

(A) The existence of a two-party system

(B) The concept of executive privilege

(C) The "Maine/Nebraska" electoral college experiment

(D) The cabinet

(E) The President's annual "State of the Union" message

46. Which of the following is true of the electoral college system?

(A) It encourages the emergence of third parties.

(B) It encourages candidates to concentrate their efforts in competitive, populous states.

(C) It ensures that the votes of all citizens count equally in selecting the President.

(D) It requires that a candidate win a minimum of 26 states to obtain a majority in the college.

(E) It tends to make presidential election results appear closer than they really are.

Question 47 refers to the quote below.

"Judge Souter agreed with the decision but cited a separate point of law than that of the other members of the court in a 9–0 decision favoring a state's right to ban private gambling."

47. The opinion described is

(A) a concurring opinion

(B) a dissenting opinion

(C) a majority opinion

(D) a defamatory decision

(E) an abstaining opinion

48. The primary reason for the current existence of only two major political parties in the United States is that

(A) the Constitution puts severe restrictions on the existence of political parties

(B) third parties are usually too moderate, while most Americans are more extreme politically

(C) a winner-take-all electoral system makes it difficult for new parties to emerge and survive

(D) voters naturally think of themselves as either liberals or conservatives

(E) straight-ticket voting is allowed

Question 49 refers to the quote below.

"Voting is partly a matter of habit: the more frequently a person has voted in the past, the more likely she or he is to vote in the current election."

49. All of the following statements support the observation above EXCEPT:

(A) Immediately after the Twenty-sixth Amendment in 1971 gave 18- to 21-year-olds the vote, the proportion of eligible voters who actually voted declined.

(B) Immediately after the Nineteenth Amendment in 1920 gave women the vote, the proportion of eligible voters who actually voted declined.

(C)   Immediately after the passage of the Voting Rights Act of 1965, the participation rate of black voters in the South was lower than that of white voters in the South.

(D)   Unmarried persons over the age of 65 are less likely to vote than are married persons in that same age group.

(E)   Newly naturalized citizens may need special inducements to vote.

50.   Which of the following constitutional amendments prevents "cruel and unusual punishment" and suggests that the amount of bail charged must fit the circumstances of the particular crime involved?

(A)   The Fifth Amendment

(B)   The Sixth Amendment

(C)   The Seventh Amendment

(D)   The Eighth Amendment

(E)   The Ninth Amendment

Question 51 refers to the cartoon below.

Connecting the Dots

Reprinted by permission of the Christian Science Monitor.

51. The cartoon implies most greatly the need for which of the following?

    (A) The Department of Homeland Security

    (B) Greater cooperation between the United States Army, Navy, Air Force and Marine Corps

    (C) The Patriot Act

    (D) An invasion of Iraq

    (E) Greater cooperation among the member states of the United Nations

52. A filibuster

    I. can be used in either the House or the Senate

    II. is a stall tactic designed to prevent the likely passage/defeat of a bill on the Senate floor

    III. is commonly blocked by the cloture rule

    (A) I, II, and III

    (B) II and III only

    (C) III only

    (D) I and II only

    (E) II only

53. Of the following, which best predicts the likelihood that citizens will vote?

    (A) Their race

    (B) Their educational level

    (C) Their religion

    (D) Their gender

    (E) Their region of residence

54. Which entertainment figure is NOT readily identified with liberal causes?

    (A) Al Franken

    (B) Michael Moore

    (C) Charlton Heston

    (D) Barbra Streisand

    (E) Ed Asner

55. All of the following statements are true of the spoils system EXCEPT:

(A) Merit by testing is one of its key aspects.

(B) Patronage is a synonym for the spoils system.

(C) The system provides a way to fill positions within the bureaucracy.

(D) It has been limited at the federal level by law.

(E) Positions are often determined by political support and apt to change as a result of elections.

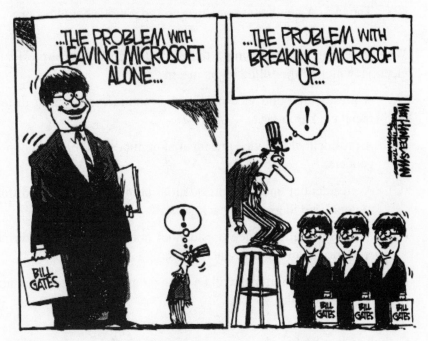

Reprinted by permission of Tribune Media Services.

56. The cartoon illustrates the federal government's concern with Bill Gates and Microsoft because of

(A) corporate scandal and insider trading

(B) faulty bookkeeping and fraudulent earnings reports

(C) intelligence sharing with potential enemies

(D) allegations of overcharging the U.S. government over military contracts

(E) anti-trust (monopoly) concerns over Microsoft's business practices

57. Which statement best describes the separation of church and state as spelled out in the First Amendment?

(A) The separation is absolute and unwavering.

(B) The separation was not addressed; it has been read into the Constitution entirely by a "liberal" interpretation.

(C) The separation was unintentional.

(D) The "wall" of separation isn't always very high, and sometimes nearly vanishes altogether.

(E) The First Amendment hints that no separation should occur.

58. When speaking of "balancing a ticket" in the context of a presidential election, which of the following is meant?

(A) A presidential and vice presidential nominee will be of different racial backgrounds.

(B) A presidential and vice presidential nominee will be from opposite genders.

(C) A presidential and vice presidential nominee will be of different regional and ideological backgrounds.

(D) A presidential and vice presidential nominee will be of different educational levels or social classes.

(E) A presidential nominee will be younger and vice presidential nominee will be older.

59. Catholic Church officials in the United States had the most trouble supporting 2004 Democratic presidential candidate John Kerry—a practicing Roman Catholic—over his support of

(A) the death penalty

(B) abortion

(C) the separation of church and state

(D) the war in Iraq

(E) equal rights for women

60. In voting on a bill, every member of Congress must balance four factors—constituents' views, party line, PAC/lobbyist support, and personal view of the issue—in deciding how to cast their vote. An incumbent in a close re-election race desiring "soft money" would probably weigh which two factors most heavily?

(A) Personal beliefs and lobbyist support

(B) Lobbyist support and the party line

(C) The party line and constituent beliefs

(D) Constituent beliefs and personal views

(E) Party line and personal beliefs

STOP
This is the end of Section I.
If time still remains, you may check your work only in this section.
Do not begin Section II until instructed to do so.

SECTION II

TIME: 100 Minutes
4 Free-Response Questions
50% of Total Grade

DIRECTIONS: Write an essay based on each of the following four questions. Be sure to pace yourself by allotting about one-fourth of your time, or 25 minutes, for each question. Where appropriate, use substantive examples in your answers. Your essays should be numbered to correspond with the questions to which you are responding.

---

1. Since about 1970 there has been an effort to shift power from the federal government to the states. Discuss the constitutional relationship of the federal and state governments, the reasons why there has been an effort to shift power in recent years, and explain some of the specific means through which the shift has been attempted.

2. Currently, the constitutional and legal validity of affirmative action is being widely discussed. Explain why affirmative action was begun in the 1960s, and the constitutional and legal issues that have been debated since that time.

3. Federal Budget Outlays (in billions of dollars)

	1970	1989 (est.)	Percent Increase 1970–1989
Fixed Costs	120.3	865.1	719.12
Variable Costs	83.8	306.3	365.51

For the purpose of this question, fixed costs are those over which the President has relatively little control. These are costs that can be adjusted only by an act of the U.S. Congress. Variable costs are those that can be changed by Presidential decision. Fixed costs include entitlement programs, interest on the deficit, and other programs approved by Congress. Variable costs include defense spending and other executive branch programs.

a)   From the information in the table above, how much responsibility does the Presidency bear for the growth in federal spending?

b)   Since politics in the real world is more complicated than a simple table, what might have to happen before federal spending is reduced?

4.   "While people complain about negative political advertisements as harmful to the political process, there is no concrete evidence that negative political campaigns have any effect on voter turnout or citizens' attitudes towards government and politics in general. What we do know is that negative political advertising has been used as long as there have been campaigns. Since politicians running for office want to appeal to as many voters as possible and are reluctant to state their specific positions on an issue, negative ads are often the only source for information about a candidate's position and action on an issue."

This claim by a political scientist seems to contradict the conventional wisdom that negative political campaigns somehow degrade the political process.

a)   Explain why negative advertisements might, in fact, help voters make a more informed election decision.

b)   Given what you know about campaigning, criticize the author's favorable position on negative political advertising.

END OF EXAMINATION

UNITED STATES GOVERNMENT & POLITICS

PRACTICE TEST 2

ANSWER KEY

1. (A)	16. (E)	31. (E)	46. (B)
2. (C)	17. (D)	32. (D)	47. (A)
3. (D)	18. (E)	33. (E)	48. (C)
4. (A)	19. (D)	34. (B)	49. (D)
5. (E)	20. (E)	35. (C)	50. (D)
6. (B)	21. (A)	36. (A)	51. (A)
7. (B)	22. (B)	37. (C)	52. (E)
8. (B)	23. (C)	38. (B)	53. (B)
9. (E)	24. (A)	39. (D)	54. (C)
10. (D)	25. (A)	40. (B)	55. (A)
11. (A)	26. (B)	41. (A)	56. (E)
12. (B)	27. (C)	42. (D)	57. (D)
13. (C)	28. (B)	43. (B)	58. (C)
14. (E)	29. (D)	44. (E)	59. (B)
15. (C)	30. (C)	45. (E)	60. (C)

DETAILED EXPLANATIONS
OF ANSWERS

TEST 2

SECTION I

1.   **(A)**

The words "under God" have caused a debate as to the constitutionality of reciting "The Pledge of Allegiance" in public schools. The issue is the separation of church and state, and also freedom of expression—both of which relate to the First Amendment. Double jeopardy relates to being charged with the same crime after first being acquitted (B), while eminent domain (D) deals with the government seizing (with compensation) private lands for greater public use. Both of these are Fifth Amendment issues. States' rights (E) could be cited by a more conservative state, likely in the South, in this issue but the Supreme Court rules for the country as a whole under Article III of the Constitution. Choice (C) simply does not relate to this issue and would be more relevant to a case like *TLO vs. New Jersey*, 1985.

2.   **(C)**

The "establishment clause" deals with the opening portion of the First Amendment that states, "Congress shall make no law respecting an establishment of religion, or prohibiting the free exercise thereof." In other words, the government cannot establish a national religion and individuals further have the right to worship whatever they want, or nothing at all. So, this issue of separating church and state is at play in the choice given concerning allowable prayer in a public school.

3.   **(D)**

Democrats, rather than Republicans, would more likely support medical care provided for all by the government. This is a liberal view that conservative Republicans would not agree with.

4.   **(A)**

The Third Amendment in the Bill of Rights is virtually meaningless today. It prevents the housing of soldiers in private homes without the consent of the property owner. This amendment has been informally repealed because it is now irrelevant. The Fourth Amendment deals with search and seizure (B), the Fifth with the right not to incriminate oneself (C), the Sixth with the right to a speedy and public trial (D), and the Eighth with fair bail and the avoidance of cruel punishments by law enforcement (E).

5.   **(E)**

Conference committees meet only after both houses of Congress pass a different bill on the same issue. The conference committee is a bi-partisan effort to reach a single, compromise bill; it would be composed mainly of members from the committee of origin, who would have the greatest stake in its final passage.

6.   **(B)**

Primaries have taken power from the major parties and given it to the states and to those relatively few voters who actually participate in primaries. Previously, the parties used the famous "smoke-filled room" scenario to broker deals and decide which candidate would be most electable and "manageable"—would carry out the party's platform. With the advent of the primaries, surprise candidates have emerged, à la Jimmy Carter in 1976 and Bill Clinton in 1992.

7.   **(B)**

Currently, a President's veto is all-or-nothing concerning a bill. A line-item veto would permit a President to knock out certain portions only of a bill, presumably pork. However, a constitutional amendment would be required to gain a President this leverage and since that process begins with Congress, it may not be forthcoming anytime soon.

8.   **(B)**

The Supreme Court has been rather split along 5–4 lines, with five justices in the more conservative camp. Among those five, the fiercely conservative triumvirate had been former Chief Justice William Rehnquist (who died in 2005) along with Associate Justice Antonin Scalia and Clarence Thomas. Generally, Anthony Kennedy and the now-retired Sandra Day O'Connor would join these three in votes, but not always. The more liberal camp has been comprised of Souter, Stevens, Ginsberg, and Breyer.

9.   **(E)**

"Casework" describes the tasks and favors that a member of Congress provides for constituents. This could include a letter of recommendation for entrance to West Point, a copy of the Freedom of Information Act requested for a college paper, and so on. This would obviously aid the member of Congress at re-election time and would lead to less public disillusionment.

10.   **(D)**

The court increased the rights of public schools to use random drug testing on students involved in extracurricular activities in the ruling of *Acton vs. Vernonia School District*.

11.   **(A)**

Presidential vetoes, or even the threat of their use, are rare in themselves. A President obviously does not want to antagonize Congress needlessly as positive executive-legislative relations will help the administration get its agenda passed into law. However, it is even rarer that a presidential veto would be overridden by Congress because that would require a 2/3 vote in each house and it is unlikely that a President would command that kind of party dominance in both houses.

12.   **(B)**

In the United States, people have freedom of religious choice, but not religious action. They may worship whatever they choose, or nothing at all. However, religious action is *not* legally protected. For instance, a Jamaican Rastafarian cannot smoke marijuana legally by claiming it is a religious ritual. Nor can a Mormon legally commit bigamy claiming a traditional church belief in the practice.

13.   **(C)**

The White House does not hold the power of formal approval of committee recommendations. Often, the party controlling a particular committee would be the opposite party from the sitting President (see Bill Clinton's administration) so this would simply be a check on presidential power.

14.   **(E)**

A "nonvoting voter" is a person who votes for some, but not all, offices listed on a given ballot. An incarcerated person is a "cannot voter," because he cannot register to vote if he desires to do so (A). Someone who doesn't vote is simply a non-voter (B), as is a person who means to register but fails to do so (D). A straight-ticket voter is the opposite of a "nonvoting voter" because she places a vote for all the races on a given ballot.

15.   **(C)**

The party holding the White House usually experiences a placid campaign as opposed to the party on the outside looking in, which holds a free-for-all among several contenders. In 2004, George W. Bush ran unopposed as the GOP incumbent while nine different Democrats fought for their party's primary and caucus delegates, with John Kerry proving ultimately successful. In 2000, the democrats held the White House and Al Gore ran against Bill Bradley (defeating him relatively early in process) while the GOP split among eight candidates into an eventual showdown between John McCain and George W. Bush.

16.   **(E)**

The Populists were strong third-party movement of the late nineteenth century. Their influence and power was greatest in the Plains states, where the farming issues they championed (inflation, railroad rates) held the most sway. In effect, the Democratic Party absorbed the Populists in 1896 with Bryan's famous "Cross of Gold" speech favoring the minting of silver. The Federalists (C), Whigs (B), and Republicans (D), respectively, have been the major parties on the right, while the Democrats (A) followed the Jeffersonian-Republicans as the major party on the left.

17.   **(D)**

Primaries pit a variety of candidates against one another and thus can divide a party's loyalties. The national convention is a time for reunification of all party factions behind the chosen candidate.

18.   **(E)**

A useful public opinion poll does not require face-to-face interviewing. In fact, that would be rather rare today. Scientific polling (+/– 3% degree of error) requires an accurate polling sample (A), which itself would necessitate careful planning (D), questions that are not leading (B), and careful analysis of results (C) to be useful to a given candidate.

19.   **(D)**

Burning the American flag has been constitutionally protected in such Supreme Court cases as *Texas vs. Johnson*, 1989.

20.   **(E)**

The federal government was not strong enough to impose any interstate controls upon the member states. Thus, interstate trade was badly stifled (C). The other choices all point to inherent weakness within the Confederation—simply, a central government so weak as to be ineffectual.

21.   **(A)**

Federal matching funds are equal to the major party candidates. Fund raising outside of this system does however favor the incumbent because of committee clout (C), franking (D), established PAC relationships (E) and generally higher name recognition.

22.   **(B)**

Any confederate system grants the greatest powers to the local governments and holds only very few powers for the federal government. Thus, issues like endangered species or air pollution would be left up to the individual state governments to solve, much as Shays' Rebellion was left to Massachusetts to handle in the 1780s.

23.   **(C)**

The "five freedoms" of the First Amendment involve religion, the press, assembly, petitioning the government, and expression or speech. Search and seizure by law enforcement is addressed in the Fourth Amendment.

24.   **(A)**

"Spin control" refers to a politician's attempt to—in effect—manipulate the media and use them to his or her advantage. (E) is probably the best of the remaining choices, but it ignores the fact that the politician does answer the question, perhaps only dealing with half-truths or certainly avoiding potential realities.

25.   **(A)**

Although law enforcement, defense attorneys, and prosecutors all see plea bargaining as a necessity, given clogged courts and prisons and the need for information to aid ongoing police investigations (answers B through E), the public sees plea bargaining as a negative, a sort of "easy way out" for accused felons.

26.   **(B)**

(B) is the correct answer. The votes in the Judiciary Committee do serve as a fair barometer as to how easy or difficult the ultimate confirmation will be. Both

Bork and Clarence Thomas illustrate that the Judiciary Committee need not support a nominee for him/her to gain a full Senate hearing (A). Committees are filled proportionally to party strength in the full Senate, thus neither party would ever hold every seat in a permanent committee (C). In a high-profile vote, such as Supreme Court nomination, it makes wise political sense for a senator to actually show up and vote, but it is not required (D); Robert Bork failed to gain Senate confirmation—thus he never served on the Supreme Court (E).

27.   **(C)**

Ford was not concerned about the "chemistry" or harmony of the Supreme Court. No President would worry about that. Instead, political considerations like getting a nominee past a Senate controlled by the opposite party (A) often lead to somewhat surprising choices. Stevens has been perceived to have become a justice firmly in the "more liberal" camp of the Supreme Court (B) even though his lower court rulings were not generally controversially liberal (E). Furthermore, Gerald Ford, in following Nixon's scandal-ridden presidency, was seen as a more moderate conciliator (D).

28.   **(B)**

Proving libel (written defamation) or slander (oral defamation) is extremely difficult under the First Amendment and the United States court system. The deck is stacked in favor of the person making the statement in terms of legal protection. Generally, to be awarded monetary damages in a libel or slander case, a defendant must prove that the uttered or written expression made was false and that the accused knew this and that the expression made cost the defendant a reasonable opportunity to earn a living in their chosen profession. Obviously, a slander/ libel case is extremely difficult to prove and, thus, to win.

29.   **(D)**

The courts ruled against "prior restraint" in the *Near* case. Expression may not be censored before the fact due to the potential danger it might cause. Instead, the expression must be allowed to occur and law suits (slander, libel, reckless endangerment, etc.) may only occur after the fact should the need arise.

30.   **(C)**

Eminent domain is referred to in the Fifth Amendment of the Bill of Rights and is the idea that private property can be seized with compensation by the government for greater public use, such as taking private land to widen a busy street or expand an airport. *Ex post facto* criminal laws are illegal (A). They involve punishing a person for an act that wasn't a crime when it was committed. Prior restraint (B) is covered in the previous explanation to question 29. Extradition involves the return of an accused felon from one state to another (D), while the Twenty-seventh Amendment prohibits Congress from voting themselves an immediate pay raise.

31.   **(E)**

The graphs basically show an increasing number of convicted felons, including those released, and the loss of suffrage that accompanies conviction in certain states, especially in the South. The increase in the number of incarcerated would increase the amount of felons who are disenfranchised (A), would create a need for more parole officers (B), public defenders (D) and for more prison and jail space (C). The graphs indicate no gender differences among the incarcerated (E).

32.   **(D)**

Cabinet members are torn between competing agendas; they advise and serve the President but also administer a large bureaucratic department of various programs and personnel. Presidents have great latitude in choosing cabinet members (A), but must also pick someone that the Senate will confirm. This has historically not been a problem. Cabinet members have support of interest groups and of the U.S. Senate, which confirms them (B). Cabinet members sometimes come from within Congress, but must resign their seat if they are to serve in the cabinet (C). The cabinet rarely meets collectively, and some members are more important than others to a given President, but individual contact would be much more likely than a collective meeting of all cabinet members (E).

33.   **(E)**

Although incumbency is a great advantage to members of both houses of Congress, the return rate in the House of Representatives is generally above 90 percent, while it runs 60–70 percent in the Senate. While (C) may have appeared to be a tempting choice, it is true because members of the House face election every two years, while Senators face election only every six years.

34.   **(B)**

The so-called faith-based initiatives allowed federal government funds to be used by church organizations in various social and volunteer service programs. The invasions of Iraq and Afghanistan (A) and the Patriot Act (C) were components of the "war on terrorism." The No Child Left Behind Act (D) deals with public schools and special education (D), and while the opposition of stem-cell research (E) by George W. Bush does have religious overtones, (B) is a stronger, more direct answer.

35.   **(C)**

Raising the prime interest rate would be a way to stem spending (via loans) and thus would curb inflation. (B) would lead to the opposite and would increase inflation. (A) is irrelevant and Congress, not the Federal Reserve, would control the levels of tariffs (D) and (E).

36.   **(A)**

Executive agreements are simply between heads of government and hold the same force of law as treaty (B) and (C). They hold one large advantage for a U.S. President: the Senate does not need to ratify them. Executive agreements do not require previous Senate approval (E). The *Miller* case dealt with obscenity and is irrelevant to this issue (D).

37.   **(C)**

Suburban residence is much more commonly a GOP voting trait. The "gender gap," resulting from females being significantly more likely than males to be liberal, prevents (E) from being the correct answer.

38.   **(B)**

Governor has been the most common launch pad to the presidency since 1970. Jimmy Carter, Ronald Reagan, Bill Clinton, and George W. Bush all ascended to the presidency having been governors prior to their successful White House bids. Nixon (1972) and George H.W. Bush (1988) had been Vice Presidents prior to their election as President.

39.   **(D)**

The Kyoto Accords of 1997 placed limits on global warming. President Clinton had signed the U.S. on to the protocol agreement along with nearly 100 other countries. President Bush pulled the U.S. out of the agreement in 2002.

40.   **(B)**

Garfield was assassinated in 1881 shortly after assuming office. Generally, presidents with very short terms are not subjected to a ranking because too little evidence of their successes or failures exists. Buchanan's inaction in the years prior to the Civil War has seen history treat him unkindly (A), although at the time he was a popular President, which shows how historical perceptions can and do change. Carter was plagued by a very poor economy and the Iran hostage crisis (C) although he has become a highly respected former President, winning the Nobel Peace Prize. Both Grant and Harding (D) and (E) were personally honest but presided over corrupt administrations that they could not control.

41.   **(A)**

The Twenty-second Amendment limits a President to two elected terms. Ten years total could be served if a President finishes a predecessor's term, serving two years or less time. (B) describes the Twenty-fifth Amendment; (C) was repealed by the Twentieth Amendment (D); and the electoral college itself was always formally part of the Constitution (E), although some of its aspects have been informally amended.

42.   **(D)**

Human nature leads to the overrating of one's own level of knowledge and expertise in any given field. Political pollsters find this to be true in their efforts to gauge accurate public opinion. This also explains why (E) is not the correct answer. The other choices reflect common polling realities or obstacles.

43.   **(B)**

The coattail effect is the carry-over from a popular candidate to lower party members appearing further down the ticket. Straight-ticket voting is merely pulling a lever for the Republican or Democratic Party to vote strictly for that party's candidates (A). Logrolling is a trade-off of votes between members of Congress on a bill that is essential to one member but not to the other (C). A mandate is a go-ahead sent to a candidate to enact their program (D) and it results from a landslide victory (E), which is generally considered to be a popular vote of 60 percent or greater.

44.   **(E)**

The revision of bills, called a mark-up session, generally occurs in subcommittee or less likely, in full committee. Committees serve as a screen for bills, and most generally kill them at a rate of 90 percent.

45.   **(E)**

Article II of the Constitution requires a President to annually deliver a State of the Union address to Congress. None of the other choices presented appear in the Constitution or its amendments, but rather have been informally adopted.

46.   **(B)**

The electoral college is based on the number of total representatives a state has in Congress. Since House seats are based upon population, it would make sense for candidates to concentrate in populous, competitive states. It makes no sense to spend a lot of time in a populous state if it's already won or lost, however. The "winner-take-all" aspect discourages votes from going to third parties, which are seen largely as "wasted votes" (A). The votes of citizens from the least populous states are proportionally exaggerated in importance via the electoral college (C). A candidate is required to win 270 electoral college votes, which is a majority of the total available without regard to how many states that candidate wins (D). Currently, this could be done by winning as few as 11 states if they were the most populous 11 states in the country. The electoral college tends to exaggerate the margin of victory as compared to the popular vote because of the "winner-take-all" aspect (E).

47.   **(A)**

A concurring opinion agrees with the majority decision yet cites a different constitutional precedent for doing so. A majority opinion (C) is written by a justice representing the main body of thought used by the justices in ruling on a case. A dissenting opinion (B) is written by a justice who opposes the majority's ruling in a case. Neither choice (D) nor (E) represents a realistic Supreme Court opinion.

48.   **(C)**

Whether at the local level in a mayoral race, in a single Congressional district, or for the presidency, the U.S. system of "winner-take-all," or single member district plurality (SMDP), helps to promote a "wasted vote" syndrome in regard to third party candidates. Many people contend that since only a Democrat or Republican has a realistic chance of winning a race, voting for a third party is simply throwing a vote away. The Constitution does not mention political parties (A). Third parties are generally farther to the right or left of the major parties, while most Americans would described themselves as moderate over more extreme political adjectives (B). Increasingly, voters think in independent terms (D) and thus, straight-ticket voting is on the decline (E).

49.   **(D)**

Each of the other choices illustrates that a newly enfranchised group does not necessarily vote in large numbers, and thus supports the quote that voting is a learned habit. Marital status is not relevant to this question.

50.   **(D)**

The Eighth Amendment of the Bill of Rights deals with defining proper legal punishment, including the fair allowance of bail for the accused.

51.   **(A)**

The cartoon implies the need for the Department of Homeland Security to coordinate and share intelligence, which may have shed light upon and prevented the 9/11 attacks. The DHS was created as the fifteenth, and newest, cabinet department in light of the 9/11 attacks.

52.   **(E)**

A filibuster is stalling tactic used by a minority group of Senators to thwart the presumed path of a bill. Senators seize the floor via marathon talking—often about unrelated events—to keep a bill from being voted on in a third reading. While this is occurring, supporters of the filibuster who are not holding the Senate floor attempt to persuade their colleagues to support their measure. At the very least, Senators involved in a filibuster can tell their constituents, "I went to extreme measures and fought the good fight—they just wouldn't listen to reason."

A filibuster may not be used in the House of Representatives, where debate must be germane, or on-subject (A) and (D). The Senate prides itself on much freer rules of debate and thus, is loathe to censor even a filibuster. Although a cloture motion can bring a bill to a vote, ending a filibuster, it is rarely invoked (A) and (B). Cloture requires the vote of 60 Senators. Filibusters are rarely seen in the Senate today.

53.   **(B)**

Educational level most correlates to likelihood to vote; the more education one has, the more likely one is to exercise suffrage. This factor overrides gender, race, income, and area of residence in correlation to likeliness to vote.

54.   **(C)**

Entertainers are typically more associated with liberal causes and the Democratic Party rather than conservatism and the Republican Party, although California Governor Arnold Schwarzenegger is an obvious exception to this rule. Former actor Charlton Heston is a long-time spokesman and leader of the National Rifle Association, a conservative lobby for gun ownership rights.

55.   **(A)**

Testing to determine merit for a government's position is the key component of the civil service system. Patronage is synonymous with the spoils system

(B) and is used to fill positions within both local and federal bureaucracies (C). The Pendleton Act of 1883 limited the use of patronage in the wake of the assassination of President Garfield over the spoils issue (D). Positions gained as a result of political support would obviously be in jeopardy should the opposing party win a subsequent election (E).

56.   **(E)**

The cartoon illustrates the United States government concern with Bill Gates and Microsoft because of anti-trust (monopoly) concerns over Microsoft's business practices. Insider trading was the charge that dogged Martha Stewart over her selling of ImClone stock (A). The faulty bookkeeping and fraudulent earnings reports refer to Enron, WorldCom, and the Arthur Andersen accounting firm (B). Microsoft was never alleged to share intelligence with potential enemy states or organizations (C). Allegations of overcharging the U.S. government over military contracts involved Halliburton, the company whose former CEO was Vice President Richard Cheney (D).

57.   **(D)**

The "wall" of separation between church and state indeed isn't always very high, and sometimes nearly vanishes. Some examples: "In God We Trust" inscribed on U.S. currency; the President placing his hand on the Bible when taking the oath of office; witnesses swearing "So help me God" before testifying, and so on. However, the "wall of separation" is *not* an informal amendment; see the first part of the First Amendment for the "establishment clause" (A and B). The separation was obviously intentional if it was included in the Bill of Rights (C) and (E).

58.   **(C)**

When speaking of "balancing a ticket" in the context of a presidential election, what is generally meant is a balance between the geographical region of the candidates and their ideology. Age (E) is less of a factor. The candidates on a ticket generally come from the same educational background and social class (D). Race (A) has not been a factor in balancing the presidential ticket thus far and gender (B) has been a consideration in only one presidential election.

59.   **(B)**

Catholic Church officials in the United States had the most trouble supporting 2004 Democratic presidential candidate John Kerry—a practicing Roman Catholic—over his support of a woman's right to choose an abortion. On the other issues, including opposition to the death penalty (A), Kerry lines up with mainstream Catholic positions. Some church officials in the U.S. went so far as to suggest refusing Kerry communion for his stance on abortion.

60.   **(C)**

Remember the two issues here—a candidate in a close race and desiring "soft money"—would need to follow the party line in voting and obviously, would need constituent support to gain re-election. Thus, these two issues together would trump any other combination that involved PAC/lobbyist support and the candidate's own views.

SECTION II

Question 1–Sample Essay that Would Achieve a Top Score

Under the United States Constitution, governmental power is shared by the national government and state governments. Local governments—including county, city, school districts, transportation districts, and others—provide a third layer of government. This system of shared power is called the federal system, or federalism. Throughout American history, there has been continual struggle over how this power is to be shared.

The Constitution specifies that the national government has certain specific or *enumerated* powers (Article 1). The Supreme Court has also concluded that the national government has *implied* powers (*McCulloch v. Maryland*, 1819) and *inherent* powers (*U.S. v. Curtiss-Wright Export Corporation*, 1936). Finally, the national government has *concurrent* powers, such as taxation, that it shares with the states and local governments. Thus, the power of the national government is extensive and changing.

Today debate centers on what is popularly called "big government." Franklin Roosevelt established Social Security (1930s) and Lyndon Johnson obtained civil rights legislation and Medicaid (1960s) directed at social problems. National government power has also grown through its expanding regulatory powers such as the Clean Air Act (1970) and the Clean Water Act (1983), which sought to achieve national environmental standards.

Beginning with Richard Nixon (1969–1974), presidents have attempted to reduce the power of national government and turn more responsibility over to the states. Money has been returned to the states in the form of grants, which include: (1) block grants for "broad functional" areas such as health care and community development, (2) categorical grants for specific purposes, Medicaid and Food Stamps being two examples, and (3) general purpose grants, which largely can be used by the recipients as they see fit. Revenue sharing, used between 1972 and 1986, has been the major example of general purpose grants.

The national debt, limits on the freedom of states, local governments, and individual citizens, and social problems such as poverty and crime have prompted considerable criticism of big government. As a result, there have been repeated efforts to reduce the regulatory burden of the federal government. In 1995, the Republican dominated Congress frequently clashed with the Clinton administration over such issues as cost-benefit analysis of regulations and reduction of environmental legislation, but they did agree on speed-limit repeal and telecommunications reform (1996). The leading example of the effort to return power to the states is the welfare reform bill (1996), which replaced the Aid to Families with Dependent Children program with block grants to the states that could then develop and operate their own welfare programs with little interference from Washington.

It is unlikely that the limits of national government power will ever be strictly defined. As long as state and local governments have problems for which their resources are inadequate, they will look to the national government for help. But that help will always bring with it intrusiveness and standardization that will never be entirely acceptable to other entities that desire a degree of independence.

Question 2–Sample Essay that Would Achieve a Top Score

Affirmative action—programs to compensate for past discrimination by favoring minorities—arose out of the demand, first from African Americans in the 1950s and 1960s, for equal treatment by the legal system and social institutions. Legalized segregation in the south and discrimination against African Americans elsewhere in the United States were increasingly challenged after the 1954 *Brown v. Board of Education* decision that declared school segregation unconstitutional on the basis of the Fourteenth Amendment guarantee of equal protection of the laws. The Montgomery Bus Boycott (1955–56), Sit-ins and Freedom Rides (beginning 1961), and the March on Washington (1963), led to the Civil Rights Act (1964) and Voting Rights Act (1965), which dismantled legalized segregation.

Within this context, President John F. Kennedy issued an order in 1961 that prohibited contractors hired by the federal government from

discriminating against minority groups. He further instructed these contractors to hire and promote minorities. After passage of the 1964 Civil Rights
Act, many employers and universities developed affirmative action programs
that gave preference to minorities, later extended to women, in hiring or admissions. It was hoped that such an approach would make up for past discrimination and move society more quickly toward equality of both opportunity and results.

Almost immediately critics charged that such affirmative action pro-
grams constituted "reverse discrimination" that was illegal under both the
Fourteenth Amendment to the Constitution and the 1964 Civil Rights Act.
Alan Paul Bakke, who had applied to the medical school of the University of
California at Davis, was denied admission even though minority students with
lower qualifications were admitted. He sued the University on the grounds
that he had not been accepted because of his race. In 1978 the Supreme
Court ordered, citing the Fourteenth Amendment, that the University admit
Bakke but at the same time stated that special preference could be given to
minorities as long as no quotas were established.

Over the next several years the Court generally upheld affirmative action
programs. By 1987 it stated that even when there is no evidence of past
discrimination, an employer may promote women and minorities over white
males. Shortly thereafter, however, it began moving in a more conservative
direction and through a series of decisions made discrimination suits against
employers increasingly difficult. A 1991 civil rights bill essentially reversed
these rulings, as civil rights advocates turned to the legislature in the face of
an unsympathetic Court.

The debate over "reverse discrimination" has not been resolved, although
the arguments remain much the same. In 1995, the University of California decided to ban racial and sexual preferences beginning with admissions for the
1997–98 academic year (later delayed to 1998–99). About the same time,
a federal court struck down a race-based admissions policy at the University
of Texas School of Law. Similar reversals of affirmative action programs took
place at other institutions.

Although opposition to affirmative action appears to be increasing, the
Fourteenth Amendment to the Constitution and federal civil rights laws

ensure that the issue will continue to be a live one. How to balance the need to help historically oppressed minority groups with the need to avoid "reverse discrimination" will be an ongoing struggle.

Question 3–Sample Essay that Would Achieve a Top Score

While the President has control over a significant portion of the federal budget, the growth in federal spending cannot be attributed solely to the President. In fact, most of the growth in federal spending is a result of either acts of Congress, or other items over which the President has little or no control. In fact, over the past 30 years or so, while both kinds of spending have grown considerably, the portion of the budget over which the President has relatively less control has grown twice as fast. In order for this growth to be curtailed (if one assumes that federal spending is too high), some change in how budgets and spending are approved would most likely have to occur.

It is too simplistic to say that Congress should just limit spending. If the answer were as easy as that, it seems likely that the federal budget would not have grown so much in the first place. Over the years, various Presidents have suggested means by which they could gain more control over the budget, and supposedly cut wasteful spending and programs.

One popular suggestion has been a "line item veto," a method by which the President could veto, or reject, parts of a bill—in this case, the federal budget—rather than being forced to choose to either accept or reject the bill in full. This would give the President the ability to cut programs that the President does not think would benefit the nation as a whole. Some argue, however, that this change would violate the Constitution and the doctrine of separation of powers.

Congressional opponents of the line-item veto brought their case to the U.S. Supreme Court in the belief that the shift in power brought about by the veto authority would change "the legal and practical effect" of their votes. Thus, the lawmaking procedure set forth in the Constitution would, in effect, have the rug pulled out from under it. But the high court, in a decision read from the bench by Chief Justice Rehnquist, said members of Congress "are not the right people to bring this suit" because they lack legal standing to do so. Ironically, the court noted that the requirement for legal standing stemmed from the general principle of separation of powers among the three branches of government.

But back on the legislative front, there is growing reason to be cautiously sanguine about the prospects for bringing federal spending under control. In July 1997, with both Republicans and Democrats practically falling over each other to claim victory and credit, the House overwhelmingly approved landmark legislation to balance the federal budget by 2002. The Senate was expected to follow suit. This kind of bipartisan effort, the result of tortuous negotiations, is encouraging in and of itself. But at the same time, one needs to take note of the uncontrollable urge a lawmaker must feel to attach himself or herself to such legislation. To vote against a package that combines long-promised tax cuts with a balanced budget is politically suicidal. The bill's most worrisome aspect is its so-called backloading, whereby tax breaks are planned to bring about the greatest revenue losses after 2002. Add to that the fact that legislators avoided dealing with the hydraheaded issue of medical or pension cost containment, and you have a potentially explosive witch's brew of budget busters.

Ultimately, if politicians or citizens want to decrease public spending, there will have to be a change in the way federal budgets are developed, either through a formal change in law, or in the informal way Congress and the President draw up a budget agreement. But the issue of whose ox is being gored can never be expected to be far from the surface.

Question 4–Sample Essay that Would Achieve a Top Score

In evaluating negative advertisements, one has to take into account what exactly about the candidate is being criticized. Some negative advertisements can inform voters about important positions and activities of the candidate. However, some negative ads are less than helpful, especially those which attack the candidate's character, rather than his or her politics. The information on issues is important for voters, because candidates themselves, in an effort to appeal to all voters, will say that they are against crime, but may be reluctant to say that their programs to eliminate crime include specific proposals—like gun control—that are unpopular with many voters. In this case, a negative advertisement stating the candidate's specific position on an issue can be helpful to voters. Nevertheless, there are problems with relying on negative ads for information.

Often, if not usually, the information in such an ad is presented in a biased and possibly misleading way. That is, an opponent will cast a candidate's policy stand in as unappealing a way as possible, in order to alienate as many voters as possible. This might border on presenting inaccurate information. In fact, it is often difficult for voters to check the accuracy of any statement provided in a campaign advertisement.

At the very least, negative ads often lack the kind of context that would enable voters to make an informed choice. Such ads can be extraordinarily powerful in the way they play upon emotions, as witness President Johnson's anti-Goldwater ad featuring a little girl picking daisies in the foreground as an explosion occurs and an atomic mushroom cloud appears behind her. This ad was so controversial—its implication being that Barry Goldwater was capable of plunging the United States into nuclear war—that it ran only once. And by then, of course, it had already achieved its purpose: planting doubt.

Today's negative ads are more "hot-button" oriented, appealing to what voters tell pollsters would most upset them to learn about a candidate. If the advertising messages come across as *ad hominem* attacks, negative advertisements can damage the credibility of both candidates, increasing the level of voter dissatisfaction with all politicians. This can result both from the content of the ads and from the rising frequency of such advertising in recent years: the sheer amount of it risks turning the public off to the whole political scene, causing a spiraling decrease in voter turnout. Such ads from opposing camps can end up, in effect, canceling each other out, and voters may stay away from the polls, frustrated that they can't find a reason to vote for someone.

While the author of the passage claims that there is little empirical evidence of actual damage, it does not seem that these negative effects would be easy to measure. Moreover, by the time one could gauge the harm that these ads do, it might, in essence, be too late. It seems likely that if both candidates are attacked, voters will think a little less of both of them in the end, even if they end up supporting one or the other. Negative advertisements may be a good source of information, but that information may come at a price.

PRACTICE TEST 3
AP United States
Government & Politics

AP UNITED STATES GOVERNMENT & POLITICS

PRACTICE TEST 3

SECTION I

TIME: 45 Minutes
60 Multiple-Choice Questions
50% of Total Grade

(Answer sheets appear in the back of this book.)

DIRECTIONS: Read the following questions and incomplete sentences. Each is followed by five answer choices. Choose the one answer choice that either answers the question or completes the sentence. Make sure to use the ovals numbered 1 through 60 when marking your answer sheet.

1. When a member of the House of Representatives helps a citizen from his or her district receive some federal aid to which that citizen is entitled, the member's action is referred to as

    (A) casework   (D) logrolling

    (B) pork barrel legislation   (E) filibustering

    (C) lobbying

2. One advantage incumbent members of Congress have over challengers in election campaigns is the use of

    (A) unlimited campaign funds

    (B) national party employees as campaign workers

    (C) the franking privilege

(D) unlimited contributions from "fat cat" supporters

(E) government-financed air time for commercials

3. Major differences between procedures in the House of Representatives and the Senate would include:

  I. In the House, time for debate is limited, while in the Senate it is usually unlimited.

  II. In the House, the rules committee is very powerful, while in the Senate it is relatively weak.

  III. In the House, debate must be germane, while in the Senate it need not be.

  (A) I only

  (B) II only

  (C) III only

  (D) I and II only

  (E) I, II, and III

4. Which of the following statements about the cabinet is FALSE?

  (A) The Department of Homeland Security was created in the wake of the 9/11/01 tragedy and subsequent anthrax scare.

  (B) It includes the heads of the executive departments, but not the heads of the independent agencies.

  (C) It was created by an informal amendment to the Constitution.

  (D) Important members of the U.S. Senate often serve concurrently in the cabinet.

  (E) Some presidents have relied heavily on advisors from outside the cabinet.

5. A "third party," such as the Libertarian Party, would hold the most chance for success in which of the following elections?

  (A) The governor's race in a populous state

  (B) The governor's race in a less populous state

  (C) A mayoral election

  (D) A U.S. Senate seat vacated by a long-time incumbent

  (E) A city-council election

6. The states of Maine and Nebraska have been utilizing an alternate electoral approach since 2000. In these two states, how is the electoral college applied?

    (A) A strict winner-take-all formula is used, applying the popular vote to the state's total electoral votes.

    (B) The state legislatures of Nebraska and Maine ultimately decide how to divide the state's electoral votes.

    (C) The winner-take-all formula has been jettisoned in favor of a formula that reflects the popular vote within each state's congressional districts.

    (D) The second-place finisher in each state is guaranteed the two "at large" electoral college votes, represented by the state's U.S. Senate seats.

    (E) Neither state has been participating in the electoral college at all; this began with the 2000 presidential election.

7. According to the information in the tables on the next page, which of the following statements is true?

    (A) A black female in a service occupation is more likely to vote Democratic than a white male skilled worker.

    (B) A white female earning under $10,000 is more likely to vote Republican than a white male earning over $50,000.

    (C) A white male with no high school diploma is less likely to vote Democratic than a white male with some college education.

    (D) A black male earning $10,000–$19,999 is more likely to vote Republican than a white male earning $20,000–$29,999.

    (E) A white female with a high school diploma is more likely to vote Democratic than a black female with no high school diploma.

PARTY IDENTIFICATION BY SEX

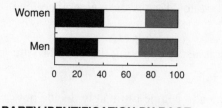

PARTY IDENTIFICATION BY OCCUPATION

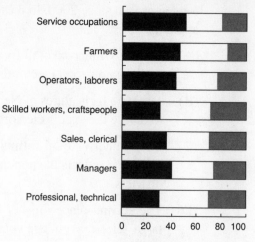

PARTY IDENTIFICATION BY RACE

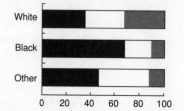

PARTY IDENTIFICATION BY EDUCATION

PARTY IDENTIFICATION BY INCOME

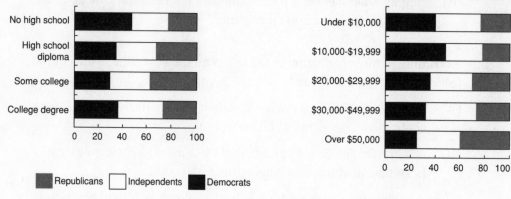

Republicans | Independents | Democrats

From Janda, Berry, Goldman, *The Challenge of Democracy,* p. 286. Reprinted with permission.

8. Which of the following were LEAST likely to have voted for Franklin Roosevelt in 1940?

    (A) Southerners

    (B) White northern business leaders

    (C) Blue-collar workers

    (D) Racial minorities

    (E) Union members

9. For much of the Clinton and George W. Bush presidencies, the Supreme Court faced a 5 to 4 conservative/liberal split. Which of the following justices does NOT belong in the "conservative camp of five"?

    (A) Antonin Scalia

    (B) Chief Justice William Rehnquist

    (C) Sandra Day O'Connor

    (D) David Souter

    (E) Clarence Thomas

Question 10 refers to the following excerpt from a Supreme Court decision.

It is emphatically the province and duty of the courts to say what the law is... If two laws conflict with each other, the courts must decide on the operation of each... If, then, the courts are to regard the Constitution, and the Constitution is superior to any ordinary act of the legislature, the Constitution and not such ordinary act, must govern the case to which they both apply.

10. This decision of the Supreme Court upheld the principle that

    (A) a law contrary to the Constitution cannot be enforced by the courts

    (B) Congress has the power to pass laws to carry out its constitutional duties

    (C) interpretation of laws is a legislative function

    (D) a law passed by Congress overrides a constitutional provision with which it conflicts

    (E) courts are not equipped to decide questions of constitutional law

11. Which of the following has chief responsibility for assembling and analyzing the figures in the presidential budget submitted to Congress each year?

    (A) Department of Commerce

    (B) Department of Treasury

    (C) Federal Reserve Board

(D) Office of Management and Budget

(E) Cabinet

12. The term "executive privilege" refers to

(A) the right of the President to veto legislation proposed by Congress

(B) the limited right of the President to withhold certain information from Congress and the public

(C) the right of the President to appoint and receive ambassadors

(D) the limited right of the President to pardon persons convicted of federal crimes

(E) the limited immunity of the President from prosecution for certain misdemeanors

13. All of the following are formal or informal sources of presidential power EXCEPT

(A) the fact that the President is elected indirectly by the public, not by Congress

(B) Supreme Court decisions that have expanded the President's emergency powers

(C) high public approval ratings

(D) the veto power

(E) the ability to introduce legislation in either house of Congress

14. Which of the following items are current examples of informal amendments to the Constitution?

   I.   The two-term presidential limit

   II. The ban on the poll-tax in the South

   III. The two-term vice presidential limit

   IV. U.S. military action without a congressional declaration of war

(A) I, II, and III only   (D) III and IV only

(B) I, III, and IV only   (E) II and III only

(C) I and II only

15. Which of the following is a FALSE statement about the Democratic Party's national convention?

    (A)   It selects the state party chairmen.

    (B)   It determines the national party platform.

    (C)   It nominates the party's candidate for President.

    (D)   It has "super delegates" not chosen by state primaries and caucuses.

    (E)   It sets the time and place for the next national convention.

16. All of the following statements represent positions the Supreme Court has taken on the First Amendment right to freedom of religion EXCEPT:

    (A)   Public school officials may write a nondenominational prayer for school children to recite at the beginning of each school day

    (B)   Public school teachers may not conduct devotional readings of the Bible in class

    (C)   A copy of the Ten Commandments may not be posted on the walls of public school classrooms

    (D)   Creation Science may not be taught in public schools

    (E)   States may not outlaw the teaching of evolution in the public schools

17. The Constitution, as ratified in 1788, provided for popular vote for

    (A)   election of the President

    (B)   election of senators

    (C)   ratification of treaties

    (D)   ratification of constitutional amendments

    (E)   members of the House of Representatives

18. Which of the following best defines the term "judicial restraint"?

    (A)   A decision by judges to limit the number of cases they decide per year

    (B)   Refusal by judges to lobby Congress for funds

    (C)   A practice by which judges remove themselves from cases in which they have a personal interest

(D)   The tendency of judges to interpret the Constitution in light of the original intent of its framers

(E)   Willingness of judges to decline participation in partisan political campaigns

19.   Which of the following is true of independent regulatory commissions?

(A)   They exercise quasi-legislative, quasi-judicial, and executive functions.

(B)   They each form part of one of the 14 cabinet-level executive departments.

(C)   They regulate certain parts of the federal bureaucracy.

(D)   They are directly responsible to the President.

(E)   They were created by the executive branch to help execute federal law.

20.   The subject of the cartoon below is most likely

(A)   the influence of environmental issues on Congressional behavior

(B)   a gerrymandered Congressional district

(C)   the role of money in influencing the outcome of an election

(D)   the beastly effect of politics on the character of a congressman

(E)   "dinosaur bills," which congressmen sponsor for the folks back home

Questions 21 and 22 are based on the following excerpt from a major Supreme Court decision.

The object of the [14th] amendment was undoubtedly to enforce the absolute equality of the [white and black] races before the law, but in the nature of things, it could not have been intended to abolish distinctions based upon color, or to enforce social, as distinguished from, political, equality, or a commingling of the two races upon terms unsatisfactory to either. Laws permitting, even requiring, their separation, in places where they are liable to be brought into contact, do not necessarily imply the inferiority of either race to the other, and have been generally, if not universally recognized as within the competency of the state legislatures in the exercise of their police power. The most common instance of this is connected with the establishment of separate schools for white and colored children, which have been held to be a valid exercise of the legislative power even by courts of states where the political rights of the colored race have been longest and most earnestly enforced.

21.   The decision quoted, which upheld the doctrine of "separate but equal," was from the case

(A)   *Dred Scott vs. Sanford,* 1857

(B)   *West Virginia Board of Education vs. Barnette,* 1943

(C)   *Plessy vs. Ferguson,* 1896

(D)   *Columbus Board of Education vs. Penick,* 1979

(E)   *Mapp vs. Ohio,* 1961

22.   The case that overturned the aforementioned decision was

(A)   *Brown vs. Board of Education,* 1954

(B)   *Swann vs. Charlotte-Mecklenburg County Board of Education,* 1971

(C)   *Engel vs. Vitale,* 1962

(D)   *Luther vs. Borden,* 1849

(E)   *Cantwell vs. Connecticut,* 1940

23. The concept of "dual federalism" is best characterized by which of the following statements?

    (A) The states may exercise only those powers delegated to them by Congress.

    (B) The states have reserved powers which Congress may regulate as it sees fit.

    (C) The powers of the states and the federal government overlap to such a degree that it is impossible to distinguish the two in practice.

    (D) The state and federal governments are each sovereign and independent within their respective spheres of influence.

    (E) The states created the federal government and have the right to nullify laws which, in their opinion, violate the federal Constitution.

24. Which of the following issues was left by the Constitutional Convention for the states to decide?

    (A) The method of electing the President

    (B) Qualifications of the electorate for voting in federal elections

    (C) The method of ratifying amendments to the Constitution

    (D) Qualifications for members of the House and Senate

    (E) Whether or not to levy protective tariffs on imported goods

25. Given the current method of electing the President, which of the following is NOT possible?

    (A) The presidential candidate with the most electoral votes fails to be elected President.

    (B) A presidential candidate with a majority of the popular votes fails to be elected President.

    (C) A presidential candidate with less than a majority of the popular vote is elected President

    (D) A presidential candidate with less than a majority of the electoral votes is elected President.

    (E) A presidential candidate with a majority of the electoral vote fails to be elected President.

26. A discharge petition is used in the House of Representatives to

    (A) kill a bill that is under consideration on the House floor

(B) force the rules committee to discharge a bill back to a standing committee that has reported the bill out with unacceptable amendments

(C) force a discharge rule on a bill under consideration on the House floor so that amendments may be made to the bill

(D) force a bill out of a committee which has held it for 30 days without reporting it out

(E) send to the Senate a bill that has been approved by the House

27. Which of the following Supreme Court decisions involved the Fourth Amendment prohibition against unlawful search and seizure?

(A) *Baker vs. Carr,* 1962

(B) *Roe vs. Wade,* 1973

(C) *Mapp vs. Ohio,* 1961

(D) *Korematsu vs. United States,* 1944

(E) *Gideon vs. Wainwright,* 1963

28. The Thirteenth, Fourteenth, and Fifteenth amendments to the Constitution were intended primarily to

(A) protect the rights of Blacks against infringement by southern state governments

(B) expand the suffrage to women, Blacks, and 18-year-olds

(C) protect freedom of speech, religion, and assembly

(D) increase the power of the federal government in order to prevent the outbreak of another civil war

(E) apply the Bill of Rights to the state governments

29. When the House rules committee issues a closed rule

(A) the House gallery is closed to the public during debate of a bill

(B) a particular bill may not be amended during floor debate

(C) vote on a bill is closed to those members who were not present during debate on the bill

(D) a particular bill may not be calendared without going first to the rules committee

(E)   a bill passed in the House is closed to amendment in the Senate

30.   One of the major problems with national government under the Articles of Confederation was that

(A)   the executive branch was too strong vis à vis the legislative branch

(B)   the government had no power to levy direct taxes

(C)   the national judiciary failed to exercise judicial review

(D)   the Articles of Confederation were amended too frequently

(E)   the bicameral legislature deadlocked frequently on controversial, but necessary, legislation

31.   Which of the following statements about the national media is/are TRUE?

I.   Magazines and newspapers need no license to publish in the United States.

II.   It is more difficult for a public figure or official to win a libel suit against the media in the United States than in any other country.

III.   The U.S. government can exercise restraint over the media to prevent the publication of sensitive government information.

(A)   I only   (D)   I and II only

(B)   II only   (E)   I and III only

(C)   III only

32.   Which of the following statements is true about political action committees (PACs)?

(A)   PACs have been an important part of American politics since the Great Depression.

(B)   PACs gain influence over certain candidates by heavily subsidizing their campaigns.

(C)   The number of PACs has grown dramatically between 1973 and the present.

(D)   Formation of PACs is restricted to business and labor groups.

(E)   The number of ideological PACs has increased much more slowly than the number of business or labor PACs.

33.   During the past three decades, all of the following changes have occurred in political behavior and public opinion in the United States EXCEPT

(A)   the declining importance of political ideology as a factor influencing presidential nominations to the Supreme Court

(B)   an increase in support for Republican presidential candidates in the South

(C)   an increase in the influence of the conservative wing of the Republican Party

(D)   a drop in voter turnout for congressional and presidential elections

(E)   an increase in the number of voters who declare themselves to be Independents

34.   The first party competition for public offices in the United States occurred between which parties?

(A)   Federalists and Whigs

(B)   Whigs and Jeffersonian Republicans

(C)   Federalists and Jeffersonian Republicans

(D)   Democrats and Whigs

(E)   Democrats and Republicans

35.   A successful candidate for President must receive

(A)   a majority of votes cast by the public

(B)   a majority of votes cast by the electoral college

(C)   a plurality of votes cast by the public

(D)   a plurality of votes cast by the electoral college

(E)   a majority vote of the public and of the electoral college

36. The most accurate way to measure public opinion is generally through

    (A) a stratified or quota sample

    (B) a study of letters to the editor

    (C) a random sample

    (D) a mailed survey

    (E) talking with your neighbor

	Health Care Expenditures as Percentage of GDP	Rank	Patient Access to Specialists	Health Status Indicator: Male Infant Death Rate	Rank
United States	10.7	1	Uncontrolled	12.8	6
Sweden	9.4	2	Uncontrolled	7.1	1
France	8.6	3	Uncontrolled	11.2	4
Netherlands	8.3	4	Referral only	9.2	2
West Germany	8.2	5	Uncontrolled	10.6	3
Britain	5.7	6	Referral only	12.2	5

Source: OECD, *Financing and Delivering Health Care* (Paris: OECD, 1987), pp. 36 and 55.

37. According to the table, which of the following statements is correct?

    (A) The quality of health care is consistently related to the level of expenditures.

    (B) Uncontrolled access to health care, rather than controlled access, is more likely to improve the health status index of a country.

    (C) The Health Status Index is based upon longevity of adult females.

    (D) The U.S. spends a lower percentage of its Gross Domestic Product (GDP) on health care than other societies but, because it is larger, it actually spends more money.

    (E) The U.S. has a relatively poor Health Status Index, but expends a greater percentage of GDP on health care than the Netherlands.

38. Under a federal system of government,

    (A) power is concentrated in the central government

(B) power rests primarily in subnational units which control the national budget

(C) the national government and subnational units would share power

(D) each state has a veto over national policy in areas such as defense policy

(E) states would typically have no power over local matters such as schools, roads, and police services

39. In addition to formal amendments, the U.S. Constitution has been changed by

  I. custom and tradition

  II. judicial interpretation

  III. statutory enactment by states

(A) I   (D) I and III

(B) I and II   (E) I, II, and III

(C) II and III

40. In terms of demographics, the greatest population gains, and thus gains in seats in the House of Representatives, have been made over the past three decades in the

(A) Sunbelt   (D) Plains states

(B) industrial Northeast (E) Pacific Northwest

(C) Midwest

41. All of the following are recognized functions of the major political parties EXCEPT

(A) recruiting candidates for public office

(B) aggregating interests into electoral alliances

(C) establishing channels of communication between public and government

(D) providing personnel to staff elections and run the government

(E) articulating interests

42. Which of the following persons would be most likely to vote?

    (A) A black factory worker living in the South

    (B) A white, middle-aged attorney from the West

    (C) A 19-year-old from the Midwest

    (D) A 30-year-old female secretary with three children from the Northeast

    (E) A high school dropout from the Northeast

Executions by State

From 1976 through June 1989 Total: 111

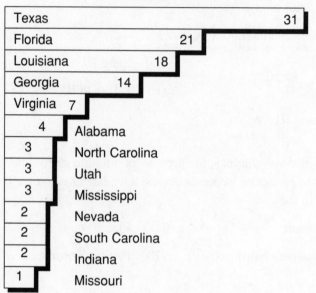

State	Executions
Texas	31
Florida	21
Louisiana	18
Georgia	14
Virginia	7
Alabama	4
North Carolina	3
Utah	3
Mississippi	3
Nevada	2
South Carolina	2
Indiana	2
Missouri	1

Source: NAACP Legal Defense and Educational Fund Inc., 1989.

43. On the basis of the graph above, one can conclude that

    (A) most people who are executed are poor

    (B) most executions have taken place in Republican-controlled states

    (C) most executions have taken place in the South

    (D) most murderers have been executed

    (E) Blacks are more likely to be executed than Whites

44. Which of these important Supreme Court decisions established the doctrine of judicial review?

    (A) *Barron vs. Baltimore*   (D) *Gideon vs. Wainwright*

    (B) *McCulloch vs. Maryland*   (E) *Roe vs. Wade*

    (C) *Marbury vs. Madison*

45. Under the U.S. Constitution, all states are required to

    (A) have a republican form of government

    (B) adopt the Equal Rights Amendment

    (C) have a strong Democratic Party

    (D) elect governors for two-year terms

    (E) maintain balanced budgets

46. The key Supreme Court case that established national supremacy by refusing to allow the states to tax the federal government was

    (A) *Marbury vs. Madison*

    (B) *Roe vs. Wade*

    (C) *Gibbons vs. Ogden*

    (D) *Brown vs. Board of Education of Topeka*

    (E) *McCulloch vs. Maryland*

47. The "pluralist" theory of American democracy contends that

    (A) everyone has about the same amount of political power

    (B) everyone should have about the same amount of power

    (C) a small elite rules

    (D) a number of elites compete for power

    (E) power should be divided between Congress, the President, and the courts

48. Presidential primaries are

    (A) required by the Constitution

    (B) used in all states

(C)   used to select members of the electoral college

(D)   an alternative to the use of caucuses to select delegates to national party conventions

(E)   used only in the Republican Party

49.   The so-called Bush Doctrine, relating to the foreign policy of George W. Bush in the post-9/11 era, offered a significant change in American foreign policy by proposing that the United States

(A)   leave the United Nations

(B)   utilize pre-emptive strikes against potential enemies

(C)   cooperate more fully on international matters with its NATO allies

(D)   re-institute a federal draft to promote military preparedness

(E)   reconsider its pro-Israel policies in relation to other Arab states

50.   Which of the following governmental agencies is not a cabinet-level department?

(A)   Homeland Security

(B)   Housing and Urban Development

(C)   U.S. Postal Service

(D)   Defense

(E)   Education

51.   If, in reaching a judicial decision, a court relies upon the reasoning in an earlier case, the court has relied upon

(A)   precedent   (D)   a statute

(B)   the Constitution   (E)   the Chief Justice

(C)   common sense

52.   Based on the seniority system as it is presently used in the House of Representatives, and assuming the Democrats are the majority party, which of the following persons on a Committee would serve as Chair?

(A)   Representative Brown, Democrat, age 43, in Congress for 12 years, member of Committee for 10 years

(B)   Representative Green, Republican, age 67, in Congress for 17 years, member of Committee for 14 years

(C)   Representative White, Democrat, age 51, in Congress for 8 years, member of Committee for 5 years

(D)   Representative Black, Democrat, age 81, in Congress for 21 years, member of Committee for 8 years

(E)   Representative Smith, Republican, age 45, in Congress for 15 years, member of Committee for 15 years

53.   The Rules Committee of the House of Representatives

(A)   determines committee assignments for members of the House

(B)   determines how bills will be handled in House debate

(C)   negotiates compromises with the Senate

(D)   has grown increasingly important in the twentieth century

(E)   selects the Speaker of the House

Questions 54 and 55 refer to the following passage:

"We come then to the question presented: Does segregation of children in public schools solely on the basis of race, even though the physical facilities and other 'tangible' factors may be equal, deprive the children of the minority group of equal educational opportunities? We believe that it does ... We conclude that in the field of public education, the doctrine of separate but equal has no place. Separate educational facilities are inherently unequal." [*Brown vs. Board of Education of Topeka,* 1954]

54.   The viewpoint which is closest to the meaning of equality in the passage above is the viewpoint that

(A)   life, liberty, and the pursuit of happiness is important

(B)   everyone should pay an equal amount in income taxes

(C)   different people should be treated differently

(D)   equality requires the elimination of signs of inferiority such as separation on the basis of race

(E)   as long as people get a good education it should not matter whether they go to an integrated or segregated school

55. The passage would most clearly support a subsequent decision to

    (A) prohibit homosexual marriages

    (B) permit single-sex educational institutions

    (C) ban restrictive covenants in property deeds that would restrict the sale of single-family homes on the basis of a purchaser's race

    (D) require public schools to mainstream handicapped students

    (E) require integration of other public facilities, such as restaurants and swimming pools

56. A "concurring opinion" by a judge means that

    (A) the judge supports the President

    (B) the judge strongly opposes the court's decision

    (C) the judge agrees with the majority reasoning, but rejects their conclusion

    (D) the judge agrees with the majority's conclusion but rejects their reasoning

    (E) the judge has refused to write an opinion on the case

57. During the past two decades, which group has shown the largest proportional gain of the total U.S. electorate?

    (A) Hispanics   (D) the elderly

    (B) Blacks   (E) Asian-Americans

    (C) women

58. Which of the following is generally regarded as a key feature of the "Reagan Revolution"?

    (A) Democrats lost control of the House of Representatives

    (B) Sharp increases in defense spending

    (C) Greater attention to education at the national level

    (D) Significant decreases in domestic spending

    (E) The appointment of more liberal federal judges

59. During "midterm" congressional elections, how likely is the President's party to increase the number of seats in Congress that it holds?

    (A) Always increases

    (B) Almost always increases

    (C) Usually increases

    (D) About as likely to increase as to decrease

    (E) Less likely to increase than to decrease

60. All of the following statements about modern congressional staffs are true EXCEPT

    (A) staff members have grown increasingly important

    (B) the number of staff members has increased dramatically since the 1950s

    (C) members of Congress are increasingly dependent on their staff

    (D) only a few members of Congress have full-time staff working in their home states and districts

    (E) staff members are appointed politically

STOP
This is the end of Section I.
If time still remains, you may check your work only in this section.
Do not begin Section II until instructed to do so.

SECTION II

TIME: 100 Minutes
4 Free-Response Questions
50% of Total Grade

DIRECTIONS: Write an essay based on each of the following four questions. Be sure to pace yourself by allotting about one-fourth of your time, or 25 minutes, for each question. Where appropriate, use substantive examples in your answers. Your essays should be numbered to correspond with the questions to which you are responding.

1. Presidents are often able to champion controversial positions successfully if they have previously established a credible opposition viewpoint in regard to the given issue.

   Examine this statement in regard to any three of the following in the success or failure of realizing the issue they supported:

   • Dwight Eisenhower: "military-industrial complex"

   • Lyndon Johnson: civil rights

   • Richard Nixon: the People's Republic of China

   • Bill Clinton: socialized health care

2. Informal amendments are a key component of U.S. constitutional law.

   a) Define an informal amendment.

   b) Why are informal amendments an enduring aspect of American constitutional law?

   c) Describe how informal amendments have been used to alter the meaning of any two different formal amendments.

3. A President in a second term no longer has to worry about re-election. Given this, what checks on power exist for a second-term President? Discuss any two checks, formal or informal, on presidential power that exist for a President in the second term. Illustrate with reference to any second-term President(s) since 1950 when answering.

4.   Refer to the data below:

Party Identification in the United States, 1952-2000[a]

YEAR	DEMOCRATS	INDEPENDENTS	REPUBLICANS
1952	48.6	23.3	28.1
1956	45.3	24.4	30.3
1960	46.4	23.4	30.2
1964	52.2	23.0	24.8
1968	46.0	29.5	24.5
1972	41.0	35.2	23.8
1976	40.2	36.8	23.0
1980	41.7	35.3	23.0
1984	37.7	34.8	27.6
1988	35.7	36.3	28.0
1992	35.8	38.7	25.5
1996	39.3	32.9	27.8
2000	34.8	41.0	24.2

[a]In percentage of people; the small percentage who identify with a minor party or who cannot answer the question are excluded.
Source: 1952-2000 National Election Studies conducted by the University of Michigan, Center for Political Studies.

a)   Explain the overall trends shown on the chart.

b)   Define what is meant by an "independent" voter.

c)   Explain one specific strategy that either or both major parties might adopt to reverse this trend.

END OF EXAMINATION

UNITED STATES GOVERNMENT & POLITICS

PRACTICE TEST 3

ANSWER KEY

1. (A)	16. (A)	31. (D)	46. (E)
2. (C)	17. (E)	32. (C)	47. (D)
3. (E)	18. (D)	33. (A)	48. (D)
4. (D)	19. (A)	34. (C)	49. (B)
5. (E)	20. (B)	35. (B)	50. (C)
6. (C)	21. (C)	36. (A)	51. (A)
7. (A)	22. (A)	37. (E)	52. (A)
8. (B)	23. (D)	38. (C)	53. (B)
9. (D)	24. (B)	39. (B)	54. (D)
10. (A)	25. (E)	40. (A)	55. (E)
11. (D)	26. (D)	41. (E)	56. (D)
12. (B)	27. (C)	42. (B)	57. (A)
13. (E)	28. (A)	43. (C)	58. (B)
14. (D)	29. (B)	44. (C)	59. (E)
15. (A)	30. (B)	45. (A)	60. (D)

DETAILED EXPLANATIONS
OF ANSWERS

TEST 3

SECTION I

1.   **(A)**

(A) is the best answer since the term "casework" is used by political scientists to describe the activities of congressmen on behalf of individual constituents. These activities might include helping an elderly person secure social security benefits, or helping a veteran obtain medical services. Most casework is actually done by congressional staff, and may take as much as a third of the staff's time. Congressmen supply this type of assistance for the good public relations it provides. Answer (B) fails because pork barrel legislation is rarely if ever intended to help individual citizens. Pork barrel legislation authorizes federal spending for special projects, such as airports, roads, or dams, in the home state or district of a congressman. It is meant to help the entire district or state. Also, there is no legal entitlement on the part of a citizen to a pork barrel project, such as there is with social security benefits. (C) is not the answer because lobbying is an activity directed toward congressmen, not one done by congressmen. A lobbyist attempts to get congressmen to support legislation that will benefit the group which the lobbyist represents. Log rolling, (D), is incorrect because it does not refer to congressional service for constituents. It refers instead to the congressional practice of trading votes on different bills. Congressman A will vote for congressman B's pork barrel project and in return B will vote for A's pork barrel project. Filibustering, (E), is incorrect. It is a technique used in the Senate to postpone a vote on a piece of legislation. The Senate has a tradition of unlimited debate and nongermane debate. This means that a senator may hold the floor for as long as (s)he likes and need not confine his/her remarks to the bill under consideration. Senators opposing a bill might get control of the floor and talk until the supporters agree to withdraw the bill from consideration.

2.   **(C)**

The franking privilege is the right of congressmen to send mail to constituents at public expense. Challengers do not enjoy this privilege. Observers have noticed that the amount of free congressional mail increases during election years, as members try to keep their names before their constituents. Answer (A) is incorrect since incumbent congressmen certainly do not have access to unlimited campaign funds. Congressmen may spend as much of their own money as they wish, and they are free to raise money from contributors. But no candidate has unlimited personal funds, nor can incumbents raise unlimited funds from contributions. Answer (B) is incorrect because incumbents and challengers may both have access to national party employees as campaign workers. Both political parties have campaign committees for the House and Senate. All of the committees supply campaign managers, communications directors, and fund raising experts to challengers and incumbents during election campaigns. (D) is incorrect because the Federal Election Campaign Act of 1974 placed a limit of $1,000 per election on individual contributions to political candidates. This put an end to so called "fat cat" contributors who used to contribute vast sums to candidates. (E) is incorrect because the federal government does not finance any aspect of congressional campaigns.

3.   **(E)**

The correct response is (E), since major differences between procedures in the House and Senate include all three of the features mentioned. Because the size of the House is fairly large, with 435 members, time for debate must be limited. If each member was allowed to speak as long as (s)he wanted on every bill, the House could not complete all of its business. Also, debate in the House must be germane. That is, when a member rises to speak, his/her comments must be related to the subject under consideration. This is another time-saving mechanism. The Senate has only 100 members, and is not as rushed for time as the House. The Senate has traditionally allowed members to speak as long as they wish, and does not force them to confine their remarks to the subject at hand. In the House, the rules committee is very powerful. No bill may get to the House floor without a rule from the rules committee. The rule gives the conditions for debate. The rule sets the time limit for debate and states whether and on what conditions the bill can be amended. The rules committee in the Senate has no such powers.

4.   **(D)**

(D) is the correct answer because it is not true. Due to a conflict of interest between the legislative and executive branches of government, no member of either the House of Representatives or the Senate may concurrently hold an elected legislative position while serving on the President's cabinet. George Washington introduced the original cabinet, then consisting of four positions

(C). Independent agencies, such as the Environmental Protection Agency (EPA), are not formally represented in the cabinet (B). Congress approved a Department of Homeland Security in 2003, following the September 11 attacks and their aftermath (A). Examples of presidents relying on informal advisors outside their cabinet for advice include FDR (with his "Brain Trust") and Nixon (with his "Palace Guard").

5.   **(E)**

(E) is the correct answer because the general rule of thumb on third parties in American politics is that the smaller the size of the potential electorate, the better chance the third party has of winning. A smaller scale election, such as for a city-council seat, negates factors that generally aid the major parties, such as funding to air commercials on television and radio, news media coverage, and name recognition.

6.   **(C)**

Both Maine and Nebraska have opted for an alternative to the winner-take-all formula for determining electoral college votes. In all other states, the plurality winner of the popular vote takes all of the state's electoral college votes. For instance, if a candidate won Indiana's popular vote by just a few votes, that candidate would receive all eleven of Indiana's electoral votes. (Remember, electoral college votes are determined by a state's total representation in Congress, its number of seats in the House of Representatives plus its two Senate seats.) Maine and Nebraska have opted to use a system whereby the plurality winner within a congressional district receives one electoral college vote for that district. The candidate who wins an overall popular vote plurality in these states wins the two remaining "at large" electoral college votes. It is interesting to note that the system described above would have distorted the electoral college vote further away from the popular vote if it had been applied nationally in the 2000 election. George W. Bush, who lost the popular vote nationally to Al Gore, would have commanded a greater electoral college victory than the 271 to 267 edge he achieved under the winner-take-all format.

7.   **(A)**

The table shows party identification by social groups. The term "party identification" refers to the psychological attachment of a voter to a political party. A voter with a Republican Party identification is, of course, likely to vote Republican in a given race, while a voter with a Democrat identification is likely to vote Democrat. (A) is the correct response. We can see from the chart that blacks are more likely to be Democrats, while whites are more likely to be Republicans.

Females are more likely than males to be Democrats. About 50% of people in service occupations are Democrats, while less than 20% are Republicans. Skilled workers are slightly more likely to be Republicans than Democrats. Taking all of these factors into consideration, we may infer that a black female in a service occupation is more likely to vote Democrat than a white male skilled worker, (A). Answer (B) is false. Females are more likely to be Democrats than are males. Those making under $10,000 are more likely to be Democrats than are those making $50,000 or more. Answer (C) is false. Those with no high school diploma are more likely to be Democrats than are those with some college. Answer (D) is false. Blacks are less likely to be Republicans than are whites, and people earning $10,000–$19,999 are less likely to be Republicans than are those earning $29,999. Answer (E) is false. Whites are less likely to be Democrats than are blacks. Those without high school diplomas are less likely to be Democrats than are those with high school diplomas.

8.   **(B)**

In 1932, Franklin Roosevelt was elected President in a landslide vote, ending a 12 year period of Republican domination of the presidency. This election is considered by political scientists a "realigning election." A realigning election is one in which a sharp, lasting change occurs in the coalition of voters that supports each of the parties. In the election of 1936, Roosevelt drew into the Democratic Party a coalition of urban workers, blacks, southern whites, and Jews. Most of the urban workers were also union members. The coalition did not include large numbers of business interests, which continued to vote for the Republican Party. This coalition continued to support the Democratic Party until approximately 1968, when white Southerners began to vote for the Republican candidate for President more often than for the Democratic candidate. The answer is (B), northern business leaders, since most of these voters supported the Republicans in each of the years Roosevelt ran for President (1932, 1936, 1940, and 1944). Answer (A) is wrong because most Southerners, white and black alike, voted for Roosevelt each time he ran for President. Answer (C) is wrong because blue-collar workers heavily supported Roosevelt in each of his elections. Answer (D) is wrong because blacks and Jews, two prominent racial minorities, voted for Roosevelt. Answer (E) is false because union members, who were mostly blue-collar workers, heavily supported Roosevelt.

9.   **(D)**

(D) is the answer. Souter, along with justices Stevens, Ginsberg, and Breyer, is considered to reflect more liberal political views in his rulings than do Scalia (A), Rehnquist (B), O'Connor (C), Thomas (E), or Anthony Kennedy, who was not listed among the answer choices.

10.   **(A)**

The passage is taken from the landmark case *Marbury vs. Madison,* 1803. What the passage means, in everyday language, is:

1. Interpreting laws is a judicial function. 2. When two laws conflict, the courts must decide which will be enforced. 3. The Constitution is superior to laws passed by Congress or state legislatures (called statutory law). 4. Therefore, if a statute conflicts with the Constitution, the statute cannot be enforced by the courts.

Answer (B) is incorrect because the passage says nothing about Congress's right to pass laws to carry out its duties. Rather, the passage deals with a conflict between statutory and Constitutional law. Answer (C) is incorrect because it contradicts the main thesis of the passage. The passage clearly says that it is the duty of *courts*, not legislatures, to "say what the law is," which means the same as "interpretation of laws." Answer (D) is incorrect because the passage says when an act of the legislature and the Constitution conflict, the Constitution governs the case. Answer (E) is incorrect because the passage states specifically that if two laws conflict, the courts must decide the operation of each. It then posits a case where the two laws in conflict are an act of the legislature and the Constitution. The clear implication is that, in such a case, the courts must decide on the operation of the Constitution, which means deciding questions of Constitutional law.

11.   **(D)**

The Office of Management and Budget is the chief presidential staff agency. Its primary responsibility is to put together the budget that the President submits to Congress. Each agency and office of the executive branch must have its budget requests cleared by OMB before it gets into the President's budget. The OMB also studies the organization and operations of the executive branch, to ensure that each office and agency is carrying out its appropriate duty, as assigned by law. Answer (A) is incorrect because the Department of Commerce does not help the President draw up his annual budget. The Department of Commerce was created in 1903 to protect the interests of business people at home and abroad. Answer (B) is incorrect because the Department of Treasury is not involved in drawing up the President's budget. The functions of the Treasury Department include collecting taxes through the Internal Revenue Service, an administrative unit of Treasury, administering the public debt, and coining money. Answer (C) is incorrect because the main responsibility of the Federal Reserve Board is the implementation of monetary policy (see explanation for question 7). It has nothing to do with drawing up the President's annual budget. Answer (E) is incorrect because the Cabinet does not help the President draw up his budget. It advises the President on the administration of the executive departments.

12.   **(B)**

In 1974, in the case *United States vs. Nixon,* the Supreme Court declared that the President has an executive privilege to protect military, diplomatic, and sensitive national security secrets from disclosure. However, the material may be successfully subpoenaed if needed by either the defense or the state in a criminal prosecution. (A) is incorrect since the right of the President to veto proposed legislation is called the veto power. It has nothing to do with the President's right to protect information from disclosure. (C) is incorrect because the right of the President to appoint and receive ambassadors is unrelated to the executive privilege of withholding certain information. (D) is incorrect because the President's power to pardon is unrelated to executive privilege. Also, the President has an unlimited, not a limited, right to pardon persons convicted of federal crimes. (E) is incorrect because the President enjoys no immunity from prosecution for misdemeanors or felonies.

13.   **(E)**

The President does not have the ability to personally introduce legislation in either house of Congress. To introduce legislation in either house, one must be a member of that house. (A) is incorrect because the fact that he is elected indirectly by the people, not by the legislature as in parliamentary systems, is a source of power and independence for the President. (B) is incorrect because the Supreme Court has expanded the President's emergency powers. See, for example, the Prize Cases,1863; and *Korematsu vs. U.S.,* 1944. (C) is incorrect because when the President has high public approval ratings, as measured in opinion polls, he is in a much better position to push his legislative proposals through Congress. (D) is incorrect because the veto power can be wielded very effectively by presidents to prevent the passage of legislation they don't like. President Bush had vetoed more than 20 bills by January 1992, and none of the vetoes had been overridden by Congress.

14.   **(D)**

Informal amendments are understood and accepted, but not formally written into the Constitution. Thus, the answer cannot include choices I or II, as both are reflected in the Constitution (the presidential term limit is dictated by the Twenty-second Amendment and the Twenty-fourth Amendment bans the poll tax). This rules out answers (A), (C), and (E). (B) is not correct because both choices III and IV, the vice presidential term limit and the increasing power to wage war without a formal declaration from Congress (Korea, Vietnam, and both Gulf wars were waged without a formal declaration), are valid examples of informally amending the Constitution.

15.   **(A)**

The question asks which statement is false. (A) is the correct response because the state party conventions choose their respective state party chairmen. (B) is a true statement. The party platform is written at the national party convention. (C) is a true statement, since the convention does nominate the party's candidate for President. (D) is a true statement since the Democratic Party, unlike the Republican Party, has several hundred "super delegates" who are free to vote for the nominee of their choice at the convention. The super delegates are Democratic governors, congressmen, and other distinguished party members. (E) is a true statement because one of the functions of the convention is to set the time and place of the next convention.

16.   **(A)**

The question requires you to identify the false statement. The correct response is (A), since the Court declared in *Engel vs. Vitale,* 1962, that a non-denominational prayer written by New York officials for recitation in public schools at the beginning of each school day was unconstitutional. (B) is a true statement because the Court declared in *Abington School District vs. Schempp,* 1963, that a Pennsylvania law which required daily Bible reading in public schools was unconstitutional. (C) is a true statement because in *Stone vs. Graham,* 1980, the Court held unconstitutional a Kentucky statute that required the posting of a copy of the Ten Commandments, purchased with private funds, on the wall of every classroom in the state. (D) is a true statement because in *McLean vs. Arkansas Board of Education,* 1982, the Court held unconstitutional a law requiring that creation science be taught in public schools. (E) is a true statement because in *Epperson vs. Arkansas,* 1968, a law prohibiting the teaching of the theory of evolution in public schools was declared unconstitutional by the Court.

17.   **(E)**

The Great Compromise, promoted by Roger Sherman, provided for a bicameral legislature, with members of the House to be directly elected; members of the Senate were originally chosen by the state legislatures (B). The President is elected not by direct popular vote but by the electoral college. Originally, state legislatures chose the electors who made up the electoral college. The Seventeenth Amendment, adopted in 1913, provides for popular election of senators, but the question asks you to make your choice based on how the constitution emerged from the Constitutional Convention in the eighteenth century. (C) is incorrect because treaties are ratified by a two-thirds vote of the Senate. (D) is incorrect because constitutional amendments are ratified in one of two ways. The first is by three-fourths of the state legislatures. The second is by three-fourths of state ratifying conventions. Congress determines which method will be used.

18.   **(D)**

There are two schools of thought on the proper method of constitutional interpretation by the judiciary. One is called "judicial activism." Advocates of this school believe that the intentions of those who wrote the Constitution should not be authoritative for the decision of controversial matters in the present. They say that judges should be free to adapt the Constitution to changing political and social circumstances. The other school is called "judicial restraint." Advocates of this school stress that the Constitution was a great contract by which the American people created a government. This contract laid the ground rules for the operation of the government, and it provided a formal process of amendment for changing those ground rules. In order to understand the ground rules, say advocates of restraint, one must determine the original intentions of those who wrote and ratified the Constitution. For unelected judges to assume for themselves the power to change the Constitution, according to this school, is for the judges to usurp a power that was not given them by the Constitution or the people. Therefore, the correct answer is (D). Answer (A) is incorrect because there is no general process by which judges limit the number of cases they hear in a year. Justices on the Supreme Court do have a lot of control over which cases they hear, through a process called "certiorari." When litigants appeal to the Court to have their cases heard, the justices vote on the merits of the cases. If four justices vote to hear a particular case, they issue a "writ of certiorari" to the lower court, ordering all documents relevant to the case to be sent up to the Supreme Court. Answer (B) is incorrect because judges do not lobby for funds from Congress. Answer (C) is incorrect because when judges remove themselves from a case they are said to recuse themselves. Answer (E) is incorrect because judicial restraint refers to a method of interpreting the Constitution and has nothing to do with political campaigns.

19.   **(A)**

When it created the independent regulatory commissions, Congress gave them the power to pass regulations (legislative), enforce the regulations (executive), and conduct hearings to determine the punishment for violators of the regulations (judicial). Answer (B) is incorrect because independent regulatory commissions, while nominally in the executive branch, are not included in any of the 14 executive departments. Answer (C) is incorrect because the regulatory commissions do not regulate the federal bureaucracy. Rather, some guard against unfair business practices, others police the side effects of business, such as pollution, and others protect consumers from unsafe products. Answer (D) is incorrect because the commissions were set up by Congress to be independent of the President. They are headed by commissioners who are appointed for fixed terms and are not removable by the President. The commissions must also be bipartisan in membership. Answer (E) is incorrect because the commissions were created by Congress.

20.   **(B)**

This is a famous political cartoon from 1812, when the Massachusetts state legislature created a misshapen district which would be a "safe district" for Congressman Elbridge Gerry. A safe district is one in which a particular political party, or in this case a particular person, is almost certain to win. When cartoonist John Gilbert saw the district he added a head, wings, and claws and called it a salamander. Newspaper editor Benjamin Russell replied that it should be called a "Gerrymander." The term has been used ever since to describe any congressional district of contorted boundaries that is created as a safe seat for a political party or candidate. Answer (A) is incorrect because the cartoon has nothing to do with environmental issues or congressional behavior. Answer (C) is incorrect because the cartoon has nothing to do with the influence of money on elections. Answer (D) is incorrect because the cartoon has nothing to do with the character of congressmen. Answer (E) is incorrect because the term "dinosaur bill" is a fictitious term concocted as a distractor for this question.

21.   **(C)**

The quotation is from *Plessy vs. Ferguson,* 1896. (A) is incorrect because in the Dred Scott case, which was before the Civil War, the Supreme Court held that Blacks had no political rights under the Constitution. In the last sentence of the quotation, the Court mentions the political rights of Blacks, and that these rights had been earnestly enforced in some states. Therefore, the case the quotation is an excerpt from must have been subsequent to the Dred Scott case. (B) is incorrect because in *West Virginia vs. Barnette,* the Court struck down a West Virginia law which required children in public schools to salute the flag and say the Pledge of Allegiance at the start of each school day. (D) is incorrect because in *Columbus Board of Education vs. Penick,* the Court declared that the public schools of Columbus, Ohio, were racially segregated in violation of the desegregation decision of *Brown vs. Board of Education,* 1954. (E) is incorrect because *Mapp vs. Ohio* dealt with a Fourth Amendment illegal search and seizure issue.

22.   **(A)**

In *Brown vs. Board of Education,* the Supreme Court declared racial segregation of public schools unconstitutional, even though the facilities of the White and Black schools were equal. This effectively overturned the decision in Plessy, which had upheld the doctrine that racial segregation in public schools was constitutional so long as the facilities were of equal quality (separate but equal). (B) is incorrect because *Swann vs. Charlotte-Mecklenburg* did not itself establish the principle that state-sponsored segregation was unconstitutional. Rather, *Swann vs. Charlotte-Mecklenburg* dealt with the question of how to implement the *Brown vs. Board of Education* decision. (C) is incorrect because *Engel vs. Vitale* dealt with state-sponsored prayer in public schools. It had nothing to do with desegregation. (D) is incorrect because *Luther vs. Borden* was a "political question" case. It established the rule that certain political controversies would not be decided by the federal courts. The most common type of political question involves a dispute between the executive and legislative branches over the scope of their respective powers. (E) is incorrect because *Cantwell vs. Connecticut* dealt with the issues of freedom of speech and religion. It had nothing to do with desegregation of public facilities.

23.   **(D)**

The concept of dual federalism was predominant in American government from the post-Civil War period until approximately the 1930s. A typical description of this concept was given by the Supreme Court in the Tarbells case, 1872:

> There are within the territorial limits of each state two governments (state and national), restricted in their spheres of action, but independent of each other, and supreme within their respective spheres. Each has its separate departments, each has its distinct laws, and each has its own tribunes for their enforcement. Neither government can intrude within the jurisdiction of the other nor authorize any interference therein by its judicial officers with the action of the other.

(A) is incorrect because dual federalism held that the states had certain powers which were specifically reserved to them by the Tenth Amendment. These could be exercised regardless of congressional action. (B) is incorrect because it describes the current concept of federalism, which might be called one of national supremacy. In the case *Garcia vs. San Antonio,* 1985, the Supreme

Court declared that henceforth Congress should decide for itself to what extent it ought to regulate those powers that were originally reserved to the states by the Tenth Amendment to the Constitution. This means, in effect, that there are no longer any reserved powers of the states upon which Congress may not encroach. This concept is radically different from that of dual federalism. (C) is incorrect because the term for this concept of federalism is cooperative federalism. (E) is incorrect because it expresses a view typically referred to as the theory of nullification. This theory was held by many in the South before the Civil War. Perhaps the most famous advocate of this theory was John C. Calhoun.

24.   **(B)**

The original Constitution said nothing about what qualifications would be required for voting in federal elections. Article I, section 4, states:

> The times, places and manner of holding elections for Senators and Representatives, shall be prescribed in each state by the legislature thereof; but the Congress may at any time by law make or alter such regulations, except as to the places of choosing Senators.

The Fifteenth Amendment prevented the states from denying persons the right to vote on the basis of race; the Nineteenth Amendment extended the right to vote to women; the Twenty-Fourth Amendment outlawed the use of the poll tax by states; and the Twenty-Sixth Amendment extended the right to vote to persons eighteen years of age or older. (C) is incorrect because two methods of ratifying amendments are given in Article V. Congress is given the power to decide which method will be used for any proposed amendment. (D) is incorrect because the qualifications for members of the House and Senate are stipulated in Article I. (E) is incorrect because Article I, section 10, of the Constitution says that a state cannot, without the consent of Congress, levy duties on imports or exports "except what shall be absolutely necessary for executing its inspection laws."

25.   **(E)**

The Constitution states in the Twelfth Amendment that "The person having the greatest number of [electoral] votes for President, shall be President, if such number be a majority of the whole number of Electors appointed...." (A) is incorrect because to win in the electoral college a candidate must receive a majority of the electoral votes, not merely a plurality. If three or more candidates received electoral votes, it would be possible that none received the necessary majority. In that case the decision would be made in the House of Representatives. In 1824, Andrew Jackson received 99 electoral votes, John Quincy Adams

84, William Crawford 41, and Henry Clay 37. The House of Representatives chose John Quincy Adams as President, despite the fact that Jackson had the most electoral votes. (B) is incorrect because the President is not elected directly by popular vote, but rather by the electoral college. Whichever candidate wins a plurality of the popular vote in a state wins that state's electoral vote. It is possible for a candidate to win a majority of the popular vote nationwide, but not win a majority of the electoral votes. This happened in 1876, when Samuel J. Tilden won 51% of the popular vote, but lost the presidency to Rutherford B. Hayes by an electoral vote of 184 to 185. (C) is not correct because several presidents have won less than a majority of the popular vote, but a majority of the electoral vote. This happened in 1876, as explained above. It has also happened several times when three or more candidates split the popular vote, with the President-elect winning a majority of the electoral vote (1824, 1844, 1848, 1856, 1860, 1880, 1884, 1888, 1892, 1912, 1948, 1968, 1992, 1996 and 2000). (D) is incorrect because if no candidate wins a majority of the electoral vote, the House of Representatives selects the President from among the top three popular vote-getters.

26.   **(D)**

A discharge petition is used to force a bill out of a standing committee which has refused to report the bill out to the full House. In the House, a bill cannot reach the floor unless reported out of a committee. A bill that has not been reported out within 30 days after referral to committee may be subject to discharge. The discharge petition must be signed by an absolute majority of House members (218). The motion to discharge is then voted on, and carries with a majority vote of those present and voting. The rules committee may be discharged of a bill after 7 days, rather than the 30 required for other committees. (A) is incorrect because the only way for a bill on the floor to be killed is by a negative vote by a majority of those present and voting. (B) is incorrect because a discharge petition cannot be used to force the rules committee to send a bill back to the committee to which the bill was originally referred. (C) is incorrect because a discharge petition is not used to open a bill up to amendments on the floor of the House. In the House, bills reported out of a standing committee go to the rules committee. The rules committee gives each bill a rule which specifies the time limit for debate on the bill, and whether or not the bill may be amended during floor debate. When the bill comes to the floor for debate, the first thing voted on is the rule assigned by the rules committee. Most of the time the rule is routinely approved. If it is rejected, its opponents may substitute a rule more to their liking. This process does not involve a discharge petition. (E) is incorrect because a bill approved by the House is certified by the clerk, printed on blue paper, and automatically sent to the Senate for its consideration.

27.   **(C)**

Although the Fourth Amendment protects the public against unreasonable search and seizure, the precise way by which that protection is to be enforced is not stipulated in the Amendment. Before 1914, any person whose Fourth Amendment rights were violated by federal authorities had as their only recourse a civil suit for damages against the offending official. Any evidence gained through the illegal search was admissible in court. Persons whose Fourth Amendment rights were violated by state officials had no recourse whatsoever under the Fourth Amendment, since it did not originally apply to the states. In 1914, in *Weeks vs. U.S.,* the Supreme Court established the exclusionary rule, which allowed evidence obtained illegally by federal officials to be excluded from trial in federal courts. In *Wolf vs. Colorado,* 1949, the Court applied the Fourth Amendment to the states, but did not apply the exclusionary rule to the states. This meant that, while evidence seized illegally by a state official was still admissible in a state court, the person whose rights were violated could now sue the offending official for violation of the person's civil rights. In *Mapp vs. Ohio,* 1961, the Court finally applied the exclusionary rule to state officials and courts. (A) is incorrect because *Baker vs. Carr* dealt with the reapportionment of the Tennessee State Assembly. (B) is incorrect because *Roe vs. Wade,* 1973, dealt with a woman's right to an abortion. (D) is incorrect because *Korematsu vs. U.S.,* 1944, dealt with the President's power to exclude Japanese Americans from military districts during World War II. (E) is incorrect because *Gideon vs. Wainwright,* 1963, dealt with the right of indigents accused of felonies to have lawyers appointed at state expense to defend them.

28.   **(A)**

Amendments Thirteen (1865), Fourteen (1868), and Fifteen (1860) were adopted in order to protect the rights of former slaves after the Civil War. The Thirteenth Amendment forbids slavery or involuntary servitude anywhere in the United States or in any place subject to its jurisdiction. It therefore prevented the reimposition of slavery in the southern states. The Fourteenth Amendment restricts the powers of states; the most important provisions are those that forbid a state to deprive any person of life, liberty, or property without due process of law, or to deny any person equal protection of the law. The Fifteenth Amendment prohibits states from denying anyone the right to vote on the basis of race, color, or previous condition of servitude. This was clearly meant as a precaution against attempts by southern states to prevent blacks from voting. (B) is incorrect because the Nineteenth Amendment extended the suffrage to women, and the Twenty-Sixth Amendment extended it to 18-year-olds. (C) is incorrect because the First Amendment provides protection for speech, religion, and assembly. (D) is incorrect because these amendments did not increase the power of the federal government in any way which could help prevent another civil war. The due process clause of the Fourteenth Amendment has been used by the Supreme Court to apply the Bill of Rights to the state governments. However, it is not at all clear from the debates which took place in Congress when the amendment was proposed that this use of the due process clause was intended by the authors of the amendment. In addition, it was not until *Gitlow vs. New York,* 1925, that the Court thought to use the due process clause of the Fourteenth Amendment for that purpose. Therefore, (E) is incorrect.

29.   **(B)**

A bill's route to the floor of the House lies through the House rules committee. First, a bill is introduced by a member. The presiding officer refers the bill to a standing committee, which often sends it to a subcommittee. After being referred out of committee, the bill goes on one of the calendars. Next, the bill goes to the rules committee. The bill's sponsor and the chairman of the committee which reported the bill will appear before the rules committee to request a rule on the bill. The rules committee will issue either a closed or open rule on the bill. A closed rule means that no amendments, or only those proposed by the committee that reported the bill, can be considered during floor debate. An open rule means that amendments may be proposed by any participant in the debate on the floor. Answer (A) is incorrect because the rules committee does not have the power to close the gallery to the public. Answer (C) is incorrect because there is no House procedure to prevent members from voting on a bill if they miss all or part of the debate on the bill. Answer (D) is incorrect because bills are calendared after being reported out of committee, before going to the rules committee. Answer (E) is incorrect since one house of Congress cannot prevent the other from amending any bill passed by the first house.

30.   **(B)**

The Continental Congress was not given the right to levy direct taxes on individual citizens. Instead, the Articles of Confederation only allowed the Congress to requisition money from the state governments. A requisition amounted to the same thing as a request. When the state governments fell behind in making their requisition payments, Congress was unable to force payment of the money. For this reason, the continental treasury was constantly empty. (A) is incorrect because there was no separation of powers under the Articles of Confederation. The government consisted of a Congress alone, made up of delegates from each of the states. (C) is incorrect since there was no national judiciary under the Articles of Confederation. (D) is incorrect because the Articles of Confederation were very difficult to amend. Amendment required unanimous consent of the 13 states, and Rhode Island always refused to go along with any proposed amendments (for which it came to be known as Rogue Island). (E) is incorrect because the Continental Congress was a unicameral body.

31.   **(D)**

Whereas television and radio stations must be licensed to operate in the United States, newspapers and magazines need not be. Therefore, statement I is true. It is more difficult for a public figure or official to win a libel suit against the media in the United States than in another country, so statement II is true. The Supreme Court has held that before the news media can be found guilty of libeling a public figure or official, the person must show not only that what was published was false and damaging to his/her reputation, but also that it was published with "actual malice," a rule not used in other countries. The legal definition of actual malice is reckless disregard for the truth or falsity of the story. Since reckless disregard is difficult to prove, winning libel suits is difficult for public officials and figures in the U.S.

32.   **(C)**

The Campaign Finance Reform law of 1973 made it legal for corporations and labor unions to form PACs. PACs quadrupled in number between 1975 and 1982, and are still forming. (A) is incorrect because PACs were unimportant in American politics before the campaign reform law of 1973. Indeed, one well-known dictionary of American politics, copyrighted in 1972, does not even have an entry for political action committee. (B) is incorrect for two reasons. First, by law a PAC can contribute no more than $5,000 to a candidate for a primary campaign, and no more than $5,000 during a general election campaign. A total contribution of $10,000 is not likely to buy a PAC a great deal of influence these days, when campaigns for Congress cost in the hundreds of thousands of dollars. Secondly, there are literally thousands of PACs, so there is PAC money available on every side of every issue. Candidates can accept PAC money and still decide for themselves how to vote on the issues. (D) is incorrect because PACs may be formed by a variety of groups, or even by an individual. When Representative Charles Rangel was running for Whip of the Democratic Party in the House, he set up a PAC that made campaign contributions to other representatives' campaigns, hoping they would then vote for him as Whip. (E) is incorrect because the number of ideological PACs has increased at a faster rate than business or labor PACs in recent years. In the 1988 election there were nearly 600 ideological PACs. Ideological PACs now raise more money than business or labor PACs, although they contribute less to candidates. This is due to the fact that they spend more than other PACs on advertising per dollar raised.

33.   **(A)**

Presidents Reagan (1981–1989) and Bush (1989–1993) emphasized political ideology as a factor in choosing their nominees to the Supreme Court. The single most important issue has been a potential candidate's stand on *Roe vs. Wade,* 1973. In that case, the Supreme Court held that the right to privacy included a woman's right to choose an abortion, at least in the first trimester of pregnancy. Roe is perhaps the most controversial decision of the Court in the last 30 years. Republican presidents have tried to nominate Justices who would vote to overturn Roe, while Democratic senators have done their best to thwart those nominations. (B) is incorrect because there has, in fact, been an increase in support for Republican presidential candidates in the South in the last 30 years. From the end of Reconstruction until the 1950s, the Democratic candidate for President could count on solid support from the states of the old Confederacy. However, that began to change in the 1960s. In the six elections since 1964, the Democratic candidate for President has won a majority of the southern states only once, in 1976. The Democratic candidate has not won Virginia and has won Mississippi, Alabama, Florida, South Carolina, and North Carolina only once each, since 1964. (C) is incorrect because the conservative wing of the Republican Party has increased in influence in the past 30 years. After a bitter battle at the 1964 Republican National Convention, conservative Republicans managed to nominate Barry Goldwater as the party's candidate for President. This was the beginning of the takeover of the party by its conservative wing. In 1968, the party nominated Richard Nixon, a strongly anticommunist conservative. In 1980 and 1984, the party nominated Ronald Reagan, long a conservative influence within the party. The conservative wing of the party has also managed to dominate the party's platform at most of the last seven party conventions. (D) is incorrect because voter turnout has decreased in the last 30 years. In 1960, about 62% of the voting age population voted in the presidential election. In 1988, less than 50% did. (E) is incorrect because the number of people declaring themselves to be Independents increased from about 21% in 1962 to 33% in 1986.

34.   **(C)**

The first political parties to compete for public office in the United States were the Federalists and Jeffersonian Republicans, sometimes called the Democratic Republicans. An earlier alignment of political sentiment took place between the Federalists and Antifederalists. Of these two groups, the former supported ratification of the Constitution, while the latter opposed ratification. These two groups did not compete against each other for public office, because the Antifederalist organization ceased to exist after the Constitution was ratified. After the Constitution was ratified, the Federalists won most of the offices in the new government. Many former Antifederalists joined the Jeffersonian Republicans, who began to organize in the early 1790s in opposition to Federalist policies. The Jeffersonian Republicans won control of Congress and the presidency in the election of 1800. The Federalists soon faded from the scene, and were almost nonexistent by 1820. (A) is incorrect because the Whigs organized in the 1830s, after the Federalists had passed from the political scene. (B) is incorrect because the Whigs appeared after the Jeffersonian Republicans had lost power. (D) is incorrect because the Whigs and Democrats competed in the 1830s, after the initial competition between the Federalists and Jeffersonian Republicans had occurred. (E) is incorrect because the Democrats and Republicans began to compete in the 1850s, long after the initial competition between the Federalists and Jeffersonian Republicans had occurred.

35.   **(B)**

To be elected President a person must receive a majority of electoral college votes. To win the presidency a candidate need have neither a majority (A) nor a plurality (C) of the popular vote. Since that is so, (E) is also incorrect. Although unlikely, it is possible to obtain a majority of the electoral votes without winning the popular vote. In the absence of an absolute majority of the electoral college vote (D), the election is thrown into the House of Representatives, where the plurality winner in the electoral college could lose.

36.   **(A)**

A stratified or quota sample (A) selects survey respondents randomly within identified segments (or strata) of the population in proportion to what the segments share of the total population. Such surveys can be quite accurate with 1,000–1,500 respondents. A random survey (C) would have to be much larger (and more expensive) to achieve the same accuracy. Letters to the editor (B) and mailed surveys (D) are often heavily biased because people who feel strongly about issues but whose attitudes are not necessarily representative of the majority, are more likely to write letters or return mailed surveys. Talking with your neighbor (E) is obviously far too limited to accurately represent the population.

37.   **(E)**

The quality of health care is not consistently related to the level of expenditures (A); otherwise, the ranking would be essentially identical on both factors. (B) is incorrect because there is also no consistent difference in the Health Status Index based on whether access is controlled or uncontrolled (average rank is 3.5k for controlled and uncontrolled access). The Health Status Index is based upon male infant mortality, not the longevity (C) of adult females. (D) is incorrect because the U.S. actually spends a higher percentage of its Gross Domestic Product on health care than any other country listed on the table.

38.   **(C)**

In a federal system power is shared. A system with power concentrated at the national level (A), or in which states have no power over local matters (E), is unitary; one with power concentrated in subnational units, particularly if those units controlled the national budget (B) or where subnational units (D) had veto power would be a confederate system.

39.   **(B)**

The Constitution has been changed by custom, tradition (I), and judicial interpretation (II). Examples include the two-term limitation (only added as a formal amendment in the twentieth century), emergency powers of presidents, and the interpretation of the "equal protection" clause. State statutes (III) do not directly affect the meaning of the Constitution.

40.   **(A)**

The Sunbelt encompasses areas ranging from South Carolina to southern California. Since the 1980s, these areas have gained population in a greater proportion than other regions of the country. Arizona, Texas, and Florida have each gained significant numbers of House seats due to this trend. The other regions mentioned have indeed gained population in the last three decades, but proportionally have gained much less than the Sunbelt, and thus may have lost Congressional representation as a result—the state of New York is a good example.

41.   **(E)**

Articulating interests is generally thought of as the special task of interest groups. Parties, on the other hand, bring together or "aggregate" interests (B) in order to create a working majority to run government. Parties also play a significant role in recruiting candidates (A), serving as channels of communication (C), and staffing elections (D).

42.   **(B)**

On the average a white, middle-aged attorney would be the most likely to vote. Except for the South, region is not a significant vote predictor. Younger people (C), those who are less educated (E), those with lower paying occupations (D), and those from minority groups (A) are less likely to vote. Overall, women are only slightly less likely to vote than men, a fact offset by their greater numbers in the electorate. Here the age and probable education level of the secretary (D), rather than gender, make her a less likely voter than the attorney, whose sex is not identified.

43.   **(C)**

Of the 111 executions from 1976 through June 1989 indicated on the graph, all but seven occurred in the states of the old Confederacy. The data presented in the table simply does not indicate whether those who were executed were poor (A) or black (E). (D) is incorrect because only a small percentage of murderers have been or are ever likely to be executed. Although the Republican Party has become more influential in the formerly Democrat-controlled "solid South," it is not accurate to characterize the states on the graph as "Republican-controlled" (B).

44.   **(C)**

Marbury vs. Madison is the correct choice. The *Barron* decision (A) determined that the Bill of Rights did not apply to the states. (B) is best known for the "implied powers" doctrine and (D) was the mid-twentieth century decision that gave poor people the right to state-provided legal representation in criminal cases. *Roe vs. Wade* (E) is the controversial abortion rights decision.

45.   **(A)**

Although we commonly use the term "democratic" today to describe our government, that term is not used in the Constitution, which instead requires each state to have a "republican" form of government. As used in the constitution, "republican" meant roughly a "representative" government. State law, not the federal constitution, determines whether states adopt the ERA (B), elect governors for two-year terms (D) or maintain balanced budgets (E). There is no constitutional requirement, state or federal, with regard to having political parties.

46.   **(E)**

McCulloch vs. Maryland involved the question of whether the state of Maryland could tax a federally chartered bank. The Court held that it could not, because to do so would infringe on the power of the national government. (A), (B), (C), and (D) are all well-known cases, but their importance is based upon other issues. (A) is incorrect, although important, because it established the principle of "judicial review." Similarly, (C) is an important early case involving the meaning of the "Interstate Commerce" clause. Although important, (B) involves abortion rights and (D) is a contemporary case dealing with the question of segregation in public schools.

47.   **(D)**

Pluralist theory, sometimes called "plural elitism," argues that multiple elites contend for power and that the essence of democracy is preserved by their need to compete for mass support. (A) is incorrect and corresponds to a simple classical concept of democracy that exists, if at all, in small communities. (B) is a value statement about what ought to be, but does not necessarily reflect the view of pluralists who see both necessity and value in elites' competition. (C) is incorrect since it is a belief held by "elitists," whose views are in sharp contrast to those of the "pluralists." (E) is a statement about separation of powers, not pluralism, and is therefore incorrect. Although compatible with a pluralist viewpoint, it is not a necessary component of that perspective.

48.   **(D)**

Primaries and caucuses are the two alternative methods used to select delegates to the national conventions for the two major political parties. (A) is incorrect since primaries are neither mentioned nor required by the Constitution. (B) is incorrect since primaries are used in many but not all states. (C) is incorrect since primaries play no direct role in the selection of electors. (E) is incorrect because primaries are also used by the Democratic Party.

49.   **(B)**

The controversial "Bush Doctrine" was issued after 9/11, and after George W. Bush's provocative announcement of an "axis of evil" involving Iran, Iraq, and North Korea. The doctrine attempted to justify pre-emptive attacks in the wake of the terror of 9/11. Although the Bush administration ignored the will of the United Nations Security Council regarding Iraq in 2003, the U.S. has never proposed leaving the organization (A). The NATO allies split over the course of action to take regarding Iraq; some member nations supported military action, while others supported continued UN weapons inspections (C). The U.S. has not reinstituted a federal draft since the end of the Vietnam War (D). Finally, the U.S. has not fundamentally altered its support of Israel as its key ally in the Middle East (E).

50.   **(C)**

The U.S. Postal Service, formerly the Post Office Department, lost its Cabinet status in the 1970s. The newest Cabinet department is Homeland Security (A), while (B) Housing and Urban Development and (D) Defense have been Cabinet departments for some years and (E) Education was elevated to the Cabinet in the 1970s.

51.   **(A)**

Precedent means to follow the rule in the "preceding" case, hence (A) is the correct response. Following the decision in an earlier case is a "rule" of the courts themselves, but is not required by the Constitution (B), nor by a statute (D), a law enacted by the legislative branch. (C) is incorrect since a major reason to follow earlier cases is consistency, rather than "common sense." (E) is incorrect, because the Chief Justice may or may not have agreed with the earlier decision.

52.   **(A)**

Committee chairmanships in the House of Representatives are generally given to the member of the majority party (Democratic in this example) that has served the longest on the particular committee, in this case (A). (B) and (E) are incorrect because they are not Democrats. (C) and (D) are incorrect because seniority is not based upon age, but on length of service to the committee.

53.   **(B)**

The Rules Committee determines the rules for house debate on most bills, giving it substantial power. (A) is incorrect since the Rules Committee does not make committee assignments and (C) is incorrect because negotiating compromises is a function of conference committees, not the Rules Committee. (D) is incorrect because the Rules Committee, although still powerful, has declined in importance in recent decades. Selection of a speaker (E) is done by the majority party caucus and is not a function of the bi-partisan Rules Committee.

54.   **(D)**

An important aspect of the Court's argument in *Brown* was that the intangible badge of inferiority that accompanied segregated schools deprived children of equal educational opportunities and made separate educational facilities "inherently" unequal. The passage expresses the view that segregation itself, rather than the quality of education narrowly defined, is the issue. Therefore, (E) is incorrect. The statement makes no reference to how "different" people

(C) should be treated, except to indicate that treatment should not differ on the basis of race. Answers (A) and (B) are not responsive. (A) does not refer directly to equality and (B)'s reference is to an aspect of equality that is remote from the issues of race.

55. **(E)**

Within a few years after the *Brown* decision, the Court handed down decisions requiring the integration of other public facilities. Racial discrimination, unlike discrimination based upon sex (B), sexual preference (A), or the physical/mental capabilities (D) of students, is clearly prohibited by the Fourteenth Amendment. Protections against other forms of discrimination is less certain. Although racially restrictive covenants (C) are banned in a manner consistent with the results in *Brown,* the reasoning was different because it involved private discrimination. Equally important, the Supreme Court decision on restrictive covenants predated the *Brown* decision by several years.

56. **(D)**

In a "concurring opinion" the judge "concurs" or agrees with the majority conclusion but bases his or her answer on different reasons. (C) is incorrect because it reverses what the opinion concurs with, while (B) describes a "dissenting opinion," not a "concurring opinion." (A) is incorrect since it is agreement with the rest of the court, not the President that is the issue. (E) would refer to an abstention, not a "concurring opinion," which would necessarily be in writing.

57. **(A)**

Hispanics now make up the largest minority population in the United States, according to the 2000 U.S. census, surpassing Blacks (B). Neither women (C) nor the elderly (D) made significant demographic gains in the past two decades, though both comprise large and important sectors of the electorate, and indeed comprise a total population much larger than that of Hispanics. Asian-American immigration continues to increase, but does not proportionally match that of Hispanic population growth (E).

58. **(B)**

The Reagan administration advocated significant increases in defense spending. Although domestic spending (D) was downplayed, those expenditures also grew under Reagan. (A) is incorrect since the Democrats retained control of the House throughout the Reagan administration, although Republicans captured control of the Senate for several years. Education (C) was not a priority of the administration and Reagan advocated the appointment of conservative, not liberal judges (E); hence, these responses are also incorrect.

59.   **(E)**

During a presidential election year, the "coattail effect" of the presidential winner usually means that the President's party gains some seats at that time which it may not be able to retain two years later at a "midterm" election when the President is not running. Therefore, (A), (B), (C), and (D) are incorrect because it is less likely that the President's party will increase the number of seats held in Congress than it will experience some decrease.

60.   **(D)**

This answer is correct because it is the only statement which is not true. Actually most members of Congress have full-time staff working in their home states and districts. The size (B) and importance (A) of staff has increased as members of Congress have become increasingly dependent (C) on the knowledge and expertise of these political appointees (E).

SECTION II

Question 1–Sample Essay that Would Achieve a Top Score

Whether domestically or in foreign affairs, a President seems more likely to successfully guide a controversial policy if he has previously established credentials opposed to that policy. The administrations of Eisenhower, Nixon, and Clinton each bear out this generalization.

Dwight Eisenhower used his televised "farewell address" to the country in 1961 to warn against what he perceived as the dangers of the growing "military-industry" complex to shape policy to their own benefit. During the height of the Cold War, Eisenhower perceived that military-related firms like Lockheed Martin Aviation or Bell Helicopter might lobby powerful allies in the government to pursue policies (war) that would profit them.

Eisenhower, a staunch foe of communism and the former Allied commander during World War II who led the D-Day invasion, held a track record that could prevent the media, public, or military from declaring that he was "soft" militarily. Thus, Eisenhower's past military association gave him credibility in making his critique against the "military-industrial complex" and its worrisome possibilities.

Eisenhower's Vice President, Richard Nixon, had also gained a fierce reputation as an anti-communist. His battles and victories against such accused communists as Alger Hiss were well-known American political lore. Nixon had also established anti-communist credentials by serving in the House Un-American Activities Committee in the late 1940s.

Decades later, Nixon was able to turn this reputation to his advantage. In 1972, Nixon's historic visit to the People's Republic of China led to the eventual U.S. recognition of communist China as opposed to "free" Taiwan. Mainland China could eventually be an important U.S. market and ally, Nixon believed. Nixon knew he could take this bold move given his past stance opposing communism whereas another President without this background may have stumbled in the attempt.

Bill Clinton failed to realize a couple of early controversial proposals in his first term: allowing gays into the military and a government health care plan. Clinton, a moderate liberal from Arkansas, ran into opposition on both policies even though his party held control of Congress at the time. An inexperienced liberal President promoting controversial liberal causes ultimately led to failure for both policies. Political cartoonists, special interests like the American Medical Association, radio talk show hosts, and ultimately, the American public and Congress opposed these policies. Clinton lacked the background to convince these various interests that he could successfully administer these policies.

Question 2–Sample Essay that Would Achieve a Top Score

(A)   An informal amendment is defined as an unwritten, yet understood and generally accepted, change to the United States constitution. While only 27 formal (written) amendments exist, there are thousands of informal amendments in existence. Thus, the informal amendments comprise a key component of constitutional law. Some examples include the existence of a cabinet, the "winner-take-all" aspect of the electoral college or that the committee system would exist and become the key organization in handling congressional business. However, the most important informal amendment of all is simply that informal amendments may exist at all.

(B)   Informal amendments endure because they breathe flexibility and life into U.S. Constitution. Formally amending the constitution requires the unlikely combination of 2/3 passage in both houses of Congress followed by ratification of 3/4 of all state legislatures. This difficulty explains why only 27 such amendments have occurred since 1788. Meanwhile, thousands of informal amendments have come and gone during these centuries. Since the Founding Fathers could not have imagined such issues as AIDS, nuclear warfare, the spread of communism, or women's liberation, informal amendments have proven a necessary lifeline to the U.S. Constitution.

(C)   An interesting application of informal amendments has been to change aspects of the formal amendments. For instance, the Second

Amendment calls for the need of the American populace to serve as a "well regulated militia." This assertion has been nullified over the centuries by the lack of invasions—the last being the War of 1812—and by the advent and might of a professional military and the 50 state national guards serving in reserve. So the opening clause the amendment has been repealed, while the second part, which ensures the right of Americans to "keep and bear arms," remains meaningful.

Another amendment that has been informally altered is the Sixth Amendment, which guarantees the accused the right to a "speedy and public trial." Informally, this amendment has been changed and is now understood to mean "not TOO speedy nor TOO public" of a trial, however. For example, a trial is generally held months, not weeks, after an indictment so that the accused and the defense lawyer(s) have ample time to mount an adequate defense, locate and interview witnesses, and plan an overall defense strategy. Also, a trial will be public, but not staged in an athletic arena were large crowds could cheer and chant, and attempt to influence a witness, judge, or a jury. This would be a sort of "burlesque" of justice. Instead, "public" has come to mean staged in a courtroom (sometimes televised) before a relatively small audience of spectators, members of the press, and the assorted participants in a trial.

Many of the 27 formal amendments have been informally amended and these are but two examples. Others of note include the addition of a "winner-take-all" aspect to the Twelfth Amendment and the electoral college or applying the two-term limit of the Twenty-second Amendment to the Vice President as well as the President.

Question 3–Sample Essay that Would Achieve a Top Score

It is obviously simplistic to contend that a President serving a second term can do whatever he pleases with no worries of political consequence since he cannot be re-elected. Several formal and informal checks on presidential power, even that of a very popular two-term President, exist.

One informal check that restrains presidential action is the President's concern about his own place in history. During the second term, the President realizes his tenure of office is nearing its twilight and becomes more concerned with how history will recall the administration. This inhibits a President from perhaps embarking on a risky foreign policy, such as war, or on a bold domestic policy that might fail, such as attempting to radically change the social security system.

It is interesting to note that the last three of four two-term presidents of the twentieth century, despite their concern with their place in history, were plagued by unwelcome scandals in their second terms. Nixon, Reagan, and Clinton were dogged by Watergate, Iran-Contra, and the impeachment over perjury during a sex scandal, respectively.

Another informal check on a President's actions in the second term is his desire to see his own party succeed in subsequent elections. For instance, a President generally would like to see his Vice President succeed him in the White House. Reagan wanted the elder Bush to win in 1988 while Clinton hoped for a Gore victory in 2000. Moreover, the President wants his own party to control Congress in the upcoming elections. This prevents a President from "burning bridges" and pursuing policies that might cost their party. A needed tax hike to fund government services may very well be postponed until after the next election to reflect well on the President's party.

Several other checks exist, from Congress to the media to public opinion polling. It is fair to say, given the reality of American politics, a second-term President still has many checks to contend with, although some of them are self-imposed.

Question 4–Sample Essay that Would Achieve a Top Score

(A)   The general trend shown on the graph in the past half-century is that the major parties are losing membership as more Americans consider themselves independent voters. In 1952, more than 75 percent of all voters placed themselves in a major party. Today, that figure is closer to 50 percent. While both major parties have lost membership as a proportion of the total electorate, the Democrats have lost the most.

(B)   An independent voter is one whose allegiance may change from race to race and election to election. They probably do vote for major party candidates, it's just that they vote for either party from election to election depending on whatever factors are important to them as a voter, from personality of the candidate to a particular issue like education or taxes. An independent voter may of course also vote for third parties in casting their ballot.

(C)   Both the GOP and Democratic Party would like to reverse this trend and reclaim some of these independent voters for their own. One specific strategy that might be employed is to recruit and attract candidates that more Americans can relate to, especially at the local level. For example, Hispanics are the fastest growing group in the U.S., so both the Republicans and Democrats could run more Hispanics in sunbelt states such as Arizona, Texas, and Florida. This could also entail running more female candidates, such as a "soccer mom" candidate in a suburban region. A less candidate-centered strategy might be more effective in the long run. Here, each party would probably have to become less moderate and go farther to the right (GOP) or to the left (Democrats) to gain more followers. This strategy risks losing the votes of the moderate independents in the middle, so while it would likely increase party identification, it also holds some electoral risks, which explains why the major parties have generally avoided this tactic. Yet, "playing it safely moderate" clearly has not increased either party's base.

PRACTICE TEST 4
AP Comparative Government & Politics

AP COMPARATIVE GOVERNMENT & POLITICS

PRACTICE TEST 4

SECTION I

TIME: 45 Minutes
55 Multiple-Choice Questions
50% of Total Grade

(Answer sheets appear in the back of this book.)

DIRECTIONS: Read the following questions and incomplete sentences. Each is followed by five answer choices. Choose the one answer choice that either answers the question or completes the sentence. Make sure to use the ovals numbered 1 through 55 when marking your answer sheet.

1. Iran, Nigeria, and Mexico can all be accurately described as

    (A) theocracies

    (B) liberal democracies

    (C) authoritarian regimes

    (D) developing states

    (E) Newly Industrialized Countries

2. The "first past the post" electoral system used in Great Britain is LEAST characterized by which of the following?

    (A) An over-representation of the strength of the two major parties

    (B) Encouraging national parties in Scotland, Wales, and Northern Ireland to field individual candidates to win seats via regional support

    (C) Ensuring that a single party wins a parliamentary majority

(D) Generally under-representing the Liberal Democrats

(E) Assuring that individual MPs maintain majority support within their electoral districts

3. Socialism in the wealthy states of Western Europe has tended to promote all of the following EXCEPT

(A) a very high taxation rate for the wealthiest citizens

(B) a fundamental change in the responsibility of the government to provide health care

(C) the necessity for industrial development at the expense of the service sector of the economy

(D) politically influential labor movements on the left

(E) the maintenance of a semi-rigid class structure

4. Proponents of the "dependency theory" would be most likely to point to which of the following to support their beliefs?

(A) The Group of Seven (G-7)

(B) Global warming

(C) NGOs such as Doctors Without Borders

(D) GATT/WTO

(E) The United Nations General Assembly

5. From 1994–2004, the Conservative Party unsuccessfully followed which strategy in an attempt to combat the growing popularity and electability of New Labour?

(A) They repudiated Thatcherism as an "outmoded, unworkable philosophy."

(B) They offered massive tax hikes to fund social welfare programs such as the NHS.

(C) They moderated their policies on issues such as European integration and asylum seekers.

(D) They held steadfast to right wing policies on taxation, asylum and EU integration.

(E) They held on to unpopular shadow leaders for far too long.

6. All of the following occurred under the rule of Deng Xiaoping EXCEPT the

    (A) Tiananmen Square massacre of June 4, 1989

    (B) end of the policies of xiafing and "re-education through labor"

    (C) arrest and prosecution of the "Gang of Four" for their role in the Cultural Revolution

    (D) establishment of Special Economic Zones buffering Hong Kong

    (E) "Four Modernizations" campaign to strengthen China industrially, agriculturally, educationally, and militarily

7. The two-ballot system for presidential elections, provided for in both the Nigerian and Russian constitutions, is designed to accomplish all of the following EXCEPT

    (A) forming coalitions of varied interests and increasing cooperation among the electorate

    (B) increasing public efficacy

    (C) increasing the legitimacy of the government

    (D) ensuring that the legislative and executive branches are governed by the same political party

    (E) promoting an environment of consensus and compromise

8. Which of the following is NOT a condition typically found in a "state socialism" system, such as the former Soviet Union or in China under Mao?

    (A) Only one political party is permitted.

    (B) Workers often believe that theft on the job is acceptable.

    (C) All prices and production are set in the national capital by a central economic agency.

    (D) All property is jointly owned by the people; no property is private.

    (E) All business and services are run by the state and are generally inefficient.

9. Leaders in authoritarian regimes—such as Iran under the Ayatollah Khomeini or Nigeria under General Sani Abacha—tend to promote

    (A) a cult of personality

    (B) higher legitimacy

(C)   increased efficacy

(D)   religious toleration

(E)   labor union activism

10.   The currency pictured at right would be legal tender in which of the following locales?

(A)   London & Glasgow

(B)   Ireland & Portugal

(C)   Stockholm, Sweden

(D)   Denmark & Norway

(E)   Poland & Hungary

11.   Which of the following statements accurately compares the attempted Soviet coup in August 1991 to the Tiananmen Square episode of June 4, 1989?

(A)   Deng Xiaoping authorized the crushing of a student revolt while Mikhail Gorbachev was the target of hard-liners within his own party.

(B)   Both actions centered around the desire for increased democratization of the CPSU and the CCP, respectively.

(C)   The Soviet coup was crushed by CPSU elites, while CCP elites supported the Tiananmen Square actions.

(D)   Most Chinese citizens oppose the CCP's actions in Tiananmen Square, while most Russians supported the attempted Soviet coup.

(E)   Deng Xiaoping's powers were weakened in the aftermath of the Tiananmen Square massacre, while the results of the failed 1991 coup strengthened Mikhail Gorbachev's political position.

12.   Mexico has a more advanced economy than either Nigeria or Iran because it

(A)   has greater oil wealth

(B)   lacks any significant cleavages that lead to violence

(C)   has a greater infrastructure and a beneficial location near liberal democracies

(D) avoids splits between the executive and legislative branches

(E) lacks serious crime problems

13. The Confucianist legacy in China promotes a notion of

(A) family hierarchy with male authority most respected and valued

(B) equality among all social classes

(C) value of the peasant position within the Chinese Communist Party

(D) the Mandate of Heaven

(E) invincibility for party cadre

14. Challenges to national sovereignty in the twenty-first century include

  I. the Kyoto Accords on global warming

  II. oceanic oil spills

  III. Coca-Cola, Microsoft, and other multi-national corporations

  IV. the European Union (EU)

(A) IV only   (D) I only

(B) I, II, III, and IV   (E) II only

(C) II and III only

15. Which of the following is NOT associated with the Protestants of Northern Ireland?

(A) Clashes with Catholics during the "marching season"

(B) The Ulster Unionist Party

(C) A more likely political alliance with the British Conservative, rather than Labour, Party

(D) The Union Jack as a treasured national symbol

(E) Sinn Fein and the Irish Republican Army

16. Vladimir Putin was vaulted to national political prominence in the Russian Federation during 1999 by

(A) the power inherent to the office of Prime Minister

(B) Boris Yeltsin's personal endorsement

(C)   his perceived actions in combating the Chechen rebels

(D)   the leaders of the G-7 nations

(E)   rapid improvement in the national economy

17.   The upper house of the Russian Federation, the Federation Council,

    (A)   holds more relative power than does the House of Lords in Britain or the French Senate

    (B)   has more legislative power than does the Duma

    (C)   has about the same power as the House of Lords and the French Senate, only respected advisory powers to delay legislation

    (D)   has more legitimacy to most Russians than does the Duma

    (E)   represents areas proportionally according to their population size

18.   Deng Xiaoping's policy approaches differed from those of Mao Zedong in all of the following ways EXCEPT:

    (A)   Deng accepted the need for concrete rewards to motivate the Chinese, rather than continuing Mao's emphasis on ideology.

    (B)   Deng was willing to tolerate greater social inequality than Mao in exchange for a higher degree of national prosperity for China.

    (C)   Unlike Mao, Deng distrusted intellectuals and preferred the peasant culture.

    (D)   Unlike Mao, Deng tolerated greater decentralization of economic planning.

    (E)   Deng was more open to establishing and strengthening ties with foreign countries.

19.   The Chinese Cultural Revolution under Mao most closely resembles which of the following Soviet events?

    (A)   The Great Purge under Stalin

    (B)   Glasnost under Mikhail Gorbachev

    (C)   The "secret speech" and de-Stalinization under Khrushchev

    (D)   The attempted 1991 coup of Gorbachev

    (E)   The Bolshevik Revolution under Lenin

20. Which of the following scenarios most clearly illustrates a government whose legitimacy is low?

    (A) A nation's flags are being burnt openly in the nation's capital.

    (B) The national crime rate is high and voter turnout is relatively low.

    (C) Street demonstrations are commonplace and government employees frequently strike.

    (D) Competing ethnic groups are engaged in civil war.

    (E) Foreign states refuse to recognize a country for diplomatic purposes.

21. Which group comprises the largest sector of the Nigerian population?

    (A) Muslims

    (B) The Ibo

    (C) Members of the military, the police, and their families

    (D) The Yoruba

    (E) Women

22. Which statement concerning Russian political parties is NOT correct?

    (A) The Yabloko party favors increased deregulation of the market.

    (B) Gennady Zyuganov led the Communist Party to second place finishes in the presidential elections of 1996 and 2000.

    (C) Although Vladimir Putin officially belongs to no party, he is associated with the Unity Party.

    (D) The Liberal Democrats' main agenda is to promote and protect Russian national interest and culture.

    (E) Nationally prominent politicians Yuri Luzkhov and Yevgeni Primakov combined in 1999 to form Our Home Is Russia.

23. Which Chinese political concept/term is NOT correctly described?

    (A) Mandate of Heaven—if divine support for a ruler is withdrawn, popular revolt is justified

    (B) Red Versus Expert—the need to balance China's need for technical expertise with the ideological demand of equal educational opportunities for the masses

    (C) Iron Rice Bowl—job security and social welfare guaranteed under the CCP

(D) The Four Olds—qualities that Mao wanted to see stripped from China during the Cultural Revolution, 1966–1976

(E) Great Leap Forward—the attempt to allow "controlled capitalism" into specific zones within China from 1958–1960

24. The global trend in the last twenty years has been

(A) fewer states and more nations

(B) more nations desiring and receiving statehood

(C) an increase in the amount of stateless-nations

(D) a dramatic trend toward diplomacy in lieu of violent conflict

(E) the formation of larger multi-national states

25. The first Soviet leader to hint at Stalin's excesses and to be critical of Stalinist tactics within the Communist Party was

(A) Vladimir Lenin   (D) Nikita Khrushchev

(B) Leonid Brezhnev   (E) Boris Yeltsin

(C) Mikhail Gorbachev

26. Which group of "liberal democracies" has the most exclusive membership?

(A) G-7

(B) The "Nuclear Club"

(C) The European Union

(D) WTO/formerly GATT

(E) Permanent members of the UN Security Council

27. Political elections in China are

(A) held only in Hong Kong, Macao, and Taiwan

(B) non-existent and strictly forbidden by the CCP and People's Liberation Army

(C) held at the village level and within the CCP hierarchy

(D) staged nationwide for seats in the National People's Congress

(E) held for all offices below that of "paramount leader"

28. Which of the following is likely to be higher in Russia than in Britain?

    (A) Per capita GDP

    (B) Efficacy

    (C) Infrastructure development

    (D) Legitimacy

    (E) NGO activity

29. The concept of the mass line in Chinese political doctrine refers to

    (A) the effort by party officials to keep the masses in line

    (B) the notion that party cadres must maintain close contact with common people and integrate mass public opinion into the policy-making process

    (C) the effort by the party to ensure successful propaganda mechanisms to preserve a pliant population

    (D) the need for continuous influence by the masses over the party through active recruitment of party members from the masses

    (E) the reeducation campaign through which party leaders are made more sensitive to mass attitudes

30. The Chinese "responsibility system" under Deng Xiaoping

    (A) included repressive forced labor camps used to punish dissidents

    (B) was aimed specifically at increasing industrial output via the rewarding of honest production figures by factory managers

    (C) was a short-lived program designed to allow the common people a greater ability to criticize the state

    (D) was designed to increase citizen loyalty to the military

    (E) allowed peasants a certain incentive to exceed government quotas for their own personal gain

31. Mexico and Russia share all of the following characteristics EXCEPT

    (A) lower houses of the legislature elected by a combined SMDP-PR hybrid system

    (B) upper houses of Congress that lack the power to block legislation

(C)   each has hosted major international events such as the Summer Olympic Games

(D)   a one-party dominance for much of the 20th century

(E)   each has faced a violent internal revolt since 1994

32.   In a state with a strong executive leader, such as Russia under Vladimir Putin, Nigeria under military rule, or Mexico under the PRI, which of the following will be true by necessity?

    (A)   A strong federal system will emerge in practice.

    (B)   Efficacy will rise.

    (C)   A strong unitary system will emerge in practice.

    (D)   Legitimacy will rise.

    (E)   A pluralist state will emerge.

33.   In which pair of states are parties most changeable and most centered around candidates and personality rather than program and ideology?

    (A)   Russia and Nigeria   (D)   Iran and Mexico

    (B)   Britain and Iran   (E)   Russia and China

    (C)   Mexico and China

34.   As Prime Minister from 1979 to 1990, Margaret Thatcher wanted to

    (A)   abolish all labor unions within the United Kingdom

    (B)   reinstate capital punishment, ban abortions, and limit gun control

    (C)   privatize the National Health Service and the British Broadcasting Company (BBC)

    (D)   decrease taxation, encourage entrepreneurship and class mobility, and increase British productivity

    (E)   allow devolution for Scotland and Wales, while negotiating with the IRA over the future status of Northern Ireland

35.   Which of the following factors distinguishes leadership in Communist systems, such as those which have existed in the former Soviet Union and China, from democratic systems such as those found in France and Great Britain?

    (A)   Leaders of Communist systems do not have to balance competing interests, as do leaders of Democratic systems.

(B) Leadership transitions in Communist systems are more uncertain and destabilizing than in Western democracies.

(C) Leaders of Communist systems are more likely to be recruited from the masses than in Democratic systems.

(D) Leaders of Communist systems rely more heavily on the support of public opinion than do Western leaders.

(E) Leadership in Communist systems requires charismatic personalities, whereas this is not true of Democratic systems.

36. All of the following are reasons why communism has not spread to the world's leading states—the liberal democracies of the former First World—EXCEPT

(A) labor unions have won widespread gains for workers, leading to an increased middle class

(B) governments increasingly passed worker safety, security, and anti-discrimination legislation in the period since Marx's death

(C) equality of taxation and equality of opportunity has been fully achieved in many liberal democracies

(D) increasingly people have rejected the notion of "equality of result" as foreign to both individual initiative and human nature

(E) communist regimes are equated with repression by many workers in the leading industrial states

Percentage of Seats in the Parliament				
42%	35%	12%	8%	3%
Party A	Party B	Party C	Party D	Party E

37. Based on the table above, assume that you are the leader of Party A. You want to build a government coalition at minimal cost to your party, but enough to capture a majority of seats to control Parliament. Which party or parties are you most likely to seek a coalition with?

(A) Party B

(B) Party C

(C) Party D

(D) Parties D and E

(E) Parties C and E

38. Parliamentary systems differ from presidential systems in that

    (A) at least three political parties must be active for the system to function effectively

    (B) the head of government is also an elected member of the legislature

    (C) the electoral system is based on proportional representation

    (D) coalition governments are necessary by definition in a parliamentary system

    (E) parliamentary systems feature socialist economies, while presidential systems feature capitalist economies

39. All of the following descriptions apply to the relationship between the so-called First (developed) and Third (developing) worlds EXCEPT

    (A) most of the First World states are located north of the equator, while most of the Third World is located south of the equator

    (B) increasingly, goods are made in the Third World with lower labor costs and shipped to First World states

    (C) the term "Third World" is a subjective political science term coined in a First World state—France

    (D) historically, First World states have taken resources from the Third World to furnish finished goods at home

    (E) Third World states remain dependent on the First World for basic foodstuffs

40. In elections for the Russian Duma, voters exercising their full suffrage will

    (A) vote twice on successive Sundays—first for a candidate from the party they choose, and then for their favorite of the top two "run-off" candidates. (A single ballot would occur only in the unlikely event that a single candidate gained a majority on the first ballot.)

    (B) vote only once, choosing a single candidate, because the Duma is filled by the SMDP formula

    (C) vote only once, choosing by party not by candidate, because the Duma is filled by proportional representation

    (D) probably not vote at all, because the Duma is elected by a select "electoral college" of elected local officials

(E)   vote twice, but all voting will occur on the same day. One vote is for a candidate to represent the local district and one vote is for a party to hold "at large" seats in the Duma

41.   The Chinese Communist Party's legitimacy is most damaged by which of the following factors?

(A)   Gaunxi allegations among party members and other "insiders"

(B)   The growth rate of the Chinese economy

(C)   The transition to a "fourth generation" of leadership in 2002

(D)   The relaxation of the one-child policy

(E)   The construction of the massive Three Gorges Dam project

42.   All of the following have been associated with New Labour since it came to power in 1997 EXCEPT

(A)   the philosophy of governing via a "Third Way," between Thatcherism and socialism

(B)   a perceived preoccupation by the party on media "spin"

(C)   an aggressive pursuit of electoral reform for both the House of Lords and the House of Commons

(D)   devolved power-sharing agreements with various regions of the United Kingdom

(E)   a deeper involvement in the European Union than had occurred under the Conservatives

43.   Differences between the Prime Minister in Britain and Russia include all of the following EXCEPT

(A)   in Britain, the Prime Minister is a party leader; in Russia, that is not necessarily the case

(B)   in Britain, the Prime Minister represents the majority party in the lower house of the legislature; in Russia, the Prime Minister represents the President's party or bloc without regard to the legislature

(C)   in Russia, the Prime Minister is much more likely to be dismissed or to serve for a shorter duration than in Britain

    (D) in Britain, the Prime Minister is an elected member of the House of Commons; in Russia, the Prime Minister may not hold a seat in the Duma

    (E) in Britain, the Prime Minister is the executive leader; this is not the case in Russia

44. Mao Zedong steadfastly believed that

    (A) Hong Kong and Taiwan were potentially disruptive areas that could not be co-opted into the communist People's Republic of China

    (B) the Communist Party must be re-energized by criticism and input from the masses

    (C) cadre could provide the stability necessary for sustained economic growth

    (D) the Soviet model of communism provided an appropriate roadmap for the Chinese to follow

    (E) women should play a subservient role in the development of communism throughout China

45. Mikhail Gorbachev's reforms unintentionally resulted in all of the following EXCEPT

    (A) press criticism of Gorbachev himself

    (B) the fall of the so-called "Iron Curtain"—the shedding by the Soviet Union of the Eastern European communist states

    (C) worker unrest over the policies of perestroika

    (D) the end of the monopoly of the CPSU's political power

    (E) the dissolution of the Soviet Union

46. Legitimacy is important to a government because

    (A) it ensures that opponents will be unable to speak out against the government's policies

    (B) when a government is regarded as legitimate, other countries will accord diplomatic recognition

    (C) it provides a legal means to force citizens to vote for the government's agenda in future elections

    (D) it facilitates the enforcement of its policies, since people feel an obligation to obey those who are seen as rightful rulers

    (E)   without high legitimacy, a government cannot stay in power for more than a few months, even with the backing of a powerful military force

47.   Russia's Liberal Democratic Party is most similar in ideology to which of the following parties?

    (A)   Britain's Liberal Democrats   (D)   the PRD in Mexico

    (B)   the Scottish National Party   (E)   Yabloko in Russia

    (C)   the British National Party

48.   Political participation in China takes place through all of the following mechanisms EXCEPT

    (A)   village elections   (D)   the Communist Youth League

    (B)   inter-party competition   (E)   mass campaigns

    (C)   small group discussion

49.   As a nation develops politically and economically,

    (A)   formal, or organized, interest groups tend to grow in power compared to informal interest groups

    (B)   informal, or unorganized, groups become more politically influential than formal interest groups

    (C)   lobbying efforts tend to be dismissed by legislative bodies

    (D)   the leader of the executive tends to become less powerful

    (E)   suffrage is tightly restricted

50.   Which of the following historical/political statements is NOT correct?

    (A)   Britain has developed a civil political climate in both the House of Lords and the House of Commons.

    (B)   Russia has little tradition of democratic institutions; before the CPSU's rule, czars had ruled Russia as imperial monarchs.

    (C)   Religion has been a central issue, causing security problems in France (re Algeria), Britain (Northern Ireland), and the Russian Federation (with Chechen separatists).

    (D)   Regionalism remains stronger in various areas of China than in either the United Kingdom or the Russian Federation.

(E) British and French voters are typically not in favor of capital punishment, ending gun control, or banning abortion.

51. The fact that Britain's Prime Minister is "responsible" to the House of Commons simply means that the government must

(A) stage a general election within five years

(B) allow free votes on matters of conscience

(C) resign if a vote of confidence is lost

(D) appear weekly for Prime Minister's Questions

(E) resign if legislation is blocked by the House of Lords

52. In which state are politicians most constitutionally limited in their effort to maintain their current office through re-election?

(A) Mexico   (D) China

(B) Iran   (E) Britain

(C) Nigeria

As former [British] Prime Minister Harold Wilson put it:

"The idea of a proletariat is nonsense. I am more interested in people as individuals than in the mass. I am interested in the family, because most happiness is family happiness. I am interested in Saturdays and Sundays and Bank Holidays."

53. The quotation above suggests that Wilson

(A) believed that most workers are not revolutionary, but instead are interested in leisure and quality of life

(B) felt that socialism was too moderate an economic philosophy for Britain

(C) held Cold War views contrary to that of most of his countrymen

(D) denied that a true working class does not exist in the United Kingdom

(E) opposed the "cradle to grave" welfare state that Britain had developed

54. Which generalization regarding Non-Governmental Organizations (NGOs) is most accurate?

    (A) They tend to originate in liberal democracies but do most of their actual work in developing countries.

    (B) They tend to originate in the developing world but lobby governments in liberal democracies.

    (C) They are completely free from the dictates of national law.

    (D) They often share the same aims as multi-national corporations.

    (E) While NGOs have greatly improved the quality of life in North America, Japan, Australia, and Western Europe, they have made little impact in Latin America, Africa, Asia, or Eastern Europe.

55. Which of the following industries are LEAST likely to be nationalized in a socialist economy?

    (A) Airlines   (D) Internet service providers

    (B) Telephone service   (E) Rail service

    (C) Petroleum

STOP
This is the end of Section I.
If time still remains, you may check your work only in this section.
Do not begin Section II until instructed to do so.

SECTION II

TIME: 100 Minutes
8 Free-Response Questions
50% of Total Grade

DIRECTIONS: Write an essay based on each of the following eight questions. Where appropriate, use substantive examples in your answers. Your essays should be numbered to correspond with the questions to which you are responding. (See the directions for ID questions that follow.)

Students will provide brief definitions or descriptions of five concepts or terms, noting their significance. Students may be asked to provide an example of the concept in one or more of the countries studied, or to contrast concepts.

1.   Define and illustrate the concept of the "stateless-nation."

2.   Explain the phrase "free trade."

3.   Define "patron-client" relationships.

4.   Describe and contrast "market economy" from "command economy."

5.   Explain the goals and methods employed by a cartel.

Refer to the following chart for question 6:

Previous EU members	2004 EU "ascension states"
Austria	Czech Republic
Belgium	Cyprus
Denmark	Estonia
Finland	Hungary
France	Latvia
Germany	Lithuania
Greece	Malta
Ireland	Poland

Previous EU members	2004 EU "ascension states"
Italy	Slovakia
Luxembourg	Slovenia
Netherlands	
Portugal	
Spain	
Sweden	
United Kingdom	

6. Discuss challenges posed to the European Union by the following expansion issues:

   a. In what way does the 2004 expansion threaten the prosperity and stability of the existing EU states?

   b. Illustrate two different specific policies the EU has created to deal with the concerns described in part (a).

7. Discuss the transfer of power that occurred in the Chinese Communist Party in 2002. What does this process reveal about political development within China?

8. Political scientists sometimes speak of "semi-democratic" systems citing Vladimir Putin's Russia as a current example. Choosing TWO of the following states—Nigeria, Iran, or Mexico—answer the following:

   a. To what extent is "semi-democratic" an accurate label for Nigeria, Iran, or Mexico?

   b. What forces in Nigeria, Iran, or Mexico are pushing for greater democratic reform?

   c. What forces in Nigeria, Iran, or Mexico are pushing for less democratic reform?

END OF EXAMINATION

COMPARATIVE GOVERNMENT & POLITICS

PRACTICE TEST 4

ANSWER KEY

1.	(D)	15.	(E)	29.	(B)	43.	(B)
2.	(E)	16.	(C)	30.	(E)	44.	(B)
3.	(C)	17.	(A)	31.	(B)	45.	(B)
4.	(A)	18.	(C)	32.	(C)	46.	(D)
5.	(D)	19.	(A)	33.	(A)	47.	(C)
6.	(B)	20.	(D)	34.	(D)	48.	(B)
7.	(D)	21.	(E)	35.	(B)	49.	(A)
8.	(D)	22.	(E)	36.	(C)	50.	(D)
9.	(A)	23.	(E)	37.	(B)	51.	(C)
10.	(B)	24.	(B)	38.	(B)	52.	(A)
11.	(A)	25.	(D)	39.	(E)	53.	(A)
12.	(C)	26.	(E)	40.	(E)	54.	(A)
13.	(A)	27.	(C)	41.	(A)	55.	(D)
14.	(B)	28.	(E)	42.	(C)		

DETAILED EXPLANATIONS OF ANSWERS

TEST 4

SECTION I

1. **(D)**

Iran, Nigeria, and Mexico can all be accurately described as developing states—a generic term for those countries who formerly were members of the Third World and whose economies are developing away from an agricultural emphasis toward industry and the service economy. Iran is a theocracy (A), or a government by holy leaders, but neither Mexico nor Nigeria fits this description. None of the three states are globally influential and wealthy liberal democracies (B). Each has in the recent past been an authoritarian regime, rather by single-party rule [Mexico and the PRI], military rule [Nigeria], or monarchy and theocracy [Iran and the Shah prior to the current regime], but only Iran currently fits this description (C). Finally, while Mexico's economy qualifies it as a Newly Industrialized Country, or NIC, neither Iran nor Nigeria have yet reached this status.

2. **(E)**

"First past the post" is the British political term for the SMDP (single-member district plurality) voting scheme used in the House of Commons. SMDP always promotes a two-party system, as in Britain, where the Labour and Conservative parties have controlled the government for nearly a century. Thus (A) is accurate, many Labour and Conservative candidates gain less than majority support in their districts, but hold total legislative input for that district. Also, a strong third party, like the Liberal Democrats, would prefer a proportional representation (PR) scheme, which would reward it with more seats in parliament (D). The SMDP system does encourage parties like the Ulster Unionists or Scottish National Party to field candidates, since a plurality may be gained within a sympathetic regional district (B). And since "first past the post" promotes a two party system, it is virtually assured that either New Labour or the Conservative Party will hold a numerical majority in the House of

Commons. In other words, no coalition government will be required under an SMDP scheme.

3.   **(C)**

Socialist economies tend to nationalize more industries and provide more government services ("cradle to grave" social welfare) than do capitalist states. This, by necessity, would make (A) and (B) true. Traditionally, labor unions tend to be aligned more with liberal than conservative parties (D), and both France and Britain do feature rather low social-class mobility (E). However, in both France and Britain, the service sector accounts for the greatest percentage of the countries' gross domestic product, making (C) the correct answer.

4.   **(A)**

Supporters of the "dependence theory" divide the world into the wealthier "Northern" post-industrial states and the "Southern" developing states. Dependency theorists contend that the wealthy liberal democracies of the north perpetuate advantageous (and even exploitive) relationships with the developing world. The G-7 consists of seven of the globe's greatest economic powers—U.S.A., Britain, Italy, Canada, Japan, France, and Germany—who meet annually to form a concerted approach to further their own economic interests. The World Trade Organization (formerly known as the General Agreement on Tariffs and Trade) supports free trade globally, which includes limiting subsidies and tariffs among member states (D). Doctors Without Borders won the 1999 Nobel Peace Prize for its humanitarian work in the developing world (C). The United Nations General Assembly is a forum in which the developing states have equal footing with the wealthy liberal democracies, as each UN country receives one vote and holds veto power. Global warming (B) remains a controversial subject, but can be linked to sources in both the wealthier liberal democracies and the developing world.

5.   **(D)**

The Tories did not repudiate the policies of Margaret Thatcher (A), but instead they clung to them even when they were past favor with the mainstream British voter. The Conservative Party did not offer massive tax hikes to fund social services (B), but instead offered tax cuts to a skeptical British public that wondered how taxes could be cut without gutting programs like the NHS. The Tories remain split over the issue of EU integration with many "euroskeptics" among their members, so they did embrace further integration and were opposed to the EU Constitution, for example (C). The Tories tended to ditch party leaders rather quickly during the period, from John Major to William Hague to

Iain Duncan-Smith to Michael Howard. Howard himself stepped down surprisingly after the 2005 election and as 2006 approached the Conservatives were slated to choose a new shadow leader (E).

6.   **(B)**

Deng Xiaoping served as China's "paramount leader" from 1978, after wresting power from the "Gang of Four" in the wake of Mao's death (C). Deng's "Four Modernizations" program began China's economic boom in the wake of Mao's destructive Cultural Revolution (E) and included the Special Economic Zones of free market enterprise and foreign investment (D). Deng's hard-line advisors eventually won out over reformers, leading to the violent ending of the Tiananmen Square protest movement in the summer of 1989 (A). Xiafing was the policy of "sending down" CCP officials and others to work with the peasantry during the Cultural Revolution. Deng, himself, endured this humiliation. However, Deng did not end the use of such similar practices as "re-education through labor" to punish suspected opponents of the CCP or those accused (but not tried) of certain crimes.

7.   **(D)**

A parliamentary system would ensure that the legislative and executive branches were governed by the same party or coalition. Efficacy—the belief that political participation matters—would be increased by the options afforded voters on the second ballot (B). Legitimacy would thus be enhanced by the greater sense of efficacy and by the fact that a majority, rather than merely a plurality, of all voters chose the eventual President (C). Coalitions and compromise (A) and (E) are both promoted by the two-ballot system in that for many voters, their initial choice for President will not make it to a second ballot thus forcing like-minded coalitions.

8.   **(D)**

"State socialism" distinguishes between the actual authoritarian systems found in the Soviet Union under leaders prior to Gorbachev and in China under Mao from theoretical Marxism. In short, state socialism was the reality and Marxism was the ideal. Thus, this question calls for knowledge of the realities of the Stalinist Soviet system and of Mao's China. (A) is obviously correct, as such events as Stalin's Great Purge and Mao's Cultural Revolution attest. Workers often rationalized theft as being against the state, as opposed to against an individual person (B). Both states employed "five-year plans" covering economic goals and production quotas (C). Property was not jointly owned by the people as Marx envisioned, but was leased from the state (D).

State-owned businesses and services, such as rail, tended to be unprofitable and inefficient (E).

9.   **(A)**

A cult of personality, typically associated with figures such as Stalin and Mao, attempts to build a leader up into a deity of sorts—a God-like character. This is done with propaganda of various sorts: large wall mural portraits, writing, music composed to honor the leader and so on. Thus, questioning the authoritarian leader would be less likely, or so the theory goes. The choices all pertain to expanded individual rights, influence, or choice and no authoritarian regime would encourage that to happen lest its own power be toppled.

10.   **(B)**

The *euros* pictured would be the legal currency in Ireland and Portugal, which adopted the single currency on its "first wave" of implementation in 2002. Neither the UK, Denmark, nor Sweden have adopted the *euro* although all are EU members (A, C, and D). Norway has never joined the EU (D), and although Poland and Hungary were admitted to the EU in 2004, it will be close to ten years before these new ascension states will be allowed to adopt the single currency (E).

11.   **(A)**

Deng Xiaoping reformed China's economy but not its political system (B). Perhaps Deng had viewed with skepticism Mikhail Gorbachev's ill-fated attempt to reform both the political and economic systems of the Soviet Union simultaneously, an experiment that unwittingly led to the downfall of the Soviet Union, the CPSU, and Gorbachev himself. Ultimately, Deng and the CCP leadership authorized the use of force to end the Tiananmen Square protests (A). The Soviet coup had been crushed by Boris Yeltsin and a lack of popular support by the Soviet military (C). The mass of the Chinese populace, the peasantry, was not supportive or involved in the Tiananmen Square protests (D). Both Deng and Gorbachev faded from power shortly after the respective episodes featured in this question (E).

12.   **(C)**

Mexico has a more advanced economy than either Nigeria or Iran because it has roads, airports, power grids, communication, and education which have led to manufacturing and export growth. Additionally, the proximity of wealthy neighbors like the U.S. and Canada (and NAFTA) provide Mexico with ready trade markets. Although Mexico does produce a significant amount of petroleum, that commodity is more integral to the economies of Nigeria and Iran, which are both OPEC members (A). Chiapas has been a serious conflict for more than ten years in Mexico (B). As a presidential system, Mexico has had a split government as Vicente Fox, the PAN President, has dealt with a Chamber of Deputies dominated by the PRI (D). Kidnapping, drug violence, and political scandals have plagued Mexico in recent years (E).

13.   **(A)**

Confucianism is an enduring, influential philosophy in China. It stresses the proper role of various parties (husband/wife, ruler/subject, etc.) in relationships. (A) reflects such a relationship. (B) reflects more a Marxist view than Confucianism, while (C) describes Mao's "mass line" theory. The Mandate of Heaven (D) is a traditional view that the gods favor a ruler who benefits China and that a poor ruler loses the mandate. CCP cadre would not be invincible under a Confucianist view, as they are subordinate to the upper echelon of party leadership, such as the Standing Committee, PLA, and paramount leader.

14.   **(B)**

Sovereignty—the ultimate law-making authority of a state within its own territory—is compromised by each of the items listed. The Kyoto Accords imposed limits on greenhouse gas emissions; ocean spills obviously affect many countries with sea borders no matter which country causes the spill; multi-national corporations cross many borders and sway national legislative and executive actions; and the European Union dictates tariff, subsidy, and economic terms to its member states.

15.   **(E)**

Sinn Fein is the political wing of the Irish Republican Army (IRA), which desires the reunification of Northern Ireland with Ireland, as opposed to remaining in the United Kingdom. All of the other choices accurately reflect Protestantism in Northern Ireland.

16.   **(C)**

Following the bombing of a Moscow apartment building in the summer of 1999, then little-known Prime Minister Vladimir Putin took a hard-line "strike back" position against Chechen rebels, whom he blamed for the bombing. His stance proved popular with the Russian people, and when Boris Yeltsin surprisingly retired from office on New Year's Eve, 2000, Putin took over as acting President. While the economy has slowly rebounded since the ruble crash of 1998 (E), and Yeltsin did endorse a Putin presidency (B), neither (B) nor (E) satisfies this question. The question asks what "vaulted [Putin] into national prominence," which indicates his initial push to Russian national importance, and not subsequent events enhancing his stature. The Russian Prime Minister has not proven to be a powerful office (A), and although Russia has been included in an expanded G-8, this was achieved under Yeltsin, not Putin (D).

17.   **(A)**

Unlike either the British House of Lords or the French Senate, the Federation Council is popularly elected and can block, and not merely delay, legislation passed from the lower house, making (A) correct and (C) inaccurate. However, the Duma is the more powerful chamber, holding the power to grant amnesty, impeach a President, and block a President's choice of Prime Minister (B). Both the Duma and the Federation Council hold relatively low legitimacy in Russia (D) and the Federation Council represents geographical regions with two members each regardless of their overall population (E).

18.   **(C)**

(C) is the correct answer because it is untrue: Deng viewed the "Red versus Expert" argument differently than Mao, favoring intellectuals and expertise for the CCP. (A) is true, as illustrated by the "responsibility system" employed in agricultural production. Deng limited the "iron rice bowl" as China modernized its economy (B). Also, Deng's "special economic zones" (D) did remove some central economic planning from Beijing and these zones called for more foreign investment, making (E) a true statement.

19.   **(A)**

The Cultural Revolution (1966–1976) included the routing of the CCP's bureaucracy to reveal rightist elements, i.e. closet capitalists, and other enemies of Mao. "Struggle sessions" occurred, in which party members and others were humiliated in public. Also, xiafing, or the sending of officials to work in the countryside with the peasantry while essentially being jailed, was common. In this way, the Cultural Revolution resembles Stalin's Great Purge, in which real or imagined rivals for power were commonly sent to the gulags. Glasnost was a policy of increased media openness in the late Soviet Union (B). Khrushchev's denunciation of Stalin was a shift away from the systematic use of the gulags (C). The 1991 coup in the Soviet Union threatened to topple the leader himself, where the Cultural Revolution never seriously threatened Mao's own power within the CCP (D). The Bolshevik Revolution more closely resembles the Chinese civil war between the CCP and the Nationalist KMT Party than it does the Cultural Revolution (E).

20.   **(D)**

Legitimacy defines the belief of a country's people that their government (the system, not the particular politicians) has the right to rule. In other words, that the current constitution should continue as a framework of government. Civil war is generally the most grave sign of low legitimacy.

21.   **(E)**

At roughly fifty percent of the population, women comprise the greatest sector of the overall population among the choices given. Muslims comprise about 40 percent of the population (A), and are outnumbered by Christians. The Yoruba (D) equal about 1/5 of all Nigerians, while the Ibo make up around 17 percent (B). The police and military, while politically important, do not comprise a large percentage of the Nigerian population (C).

22.   **(E)**

Our Home is Russia, a party led by Prime Minister Viktor Chernomerdyn (1992–1998), was the main party supporting Boris Yeltsin. The party has since faded in importance. Luzkhov, Moscow's mayor, and Primakov, one of Yeltsin's most prominent prime ministers, joined together in 1999 to form the Fatherland-All Russia Party (E). The Liberal Democrats, under Vladimir Zhirinovski, are mainly a xenophobic, pro-Russian culture party (D). Putin is supported by, but is not a member of, the Unity Party (C). Zyagunov has led the CPRF into runner-up finishes in the first two presidential elections held in the Russian Federation (B). The Yabloko Party calls for increased market reforms and is the most enthusiastic pro-market of the major Russian parties.

23.   **(E)**

Mao's "Great Leap Forward" (1958–1960) was an ill-fated attempt to rapidly industrialize China by overcoming obstacles in expertise and natural resources via human resources and revolutionary fervor. The Special Economic Zones were anathema to Maoist theory, and occurred in the 1980s under Deng (E). The other concepts listed are correctly matched to their content.

24.   **(B)**

The global trend in the last twenty years has been the creation of many new nation-states, especially in Eastern Europe given the break up of the former communist bloc. Slovakia, Ukraine and Croatia are but three examples.

25.   **(D)**

In 1956, Khrushchev made his famous "secret speech" to the Soviet Party Congress denouncing Stalin's use of terror and his cult of personality. Although Gorbachev (C) made it clear he felt the same way with his glasnost policy, Khrushchev was the initial general secretary of the CPSU to attempt to "de-Stalinize" the Soviet system.

26.   **(E)**

The liberal democracies—economically developed countries that tend to have great global influence, such as the states of Western Europe, Japan, Canada, and the U.S.—perpetuate their power with limited clubs and organizations. There are only five permanent members of the United Nations Security Council. Each of the other groupings listed contains a larger, and less permanent, membership. The veto power of the five permanent members ensures they will thwart attempts to change, or add to, their number.

27.   **(C)**

Political elections in China are held to determine village leaders and are held within the CCP to determine the membership of its higher echelons. (This is normal for any political party from those in the U.S. to elsewhere in the world.) While elections are staged for various offices in Hong Kong, Macao, and Taiwan, including the presidency in Taiwan, the word "only makes choice (A) incorrect. (B) is obviously wrong given what you have read above. The National People's Congress is not elected from a countrywide poll, but from inside the CCP (D). And it is too widespread to claim that all offices below the paramount leader are elected (E).

28.   **(E)**

Non-governmental organizations, or NGOs, are more likely to play an active role in Russia because it a less economically developed state than Britain. The ongoing Chechen War has attracted groups like Doctors Without Borders and the International Red Cross to Russia for extended stays. Additionally, the Russian government is less able to handle the financial burden associated with the growing AIDS problem than is Britain, a wealthy liberal democracy. Thus, (A) cannot be the answer. Voter turnout, marches, writing elected officials are all more likely to take place in London than Moscow (B) and (D) and infrastructure development would certainly be higher in a liberal democracy than in a C/PC state (C).

29.   **(B)**

The mass line is a version of democratic centralism that calls upon the party to take into account the attitudes and opinions of common people as they make policy for the country. Once policy is made, lower level government officials and the people as a whole are expected to obey. (B) is the best choice. The mass line is not intended primarily to impose order on the masses (A), but to encourage their participation at the earliest and lowest levels of decision making. The mass line is not primarily a vehicle for propaganda and regulation of mass behavior (C). The mass line is not intended to be a recruiting device for Communist party members (D). Although the party has engaged in reeducation programs for high-level officials—especially during the Cultural Revolution—the mass line idea does not require political reeducation (E).

30.   **(E)**

The "responsibility system" was part of Deng's Four Modernizations program, designed to increase the Chinese agricultural output by offering peasants the incentive of personal choice and gain. Once the state quota was met, peasants could grow whatever they chose and sell the excess crops at whatever prices the market would bear. (A) describes "re-education through labor." (B) was encouraged by Gorbachev in the Soviet Union under his perestroika program. Mao's short-lived Hundred Flowers episode is described in (C). Choice (D) is simply a distracter; it looks plausible, but no such program existed under Deng Xiaoping.

31.   **(B)**

Both Mexico's Senate and Russia's Federation Council hold the power to initiate and block legislation. Both are popularly elected branches that do wield comparable, if slightly less, power than do their lower houses of the legislature. Both the Russian Duma and Mexican Chamber of Deputies are elected by a combined SMDP-PR vote (A). Mexico hosted not only the 1968 Summer Olympics, becoming the first "developing state" to do so, but also the 1970 and 1986 World Cup football [soccer] tournaments. Moscow hosted the 1980 Summer Games (C). The PRI and the CPSU dominated Mexican and Soviet politics respectively throughout most of the twentieth century via single-party rule (D). Chiapas has been in revolt since 1994 in Mexico while the Chechen rebels also began their uprising against the Kremlin's rule that same year (E).

32.   **(C)**

A strong executive will result in unitary state in practice even if a constitution calls for a federal system. As Putin accumulates more power, the policies in Russia's regions will increasingly be set by the Kremlin, for example. (A) would be the opposite of what would result. Efficacy and legitimacy could rise or drop with a strong executive, depending on the state involved and other pertinent factors (B & D). Corporatism is associated with single-party rule, and not merely in states with strong executive power. With corporatism, various components of the state, such as labor, business and farmers are given official placement within a party in exchange for their unquestioning support.

33.   **(A)**

In Russia, parties have formed and then disbanded after a certain candidate made a run at the Kremlin, successful or not. Examples have included Our Home is Russia (Yeltsin), Fatherland-All Russia (Moscow Mayor Luzkhov) and currently, Unity and Putin. In Nigeria, ethnicity and religion are key components and while parties attempt to gain support across national lines, the parties themselves have not proven long lasting according to past Nigerian history. Political parties are banned in Iran, rendering both (B) and (D) incorrect. By the same token, since China is an authoritarian single-party state, neither (C) nor (E) can be the correct choice.

34.   **(D)**

Margaret Thatcher is a figure who inspired much controversy and many myths in the years since her retirement as Britain's Prime Minister. She took on the coal miners during a notorious strike in 1984–85, but did not attempt to end labor unionism throughout Britain (A). Mainstream right-wing parties in Europe are much less socially conservative than the Republican Party in the U.S.A. The views expressed in (B) are far too conservative for the average British voter, and Thatcher did not hold them. The Tories under Thatcher cut some NHS funding, but never proposed privatizing this British institution, nor so the BBC (C). Devolution was an idea greatly opposed by Thatcher; it was a New Labour concept enacted under the government of Tony Blair (E).

35.   **(B)**

One of the fundamental traits of communist systems is the power struggles that occur whenever a leader dies or begins to weaken. Since there are no elections to determine a successor, contenders often engage in very destabilizing contests to determine who is the strongest. So, (B) is the best answer. (A) is not the answer because even though interest group activity is clearly more open and widespread in democracies than in Communist systems, there are different interests in the latter that compete for control over policy, including such groups as the army, party theoreticians, bureaucrats, technocrats, intelligence agencies, and regional representatives. (C) is not the answer because leaders tend to be drawn from elite classes in both Democratic and Communist systems. In Communist systems public opinion (D) is rarely consulted, except through the highly controlled party apparatus. (E) is not the answer because charismatic leaders are found in both systems, and so are non-charismatic leaders. If anything, more charismatic leaders are to be found in democracies because they have to appeal to voters to win elections.

36.   **(C)**

Equality of taxation and equal of opportunity has not been fully achieved in any liberal democracies as of yet. In fact, liberal democracies typically have a highly graduated system of taxation, charging a high percentage rate of taxable income the more one earns. Marx believed that the most industrialized states would contain the most exploited workers and thus would be ripe for communism. Among the flaws in Marx's theory was his inability to see that the leading industrial states would takes steps to thwart worker discontent. Among those were allowing labor unions to form and gain workers benefits (A) and the passage of laws to enhance workplace safety and security (B). The example of the Soviet repression, especially under Stalin, did little to endear a communist state to many workers in other industrial states (E) and human nature has proven more apt to reject "equality of result" than to embrace it (D). Many have asked, "Why work hard if the end result will be the same for all?"

37.   **(B)**

By allying with Party C, Party A ensures a 54 percent control of Parliament, while both minimizing the number of parties in its coalition and the size of the party in coalition with it. (B) is correct. (A) is not the answer because Party B is the main competitor and very large in size; Party A would have to make too many concessions in order to rule. (C) is not correct, because Party D would only give Party A 50 percent of the seats, which is not a majority and not enough to control the Parliament. (D) is not the answer, because although Party A could choose to ally with Parties D and E and get 53 percent control, building and maintaining coalitions between three parties is more difficult than with two parties, and also because this results in fewer seats than a coalition with party C. (E) is incorrect because although this coalition would give Party A a 57 percent majority, it involves the unnecessary inclusion of Party E; with Party C alone, Party A can rule the government with a 54 percent majority, and Party E's participation becomes superfluous.

38.   **(B)**

As described earlier, a parliamentary system calls for a fusion of executive and legislative powers, and each member of parliament, including the Prime Minister, is an elected member of the legislature. Tony Blair represents the district of Sedgefield in northern England, for instance. None of the other choices pose an accurate cause-effect relationship.

39.   **(E)**

Many developing states are gross food exporters. The "green revolution" of the 1970s (consisting of the proliferation of pesticides, irrigation, aid, and increased mechanization) helps explain this occurrence. The other choices each accurately describe the relationship between developed and developing states.

40.   **(E)**

The Russian Duma is elected by a "half and half" system. Of the Duma's 450 members, 225 are selected by single-member district plurality (SMDP) and the other 225 by proportional representation (PR). Of the remaining choices, (A) probably looks best, but it is describing the French two-ballot system used for the National Assembly. Russia employs a two-ballot system for its presidency, but not for the Duma.

41.   **(A)**

Gaunxi describes the connections and/or corruption used to do business in contemporary China (to obtain licenses, government contracts, etc.). Choices (B), (C), and (D) each accurately describe a policy that would enhance, not decrease, the legitimacy of the CCP. Choice (E) is the best wrong answer, as the controversial project has displaced many Chinese and run into cost overruns. However, the project has yet to be completed and may ultimately bolster the CCP's legitimacy. Gaunxi has become such a stigma for the CCP that Jiang Zemin ordered the execution of a high-placed CCP official in 2002 for corruption.

42.   **(C)**

New Labour, under Tony Blair, has offered several reforms to the British constitutional structure, including devolution (or devolved power) for Scotland, Wales, Northern Ireland, and London (D). Blair has led a more moderated Labour Party under the "New" prefix; Article Four of the party charter was removed, for instance. It had reiterated the party's role in pursuing a socialist economy for Britain (A). Blair's government has been criticized for excessive spin (B), including the perception that Blair desires Britain's ultimate acceptance of the single European currency (E). Although New Labour indicated in its 1997 manifesto that it would alter Britain's "first past the post" SMDP election system for the House of Commons, it has never put the subsequent Jenkins Report into effect. The Jenkins Report outlined a way to combine an SMDP system with a PR aspect. Since the SMDP system has netted New Labour large parliamentary majorities in both 1997 and 2001, the party leadership is understandably less enthusiastic about electoral reform. The House of Lords has been altered not by electoral reform, but rather by the removal of hereditary peers (a hereditary aristocracy, passing seats down through generations) from the chamber.

43.   **(B)**

The British government is a parliamentary system, whereas the Russian Federation's government is a presidential system with a dual executive. In short, the Prime Minister of Britain is a much more important figure than that of Russia and choices (A), (C), (D), and (E) accurately reflect this reality. (B) is not true—and thus is the correct answer—because the Duma has agreed to a President's appointment of a Prime Minister. If the Duma rejects the same candidate three times, it is dissolved for elections itself.

44.   **(B)**

Mao Zedong believed in permanent revolution for the CCP. Toward this end, he created programs such as the Hundred Flowers movement and the Cultural Revolution, whereby the masses could criticize party officials, such as cadre. Such criticism, and subsequent "rehabilitation," could keep the party responsive to the people, Mao believed. The other choices do not accurately reflect Mao Zedong's ideology.

45.   **(B)**

Mikhail Gorbachev's reforms were designed to strengthen the Communist Party and the Soviet Union. In reality, his reforms led to the death of the Soviet system. (A) Glasnost was supposed to be limited openness of the Soviet media to criticize Stalin and Brezhnev, but not Gorbachev or the CPSU. Of course, widespread criticism of Gorbachev's policies did occur, including street protests by 1990. (B) Gorbachev willingly let the Iron Curtain of eastern European communist satellites go, thus saving the Soviet Union the cost of subsidizing these states. (C) Perestroika was designed to create a more competitive Soviet economy capable of producing consumer goods. Workers, managers, and consumers disliked it for several reasons, mainly because it did improve the Soviet economy. (D) Gorbachev's demokratatziia ("democratization") program was envisioned to allow for competitive, non-rigged elections between CPSU candidates. The Soviet people quickly demanded actual elections that included non-communist candidates, explaining Boris Yeltsin's rise to power in 1991, as he was elected President of the Russian Soviet Republic. (E) As member states such as Ukraine, Lithuania, Latvia, Georgia, etc., declared independence, Gorbachev signed the dissolution of the Soviet Union on December 25, 1991, officially ending the existence of the country that he had sought to improve.

46.   **(D)**

Legitimacy defines the belief of a country's people that their government (the system, not the particular politicians) has the right to rule. Legitimacy predisposes people to cooperate with their existing government and not to seek a different framework (i.e., a new constitution) of government. Legitimacy is high in such states as Britain, Canada, China, and the U.S.A. It is low, for example, in France and Russia. Britain has legitimacy, but protest marches in London against war policies or threats to ban fox hunting have occurred in recent years (A). Governments with very low legitimacy, such as Nigeria, are still accorded diplomatic recognition (B). Legitimacy does force the electorate to support a specific party's agenda; parties can change in a legitimate system, while the constitution remains in place (C). François Mitterrand served as the President of France for fourteen years, from 1981-1995. The French government typically has low legitimacy; this is but one example proving (E) false.

47.   **(C)**

Russia's ineptly named Liberal Democratic Party is a xenophobic party led by the flamboyant and unpredictable Vladimir Zhirinovski. Although the British National party lacks a single charismatic leader or the electoral support held by the Liberal Democrats, it holds xenophobic, extreme right views. The British Liberal Democrats are much more aptly named (A) as a left-leaning social welfare party, as is the PRD in Mexico (D). The Scottish National Party is not xenophobic and pushes mildly for a Scottish state (B). Yabloko is a much more market-oriented reform party than are the Liberal Democrats (E).

48.   **(B)**

Village elections are held for a position similar to township spokesperson (A). Small-group discussion has been a hallmark of the system since Mao's days and ideally was instituted to both reflect and shape CCP policies (C). The Communist Youth League is a mechanism for recruitment to the party (D), and mass campaigns (such as Deng's Four Modernizations or Jiang's Three Represents policy) are attempts to keep party legitimacy. Inter-party competition does not occur (B), as the CCP does not allow other parties to legally exist within China.

49.   **(A)**

As a nation develops politically and economically, the avenues to influencing power tend to formalize. For example, in Britain the Trades Union Congress is an umbrella group representing the views of labor to the government. The other choices given are typically the opposite of what occurs as a state experiences political development and modernization.

50.   **(D)**

Regionalism in China occurs mainly in the west, with Muslims in Xinjiang and Buddhists in Tibet. British regionalism is much greater, with nationalist parties existing in Scotland, Wales, and Northern Ireland. In addition, England is split; the south, including London and its environs, is generally considered wealthier and less industrial than areas north (Liverpool, Manchester, Hull, etc.). (A) The British parliament, although very raucous and coarse at times—especially when the television cameras are rolling for Prime Minister's Questions—does have a veneer of civility with comments not directed at members of the body, but rather the speaker, and with respectful phrasing, such as "My right honorable friend" used as a prefix to responses. (B) Indeed, before the authoritarian reign of the Communist Party, Russia had been led for centuries by czars who viewed themselves as embued with a "divine right" to rule. Before Gorbachev, Russia had experienced no widespread culture of democracy. Algerian extremists bombed Paris in 1995 protesting France's recognition of a more secular government that had apparently been defeated at the polls in 1992. Britain is plagued by its Protestant/Catholic split and Chechnya is an Islamic region desiring independence from the Orthodox Christian Russian Federation (C). The states of western Europe are generally more liberal on social issues than is the United States. Even members of the British Conservative Party or the French UDF, mainstream rightist parties, would not favor these measures, which would be seen as radical (E).

51.   **(C)**

Given Britain's parliamentary model, its SMDP voting system, and its strong party discipline through mechanisms like safe seats, collective responsibility, and cabinet reshuffles, if a government cannot secure a favorable vote on normal legislation—i.e., anything but a "free vote" (B), in which party discipline is not enforced on a bill that involves a moral issue or a "matter of conscience"—then the notion exists that it is no longer "the government." In such a case, a vote of confidence is held on a bill, and, providing the government could secure a majority, general elections would be called. The British constitution demands that general elections be called within five years of a government coming to power (A). Similarly, Prime Minister's Questions is mandated under the British constitution, where the government is held accountable for its policies and performance thirty minutes each week that Parliament is in session (D). The House of Lords can delay, but not defeat, legislation from the House of Parliament. When this occurs, the government does not resign (E).

52.   **(A)**

In Mexico, the President is limited to a single six-year term, called the *sexenio*. Also, members of other offices, such as the Chamber of Deputies and Senate, are prohibited from hold the same office in succession. Although the Council of Guardians in Iran may void candidates from running, the question asks about succession of office. The President in Iran may hold office for two four-year terms, for example (B). Nigeria's President has the same limit, while members of congress may repeat as often as they are elected (C). The CCP manages its offices largely as it sees fit and has promoted more rotation of senior positions in recent years (D). In Britain, members of the House of Commons and indeed, the Prime Minister, may be returned to power indefinitely depending upon the voters' preferences (E).

53.   **(A)**

The quotation suggests that Wilson believed that people are motivated by quality of life and family connections as opposed to revolutionary movements or the working class struggle. He does not deny that a working class exists in Britain (D) or that his government should roll back the social welfare state that had become entrenched in Britain (E). The statement is a critique against Marxism, and does not imply that socialism is too moderate an economic policy for the United Kingdom (B). The quote doesn't relate to the Cold War (C).

54.   **(A)**

Non-Governmental Organizations (NGOs), such as Greenpeace, Doctors Without Borders, the International Red Cross, or Amnesty International, tend to come from wealthy liberal democracies but to focus their work in needy areas of the developing world, such as Africa, Asia, and Latin America (E). (B) is incorrect. NGOs are formal interest groups that raise their own funds and follow their own agenda (generally humanitarian in nature and not-for-profit) (D). NGOs are certainly not above national law in the areas where they operate (C).

55.   **(D)**

Internet service providers would not be "nationalized"—operated as monopolies by a state's government. The other items listed involving transportation (A and E), communications (B), or petroleum (C), all have commonly been nationalized under governments with socialist economies.

SECTION II

Example of ID Essays That Would Achieve a Top Score

1.   A nation and a state are synonymous. A state (country) is a political entity having the following four characteristics: population, territory, government, and sovereignty. A nation on the other hand is a cultural entity—a single group united by a common culture, including a common language, often a common religion, sporting interests, fashion, food and so on. A stateless-nation would define a nation seeking, but not yet getting, an independent state to reflect their nationality. Examples of stateless-nations would include the Kurds in Iraq and Turkey, the Chechens within Russia and the Roma ("Gypsies") across Europe.

2.   Free trade refers to the reduction, and ultimate elimination, of trade barriers between countries. Ending tariffs is a key aspect of free trade. Tariffs, or taxes on imported goods, are a protectionist measure that countries have employed to protect domestic industries and jobs. Advocates of free trade believe that the removal of such barriers will promote a higher standard of living globally given a more level "playing field" in regard to international trade. The World Trade Organization (WTO) exists to promote free trade among its member states. Regional blocs, such as the European Union and NAFTA, also encourage tariff-free trading among the members within the group.

3.   Patron-client relationships involve an exchange of sorts. A political entity—the "patron"—such as a party, government agency or politician, offers perks such as jobs, a government contract or infrastructure improvements in return for the support (votes) of the lower-status group—the "client"—seeking advancement. Illustrations of this practice have included corporatism in Mexico under the PRI and "chop politics" favoring one ethnicity or another in Nigeria.

4.   Command economies are associated with "state socialism," more commonly referred to as the communist states such as the former Soviet Union. Central government planning was the key tenet of the command economy. In the Soviet system, Gosplan was the agency that determined production levels on products from toothbrushes to steel tonnage. This economic system was widely inefficient, producing chronic shortages and surpluses on various items. Market economies, synonymous with capitalism, are driven by supply and demand rather than by central planning. Privately owned business and competition are hallmarks of the command economy. When Boris Yeltsin spoke of "shock therapy" in the early 1990s, he was suggesting that Russia make the transition from a command economy to a market economy immediately, absorb the "pain" get to more quickly reap the "gain." Obviously, such a traumatic economic change would be neither quick nor easy.

5.   A cartel can be defined as a group attempting to coordinate and limit production of a single commodity. It's an attempt to maximize profits on that commodity by keeping supply lower than it would be otherwise. A cartel may exist on any commodity, legal or otherwise, from coffee to sugar to cocaine. Perhaps the best-known cartel globally at present is OPEC, the Organization of Petroleum Exporting Countries. Contrary to the views held by many Americans, OPEC does not hold anything near a monopoly on the global oil market. However, the 11 OPEC member states do produce 40 percent of the world's oil, certainly influencing global prices. This cartel decides how much oil to produce based on such variables as current global weather trends, consumption, prices and predicted demand. Iran and Nigeria are both OPEC members, while other large producers of oil, such as Mexico and Russia, are not members.

Question 6 –Example of Essay that Would Achieve a Top Score

a.   The addition of ten new, mostly former communist Eastern bloc states to the European Union brings with it a variety of concerns for the fifteen previous member states. The older members are affluent liberal democracies from Western Europe, led by G8 members Germany, France, Britain, and Italy. The remaining members, from Ireland to Finland and Greece to Scandinavia, have prospered under the tariff-free trade zone within the EU and twelve of the fifteen states have employed the EU's monetary unit, the *euro*, as their currency.

The ten states joining the EU have been labeled as "poorer cousins" to the previous members. The per capita GDP in the new member states is about half what it is for the Western European EU states. The expansion thus threatens the existing states in several ways.

First, the EU is not only a free trade zone, but a "freedom of movement" zone for workers as well. Immigration from state to state is very easy. Thus, the expansion poses worries for say Spain, Italy, or Britain that they would be inundated with "economic migrants" from the poorer new EU member states.

Secondly, the existing EU members feared that they might be outvoted on EU policies by the new member states in European Parliament.

Also, the EU has carefully attempted to ensure that the single currency remains a strong currency via the Stability Pact. The new member states, with weaker economies and greater inflationary concerns, could seriously weaken the *euro* and thus hurt the economies of the states using it as their currency.

b.   The existing member states have enacted "transitional barriers" to prevent the free migration of citizens from the ten new ascension states. Thus, worries that London, Berlin, or Paris will be overrun by Eastern European immigrants seeking to "steal" jobs or collect social welfare benefits have been placated. These transitional barriers are expected to be in place for the next five to seven years.

The new member states must also satisfy the terms of the Stability Pact for two consecutive fiscal years before being admitted to the single currency. The Stability Pact (SP) dictates that a country's budget deficit for a single year be no greater than 3 percent of its total GDP. This is a difficult task for Germany and France (both of whom have violated the very rules they set up in the SP the past few years) let alone for the more struggling economies of Eastern Europe. In 2002 for example, Hungary, one of the most prosperous of the new entrants, had a deficit that equaled 9.5 percent of its GDP. Thus, most estimates place the wait for the new EU members to join the single currency to be roughly a decade, preserving the currency's current strength.

Given that the new member states also will have less weight in voting in the EU parliament than their more established Western European neighbors, it is easy to see why the new members are thought of as "poorer cousins." However, the EU remains a popular prospect: Bulgaria and Romania are set to join next, with Croatia and Turkey waiting in the wings.

Question 7–Example of Essay That Would Achieve a Top Score

The Chinese Communist Party continues to adapt and evolve as China modernizes and the party attempts to maintain sole political control of the country. Part of this evolution occurred at the 16th Party Congress in Beijing in 2002, where an historic transition occurred. In most communist or authoritarian states, leadership changes have traditionally occurred only through the death of the leader, whether he be Mao, Stalin, Tito, or Pol Pot. The CCP leadership of President Jiang Zemin and premier Zhu Rongji announced, however, that they were to exit their positions in favor of a "fourth generation" of younger leaders.

Ultimately, the party announced that Hu Jintao and Wen Jaibao would assume the roles of party leader and premier, respectively. In fact, Wen has taken the reigns of the Chinese economy from Zhu. However, it remains to be seen whether Jiang Zemin has actually been superseded as paramount leader by Hu. One hint that perhaps Jiang will continue leading the CCP is that he has retained the title of "chairman of the military commission." The People's Liberation Army has always played an integral role within the CCP power structure and Jiang's position within this group may ensure that he remains the genuine head of the party. Also, as many as six of the nine members of the Politburo's Standing Committee—the body through which actual CCP policies are formulated—are loyal supporters of Jiang. It seems his power will linger strongly.

Jiang Zemin has stated that the idea of a transition to a "fourth generation" of CCP leadership occurred to him after meeting with comparatively youthful heads of state, such as Tony Blair, Vladimir Putin, and George W. Bush. He felt China needed a younger leader as well (Jiang is 76 and Hu is 59). So, one aspect of the leadership change of 2002 may be that China heads toward a tradition of younger leaders.

Furthermore, this leadership transition may herald a two-term limit on China's top leadership. Both Jiang and Zhu had held their party posts through two five-year terms. Hu Jintao has claimed that this form of transition shows the maturity of the CCP and will allow it to "groom reliable successors" for the future. That remains to be seen.

Question 8–Example of Essay That Would Achieve a Top Score

(NOTE: Although the essay only called for two countries to be examined, this sample response will cover all three for review purposes.)

a.   Iran is a semi-democratic system. However, that label fits Nigeria slightly less well (but arguably still) and no longer fits Mexico at all.

In Iran, the mullahs, or Islamic clerics, along with the Faqih, a supreme Islamic leader, holds veto power over the elected President and the Majlis, or parliament. Mahammed Khatami, a reform-minded President, was consistently thwarted by the conservative clerics and the supreme leader. In fact, many reform candidates were barred from running in the 2004 Majlis elections by the conservative clerics.

Nigeria has alternated between civilian and military regimes since its independence in 1960. The current civilian government, the Fourth Republic, was instituted in 1999. Opponents of President Obasanjo and his Peoples Democratic Party (PDP) have claimed that widespread ballot fraud occurred in the 2003 elections for both the President and the federal congress. If true, these allegations indicate Nigeria is a semi-democracy. It certainly is a fledgling democracy and one of the interesting characteristics it holds currently is that key political players must be "okayed" by the military elite. Hence, both Obasanjo and his rival in the 2003 Buhari, were themselves not only former generals but also former military rulers. If acceptable candidates must have direct ties to the military elite, than this too makes the label of "semi-democratic" applicable for Africa's most populous state.

Mexico was accurately described as semi-democratic during the lengthy heyday of the PRI. However, the one-party PRI domination was chipped away in the 1980s and 1990s and then done in for good with the victory of the PAN's Vicente Fox for the presidency in 2000. The creation of IFE as an independent and powerful monitor of elections has spurred both legitimacy and multi-party pluralism in Mexico. IFE has issued ID cards to voters, replete with photos and fingerprints to ensure electoral accuracy. It also monitors campaign practices, such as spending, to keep the three main parties, the PAN, PRI, and PRD, on an even playing field.

b.   In Iran, the reformers, such as President Khatami and moderates in the Majlis, are pushing for greater democratic reforms, but to little avail. The vast young of Iran tend to push for greater democarcy and other individual freedoms, but many have become cynical and have disassociated themselves with the political system.

In Nigeria, most civilians support the democratic movement. However, the various ethnicities such as the Ibo, Yoruba and Hausa-Fulani distrust and fight one another for scarce political spoils. These inter-ethnic battles do little to further Nigeria's democratic reforms and threaten the chaos that has brought about military rule in the past. The media is rather outspoken in Lagos especially and it is a voice that consistently pushes for democratic reform.

In Mexico, the PRI itself pushed for greater democratic reform under President Ernesto Zedillo from 1994–2000. With the introduction of IFE and the ending of the *dedazo*, the hand-picking of a successor candidate by the incumbent President, the Mexican system has greatly opened up. Additionally, Mexico's expanding economy under NAFTA has led to a larger middle class and more demands for political pluralism. The Mexican media has also become much less controlled by the PRI and truly an independent voice promoting political reform. Other problems, such as escalating drug violence, encouraged voters to look for alternatives outside the PRI.

c.   The Islamic clerics, or Mullahs, lead the conservative forces attempting to block reform in Iran. They fear that reform will erode their own power and perhaps challenge the primacy of fundamentalist Islam in Iranian culture. This group was able to ban many reformers from running for election in 2004, so that the conservative clerics now readily control the Majlis and the levels above the presidency, such as the Faqih (Supreme Leader) and the Council of Guardians. Thus Iran remains a theocracy, ruled by clerics, rather than a full fledged democacry, ruled by secular politicians.

President Obasanjo has claimed that politicians and ethnicities lack the ability to admit when they lose an election and to instead claim fraud and threaten strikes if re-elections are not called. So the inter-ethnic jealousy hinders Nigeria's democratic reforms and often leads to violence around election times. Additionally, the military looms as a shadown over democratic reform. It seems that if the candidates do not have ties to the military, they are not "okayed" for national office, or at least for the presidency.

They fought a losing battle, but the "dinosaurs," or *los dinos*, within the PRI were the old guard who attempted to block the reforms proposed by Zedillo. They wanted the PRI to continue with "business as usual," but failed to realize that too much had changed in Mexico for election-time bribes and strategic vote rigging to any longer carry the day.

PRACTICE TEST 5
AP Comparative
Government & Politics

AP COMPARATIVE GOVERNMENT & POLITICS

PRACTICE TEST 5

SECTION I

TIME: 45 Minutes
55 Multiple-Choice Questions
50% of Total Grade

(Answer sheets appear in the back of this book.)

DIRECTIONS: Read the following questions and incomplete sentences. Each is followed by five answer choices. Choose the one answer choice that either answers the question or completes the sentence. Make sure to use the ovals numbered 1 through 55 when marking your answer sheet.

1. Britain's "New Labour" government, which swept into power in 1997, has contemplated or instituted all of the following constitutional changes EXCEPT

    (A) limiting the role and number of hereditary peers in the House of Lords

    (B) increasing regional autonomy for Wales, Scotland, London, and Northern Ireland

    (C) increasing the use of the referendum as a tool toward further European integration

    (D) a reduced political role for the monarchy and its institutions

    (E) introducing proportional representation into the British political debate via the Jenkins Report

2. Which of the following groups are NOT examples of "stateless nations"?

    (A) Kurds   (D) The Dutch, Danish, and Poles

    (B) The Yoruba, Ibo, and   (E) Chechens
        Hausa-Fulani

    (C) The Roma

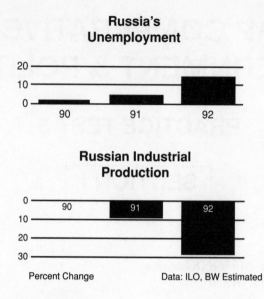

Russia's Unemployment

Russian Industrial Production

Percent Change   Data: ILO, BW Estimated

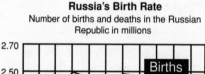

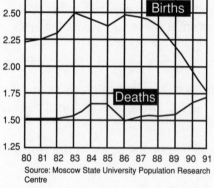

Russia's Birth Rate
Number of births and deaths in the Russian Republic in millions

Births

Deaths

Source: Moscow State University Population Research Centre

How it Adds Up

It isn't clear yet where all the money will come from, but Washington and its G-7 allies have finally promised to help Russia.

	G-7 Plan	US state
Bilateral aid*	$11.0	$2.8
I.M.F. and World Bank Loans	S4.6	$0.2
Debt rescheduling	$2.5	$0.0
Public stabilization	$6.0	$1.5
TOTAL	$24.0	$6.0

*EXCLUDES GENERAL AID, COMMODITY CREDITS, HUMANITARIAN AID, SOURCE: OMD

Source: Newsweek, April 10, 1992

3. Based on the charts above, which of the following influenced the G8 action?

(A) Unqualified support toward Mikhail Gorbachev's reforms, including *perestroika* and *glasnost*.

(B) A self-interested desire to see a capitalist, democratic, and non-threatening Russia succeed.

(C) Yeltsin's "shock therapy" program.

(D) The sudden and unexpected crash of the ruble.

(E) The IMF and World Bank pressured these states to take action.

4.   Of the following, the greatest indicator of political legitimacy would be

    (A)   a state's ability to put down civil unrest

    (B)   an informed, educated electorate

    (C)   frequent changeover of political control

    (D)   direct democracy

    (E)   electoral results that are accepted by the public as accurate and meaningful

5.   Iran and Nigeria are similar in all of the following ways EXCEPT

    (A)   OPEC membership and oil-dependent economies

    (B)   the use of *shari'a* law

    (C)   culturally, football [soccer] holds a very strong popular sway in each state

    (D)   a constitution strongly influenced by U.S. political institutions

    (E)   both are considered "developing states"

6.   Which of the following is LEAST characteristic of liberal democracies?

    (A)   A politically influential military elite

    (B)   A stated respect for human rights and equality

    (C)   Driving leadership in globally influential organizations

    (D)   Per capita GNP rates among the highest in the world

    (E)   Social welfare is considered part of the government's accepted responsibility

7.   Political parties in the Russian Federation tend to be

    (A)   personality-based and short-lived

    (B)   coalition-centered

    (C)   in control of the Kremlin

    (D)   flexible in their policies

    (E)   ideologically consistent and long lasting

8. The current Mexican government most fears China in regard to its

   (A) massive military power

   (B) human rights abuses

   (C) potential to take *maquiladora* jobs from Mexico

   (D) growing population

   (E) massive overuse of available resources such as coal and oil

9. All of the following were key tenets of the "Stalinist state" EXCEPT:

   (A) Political dissidence was suppressed by *gulags* and continuous purges.

   (B) Stalin was deified as an all-knowing, all-seeing leader.

   (C) Widespread CPSU membership was extended into the outlying republics to ensure their loyalty to the Kremlin

   (D) The *kulaks* were eliminated as a social class.

   (E) A class of elitist *apparatchiks* evolved.

Jin Meisheng, 1964
The seeds have been well selected, the harvest is more bountiful every year
Publisher: Shanghai People's Fine Arts Publishing House

10. The Chinese Communist Party poster shown on the previous page could be promoting which of the following programs CCP campaigns?

    (A) Three Represents and Strike Hard

    (B) Cultural Revolution and Hundred Flowers

    (C) Poisonous Weed and *guanxi* eradication

    (D) One Child Policy and Four Modernizations

    (E) Responsibility System and Great Leap Forward

11. Under Mikhail Gorbachev's policy of *glasnost*, which of the following was NOT intended by the CPSU leadership?

    (A) Soviet citizens would now have a voice with which to demonstrate dissatisfactions over economic and political issues.

    (B) Policies of Khrushchev could be examined and praised.

    (C) The practices of Josef Stalin and Leonid Brezhnev could be criticized.

    (D) Accurate and timely international reporting by *Pravda* was to be encouraged.

    (E) Political prisoners and dissidents were to be released from asylums and sanitariums.

12. The use of referendum by a government most likely signifies a high level of

    (A) efficacy   (D) regime stability

    (B) legitimacy   (E) lobbyist influence

    (C) political integration

13. Which regional political cleavages does/did NOT represent a desire for an independent state?

    (A) Chiapas and Ulster   (D) Tibetan Buddhists

    (B) Chechnya   (E) the SNP and Plaid Cymru

    (C) Biafra

14. The fact that in recent years China has been awarded the right to host elite international sporting events, such as the Summer Olympic Games and Formula One racing, can best be explained by the fact that

    (A) China has shown greater respect and tolerance toward Taiwan

    (B) the Chinese record on human rights issues has drastically changed

    (C) China was admitted to the World Trade Organization

    (D) the Chinese economy and infrastructure continue to significantly improve

    (E) a new, younger generation of leadership assumed power in 2002

15. The main desire of the Eastern European states that joined the European Union [EU] in 2004 was to gain

    (A) immediate acceptance of the euro as a common, stable currency

    (B) access to the common, tariff-free market of Western Europe

    (C) proportional influence in the European Parliament

    (D) influence to offset growing Russian economic power in Eastern Europe

    (E) greater agricultural subsidies

16. Consider that in "Country A" as efficacy increases, legitimacy decreases. This illustrates which of the following?

    (A) Dependency theory   (D) An inverse relationship

    (B) Regime stability   (E) A social cleavage

    (C) Political integration

Question 17 refers to the passage below.

"The districts are larger, and each district elects several representatives. Each party presents a list of candidates for these legislative seats....When the votes are counted, Party A with 25 percent of the vote would get 25 percent of the seats from that district."

17. The system described above commonly leads to

(A) a strict two-party system   (D) electoral fraud

(B) economic difficulty   (E) low voter turnout

(C) a coalition government

18. In which state is a common and strategic path to political power NOT correctly described?

   (A) The Russian Federation—gain *nomenklatura* access; climb the CPRF ladder.

   (B) Britain—"public school" to Ox-Bridge.

   (C) Mexico—Creole; UNAM to Ivy League economics degree to *camarilla* leadership.

   (D) Iran—Shi'a cleric; mullah; ayatollah.

   (E) Nigeria—Hausa or Fulani; northerner; probably Muslim; definitely have ties to military.

19. Which of the following statements is NOT true of the House of Lords?

   (A) It has the power to delay money bills for several weeks.

   (B) Politically, it holds more prestige and status than does the House of Commons.

   (C) As a dignified institution of government, it may not initiate legislation on its own accord but instead is merely a consultative body to the House of Commons.

   (D) It has traditionally been Britain's final court of appeal, but that role may be usurped by the European Court of Justice [ECJ].

   (E) It is an unelected chamber, mainly comprised now of Life Peers with some residual influence from both the Anglican Church and the aristocracy.

20. To be considered a party of the "extreme right" a Western European party must

   (A) promote privatization at the expense of nationalized industries

   (B) espouse policies such as capital punishment, minority deportations, and withdrawal from the European Union

   (C) protect the national culture [religion, food, sport, music, etc.] and economy

   (D) oppose any further integration into the EU

    (E)   support strict limits on foreign immigration to keep domestic unemployment at a minimum

21.   Which of the following does the Peoples Republic of China NOT have in common with Great Britain and the Russian Federation?

    (A)   Permanent membership in the United Nations Security Council

    (B)   A growing service economy

    (C)   The increasing privatization of former state-owned industries

    (D)   An openness to foreign investment

    (E)   A unitary form of government

22.   Why are human rights abuses an issue of concern for an authoritarian government, whether that government is clerics in Iran, a military ruler in Nigeria, or the Communist Party in China?

    I.   A poor human rights record can lead to international trade sanctions.

    II.   All states and nations hold a common definition of what "human rights" entail.

    III.   International courts, such as the Hague tribunal, hold power to prosecute war criminals.

    IV.   Authoritarian governments also desire legitimacy to precipitate policy successes.

    (A)   I and IV only   (D)   II and III only

    (B)   I and II only   (E)   III only

    (C)   I, II, and III only

23.   Which action by Margaret Thatcher united rather than divided the British populace as a whole?

    (A)   The selling of council homes to private home owners

    (B)   Her management of the British economy concerning inflation, privatization, and unemployment

    (C)   The execution of the Falkland Islands War against Argentina

    (D)   The government's prolonged "war" against the Coal Miners strike

    (E)   Her support of American nuclear sites on British soil as part of the "special relationship" with the United States and of her warm relationship with Ronald Reagan

24. Under the leadership of Vladimir Putin, which statement is true of the Russian Federation?

    (A) His popularity has skyrocketed; legitimacy and the economy have risen; constitutional federalism and separation of powers have both waned.

    (B) The freedom of the press, the economy, and Putin's popularity have all plummeted.

    (C) The execution of the Chechen War has remained constant and positive.

    (D) His popularity has skyrocketed; legitimacy and the economy have risen; constitutional federalism and separation of powers have both increased.

    (E) Pluralism has waned as the Oligarchs have increased their political control of the Kremlin.

25. Which has NOT contributed to an increased mandate of heaven under the "Fourth Generation" of CCP leadership?

    (A) An easing of the one-child policy, particularly among the peasantry

    (B) A continued economic boom in the first years of WTO membership

    (C) Steady progress with Taiwan [the Republic of China] in talks toward reunification and a further implementation of the "one country/two systems" policy

    (D) The 2008 Summer Olympics in Beijing; Formula One racing in Shanghai; and the Chinese space program

    (E) A vast increase in the amount of car ownership, especially among urban Chinese

26. All liberal democracies are characterized by

    (A) social, political, and economic equality

    (B) *laissez-faire* economics

    (C) equality of result

    (D) judicial review of legislative acts

    (E) the possibility of alternating parties in government

27. A state is distinguished from other forms of social organization in that it

    (A) has a monopoly on the legitimate use of force within society

    (B) has linguistic and cultural homogeneity

    (C) promotes debate within decision-making institutions

    (D) has a stable and democratically elected leadership

    (E) separates religion from government

28. The 419 Law, *la mordida* and *guanxi* are issues in Nigeria, Mexico and China, respectively, that all deal with

    (A) corruption   (D) foreign policy

    (B) suffrage   (E) human rights

    (C) income disparity

29. The term "corporatism" refers to a pattern of interactions between interest groups and the government in which

    (A) parties compete to gain votes from a variety of special interests

    (B) politicians gain popular support by dispensing jobs and other economic rewards to political supporters

    (C) interest groups have the opportunity to argue their cases before appropriate legislative committees

    (D) policy is formed through intertwined consultation between high levels of the bureaucracy and certain leaders of key sectors of society

    (E) private corporations contribute money to the politicians who promise to favor their causes

The green summit

Just in case you thought big, global conferences were an endangered species, look out for a huge one in Johannesburg, South Africa, in September 2002. Some 50,000 delegates will participate in the World Summit on Sustainable Development; all countries will be represented, more than half by their heads of state NGOs will also be out in force. Delegates will discuss everything from fresh water to desertification to human rights. Protocols on, among other things, "bio-safety," will be argued over and signed. The Kyoto protocol on climate change will be revived. Progress towards various targets (halting the spread of HIV/AIDS by 2015; eliminating gender disparity in education by 2005) will be reviewed. Not happy with such bread-and-butter issues, some malcontents will want to talk about globalization too. Expect to hear much about accountability, equity and justice. Activists hope that Jo'burg, coming ten years after a similar conference in Rio de Janeiro, will set the world's green agenda for the next decade. Yet the sheer breadth of topics, and the impossibility of pleasing everyone sitting around the table, may make the whole thing unmanageable. If so, expect calls to make summits like this extinct.

Cloudy outlook

Global CO_2 emissions, tonnes bn

Sources: The World Energy Outlook.
The World in 2002.

30. As illustrated in the passage above, the issue that hurts the Kyoto Protocol and other potential summits like it is/are the

    (A) demands of women for equality

    (B) poor attendance of developing states

    (C) cynicism of environmental activists

    (D) lack of political power held by "green" parties globally

    (E) clash between environmental concerns and economic gain

31. The mass line concept is supported by all of the following EXCEPT

(A) village democracy

(B) PLA harvest support programs

(C) relaxation of the one-child policy

(D) the responsibility system

(E) strict enforcement of *hukou*

32. Heading into the year 2000, which party had governed for the longest consecutive period of any party in the world?

(A) Chinese Communist Party

(B) Britain's Conservative Party

(C) The PRI in Mexico

(D) The CPSU

(E) The CPRF

33. Deng Xiaoping's policy approaches differed from those of Mao Zedong in all of the following ways EXCEPT:

(A) Deng accepted the need for concrete rewards to motivate the Chinese, rather than Mao's emphasis on ideology.

(B) Deng was willing to tolerate greater inequality than Mao in exchange for a higher degree of prosperity.

(C) Unlike Mao, Deng distrusted intellectuals and preferred the peasant culture.

(D) Unlike Mao, Deng tolerated greater decentralization of economic planning.

(E) Deng was more open to establishing and strengthening ties with foreign countries.

34. Which of the following pairs of countries have the highest degree of regime stability?

(A) China and Russia   (D) Britain and Nigeria

(B) Iran and Nigeria   (E) Mexico and Britain

(C) Mexico and China

35. NGOs (non-governmental organizations), such as Amnesty International and Habitat for Humanity, generally

    (A) rely heavily on government funding from liberal democracies

    (B) avoid volunteering their services in states with poor human rights records

    (C) approach not states, but organizations like the IMF and World Bank for funding

    (D) raise money and do their work in the developing world

    (E) raise money in the Northern Hemisphere, but apply their work in the developing world

36. Which is NOT a characteristic of a state, as the term is used in international politics?

    (A) It holds internal defensive capabilities.

    (B) It exercises sovereignty and decides when and if to cede it.

    (C) It has definite and recognized territorial boundaries.

    (D) It is politically organized by some form of written or unwritten constitution.

    (E) It has a permanent population.

37. Which of the following is NOT a common social belief among most Western Europeans?

    (A) Government-provided daycare for children is a right that working mothers should receive; quality educational care free of charge at point of service.

    (B) Gun control is only logical; it lowers murder rates and does not infringe on individual freedoms.

    (C) Capital punishment is counterproductive and nearly barbaric.

    (D) States should cede more of their sovereignty to Brussels and the EU.

    (E) Abortion is definitely a family matter and nothing to protest against.

38. Which of the following qualify as a "significant shift in economic, social, or governing strategy" given the country and time period given?

    I.   Iran in 1979

    II. Britain in 1979

    III. China in both 1949 and 1978

    IV. Mexico in 1917

    V.   Soviet Russia in both 1917 and 1991

    (A) All of the above   (D) II, IV, and V

    (B) II, III, and IV   (E) I and III only

    (C) I and V only

39. Vladimir Putin has been most similar to Boris Yeltsin in his

    (A) personality and health

    (B) relationship to both the *Duma* and to Russia's regions

    (C)   execution of the Chechen War

    (D) weakening of the oligarchs

    (E) association with former KGB and military officials within his government

40. It would be most accurate to describe Iran as a

    (A) democracy   (D) dictatorship

    (B) theocracy   (E) fascist state

    (C) absolute monarchy

41. Commonly, a head of government is more popular abroad than at home when ruling. Which leader listed below is an exception to this description?

    (A) Margaret Thatcher   (D) Mao Zedong

    (B) Olesegun Obasanjo   (E) Carlos Salinas

    (C) Mikhail Gorbachev

42. When New Labour, under the leadership of Tony Blair, spoke of a "Third Way," it was addressing a middle ground between

    (A) the social rigidity of the working class and middle class

    (B) Britain's colonial and imperial past and its high-tech future

    (C) the EU and the U.S.

    (D) the Liberal Democrats and the Conservative Party

    (E) Thatcherism and socialism

43. In which state listed have recent political election results been considered most meaningful and accurate by citizens of the state and by international observers?

    (A) Iran   (D) Nigeria

    (B) Mexico   (E) China

    (C) Russian Federation

44. Which of the following activities most approximates "direct democracy"?

    (A) Writing a letter to one's elected representative to express a constituent's views on a particular issue.

    (B) Striking workers march in the street attempting to gain government support for their demands.

    (C) Staging a referendum on a controversial bill.

    (D) Advocating revolution and the civil overthrow of the current regime.

    (E) Encouraging the government to make voter registration automatic and to hold elections at "voter friendly" times, such as over a weekend.

45. Each of the following groups has presented a challenge to the ruling Chinese Communist Party EXCEPT

    (A) the Falun Gong since 1999

    (B) Tibetan Buddhists since 1950

    (C) the Tiananmen Square student movement in 1989

(D)   village peasants since 1978

(E)   Hong Kong civil rights advocates since 1997

46.   China and the former Soviet Union are similar in all of the following ways EXCEPT

(A)   communism was a dominant political influence in both countries in the twentieth century

(B)   both countries experienced violent revolutions in order to install communist governments

(C)   leaders in both countries resorted to "cult of personality" tactics in order to consolidate national power

(D)   workers have dominated the Communist Party in both countries

(E)   the pre-revolutionary economies of both countries were largely agricultural and non-industrial in character

47.   Although Mexico is more economically developed and politically stable than Nigeria, one advantage Nigeria holds over Mexico is greater

(A)   national homogeneity and social cohesion

(B)   regime stability and legitimacy

(C)   infrastructure development and educational development

(D)   control and punishment of corruption

(E)   total amount of arable land and resource base

48.   Which of the following distinguishes democratic regimes from authoritarian regimes?

(A)   democratic regimes stage elections

(B)   in democratic regimes, leaders can be voted out of office

(C)   in democratic regimes, private citizens control the means of production

(D)   in democratic regimes, schools and the mass media are unimportant as agents of political socialization

(E)   democratic regimes lack an ideology to legitimate the exercise of political power

49. A greater challenge to liberal democracies than to C/PC states, NICs, or LDCs is

    (A) controlling health care costs as populations "gray"

    (B) enforcing the rule of law

    (C) funding the military

    (D) internal security

    (E) management of available resources

50. A "free vote" within the British House of Commons occurs if and when

    (A) the Government agrees to stand for election if the vote fails

    (B) a matter of conscience issue ensures that no party discipline will be enforced

    (C) a cabinet is "reshuffled" based on collective responsibility

    (D) a referendum issue has been defeated by the British electorate

    (E) backbenchers revolt against a position held by the Government

Question 51 refers to the cartoon below.

" Apparently it can be fatal for really old people like them."

By Kes. Reprinted by permission.

51. The CCP leadership handled the crisis referenced in the cartoon on the previous page by

    (A) labeling the Rolling Stones as a "poisonous weed"

    (B) issuing nationwide curfews

    (C) allowing free and accurate media coverage

    (D) firing the Minister of Health and Mayor of Beijing

    (E) initially granting the World Health Organization complete access to patients and records

52. All of the following are included in the European Charter of Fundamental Rights, proposed in the EU Constitution, EXCEPT

    (A) No member state has the right to use capital punishment for any reason.

    (B) Child labor is prohibited.

    (C) Labor unions have the right to organize, exist, and strike if necessary.

    (D) Gender equity must be ensured in all areas, including work, employment, and pay.

    (E) All member states must permit marriage between consenting adults, including homosexuals.

53. Great Britain may be more accurately described as the "Disunited Kingdom" given all of the following factors EXCEPT

    (A) its four separate World Cup football sides

    (B) its devolved government under the New Labour

    (C) the general public view of the monarchy and Queen Elizabeth II

    (D) northern resentment of London's wealth and power

    (E) Sinn Fein, the SNP, and Plaid Cymru

54. Marx would have likely considered Russia and China as

    (A) model staging grounds for a communist revolution because of their centuries of feudal repression

    (B) too industrialized for a successful communist revolution

    (C) too backward and agricultural for a successful communist revolution

    (D) ideal capitalist states

    (E) geographically too large to organize under Marxist rule

55. The current party system has proven to be most stable in which of the following countries?

    (A) Mexico

    (B) Britain

    (C) Iran

    (D) China

    (E) Russia

STOP
This is the end of Section I.
If time still remains, you may check your work only in this section.
Do not begin Section II until instructed to do so.

SECTION II

TIME: **100 Minutes**
8 Free-Response Questions
50% of Total Grade

DIRECTIONS: Write an essay based on each of the following eight questions. Where appropriate, use substantive examples in your answers. Your essays should be numbered to correspond with the questions to which you are responding. (See the directions for ID questions that follow.)

Students will provide brief definitions or descriptions of five concepts or terms, noting their significance. Students may be asked to provide an example of the concept in one or more of the countries studied, or to contrast concepts.

1. Define "privatization" and discuss one political consequence involved.

2. Explain and illustrate what "NGOs" are.

3. Discuss the concept of the "unitary state" and how this applies to China.

4. Discuss "personalism" and identify its tradition importance to the Mexican political system.

5. Explain what a referendum is.

6. Internal conflict management is often a challenge faced by a government.

    a. Describe an ongoing internal conflict in the United Kingdom and the Russian Federation.

    b. What response has each government proposed to control the conflict described?

    c. How successful has the response described in (b) been in resolving the conflict?

7. Political reform is a common reality for many developing states. Describe political reform in Mexico, Nigeria, and Iran since 1990.

    a. Describe an attempted political reform in Mexico and one consequence that has resulted.

    b. Describe an attempted political reform in Nigeria and one consequence that has resulted.

    c. Describe an attempted political reform in Iran and one consequence that has resulted.

8. Intra-party dissension can be politically damaging to a political party.

    a. Describe an intra-party split in a political party from among the core state countries that has occurred since 1980.

    b. Choose a party in another case study country and describe an intra-party split that has occurred since 1980.

    c. Explain one political consequence for the party dissension described in both (a) and (b).

    d. How have the parties examined in your essay attempted to solve their intra-party dissension?

END OF EXAMINATION

COMPARATIVE GOVERNMENT & POLITICS

PRACTICE TEST 5

ANSWER KEY

1. (B)	15. (B)	29. (D)	43. (B)
2. (D)	16. (D)	30. (E)	44. (C)
3. (B)	17. (C)	31. (E)	45. (D)
4. (E)	18. (A)	32. (C)	46. (D)
5. (D)	19. (C)	33. (C)	47. (E)
6. (A)	20. (B)	34. (E)	48. (B)
7. (A)	21. (E)	35. (E)	49. (A)
8. (C)	22. (A)	36. (A)	50. (B)
9. (C)	23. (C)	37. (D)	51. (D)
10. (E)	24. (A)	38. (A)	52. (E)
11. (A)	25. (C)	39. (C)	53. (C)
12. (A)	26. (E)	40. (B)	54. (C)
13. (A)	27. (A)	41. (D)	55. (B)
14. (D)	28. (A)	42. (E)	

DETAILED EXPLANATIONS
OF ANSWERS

TEST 5

SECTION I

1. (B)

A moderate left-center government, "New Labour" hasn't broached a reduced role for the monarch. Queen Elizabeth II remains quite popular with the British public as a whole, so Tony Blair would avoid needlessly "taking her on" in the public eye. Besides, as we have seen, the dignified institutions promote pride and stability and wield little actual political power as it is. New Labour has virtually eliminated Hereditary Peerages (A) and created devolved governments for several national areas within the UK (B). It has offered or used referenda on issues ranging from devolution to adoption of the euro as Britain's currency (C). The Jenkins Report indeed offered a hybrid electoral system for the House of Commons, which would have married the "first-past-the-post" SMDP format with some proportional representation (E).

2. (D)

Remember that a nation is *not* synonymous with a country, but a state is. The Dutch, Danish, and Poles are nations residing in the states of the Netherlands, Denmark, and Poland, respectively. The other nations listed are stateless. Kurds are found mainly in Turkey and Iraq (A). Yoruba, Ibo, and Hausa-Fulani are rival ethnic groups in Nigeria (B). The Roma, commonly called Gypsies, are dispersed across the globe, but mainly in Eastern Europe (C). Chechens are fighting Russia for their own Islamic state (E).

3. (B)

The economic heavyweights of the G8 had self-interest in seeing post-Soviet Russia succeed economically and politically. Russia could become a large market for these countries and also a military ally rather than a costly and worrisome foe. (A) is a pretty good wrong answer, but the "unqualified" aspect is too strong and the answer implies idealist motives as the G7's only reason for its loans. (C) Yeltsin's "shock therapy" program, which led to hyper-inflation, had not yet occurred. The ruble did not crash until late in Yeltsin's second term and well after this graph was made, so the crash was neither sudden nor unexpected (D). Since the G7 states are among the leading forces in both the IMF and World Bank, it obviously could not pressure itself to take any actions (E).

4.   **(E)**

Electoral results that are accepted by the public as accurate and meaningful indicate that the government has the right to rule in the eyes of its citizens. The need to put down civil unrest in itself would indicate low legitimacy (A). Simply because an electorate is informed and educated, does not ensure high legitimacy—France would be an example of a state that illustrates this (B). Frequent changeover of political control may or may not indicate low legitimacy. In the United States and Britain, political control alternates frequently between the two major powers, but legitimacy is relatively high in both states (C). Direct democracy is a non-issue, as it is not practiced in any state; it is representative democracy that is practiced (D).

5.   **(D)**

Nigeria's constitution is based on the U.S. model, while Iran's is heavily influenced by the Qur'an and fundamentalist Islam. The other four answers are true of both states.

6.   **(A)**

In the liberal democracies—Western Europe, Canada, the U.S. and Japan—civilian governments control the military, not vice-versa. Individual rights are respected via tradition and constitutional law (B). These sates generally drive the G8, EU, UN Security Council, and so on (C). High quality of life indicators include a very high per capita GDP (D). A "cradle to grave" safety net of social welfare guarantees are generally provided by governments of liberal democracies, especially in Western Europe.

7.   **(A)**

Political parties in the Russian Federation tend to form around a certain individual or group and the desire to propel him/them to greater political power, including the presidency. This was true of the Our Home is Russia party, which supported Boris Yeltsin. After Yeltsin resigned the presidency, this party has faded into oblivion. Similarly, Fatherland-All Russia was born in 1999 to propel Moscow's Mayor Yuri Luzkhov and former Prime Minister Yevgeni Primakov to the Kremlin. When Vladimir Putin's meteoric rise eclipsed their bid, the party began a steady decline and today means virtually nothing. This may well prove to be true of the United Russia party, which currently supports Putin. When he leaves the Kremlin, will this party simply also fade away?

8.   (C)
The current Mexican government most fears China in regard to its potential to take *maquiladora* jobs from Mexico. Chinese labor costs are lower than Mexico's, and thus some Mexican jobs have been transplanted to China in recent years. While the other choices describe actual situations, they would not immediately concern the Mexican government.

9.   (C)
The CPSU never extended widespread membership at any point, from Lenin's reign to Gorbachev's. Estimates on total party membership among the Soviet populace have ranged from 5–7 percent. The gulags were notorious work/death prison camps (A). Stalin certainly was deified by a massive "cult of personality" (B). Kulaks, or wealthy peasants, were killed under Stalin's reign under the belief they would never cooperate with the CPSU's collectivization of agriculture (D). A class of elitist apparatchiks, or party bureaucrats, did evolve under Stalin's lengthy rule (E).

10.   (E)
The poster shown promotes agricultural production with the traditional patriotic CCP trappings. Deng's Responsibility System allowed peasants to meet state quotas and then grown whatever they chose for sale at whatever price the market might bring. Mao's Great Leap Forward was an earlier failed plan to put China on a crash course toward immediate industrialization via collectivized farming and other widespread efforts. Three Represents was a policy under Jiang that allowed entrepreneurs to join the CCP, while the Strike Hard policy dealt with discouraging crime through harsh punishments (A). The Maoist policies of the Cultural Revolution and the Hundred Flowers dealt with criticism of the CCP and the attempt to re-energize the party (B). Poisonous Weeds, i.e., negative influences as defined by the CCP—and *guanxi*, which refers to connections, nepotism and corruption in Chinese business, are items the CCP wishes to eradicate (C). The One Child Policy and Four Modernizations were both initiated under Deng. The Responsibility System was a part of the Four Modernizations, but the posters do not refer to the One Child Policy.

11.   (A)
Mikhail Gorbachev's policy of *glasnost*, or openness, was not intended to allow criticism of the then-current regime or its policies. Gorbachev admired

Khrushchev for his similar previous attempts to reform the Soviet state (B). Stalin and Brezhnev were seen by Gorbachev as negative general secretaries who led to terror and stagnation, respectively, in the USSR (C). A key component of *glasnost* was the encouragement of accurate international reporting, in place of anti-Western propaganda, for the first time in Soviet history (D). The asylums and sanitariums were relics again of the "Stalinist excesses," which Gorbachev was attempting to end (E).

12.   **(A)**

Since a referendum directly involves the voter in passing or defeating legislation, it indicates a high level of efficacy, or the notion that the citizen's political action matters. The more referenda that are offered, the lower a state's legitimacy in general (B). Political integration occurs when citizens identify themselves with the state over any other identifier, such as religion or ethnicity (C). Regime stability equates to legitimacy, and thus referenda would not be the strongest indicator of an enduring regime (D). Lobbyist influence is a non-factor in this question (E).

13.   **(A)**

Chiapas in Mexico and Ulster, or Northern Ireland, in the United Kingdom represent cleavages that have turned violent at times, but neither situation involves a group demanding an independent, or sovereign, state. The Zapatista movement in Chiapas strives for greater economic gains for the impoverished native people of the region, mainly *campesino* farmers. In Ulster, the argument is not over independence, but whether the province should remain part of Britain or reunify with the Republic of Ireland. The other examples listed involve separatist movements of Muslims in Chechnya (B), the Ibo in Biafra (C), Buddhists in Tibet (D), and minority national parties in Scotland and Wales that all attempted or currently support a move toward independence.

14.   **(D)**

Without the facilities, electricity, roads, airports, hotels, and so on, China would never gain prestigious international sporting events, such as the Summer Olympic Games or a Formula One grand prix race. China hasn't substantially changed its position toward Taiwan (A) and considers it a "rogue province" that remains part of the People's Republic. The Chinese record on human rights hasn't substantially changed in recent years on such issues as punishment without trial or the treatment of the Falun Gong (B). While China has been admitted to the World Trade Organization, that alone does not gain a country the right to host prestigious athletic events (C). Nigeria, for instance, is also a WTO member and it is light years away from hosting these major contests in terms of its infrastructure and economy. The Olympics in Beijing and F1 race in Shanghai were secured under Jiang Zemin prior to the new, younger generation of leadership assuming power in 2002 under Hu Jintao (E).

15.　　**(B)**

The main desire of the Eastern European states that joined the European Union [EU] in 2004 was to gain the economic benefits of free trade with Western Europe. The ten new ascension states will not be eligible to join the single currency for some ten years beyond joining the EU (A). Neither will these new states gain proportional membership in the EU parliament compared to the older, wealthier members of the Union (C). Russia's growing economic status, mainly due to a hike in oil prices, was not a long-term reason the Eastern European states desired EU membership (D). In the EU, the Common Agricultural Policy limits rather than enhances agricultural subsidies (E).

16.　　**(D)**

An inverse relationship reveals patterns of opposites. Something going up may cause something else to go down, for instance, as was suggested in this question. Dependency theory (A) deals with the economic relationship between the "developed" and "developing" worlds. Regime stability (B) indicates a long-lasting constitutional government for a country; e.g., a constitution that lasts for a long time as in Britain or the USA. Political integration (C) is the notion that the "state identifier" [Austrian, South African, etc.] is used above other more "localized" identifiers, such as region, ethnicity, or religion. A social cleavage (E) describes any split that inhibits political integration, such as the Protestant-Catholic strife in Northern Ireland, for example.

17.　　**(C)**

A proportional representation (PR) voting system is described in the quote. This system represents parties by the percentage of the vote gained nationally, leading to a plethora of parties holding seats and the need for a coalition government to form a majority and get bills passed. It need not lead to economic difficulty (B), electoral fraud (D), and will likely promote higher voter turnout than the single-member-district-plurality alternative (E). SMDP promotes a two-party system as in the U.S. or Britain (A).

18.　　**(A)**

All the descriptions correctly explain a path to power in Britain, Mexico, Iran, and Nigeria. However, the description for the current Russian Federation is incorrect. Instead, the description incorporates aspects of the Soviet power structure. *Nomenklatura* lists are no longer used for important posts in contemporary Russia.

19.   **(C)**

The House of Lords may indeed initiate legislation on its own. It can delay, but not defeat, bills forwarded from the House of Commons (A). As the upper house of parliament, a bit above the "grime" of everyday politics and elections, the House of Lords holds more prestige status than does the House of Commons (B). While the House of Lords has traditionally been Britain's final court of appeal, that role is being challenged by the European Court of Justice (D). The chamber is unelected and is now mainly comprised now of Life Peers as New Labourites have moved to remove most Hereditary Peers.

20.   **(B)**

To be considered a party of the "extreme right" a Western European party must espouse policies such as capital punishment, minority deportations, and withdrawal from the European Union. These policies are out of the mainstream and beyond what a party such as the Conservatives in Britain would support. Privatization (A) is a mainstream right tactic of recent decades. Opposition to further integration in the EU, while remaining in the organization, is a tactic the mainstream right (and occasionally left) might support (D). Limiting immigration (E) and protecting national culture (C) are both common policies of mainstream parties.

21.   **(E)**

As its name would indicate, the Russian Federation is a federal rather than a unitary system. Britain and China hold to a unitary framework. The comparisons are accurate of all three states.

22.   **(A)**

Even authoritarian governments are wary of criticism in the area of human rights. Organizations like the UN can call for trade sanctions against purveyors of human rights abuses. Also, domestically authoritarian rulers desire legitimacy to help promote cooperation and ruling longevity. Obviously, all states and nations do not share a common definition of what human rights entail. War crimes trials generally would entail foreign policies (like war) rather than domestic human rights concerns.

23.   **(C)**

Margaret Thatcher was certainly a divisive figure in recent British politics whose legacy remains important today. The Falkland Islands War was seen by most

Britons as an acceptable response to the Argentine "invasion" of these sparsely populated British islands off of Argentina's coast. The remaining Thatcher tenets, from privatization to battling the labor unions, tended to widen the gaps in British society between the haves and have-nots and added to Mrs. Thatcher's controversial standing.

24.   **(A)**

Vladimir Putin, a man of tough talk and action, has seen his popularity rise and helped Russian legitimacy and the economy also rise. However, constitutional federalism and separation of powers have both waned as Putin himself has asserted greater powers (D), including basically muffling any opposition media outlets, so (B) is only correct in that vein. The war in Chechnya has bogged down into stalemate and has not consistently remained popular in Russia, as during the Moscow theatre hostage crisis in 2002 and the subsequent handling of it by the government (C). Under Putin, the Oligarchs have reigned in from political activity, some jailed and some exiled (E).

25.   **(C)**

The mandate of heaven under the "Fourth Generation" of CCP leadership has not been enhanced by steady progress toward Taiwanese reunification. This split remains a political headache for the current CCP regime as it had been for its predecessors. The one-child policy has been somewhat relaxed and is at best now enforced inconsistently (A). China's economic boom continues unabated under Hu, registering nearly 8 percent growth annually by 2005 (B), which allowed more urban Chinese than ever to own their own cars (E). The 2008 Summer Olympics in Beijing; Formula One racing in Shanghai; and the Chinese space program have each added to Chinese pride and increased the current regime's mandate of heaven (D).

26.   **(E)**

All liberal democracies are characterized by the possibility of alternating parties in government via electoral change. Social, political, and economic equality along with equality of result, are tenets of Marxism and are not realities in the world's wealthiest states (A) and (C). Many liberal democracies hold socialist economies and indeed none hold strict *laissez-faire* economics unfettered by law or restriction today (B). Judicial review of legislative acts occurs in some liberal democracies but not in all (D).

27.   **(A)**

A state is distinguished from other forms of social organization in that a state has a monopoly of the legitimate use of force via the police or military within its own borders. Linguistic and cultural homogeneity describes a nation rather than a state (B). The media, local governments, interest groups and others may promote debate within decision-making institutions (C). A state need not by definition be either stable or democratic (D). Islamic states such as Iran combine religion and government (E).

28.   **(A)**

The 419 Law, *la mordida* and *guanxi* are issues in Nigeria, Mexico and China respectively that all deal with corruption. The 419 Law relates to a fraudulent investment scheme often perpetrated via e-mail from Nigeria. *La mordida*, which in English means "the bite," is the practice of Mexico City police exacting bribes from traffic offenders rather than officially issuing tickets. *Guanxi* refers to the "connections" necessary to establish business relationships in China. These relations need not be illegal, often implying nepotism, but may also involve bribery of some sort to establish commercial ties.

29.   **(D)**

The term "corporatism" refers to a pattern of interactions between interest groups and the government in which policy is formed through intertwined consultation between high levels of the bureaucracy and certain leaders of key sectors of society. Corporatism is commonly found in one-party states, such as Mexico was under the PRI in the twentieth century. When parties compete to gain votes from a variety of special interests, this is pluralism, common to liberal democracies (A & C). Politicians who gain popular support by dispensing jobs and other economic rewards to political supporters are practicing patronage or the "spoils system" (B). Private corporations do commonly contribute money to the politicians who promise to favor their causes, but this is unrelated to corporatism (E).

30.   **(E)**

The issue that hurts the Kyoto Protocol and other potential summits like it is the clash between environmental concerns and economic gain. Screens and filters that would limit greenhouse gas emissions also cost more for a producer and, ultimately, for the consumer buying the goods.

31.   **(E)**

The mass line is a concept where the CCP attempts to tangibly help the massive Chinese peasantry improve their lives. Enforcing the *hukou* or internal passport system would not accomplish this (although it is enforced) because it would keep peasants in the countryside who wish to move to the larger cities and Special Economic Zones for greater opportunity. Since those areas are already overcrowded and this leads to headaches for the government, the CCP discourages further migration by peasants. Village democracy has allowed rural citizens to choose their local representatives (A), while the PLA wisely and regularly assists with harvest and flood aid (B). The one-child policy has been ignored by certain village cadres who know that if they strictly enforce the policy, female infanticide will again rise (C). The responsibility system, initiated under Deng in the early 1980s provides a great incentive for the Chinese peasantry to grow crops efficiently, thus meeting China's vast needs. Once a state quota is reached in a specified crop, a farmer may grow whatever they please and sell it on the market for whatever they can get (D). Choice and profit are indeed powerful motivations.

32.   **(C)**

The PRI in Mexico ruled the executive branch from 1929–2000. The Chinese Communist Party has held power since 1949 (A). The Tories in Britain ruled from 1979–1997, which is impressive in any liberal democracy, but pales in comparison to other parties listed (B). The CPSU ruled the Soviet Union from 1917 to the demise of the state in 1991, so the party was extinct by 2000 (D). The CPRF has not yet ruled Russia, although it plays an important role within the system (E).

33.   **(C)**

Unlike Mao, Deng trusted intellectuals and pushed for resources to be allocated toward "experts" in a given field rather than toward CCP zealots. The responsibility system to peasants is an example of a concrete reward for increased work output (A). The Special Economic Zones were advanced economically compared to other areas of China, and Deng embraced this as the cost of advancement (B). The SEZ's were areas of foreign investment that decentralized the CCP's economic management and strengthened ties with the outside world (D) and (E).

34.   **(E)**

In terms of regime stability, the pair of countries possessing the highest degree would be Mexico and Britain, whose constitutions have lasted much longer than any other pair of states offered in the choices. The Mexican constitution dates from 1917 and Britain's dates back centuries and is largely unwritten. Regime stability refers not to the office holders or their political party, but to the system of government in place.

35. **(E)**

NGOs, such as Amnesty International and Habitat for Humanity, generally raise money in the wealthy liberal democracies of the Northern Hemisphere while applying their work where it is most needed, in the developing world. By definition, non-governmental organizations receive no government funding or no loans from the IMF or World Bank (A) and (C). NGOs typically do a great deal of work in states with poor human rights records where their services are most needed (B). Amnesty International and Doctors Without Borders are but two organizations that come to mind here. The NGOs would not raise money in the developing world, where people are generally more impoverished and less able to fund charities (D).

36. **(A)**

While it is highly likely that a state would hold internal defensive capabilities, it may opt not to. (Even neutrals like Sweden or non-aggressors like Japan under its current constitution hold capable internal militaries for defensive purposes.) The four characteristics necessary for international statehood include sovereignty (B), definite boundaries (C), some form of government (D), and a permanent population (E).

37. **(D)**

It is not just the British who resent ceding increased sovereignty to the EU. This is a common feeling among many Western Europeans. Remember, the Europeans are generally in agreement on social matters and they are not part of the political debate; this applies to gun control, abortion, banning the death penalty, and government provided daycare.

38. **(A)**

Each scenario posed fits the terms of the quote provided in the question. In Iran in 1979, the Ayatollah Khomeini led a successful fundamentalist Islamic revolt ousting the Shah. Margaret Thatcher led the Conservative Party to victory in 1979, markedly changing British society through privatization and a more divisive debate on the role of unions, Social Darwinism and government. China's communist party defeated the nationalist KMT in 1949, setting up the People's Republic of China. Then in 1978, Deng Xiaoping assumed the leadership mantle and began his massive economic reforms toward a market economy under the "Four Modernizations." The year 1917 in Mexico culminated the seven-year bloody revolution and led to Mexico's current constitution, the years 1917 and 1991 mark the beginning and the end of the Soviet Union. The beginning changed peasant Czarist Russia into a communist state and the end launched a command economy full-scale into a market economy (and democracy) via Yeltsin's "shock therapy."

39.   **(C)**

Vladimir Putin has been most similar to Boris Yeltsin in his continued execution of the Chechen War. It raged under Yeltsin in a stalemate from 1994–1996, and since Putin re-ignited the conflict in 1999 it has remained a brutal, seemingly unending, mess. Putin is seen as much more youthful, sober and vigorous than was the ailing Yeltsin, who suffered from alcohol and heart problems (A). Putin has more control over both the *Duma* and the regions than Yeltsin did, since Putin's pro-Kremlin United Russia Party holds considerable sway in both of these areas (B). While Putin has exiled or imprisoned several of the Oligarchs, Yeltsin was seemingly much more controlled by, and politically indebted to, these wealthy industrialists (D). Instead of surrounding himself with the Oligarchs, Putin has his *Siloviki*, which includes former KGB and military officials within his government. Yeltsin did not surround himself with these individuals.

40.   **(B)**

A theocracy describes rule by religious leaders and the *mullahs*, or Iranian Muslim clerics, who have the final political say over elected authorities such as the President or the *majlis* (parliament).

41.   **(D)**

China was a relatively closed society during most of Mao's rule, so the outside world's view of the People's Republic of China was very limited. Also, as a rabid communist, Mao was often feared and loathed by the West. The other leaders fit this maxim well. Thatcher was a divisive Social Darwinist who promoted much loathing throughout working class Britain, especially in coal mining regions such as Scotland and northern England (A). Obasanjo is a prominent spokesman for AIDS drugs and debt relief for the developing world, yet he is fairly despised by much of Nigeria, especially in the Muslim north (B). Gorbachev's *perestroika* reform failed and backfired on him, when Soviets took to the streets to oppose his rule (C). Salinas was the darling of his NAFTA partner neighbors, Canada and the U.S., but by the end of his term in 1994, with the peso crashing and family scandals unraveling, he was forced to flee Mexico and lives in exile today (E).

42.   **(E)**

Blair's "Third Way" was designed to be a new, more moderate path between the excesses of Thatcherism and socialism. Thus it places the party between the

Conservatives on the right and Liberal Democrats farther to the left. A key step in this process was the abolition of Clause IV of the Labour Party charter which had stipulated that Labour was fundamentally committed to socialism.

43.   **(B)**

With the advent of IFE in the 1997 mid-term elections, international observers have considered Mexico's electoral results to be the most accurate and meaningful of the states listed. In Iran, a theocracy of Islamic clerics holds a check over candidates allowed to run, and thus over the final results (A). In Russia, the opposition is muted by the media, jailings, and other mechanisms that help ensure the success of Vladimir Putin and his supporting United Russia party (C). In Nigeria, international observers have reported suspected fraud and outright violence in the past two national elections in 1999 and 2003 (D).

44.   **(C)**

Direct democracy is unwieldy, and therefore seldom used. Every citizen would get a legislative vote and the right to debate legislation. Thus, representative democracy, in which voters cede this power to elected officials is employed instead. Still, a referendum in which voters have a "yes" or "no" vote on a bill most approximates direct democracy. The remaining choices each promote greater efficacy rather than direct democracy.

45.   **(D)**

China's vast peasantry has remained a key constituency to the CCP since the civil war effort of the 1940s. Mao's mass-line philosophy has been updated to keep the CCP in good favor with the peasants. The Falun Gong has been banned as a "dangerous cult" since staging various widely publicized meetings in 1999 and 2000 (A). Tibetans continue to struggle for autonomy and statehood under the leadership of the exiled Dalai Lama (B). The Tiananmen Square student movement in 1989 was crushed by the tanks of the PLA, leading to more than 1,000 deaths along the boulevards of Beijing (C). Hong Kong civil rights advocates have protested CCP rule since the 1997 return of the coastal city from Britain to China (E).

46.   **(D)**

In neither China nor the Soviet Union did workers dominate the Communist Party. Violent revolutions did occur in both states (B), in the Soviet Union ending in about 1922 and in China ending in 1949 (A). Both Stalin and Mao developed a considerable cult of personality (C). Both states were largely agricultural and dominated by a peasant population prior to the installation of communism (E).

47.   **(E)**

A Nigerian political advantage over Mexico is greater total amount of arable land and a larger overall resource base, including a larger population. Otherwise, the advantages are all Mexico's: more homogeneity by far (A), much greater regime stability and legitimacy (B), a more highly developed infrastructure (C), and relatively less corruption, although that is a concern in Mexico as well (D).

48.   **(B)**

In democratic regimes, a leader can actually be removed from office by election. Elections have been staged in many an authoritarian regime—generally rigged, often a "yes/no" referendum on returning a ruler (A). Private control of the means of production describes capitalism (C). Schools and the mass media are certainly important as agents of political socialization in democratic, as well as authoritarian regimes (D). Democracy itself is often the ideology used to attempt to legitimize the exercise of political power (E).

49.   **(A)**

Because they have longer life expectancies, liberal democracies face a greater challenge in controlling health care costs for aging populations than do C/PC states, NICs, or LDCs. The other choices would pose similar challenges for a government no matter what political science classification the state holds.

50.   **(B)**

A "free vote" within the British House of Commons occurs if and when a matter-of-conscience issue, such as gay marriage, allows a vote in which party discipline among backbenchers will not be enforced. A vote of confidence occurs when the Government agrees to stand for election if the vote fails (A). Cabinet reshuffles occur annually based on a number of factors, including collective responsibility (C). A referendum is a vote by the citizens of a state on a particular issue (D). A backbencher revolt could lead to a vote of no confidence or a party leadership election (E).

51.   **(D)**

The CCP leadership under Hu Jintao handled the SARS crisis by firing the Minister of Health and Mayor of Beijing. The CCP did not label the Stones a "poisonous weed" [i.e., negative influence on China] or they would never have been permitted to tour China in the first place (A). Curfews were issued in certain locations in combating SARS, but were not issued throughout the country (B). Media access was of course limited by the CCP (C), as was initial access for the WHO to records and patients (E).

52.   (E)

The European Charter of Fundamental Rights addressed all of the issues shown, except for gay marriage. Certain EU member states such as the Netherlands and Belgium have moved on their own to permit gay marriage.

53.   (C)

A strong majority of all British citizens support the current monarch, Queen Elizabeth II, and the institution of the monarchy in general. The other areas raised, football (A), viz., devolved politics (B), a north-south split over wealth and opportunity (D), and regional, separatist political parties (E), all tend to divide the UK.

54.   (C)

Marx would have likely considered Russia and China as too backward and agricultural for a successful communist revolution. Marx contended that only the most industrial states, with a history of exploiting the proletariat working class, could undergo a successful communist revolt. Thus, he imagined that it would occur in Germany, Britain, France, or even possibly the United States. Among the many factors Marx could not foresee were socialist "cradle to grave" welfare state benefits, such as disability and unemployment insurance, that would make his system less attractive to mass labor.

55.   (B)

Britain's two-party system has easily proven the longest lasting of the choices given by far. The Conservative and Labour parties have led this system for nearly a century at present. Prior to that it was the Liberal and Conservative parties and tracing the evolution of the parties back to the seventeenth century, one finds the Tory Party supporting the monarchy and the Whig Party opposed to it. Mexico's party system has basically evolved into a relatively stable three-party system in the past two decades with various changes in law, such as IFE and the introduction of PR seats into the Chamber of Deputies (A). Iran has no party system at all, as its current constitution bans parties altogether (C). Nigeria's party system is in flux, as usual, given its regime's instability. However, since the enactment of the 1999 constitution, Nigeria seems to be headed toward a two-party model with an SMDP-elected legislature, a President elected under the two-ballot majority vote rule (D). Russia's party system is also still rather volatile. Parties such as "Our Home is Russia" seem to exist to propel a certain candidate to power—Yeltsin, in this case—and then fade to oblivion once that candidate leaves political office. This may also occur with Putin's "United Russia" movement. Other parties, such as the Communists, Liberal Democrats and perhaps the Union of Right Forces, seem to have a bit more ideological staying power (E).

SECTION II

Sample of ID Essays that Would Achieve a Top Score

1. Privatization involves the selling of formerly state-owned enterprises to private hands. While this practice became somewhat synonymous with Margaret Thatcher's rule of Britain, privatization has become widespread elsewhere. In Mexico, under Carlos Salinas many businesses such TelMex and the country's airline, AeroMexico, were sold off. As China's ongoing experiment in "socialism with Chinese characteristics" continues, many state-run enterprises are being sold to private investors. In fact, leading officers in the People's Liberation Army now own many lucrative businesses across China. One political consequence involved with privatization is a potential voter backlash. (This would not apply in China currently, but could and has in both Mexico and Britain.) For instance, TelMex was sold to multi-millionaire Carlos Slim, perhaps the wealthiest man in Mexico. Under Slim, telephone rates have gone up markedly as has Slim's net worth. The PRI thus, was seen as more corrupt and/or inept, leading some voters in Mexico to seek alternatives to its rule. (NOTE: The question called for one consequence of course, the student responding could cite more positive consequences, such as a potential lowering of tax rollls by selling off nationalized industries.)

2. "NGOs" are non-governmental organizations. Thus, they are officially tied to no single country, government or political party. Examples include the International Red Cross, Doctors Without Borders and Amnesty International. NGOs generally rely on money raised in the liberal democracies of Western Europe, the U.S., Canada and Japan to do their work in the more impoverished developing world. Of course, NGOs can and do try to affect political policies, but they are beholden to no single group (such as the UN) for support.

3. A unitary state is one in which the laws passed at the national level hold sway across the country. In a federal system, local legislatures have the authority to pass some laws to allow for local cultural differences. For example,

in the U.S., Utah might have laws reflecting its strong Mormon religious traditions, while Louisiana's laws reflect its local traditions. In a unitary system, the local governments exist many to administer the laws of the state, not to create separate local statutes. Thus, a unitary system generally makes the most sense in geographically small, relatively homogenous states. Most Western European states would apply to this example. In larger, more culturally diverse states, such as India or Canada, a federal system seems to make more sense. The People's Republic of China is an exception to this rule. Large geographically, it nonetheless is a unitary state. Why? Because China has an authoritarian government under the Chinese Communist Party that does not want dissent and can best maintain control, it feels, through unitary rule.

4.   Personalism is generally understood to mean "It is not what you know, but who you know" that is the key for political ascendency. In Mexico, the traditional "network" in which personalism thrived was the camarilla. The camarilla is a means by which like-minded politicians join forces to gain influence within their party and within the Mexican system. A politician could belong to more than one camarilla, and might even start their own if politically ambitious. Thus, personalism minimizes the importance of policy-expertise in a given area and maximizes the importance of political connections.

5.   A referendum is a vote on a proposed law that is decided not by a state's legislative body, such as the Russian Duma or the Iranian Majlis, but rather by a country's voters instead. Generally, a government never offers a referendum to the public that it does not want to see passed. (Otherwise, why would they offer it?) A case in point has been the issue of the single European currency in Britain. Under Tony Blair, a referendum on the issue was promised before Britain would ever accept the euro as its currency. It was widely believed that Blair supported the switch from the pound sterling to the euro as a wise economic move for Britain. However, the country as a whole remains divided on the issue and thus, in Blair's first eight years as Prime Minister, he has not offered this issue as referendum to the British voters, fearing defeat.

Question 6–Sample Essay that Would Achieve a Top Score

(a)   Both Britain and Russia are faced with significant religious cleavages that have led to internal conflict. The most notable conflict in Britain remains the Protestant versus Catholic strife in Northern Ireland. Catholics in the province wish to be reunited with the Republic of Ireland, while the majority Protestant population desires to remain part of the United Kingdom. Ireland is a Catholic country while the UK has a strong Protest tradition under the Anglican Church. What has resulted since the early '70s is "The Troubles"—a low civil war of assassinations, car bombings, and other forms of terror, led by paramilitary fighters on both sides. The IRA (Irish Republican Army) represents Catholic desires for Irish reunification while the Orange Order fights for the Protestant right to remain under the British Union Jack.

In southwestern Russia, Chechnya has been fighting for independence for more than a decade. The Chechens are Islamic by religion and Arabic by culture and feel little in common with their rulers from Moscow, who speak Russian and are largely Orthodox Christians by custom. Additionally, Chechnya is a region blessed with petroleum, which could conceivably fund a newly independent state to some degree. As opposed to the situation in Ulster, Chechnya has been an outright, for scale civil war between the Russian forces and the Chechen guerrillas, mired largely in a stalemate.

(b)   The British government under Tony Blair embarked upon the Good Friday Peace Agreement in 1998 along with the Republican of Ireland and the people of Ulster via a referenda in both places. This landmark agreement called for a devolved assembly in Northern Ireland (Stormont) and for Ireland to remove its constitutional claim to the province. More controversially, it called for the early prison release of convicts from both the Orange Order and IRA, some guilty of murder. Finally, it called for the decommissioning, or hand over to authorities, of weapons held by the paramilitaries, thus ending their ability to make "war."

In Russia, Boris Yeltsin ended the first Chechen War in 1996 by negotiating a peace with a vaguely promised future autonomy, and eventual sovereignty, for Chechnya. In 1999, then Prime Minister Vladimir Putin used a Moscow apartment blast, presumably committed by Chechen rebels, to catapult himself to national fame by talking and acting tough in regard to Chechnya. Since then, Russian forces have pounded, but not crushed, the Chechen resistance with air strikes and ground artillery. Putin has also offered a dubious referendum in 2003 on Chechen self-determination that overwhelmingly passed but was largely believed to have been voided by the lack of voter turnout, although the Kremlin claimed the turnout was quite high.

(c)   The verdict is still out in Northern Ireland, although the region has been somewhat more peaceful than it was prior to the Good Friday Agreement. Decommissioning has still not occurred, and thus sectarian violence has not totally stopped. As a result, the Stormont assembly has been suspended in Ulster on several occasions. Summer "marching season" fracases remain a way of life in the province, but large-scale bombings have not occurred since the tragedy killing nearly 30 people in Omagh in 1998. It seems the Good Friday Agreement has accomplished some positive measures while its terms remain unfulfilled.

Chechnya is less promising. The entrenched battle rages on in a bloody draw. And the Chechen have struck back at Moscow on several occasions, including the 2002 theater hostage standoff and a suicide bombing at an outdoor concert in 2003. Perhaps because of his "black belt" image, and certainly because of the precedent it would set to other largely Islamic border regions, Putin has shown little inclination toward a compromised political settlement with Chechnya.

Question 7–Sample Essay that Would Achieve a Top Score

Political reform is a common occurrence as states evolve and face new challenges. Mexico, Nigeria, and Iran have each experienced profound reform in recent decades.

(a)   Under Presidents Zedillo (PRI) and Fox (PAN) several important reforms have been forwarded. Under Fox, the Chamber of Deputies approved a measure allowing Mexican citizens living and working in the U.S. to vote in Mexican elections. This may have consequences for the 2006 Mexican presidential elections and those beyond. A landmark proposal enacted under the Zedillo administration was the creation of IFE, the federal election institute. IFE is independent of any party, most notably the PRI, and has far-reaching power to monitor not only polling stations and ballot counting, but also campaign spending by parties and candidates. Involving voter ID cards with photos, the fingerprinting of voters, and transparent ballot counting procedures, IFE has greatly increased public confidence in the electoral process in Mexico. A specific consequence has been the loss of the PRI's monopoly on political power in Mexico. In 1997, the PAN and leftist PRD gained enough seats in the Chamber of Deputies to prevent a PRI majority. In 2000, Vicente Fox gained his historic presidential victory, ousting the PRI from the presidency. Thus, a true multi-party democracy has been a result of IFE's political reform.

(b)   Nigeria has been a constant study in reform since gaining its independence in 1960. A contentious land of hundreds of rival ethnicities and religious groups, Nigeria often verges on open chaos and frequently experiences violent revolt. Consequently, Nigeria has revolved between civilian and military during its existence, necessitated by the delicate balance between freedom and security. A key reform occurred in 1999 following the death of the loathed dictator, General Sani Abacha. Nigeria once again made a transition toward democracy and civilian rule under the constitution of the Fourth Republic. A consequence that has resulted has been the political rebirth of a former military ruler, Olesegun Obasanjo. Mr. Obasanjo, a Yoruba and a Christian, has attempted to oversee such fractious events as the implementation of Shari'a, or fundamental Islamic law in Northern Nigeria. Obasanjo's People's Democratic Party (PDP) has also become a strong political entity at both the federal and local level.

(c)   Since its 1979 Islamic Revolution, which removed the Shah (monarch) from power, Iran has continued to reform its system. Under the former President, Mohammed Khatami, first elected in 1997, Iran has indeed split politically into "conservative" and "reformist" factions. As of the 2004 elections for the Majlis (parliament), the conservative faction, favoring fundamental Islam over open democracy and a freer media, has taken a stronghold of power. Reformers, like former President Khatami, appear for the moment to have taken a back seat. Many reformist candidates were in fact blocked from running in the Majlis elections by the Council of Guardians. The Council is comprised of 12 members, all fundamentalist Muslims, who not only screen bills passed by the Majlis, but also may reject any candidates for the Majlis they see fit without explanation. Choosing the Council of Guardians is Iran's supreme Islamic leader, Ali Khamenei, who thus has the power to block any liberalizing reforms, whether by the President or the Majlis. So, a result of the attempted reform by moderates like Khatami has been a backlash of conservative Islamic leaders determined to retain and enhance their own power.

Question 8–Sample Essay that Would Achieve a Top Score

a. The Conservative Party is Britain has experienced a divisive split which became obvious under the leadership of Prime Minister John Major in the mid-1990s over further integration in the European Union. One faction of the party, known as "euroskeptics," wants as little to do with the EU as possible. This wing of the party accepts the free trade zone of the EU, but otherwise resents what it sees as an invasion of British sovereignty from Brussels. Euroskeptics, led by former Prime Minister Margaret Thatcher, most certainly do not want the *euro* to replace the pound as Britain's currency. They also resent the European Court of Justice usurping the role previously held by the House of Lords as Britain's final court of appeal.

On the other hand, "europhiles" within the Conservative Party believe that further European integration will benefit the country economically. They fear that by not adopting the *euro*, the UK will be left behind not only economically, but also in terms of influence within the EU itself.

b. The PRI in Mexico went through a "life-changing experience" in the late 1980s and '90s that is still unfolding, as the party attempts to cope with the new realities of Mexican democracy and pluralism. The old guard, known as "*los dinos*," desired to halt any reforms that might endanger the PRI's electoral power. They were not above bribing voters come election time with municipal services like streets or sewers, or with more personal goodies, like groceries or a bicycle. Along with the time tested pendulum theory and corporatism, these tactics had served the PRI well for decades.

However, a younger guard of PRI technocrats, trained in economics in the Ivy League, were skeptical. Mexico was changing and the old ways were less and less successful. This generation of *Priista* pushed for a reformed system, one with cleaner elections and more transparent campaigns. Led by Ernesto Zedillo, the IFE was created in the 1990s to increase legitimacy in the years following the multiple scandals of the Salinas administration.

Zedillo gave up the long-held practice of the *dedazo* in which the incumbent hand-picks the next PRI presidential candidate. Instead, the PRI staged a country-wide primary in 1999 which was won by Francisco Labastida.

c.   As a result of their intra-party squabbles, the Tories have been relegated to a weak opposition status since 1997. Subsequent party leaders to Major, William Hague and Iain Duncan-Smith, were unable to unite the party and lead it to greater standing in the House of Commons. Given by-election results from 2004, the Liberal Democrats are threatening to replace the Conservatives in Britain's two-party system.

The PRI lost its political monopoly over Mexico. First, in 1997, the party lost its majority in the Chamber of deputies, although it did retain a plurality of seats over the PRD and the PAN. In 2000, the Labistida was soundly defeated by the PAN's Vicente Fox.

d.   2004–'05 shadow leader Michael Howard has smoothed over these EU divisions somewhat, but the Tories remain basically opposed to further integration. The party basically now seems unified in calling for a referendum on the European Union Constitution, for example. Howard has basically convinced the Tory backbenchers to let him do the talking and to avoid the perception of a perpetually split party.

The PRI seems to have settled more on the "tecnico" side of its split, emerging as more relevant to the changes occurring in Mexico. Toward this end, the party has dictated that 30 percent of all its candidates by 30 or younger, and that 40 percent of its candidates be women.

While it remains to be seen if the Conservative Party will finally heal its "euroskeptic" split, the PRI fared well in 2003 mid-term elections and has its eyes set on recapturing the presidency in 2006.

(**Note:** A student choosing this essay might also write about the Chinese Communist Party and the intra-party split that occurred from April–June 1989 concerning the student movement in Tiananmen Square.)

Glossary

UNITED STATES

ABC Programs: those implemented by Franklin Delano Roosevelt during the Great Depression to give relief to the unemployed

Administrative Law: the rules and regulations that regulate administrative agencies

Admiralty and Maritime Law: the legal code as applied to navigation and commerce on the high seas as well as upon navigable waterways

Affirmative Action: programs designed to overcome past discriminatory actions such as providing employment opportunities to members of a group that were previously denied employment because of racial barriers

Amendment: the modification of the constitution or a law

Amicus Curiae: a third-party brief filed with the permission of the court to support a litigant

Anti-Federalist: persons opposed to the creation of a strong national government out of fear that individual and states' rights would be destroyed

Appeasement: the act of making concessions to a political or military rival

Appellate Court: courts that have the authority to review the findings of lower courts

Appellate Jurisdiction: the power to review the decisions of lower courts

Articles of Confederation: union of states created in 1781 in which the national government did not have the authority to act directly upon the people and antecedent to the Constitution

Assigned Counsel System: persons who are unable to obtain legal counsel will be provided, by the courts, suitable representation

Baker vs. Carr: the Supreme Court held that congressional district reapportionment may not be used to dilute representation of minorities

Bicameralism: a two-house legislature

Bill of Attainder: legislative act that inflicts punishment on an individual or group for the purpose of suppressing that person or group

Bill of Rights: the first ten amendments to the Constitution

Bipartisan: politics that emphasizes cooperation between the major parties

Block grants: federal money provided to a state or local government for a general purpose, such as reducing crime or improving education, with relatively few requirements on how the states can spend the money

Blue States: Label given to the states that tend to support Democratic candidates and have more liberal views, including California and New York.

Brown vs. Board of Education of Topeka: the Supreme Court declared the doctrine of "separate but equal" unconstitutional

Bureaucrat: an appointed government official who insists on rigid adherence to rules

Bush doctrine: notion of pre-emptive strikes against potential enemies

Cabinet: the heads of the various departments in the Executive branch who aid in the decision-making process

Camp X-Ray: detention camp at the U.S. naval base in Guantanamo Bay, Cuba, where many detainees have been held since shortly after 9/11

Capital Punishment: the execution of an individual by the state as punishment for heinous offenses

Capitalism: an economic system in which the means of production are held by an individual for the benefit of that individual

Caucus: a closed meeting of Democratic Party leaders to agree on a legislative program

CEO (Chief Executive Officer): top officer of a corporation

Checks and Balances: constitutionally distributed power where the powers overlap so that no branch of government may dominate the other

Civil Law: the legal code that regulates the conduct between private parties

Civil Rights Act of 1964: legislative act that removed racial barriers in all places vested with a public interest

Class Action Suit: a lawsuit filed on behalf of a group of persons with a similar legal claim against a party or individual

Cloture: parliamentary procedure for ending debate and calling for an immediate vote on a pending matter

Common Law: a body of judge-made law created as court cases are decided

Concurrent Powers: powers held by both the national and state governments

Concurring Opinion: the opinion of a Supreme Court justice who agrees with the majority ruling, but for different reasons

Confederated System: a system of government created when nation-states agree by compact to create a centralized government with delegated powers, but the nation-states do not give up individual autonomy

Conference: a meeting between committees of the two branches of the legislature to reconcile differences in pending bills

Conglomerate: a corporation that has many businesses in unrelated fields

Consent Decree: an individual or party agrees to modify future behavior or activities along court or regulatory agency guidelines

Conservative: is apt to oppose change, to be more religious, to prefer smaller government and the Republican Party; also believes that people themselves, not government, should solve their own problems

Constitution: the rules that determine the scope and function of government, as well as how the government is to be run

Compassionate Conservatism: political philosophy in which conservatism and compassion go together and complement each other

Constitutional: formal limitations on how political power is granted, dispersed, or used within the framework of a government

Constitutional Body of Law: comprised of the four components (formally written U.S. Constitution, informal amendments, the most important acts of Congress, current Supreme Court case precedents)

Court Packing: the act of placing members of the same political party on the bench so that opinion of the court will be consistent with the political party's (seen most dramatically with Franklin Delano Roosevelt)

Criminal Law: the legal code dealing with the actions of all people

De Facto Segregation: segregation that results from nongovernmental action; i.e., administered by the public

Declaration of Independence: the formal declaration of the United States' secession from England

Defendant: the party in a civil action or criminal action charged with the offense

De Jure Segregation: legally established segregation

Demagogue: a person who gains power through emotional appeals to the people

Democrat: any member of the Democratic Party, one of two major parties in the U.S.; party's lineage traces to Jefferson's Democratic Republican Party (1792)

Department of Homeland Security: newest cabinet department, created in the wake of the 9/11 attacks, coordinating the efforts of the FBI, CIA, and other such agencies to create a more coordinated approach to internal security

Deregulation: the act of reducing or eliminating economic controls

Desegregation: the removal of racial barriers either by legislation or judicial action

Diffuse Support: support for the political system as a whole, as opposed to specific candidate's policies

Dissenting Opinion: disagreement with the majority opinion of the Supreme Court by another Supreme Court justice

Domestic Policy: programs, laws, and regulations focusing on the internal affairs of the nation

Double Jeopardy: the act of being tried for the same crime twice by the same level of government

Dred Scott vs. Sanford: the Supreme Court upheld the right of a slave owner to reclaim his property after the slave had fled into a free state

Eminent Domain: the power of a government to seize private property for public use, usually with compensation to the owner

Equal Pay for Equal Work: a measure by which men and women are paid equally, given similar job descriptions and similar performance evaluations

Equity of Redemption: judicial solution used when suits for money damages do not provide just compensation

Ethnocentrism: a belief that one's ethnic group is superior

Excise Tax: a tax on a specific consumer item such as alcoholic beverages

Executive Agreement: informal agreements made by the executive with a foreign government

Ex Post Facto Laws: laws created to make past actions punishable that were permissible when they occurred

Expressed Powers: powers constitutionally given to one of the branches of the national government

Federal System: governmental system in which power is constitutionally divided between a national government and its component members

Federalist: person who supported the ratification of the Constitution before 1787

Fighting Words: words that inflict injury upon persons

Filibuster: a senator who gains the floor has the right to go on talking until the senator relinquishes the floor to another

Focus Groups: about ten to fifteen people and a moderator who have an opportunity to discuss their opinions about issues and candidates in depth

Foreign Policy: treaties, agreements, and programs focusing on the relations between the United States and other nations

Franchise: the right to engage in the electing of public office holders

Gerrymander: redrawing of congressional districts in order to secure as many representative party votes as possible

Gideon vs. Wainwright: case decided by the U.S. Supreme Court in 1963 that established the right to legal representation for all defendants in criminal cases

Glass Ceiling: a reference to the perceived limits that a woman can reach compared her to male counterparts, especially in corporate America

GOP: the Republican Party

Impeachment: the process used to remove certain officials, including the President, from office. Similar to a trial, impeachment does not necessarily mean that an official will be removed from office; he or she must be found guilty of an impeachable offense

Implied Powers: powers that have been reasonably inferred for the carrying out of expressed powers

Immunity: granted exemption from prosecution

In Forma Pauperis: decision that indigents bringing cases to the Supreme Court do not have to pay regular fees or meet all standard requirements

Incumbent: a candidate currently holding a given office

Informal Amendment: an accepted (meaning understood and applied), but unwritten, change to the constitution

Inherent Powers: powers exclusively controlled by the national government such as foreign affairs

Initiative and Referendum: a procedure by which voters pass or reject laws directly. In this way, laws are approved directly by voters, not through representatives

Interest Group: group of persons who share some common interest and attempt to influence elected members of the government

Iran-Contra: the selling of arms to Iran so that the profits from these sales could be used to fund the *contras* in El Salvador

Jim Crow Laws: laws designed to promote racial segregation

Judicial Activism: using the power of the bench to broaden the interpretation of the Constitution

Judicial Restraint: using the power of the bench to limit the interpretation of the Constitution

Judicial Review: assumed power of the courts to declare an action of the president or Congress unconstitutional

Judiciary Act of 1789: congressional act which set the scope and limits for the federal judiciary system

Jus Sanguinis: citizenship acquired through one's parents

Jus Soli: citizenship established through place of birth

Kennedy, John F.: elected in 1960 as youngest President of the United States; established the Peace Corps in 1961; issued challenge to NASA to land a man on the moon; assassinated in 1963

King, Jr., Martin Luther: civil rights leader who fought for the rights of minorities by the use of peaceful civil disobedience

Lame Duck: a defeated office holder after that person has lost their re-election, but is still in office until the newly elected official is sworn in

Libel: published defamation of another person

Liberal: believes that government can and should help solve social problems, is more prone to prefer change, political experimentation and the Democratic Party, and to champion the rights of the individual over the needs of the state

Line-Item Veto: the objection by the president to a single item in a piece of legislation; this authority, signed into law by President Clinton in 1996, was unsuccessfully challenged as unconstitutional by six members of Congress, with the U.S. Supreme Court saying the plaintiffs had no legal standing to bring a case

Litigation: a law suit

Lobbying: activities aimed at influencing public officials and the policies they enact

Logrolling: mutual aid among politicians to achieve goals in each one's interests

Malcolm X: radical Muslim leader who wanted a total separation of the races

Mapp vs. Ohio: the Supreme Court recognized that evidence seized without a search warrant cannot be used

Marbury vs. Madison: the U.S. Supreme Court, in a landmark decision in 1803, established the concept of judicial review

Maverick: a person who holds no party allegiance and has unorthodox political views

McCarthyism: the act of seeking out subversives without cause or need (seen during the 1950s when Senator Joseph McCarthy stoked fear of Communism)

Media Bias: the major television networks—ABC, NBC, and CBS—along with the most respected newspapers, such as the *New York Times* and *Washington Post*, are considered to have a liberal bias

Military-Industrial Complex: the assumption that there is an alliance between the military and industrial leaders

Miranda vs. Arizona: 1966 case in which the U.S. Supreme Court decided that all persons who are detained or arrested must be informed of their rights

Misdemeanor: offense that is less than a felony with punishment ranging from a fine to a short jail term

Multilateral: a foreign policy approach in which multiple countries work in unison

National Supremacy Clause: constitutional doctrine that the actions or decisions of the national government take priority over that of the state or local governments

Naturalization: process by which persons acquire citizenship

New Deal: legislation championed by Franklin Delano Roosevelt during the Great Depression that provided a safety net (e.g., Social Security) for all members of society

New Jersey Plan: single-house legislature with equal representation for all states

9/11: a series of coordinated attacks carried out on the United States on Tuesday, September 11, 2001

Nixon, Richard M.: the only President of the United States to resign after being confronted with impeachment (because of his alleged actions in the Watergate scandal)

Nonproliferation Treaty: an agreement not to distribute nuclear arms to countries that do not have them

Obscenity: any work that taken as a whole appeals to a prurient interest in sex

Oligarchy: government by the few based on wealth or power

Ombudsman: person or office that hears formal complaints against the government

Original Intent: a doctrine of Constitutional interpretation that says Supreme Court Justices should base their interpretations of the Constitution on its authors' intentions

Original Jurisdiction: the authority of a court to hear a case being brought up for the first time

PAC (political action committee): set up by labor unions, corporations, or other special interest groups to support candidates via campaign contributions in hopes of influencing policy in their favor

Partisan: political opposition drawn along party lines

Patriot Act: passed in the aftermath of 9/11 giving extra powers to intelligence and law enforcement officers in the effort to combat terrorism. Examples include the interception of mail, phone tapping, e-mail surveillance, and so on. The law has proven to be controversial

Patronage: dispensing government jobs to persons who belong to the winning political party

Personal Property: all property held by an individual excluding real estate

Petit (or Petty) Jury: a trial jury of 12 that sits at civil/criminal cases

Plaintiff: the party who brings a civil action to court for the purpose of seeking a monetary remedy

Plea Bargain: an agreement between a prosecutor's office and the accused to avoid a trial

Plessy vs. Ferguson: the Supreme Court established the rule of "separate but equal" as being constitutional

Police Power: power to regulate persons or property in order to promote health, welfare, and safety

Political Question: constitutional question that judges refuse to answer because to do so would encroach upon the authority of Congress or the President

Poll Tax: the requirement of a person to pay for the right to vote

Precedent: judicial use of prior cases as the test for deciding similar cases

Prior Restraint: censorship enacted before the speech, publication, etc., is released to the general public

Procedural Due Process: constitutional requirement that a government proceed by proper means

Pro-choice: supports a woman's right to choose regarding abortion

Pro-life: opposed to abortion

Public Opinion: the beliefs, preferences, and attitudes about an issue that involves the government or society at large

Reagan, Ronald W.: two-term President during the 1980s whose economic policies followed supply-side theory

Rebellion: an organized military action designed to replace the existing leaders but maintain its structures

Red States: Label given to the states that tend to support Republican candidates and have more conservative views, inclduing Texas and Florida

Referendum: the process whereby a legislative proposal is voted upon by popular vote

Remand: to turn over authority of a case

Republic: form of government that derives its powers directly or indirectly from the people, and those who govern are accountable to the governed

Republican: any member of the Republican Party, one of the U.S.'s two major political parties; the GOP came into being 1854-1856, unifying anti-slavery forces

Reserved Powers: powers retained by the states

Resolution 1441: dealt with Iraqi cooperation over a UN search for "weapons of mass destruction"

Revolt: a disorganized military action aimed at gaining attention for a specific cause

Revolution: complete change of the form of government and its leaders

Roe vs. Wade: the Supreme Court established a woman's right to an abortion

Roosevelt, Franklin Delano: president of the United States during the Depression and World War II; most noted for his enactment of New Deal programs such as the Social Security Act

Rule of Four: in order for a case to be heard by the Supreme Court, four justices must agree to hear the case

Safe Seat: electoral office, usually in the legislature, for which the party or incumbent is strong enough that reelection is almost taken for granted

Sedition: conduct/language inciting rebellion against authority of the state

Slander: verbal defamation of a person's character

Spin: an attempt by a candidate or his or her staff to frame a message a certain way, generally ignoring the potential negatives to a particular policy

Stare Decisis: a rule of precedent in which an established rule of law is considered binding on all judges whenever a similar case is presented

Statism: the rights of the state over those of the citizens

Statutory Law: law enacted by a legislative body

Stay: the temporary delay of punishment, usually in a capital offense case

Substantive Due Process: constitutional requirement that government actions and laws be reasonable

Suspect Classification: racial or national origin classifications created by law and subject to careful judicial scrutiny

Symbolic Speech: nonverbal communication of a political idea

Tariff: any tax levied on imported goods

Trial Court: any court of original jurisdiction that empowers a jury to decide the guilt or liability of an individual

Unicameral Legislature: single-house legislature

Unilateral: a foreign policy approach in which the U.S. acts as it sees fit without consideration for the views of traditional allies or of the UN Security Council

Unitary System: a system of government in which power is concentrated in the central government

United States vs. Nixon: the Supreme Court ruled that material vested with a public interest could not be withheld from evidence under the rule of executive privilege

Virginia Plan: strong central government with a bicameral legislature

War Powers Act: requires Congress to approve stationing American troops overseas for more than 90 days

Watergate: the illegal entry and phone monitoring in 1972 of Democratic headquarters in the Watergate complex in Washington by members of the Republican Party

West Virginia Board of Education vs. Barnette: the Supreme Court decided that compulsory flag salute in schools is unconstitutional

WMD: weapons of mass desctruction

Writ of Appeal: formal request to have a court review the findings of a lower court

Writ of Certiorari: a formal appeal used to bring a case up to the Supreme Court

Writ of Habeas Corpus: court order requiring jailers to explain to a judge why they are holding a prisoner in custody

Writ of Mandamus: court order directing an official to perform a nondiscretionary or ministerial act as required by law

X, Malcolm: see Malcolm X

COMPARATIVE

Abuja: capital city of Nigeria

Aguiyi Ironsi (Nigeria): leader of a coup that displaced the ineffective civilian government

Anarchy: a state of absence of political authority

ANPP (Nigeria): All-Nigeria People's Party

anti-rightist campaign: revenge program of the CCP in which many of those critical of the CCP during the Hundred Flowers period were imprisoned or even killed

Apartheid: constitutionally established segregation and disenfranchisement

appratchi: a member of the government that held a position of political responsibility (with the exception of the higher ranks of management)

Assembly of Experts (Iran): 86-member body composed of *mullahs* who are elected for eight-year terms and who chose the *Faqih*

Axis of Evil: term coined in 2002 by U.S. President George W. Bush to describe regimes that sponsor terror; included Iran, Iraq, and North Korea

Ayatollah: religious leader

Backbencher: any member of Parliament who does not hold a cabinet position

Bakassi Boys: the most notorious of Nigeria's ethnic groups

Biafra: short-lived state formed by fleeing Ibos in 1967, after seceding from Nigeria

Bicameral: a two-house legislature

Blair, Tony (United Kingdom): succeeded the Tory Government of John Major as British Labour Prime Minister in 1997

Bolshevik Revolution: the Russian Revolution of 1917 that removed the Czar from power and put in its place a communist system of government

Bolsheviks: members of the extremist wing of the Russian Social Democratic party that seized power in Russia in 1917

Bourgeoisie: the capitalist class that has power over the proletariat

brain drain: describes the exodus of talented and capable people from a country where opportunity is limited. Generally more prevelant the lower a country's per capita GDP is; ex. brain drain worse in Nigeria than in Russia or Mexico

British Constitution (United Kingdom): an unwritten collection of customs, conventions, acts of Parliament, and Common Law

Brussels: the headquarters of most EU organizations

by-election: a special election to fill a vacancy in a district between general elections because of death or resignation

C/PC (Communist/Post-Communist) states: formerly the Second World

cabinet reshuffle: an event in which members of the cabinet are rotated or moved from one post to another, in some cases resulting in promotions and in others, demotions to backbenches, based on loyalty or practice of collective responsibility

Camarilla (Mexico): a political clique, of sorts, like a ladder, that one climbs to get to a higher level

Campesino: peasant farmer

Capitalism: features a market economy, meaning that demand of consumers drives production

Caudillo: politico-military leader who heads an authoritative power

Chador **(Iran):** head-to-toe black cover women must wear whenever in public

Chancellor of the Exchequer: in the United Kingdom, a position controlling the treasury and budget

Chechnya (Russian Federation): separatist and rebellious republic of the former Soviet Union seeking independence from Russia

Chinese Communist Party (China): the dominant (and only) political party that exercises a monopoly of power in the People's Republic of China

Chinese Communist Party: ruling party of the People's Republic of China

chop politics: practice by which members of nations who held political office attempted to govern in the best interest of their own ethnicity rather than in the best interest of Nigeria as a whole

Churchill, Winston (Great Britain): prime minister during World War II

coal miners strike, 1984-85: a turning point in British industrial relations in which the government under Margaret Thatcher broke the coal-miner union during a yearlong strike

collective responsibility: the right of cabinet members to disagree over a proposed policy, or with the prime minister, until the policy is set and announced, at which point all members are to publicly show support

Collectivism: state ownership of both the means of production and distribution of consumer goods

command economy: state-planned production

Common Agricultural Policy: designed to make subsidies between member states equal

common market: in the European Union, a single market with common policies on product regulation and freedom of movement of product production (goods, services, capital, and labor)

Communism: any system of government based upon Marxist theory in which state ownership of the means of production is employed for the benefit of all

Communist Manifesto: Karl Marx's plan and explanation of how Communism is to be implemented by the natural economic development of industrialized nations

Communist Party of the Soviet Union: successor of the Bolshevik Party that exercised a totalitarian-elitest one-party system until the demise of the Soviet Union in 1991

Confederal: state government holds almost no powers while the sub-state governments wield extensive legislative control

Confederation: power is concentrated in the component members of a larger system with limited grants of power given to a central government by the component members

Confucianism: an East Asian ethical and philosophical system based on the teachings of Confucius

Conservative Party/Tories: one of the United Kingdom's political parties; Margaret Thatcher, former Prime Minister, was elected under this party

Constitution of the Russian Federation: adopted in 1993 under Boris Yeltsin, contained provisions for strong presidential powers while maintaining checks and balances, a president who was allowed to rule by decree under national emergency and who could dissolve the Duma, calling for new general elections and referendums as he saw fit

Convergence criteria: the steps an EU member must satisfy in order to be eligible to join the single currency

Corporatism (Mexico): allowed the PRI's bureaucracy to pull in key sectors of Mexican society, guaranteeing those votes in return for access and influence within the party

Council of Guardians: comprised of twelve mullahs chosen by the Faqih and Iran's Supreme Court; a conservative body that reinforces the power of the Islamic fundamentalists in the Iranian political system

CPSU: Communist Party of the Soviet Union

Creole: Mexican peoples with only Iberian blood

Cultural Revolution (China): Mao Zedong's revolution which would purge the elder leaders and put in a younger generation whose zeal would not let the country self-destruct, as Mao felt the Russian Revolution did to the Soviet Union by taking the "Revisionist Road to Capitalist Restoration"

Cultural Revolution: revolutionary uprising by Chinese students and workers against the bureaucrats of the CCP

dacha: Russian summer vacation house

Das Kapital: Karl Marx's work giving his analysis of the economics of capitalism

De Facto: a political entity actually exercising power, but not by right of law

De Jure: a political entity exercising power by right of law

Dedazo: pointing the finger of blame

defence minister: in the United Kingdom, a cabinet position that controls the armed forces

Democracy Wall: a wall established in Bejing calling for the fulfillment of the "Fifth Modernization" (democracy) in accord with Deng Xiaoping's reforms; the wall was taken down after 15 months and its creator (a young dissident named Wei Jiangsheng) was imprisoned and eventually exiled

Demokratizatsia: democratization

Deng Xiaoping (China): China's paramount leader from 1982 until his death in 1997

Devolution (United Kingdom): term used by Labour Party in Britain to signify greater self-rule for Scotland, Wales, and Northern Ireland

Duma: any of various representative assemblies in modern Russia and Russian history

Efficacy: the belief that political action, whether by voting, writing to an elected official, or marching in the streets, matters and may influence policy

efficient institution: elements of government that include the House of Commons and cabinet, led by the prime minister; they are elected offices and hold most of the political power

Ejido: a communal farm, generally on poor land in Mexico's South

Engels, Friedrich: author of the first socialist theories

ethnic militias (Nigeria): formed throughout the country to settle scores in a vigilante manner

EU Constitution: includes all previous EU treaties, as well as establishing a stronger EU presidency and a more coordinated EU foreign policy

European Community: renamed from the European Economic Community in 1992 under the Maastricht Treaty, making the European Community the first of three pillars of the European Union

European Court of Justice: judicial arm of the EU holding the power of judicial review over decisions made by courts in member states (i.e., House of Lords as Britain's highest court of appeal)

European Economic Community (EEC): formed under the Treaty of Rome; one of the most important of the three European Communities

European Parliament: the parliamentary body of the EU, elected by EU citizens every five years. It comprises one half of the legislative branch of the EU, and meets in Brussels and Strasbourg (France)

European Union (EU): an intergovernmental and supranational union of 25 European countries (member states), established under the Maastricht Treaty

euroskeptics: those who disagree with the purposes of the European Union

Ex Officio: by virtue of office or position

Falun Gong: group that tested Jiang Zemin's rule in 1999

Farsi: Persian; Iran's dominant language

Fascism: a political system based on one-party militarism and nationalism

Fatwa **(Iran):** death threat

Federal: governing power is shared between the state and sub-state entities

Federalism: two or more levels of mutually autonomous governments each of which can act directly upon an individual

female infanticide: abandonment of female babies that had occurred in response to the one-child policy

First World: industrial democracy (i.e., "the free world," for example Western Europe, Japan, Canada, and the United States)

first-past-the-post: a voting system for single member district pluralities

foreign minister: cabinet member responsible for helping form the governmental foreign policy of a sovereignty

Four Modernizations: goals of Deng Xiaoping's reforms, including agriculture, industry, science and technology, and the military

Four Olds: traditional customs, culture, habits, and beliefs torn down by the Chinese Cultural Revolution

free trade: among EU members, no tariffs on most goods.

free vote: a vote on a bill in which party discipline is not to be enforced and occurs on "matters of conscience"

Fundamental Charter of Rights: basic individual rights according to the EU; includes provisions that ban capital punishment, guarantee health care for all, and mandates equal pay for equal work between the genders

Gang of Four: group of Communist Party leaders in China who were arrested and removed from their positions following the death of Mao Zedong, and were blamed for the events of the Chinese Cultural Revolution. Two were executed

glasnost: a reform under Mikhail Gorbachev that gave new freedoms to the people of the Soviet Union, such as a greater freedom of speech; the new freedoms (and freedom of the media to discuss the failure of the Soviet government) changed citizens' views and ultimately led to the collapse of the Soviet Union

Glasnost: aspect of Gorbachev's reforms for the Soviet Union meaning "openness"

Good Friday Agreement (United Kingdom): core agreement and compromise plan for government to allow self-rule in Northern Ireland for Ulster Unionists (Protestants) and Catholics; signed on April 10, 1998

Gorbachev, Mikhail (Russian Federation): former President and General Secretary of the Communist Party of the Soviet Union (CPSU) from 1985–1991

grand bargain: an agreement by which Iran would be admitted into the World Trade Organization in exchange for the curtailment of Iran's nuclear program

Great Famine: famine in which ten million people, mostly in the Ukraine, are believed to have starved to death

Great Leap Forward (China): Mao Zedong's plan to aid the agricultural peasant labor force in a "democratic" method unlike Stalin earlier; it failed miserably because authoritarian methods were used instead of peasant self-management, and led to an utter depletion of the peasant labor force

Great Leap Forward: begun in 1958, was designed to catch China up with the West industrially in a mere 15 years of concerted effort using China's massive human resources. The program was abandoned after only two years of operation and resulted in widespread misery throughout China

Great Purge: the killing of thousands of top CPSU officials, including heroes of the Bolshevik Revolution, former comrades of Lenin, and top Red Army leaders

guanxi: (China) Implied system of connections, often involving nepotism, needed for commercial success within China

Hausa-Fulani: a large ethnic group in Nigeria

hereditary peers: aristocrats who passed their seats in the House of Lords on to an heir; they have been stripped of their voting rights in the House of Lords in favor of Life Peers

House of Commons (United Kingdom): popularly elected legislative body who control all real power, but are responsible to the public

House of Commons: historically, the elected lower house, which holds greater power than the upper house

House of Lords (United Kingdom): composed of Life Peers and Hereditary Peers of Right; has no real legislative power

House of Lords: the upper house of the Parliament of the United Kingdom

hukou: internal passports or documents that control residence and freedom of movement within China

Hundred Flowers: period between 1956 and 1957 during which the Chinese Communist Party permitted criticism of the CCP. The negative criticism that resulted unleashed a sort of revenge program by the government

hyper-inflation: annual inflation rates of more than 100 percent

Ibo: ethnic group in Nigeria

Imperialism: any form of government policy in which territories are conquered or colonized for the benefit of the mother country

Iranian Revolution: in 1979, moved Iran from an autocratic, pro-West monarchy under Shah Mohammad Reza Pahlavi to an Islamic dictatorship under Ayatollah Khomeini

iron rice bowl: CCP's promise of life-long security through employment, housing, and basic medical care

Islamic states: include some 26 countries in the Middle East, North Africa, and southern Asia in which Islam and specifically the Qur'an serves as the guide for government, through a comprehensive body of law called *shari'a* and the general combination of church and state

Kulaks: wealthy peasants in the Russian Empire

Labour Party (United Kingdom): party in Great Britain whose views tend to be in opposition of and to the left of the Tory Party

Labour/New Labour: one of the United Kingdom's main political parties. Tony Blair is the party's most recently elected leader

Lagos: largest city in Nigeria

LDCs (Less Developed Countries): are a step below the NICs in terms of economic development, and have long-term potential for economic and political advancement, but this advancement is blocked by barriers, which usually involve significant cleavages, either ethnic, religious, or both, within the state

Legitimacy: the notion that a government's rule is just and that it has the right to exist

Lenin: brought Marxist ideology to Russia during World War I

Liberal Democrats: Britain's strongest "minor" political party

life peers: earn their seats in the House of Lords through meritorious service to the United Kingdom

little emperor's syndrome: in the People's Republic of China, describes generally spoiled children, who have been doted upon by their parents both economically and emotionally

Locke, John: wrote that natural law consists of man's right to life, liberty, and property

Lootocrats (Nigeria): top aides to Babingida and Abacha; lined their own pockets at expense of Nigeria's power

Maastricht Treaty: led to the creation of the European Union and the euro as the EU's currency

Machismo: male domination

Mahmoud Ahmadinejad: elected president of Iran in 2005

Majlis **(Iran):** parliament

Major, John (United Kingdom): succeeded Margaret Thatcher as prime minister in 1990, re-elected in 1992 until his defeat in the 1997 elections

mandate of heaven (People's Republic of China): the belief by the populace that the gods favored the maintenance of the current dynasty

manifesto: collection of beliefs

Mao Zedong (China): communist leader of China who began the Cultural Revolution in order to create new Chinese values

Maquiladora: a high-tech factory located in Mexico's wealthier north, near the U.S. border

market economy: the demand of consumers drives production

Marx, Karl: author of the *Communist Manifesto*

mass line: an attempt to make Marxism "work" in a non-industrial, peasant country

MEP: Member of the European Parliament

Mestizo: Mexican peoples who are a mixture of Iberian and indigenous natives

Militarism: any system of government in which the military forces have absolute power within the country

Miss World 2002 contest: pageant during which a journalist wrote that the Muslim prophet Mohammed would have been proud to wed any one of the contestants, resulting in riots leading to the deaths of more than 200 people. The pageant was relocated to London

Monarchy: a system of government in which all power is vested within a king who is chosen by right of heredity

MP: Member of Parliament

***Mullahs* (Iran):** educated Muslims trained in traditional religious law; usually holds an official post

NAFTA (North American Free Trade Agreement): agreement between Mexico, Canada, and the United States, reducing tariffs and eliminating quotas between the three countries

Nation: a cultural (rather than political) grouping and generally shares a common language and religion

National Leader System: legislature is responsible to the executive, and legitimizes the executive's decisions

National People's Congress: in theory, this is the legislative branch of China's federal government

NEPA: Nigeria's power monopoly

NGOs (Non-governmental organization): usually non-profit advocacy groups that gain a portion of their funding from private sources; usually used to describe social, cultural, legal, and environmental groups

NICs (Newly Industrialized Countries): developing countries formerly part of the Third World

nomenklatura: a privileged list of candidates to fill CPSU positions

Nuclear Non-Proliferation Treaty: treaty that restricts the possession of nuclear weapons

Oligarchy: all power in the state is vested in the minority ruling class

one child policy: enacted early in Deng Xiaoping's administration, limited families to a single child without taxation penalties

one country/two systems: idea proposed by Deng Xiaoping for the unification of China

OPEC (Organization of the Petroleum Exporting Countries): international organization whose purpose is to negotiate with oil companies on matters concerning petroleum production, pricing, etc

Open Sore of a Continent (Nigeria): written by Nobel literature laureate Wole Soyinka, after being driven into exile and teaching in the United States; decries the pitiful state of Nigeria under General Sani Abacha

Our Home is Russia: political party in Russia which backed Boris Yeltsin

Ox-bridge: Referring to Oxford and Cambridge in the United Kingdom, as the natural path of students for political office

PAN (Mexico): National Action Party, rival party to the PRI

parallel hierarchies: in an attempt to ensure CCP power, concept that for every government position, a corresponding CCP position will exist to "shadow" it

Parliamentary System: executive is chosen by and is responsible to the legislature

party discipline: a political party's ability to get its members party leadership policies

PDP (Nigeria): People's Democratic Party

PEMEX: Mexican oil monopoly

pendulum theory (Mexico): technique employed by the PRI (Institutional Revolutionary Party) allowing it to sway from left to right to fit the mood of the Mexican electorate

People's Liberation Army (China): a major political lobby and force in exercising power with the CCP in the People's Republic of China

People's Liberation Army (PLA): military force of the People's Republic of China

People's Republic of China: founded in 1941 and led by the Communist Party, it is the world's most populous country

Perestroika: aspect of Gorbachev's reforms for the Soviet Union meaning "restructuring"

perestroika: the reform of Soviet industry

Pluralism: a framework by which different groups interact while showing respect and tolerance of each other

Politburo: the chief political and executive committee of the Communist Party

political elites: those who have access to political positions in the upper bureaucracy, parliament, the cabinet, and so on

political integration: the notion that the citizens of a state will primarily identify themselves with the state, as opposed to their ethnicity or religion

PR (Proportional Representation): voters choose a party with their vote; votes are then tallied country wide, and the percentage won by a party translates into the percentage of seats they have earned in the legislature

Pravda: newspaper of the Soviet Union (an official publication of the Communist Party between 1918 and 1991)

PRD (Mexico): Democratic Party of the Revolution, formed in the late 1980s by disaffected PRI deputies

Premier: prime minister of the Communist Party

Presidential System: the executive is chosen separately from the legislature and is not responsible to the legislature

PRI: Institutional Revolutionary Party of Mexico

Prime Minister (United Kingdom): the head of government and majority party leader who is selected by the Sovereign from the House of Commons

Privy Council (United Kingdom): ex officio officers/cabinet members appointed as honor; life membership; no important function except Judicial Committee which acts as Appellate Court

Pro Forma: done or carried out in a routine manner

Proletariat: Marx's term for the exploited industrial working class

protest vote: demonstrates the voter's unhappiness with the candidate selection or with the current political system

public school: the British label for what Americans would call a private boarding school. The name draws from the fact that these schools often prepare students for a life of public service to Britain via political office

Putin, Vladimir (Russian Federation): last prime minister under Yeltsin and heir apparent who was elected President of Russia in 2000

Red Guards: high school and college students unleashed by Mao Zedong to implement the Chinese Cultural Revolution

regional parties: smaller political parties in the United Kingdom, for example the Scottish National Party or Sinn Fein

Republic of China (Taiwan): country set up by fleeing Nationalist forces when defeated by the Communist Party and the People's Liberation Army

Republic: a political entity in which the supreme power lies with the voting public

responsibility system: a system by which the peasants of China were free to grow whatever they chose at market value once they met the state quota for a certain crop (often wheat)

Russian Federation: formerly part of the USSR, Russia is now an independent country

safe seat: a district from which a political party generally wins

SARS (Severe Acute Respiratory Syndrome): 2002 outbreak that originated in Hong Kong and became a world health scare as it was both extremely contagious and lethal

Second World: industrialized but not democratic. (i.e., "the communist bloc," basically the Soviet Union and its Eastern European satellite states like Poland, East Germany, Czechoslovakia, etc.)

shadow cabinet: in the United Kingdom, a group of opposition party representatives who form an alternative cabinet with the responsibility to criticize the government and its legislation

Shah (Iran): ruler

Shi'a: one of the two main branches of Islam

shock therapy: in the Russian Federation under Boris Yeltsin, an immediate leap to a market economy without any safety net or transitional period. Hyper-inflation resulted during the mid-1990s

SMDP (Single Member District Plurality): sometimes called "First Past the Post"; a country is broken down into districts of roughly equal population; parties run a single candidate in each district and the candidate gaining the most votes—a plurality—represents the district politically

Socialism: a system of government in which the state is responsible for the general welfare of its citizens

Sovereignty: having ultimate political authority within one's own soil

Soviet Union/USSR: socialist state founded in 1922, centered on Russia; the state was dissolved in 1991. The only ruling political party was the Communist Party of the Soviet Union

Soviet: a form of government in which the political party, e.g., the Communist Party, is the decision-making branch of the government while the government is reduced to implementing party decisions

Special Economic Zones: to buffer Hong Kong's influence on mainland China, these zones were set up in which foreign investment and capitalism were encouraged

Stability Pact: an agreement by EU member states regarding fiscal policy in order to use the euro as that state's currency

Stalin, Joseph: absolute leader of the Soviet Union who modified communist doctrine into totalitarian doctrine by the suppression of his people

State: used in its international sense, synonymous with *country*. For a state to exist, the following four conditions must be met: permanent population; defined territory; organized government; and sovereignty

struggle sessions: occurred during the Chinese Cultural Revolution when the Red Guards publicly questioned the loyalty and/or Maoist credentials of authority figures such as CCP cadre (bureaucrats), school teachers, parents, or any other authority figure they might have a grudge against and wished to publicly humiliate

Subsidy: a guaranteed payment from a government to a producer, usually farmers, for a certain commodity

Sunni: the larger of the two main branches of Islam

Super Eagles: Nigeria's national football (soccer) team

Thatcher, Margaret (United Kingdom): prime minister of Great Britain 1979–1990

the dash (Nigeria): an accepted practice of political corruption

Theocracy: rule by religious leaders

Third World: a grouping of a widely disparate group of states

Tiananmen Square (1989): after a group of university students gathered to mourn the passing of Hu Yaobang, a moderate reformer, a democracy movement blossomed, but was ended with the massacre of 1,400 students in the square; this marked the end of Deng

Totalitarian: form of government in which person/party has absolute power and rival parties are not allowed to exist

Treaty of Nice (1991): the treaty's primary purpose was to reform the institutional structure of the EU to allow for expansion

Treaty of Rome: in the European Union, treaty that established the European Economic Community (EEC)

Treaty of Versailles: treaty that formally ended World War I

tyranny of law: a crackdown on both organized crime and on the powerful Oligarchs in Russia

unitary mistake: announcement by Aguiyi Ironsi that Nigeria would be run as a unitary system under his military rule

Unitary: all power is concentrated in a central government

United Russia: political party in Russia; backs President Vladimir Putin

village democracy (China): grass roots movement where villagers elect their own representative, to promote greater profit among local crops, help peasants understand and implement the latest CCP directives, and so on

Welfare State: government takes responsibility for the personal welfare of its citizens

Yeltsin, Boris (Russian Federation): took office in 1991 as President of the Russian Federation, re-elected in 1996, and resigned at the end of 1999

Yoruba: second largest ethnic group in Nigeria

Zapatista: peasant farmers who revolted against local and federal authorities to display their anger at NAFTA and its perceived economic aid only for Mexico's already wealthier north

Zemin, Jiang (China): head of CCP (1989), head of state (1993), and the pre-eminent political leader of the PRC since Deng Xiaoping's death in 1997

zero-sum politics: a situation in which a participant's gains or losses is exactly equal to that of the other participants

Answer Sheets

AP U.S.
GOVERNMENT & POLITICS
PRACTICE TEST 1

ANSWER SHEET

1. Ⓐ Ⓑ Ⓒ Ⓓ Ⓔ	21. Ⓐ Ⓑ Ⓒ Ⓓ Ⓔ	41. Ⓐ Ⓑ Ⓒ Ⓓ Ⓔ
2. Ⓐ Ⓑ Ⓒ Ⓓ Ⓔ	22. Ⓐ Ⓑ Ⓒ Ⓓ Ⓔ	42. Ⓐ Ⓑ Ⓒ Ⓓ Ⓔ
3. Ⓐ Ⓑ Ⓒ Ⓓ Ⓔ	23. Ⓐ Ⓑ Ⓒ Ⓓ Ⓔ	43. Ⓐ Ⓑ Ⓒ Ⓓ Ⓔ
4. Ⓐ Ⓑ Ⓒ Ⓓ Ⓔ	24. Ⓐ Ⓑ Ⓒ Ⓓ Ⓔ	44. Ⓐ Ⓑ Ⓒ Ⓓ Ⓔ
5. Ⓐ Ⓑ Ⓒ Ⓓ Ⓔ	25. Ⓐ Ⓑ Ⓒ Ⓓ Ⓔ	45. Ⓐ Ⓑ Ⓒ Ⓓ Ⓔ
6. Ⓐ Ⓑ Ⓒ Ⓓ Ⓔ	26. Ⓐ Ⓑ Ⓒ Ⓓ Ⓔ	46. Ⓐ Ⓑ Ⓒ Ⓓ Ⓔ
7. Ⓐ Ⓑ Ⓒ Ⓓ Ⓔ	27. Ⓐ Ⓑ Ⓒ Ⓓ Ⓔ	47. Ⓐ Ⓑ Ⓒ Ⓓ Ⓔ
8. Ⓐ Ⓑ Ⓒ Ⓓ Ⓔ	28. Ⓐ Ⓑ Ⓒ Ⓓ Ⓔ	48. Ⓐ Ⓑ Ⓒ Ⓓ Ⓔ
9. Ⓐ Ⓑ Ⓒ Ⓓ Ⓔ	29. Ⓐ Ⓑ Ⓒ Ⓓ Ⓔ	49. Ⓐ Ⓑ Ⓒ Ⓓ Ⓔ
10. Ⓐ Ⓑ Ⓒ Ⓓ Ⓔ	30. Ⓐ Ⓑ Ⓒ Ⓓ Ⓔ	50. Ⓐ Ⓑ Ⓒ Ⓓ Ⓔ
11. Ⓐ Ⓑ Ⓒ Ⓓ Ⓔ	31. Ⓐ Ⓑ Ⓒ Ⓓ Ⓔ	51. Ⓐ Ⓑ Ⓒ Ⓓ Ⓔ
12. Ⓐ Ⓑ Ⓒ Ⓓ Ⓔ	32. Ⓐ Ⓑ Ⓒ Ⓓ Ⓔ	52. Ⓐ Ⓑ Ⓒ Ⓓ Ⓔ
13. Ⓐ Ⓑ Ⓒ Ⓓ Ⓔ	33. Ⓐ Ⓑ Ⓒ Ⓓ Ⓔ	53. Ⓐ Ⓑ Ⓒ Ⓓ Ⓔ
14. Ⓐ Ⓑ Ⓒ Ⓓ Ⓔ	34. Ⓐ Ⓑ Ⓒ Ⓓ Ⓔ	54. Ⓐ Ⓑ Ⓒ Ⓓ Ⓔ
15. Ⓐ Ⓑ Ⓒ Ⓓ Ⓔ	35. Ⓐ Ⓑ Ⓒ Ⓓ Ⓔ	55. Ⓐ Ⓑ Ⓒ Ⓓ Ⓔ
16. Ⓐ Ⓑ Ⓒ Ⓓ Ⓔ	36. Ⓐ Ⓑ Ⓒ Ⓓ Ⓔ	56. Ⓐ Ⓑ Ⓒ Ⓓ Ⓔ
17. Ⓐ Ⓑ Ⓒ Ⓓ Ⓔ	37. Ⓐ Ⓑ Ⓒ Ⓓ Ⓔ	57. Ⓐ Ⓑ Ⓒ Ⓓ Ⓔ
18. Ⓐ Ⓑ Ⓒ Ⓓ Ⓔ	38. Ⓐ Ⓑ Ⓒ Ⓓ Ⓔ	58. Ⓐ Ⓑ Ⓒ Ⓓ Ⓔ
19. Ⓐ Ⓑ Ⓒ Ⓓ Ⓔ	39. Ⓐ Ⓑ Ⓒ Ⓓ Ⓔ	59. Ⓐ Ⓑ Ⓒ Ⓓ Ⓔ
20. Ⓐ Ⓑ Ⓒ Ⓓ Ⓔ	40. Ⓐ Ⓑ Ⓒ Ⓓ Ⓔ	60. Ⓐ Ⓑ Ⓒ Ⓓ Ⓔ

AP U.S.
GOVERNMENT & POLITICS
PRACTICE TEST 2

ANSWER SHEET

1. Ⓐ Ⓑ Ⓒ Ⓓ Ⓔ	21. Ⓐ Ⓑ Ⓒ Ⓓ Ⓔ	41. Ⓐ Ⓑ Ⓒ Ⓓ Ⓔ
2. Ⓐ Ⓑ Ⓒ Ⓓ Ⓔ	22. Ⓐ Ⓑ Ⓒ Ⓓ Ⓔ	42. Ⓐ Ⓑ Ⓒ Ⓓ Ⓔ
3. Ⓐ Ⓑ Ⓒ Ⓓ Ⓔ	23. Ⓐ Ⓑ Ⓒ Ⓓ Ⓔ	43. Ⓐ Ⓑ Ⓒ Ⓓ Ⓔ
4. Ⓐ Ⓑ Ⓒ Ⓓ Ⓔ	24. Ⓐ Ⓑ Ⓒ Ⓓ Ⓔ	44. Ⓐ Ⓑ Ⓒ Ⓓ Ⓔ
5. Ⓐ Ⓑ Ⓒ Ⓓ Ⓔ	25. Ⓐ Ⓑ Ⓒ Ⓓ Ⓔ	45. Ⓐ Ⓑ Ⓒ Ⓓ Ⓔ
6. Ⓐ Ⓑ Ⓒ Ⓓ Ⓔ	26. Ⓐ Ⓑ Ⓒ Ⓓ Ⓔ	46. Ⓐ Ⓑ Ⓒ Ⓓ Ⓔ
7. Ⓐ Ⓑ Ⓒ Ⓓ Ⓔ	27. Ⓐ Ⓑ Ⓒ Ⓓ Ⓔ	47. Ⓐ Ⓑ Ⓒ Ⓓ Ⓔ
8. Ⓐ Ⓑ Ⓒ Ⓓ Ⓔ	28. Ⓐ Ⓑ Ⓒ Ⓓ Ⓔ	48. Ⓐ Ⓑ Ⓒ Ⓓ Ⓔ
9. Ⓐ Ⓑ Ⓒ Ⓓ Ⓔ	29. Ⓐ Ⓑ Ⓒ Ⓓ Ⓔ	49. Ⓐ Ⓑ Ⓒ Ⓓ Ⓔ
10. Ⓐ Ⓑ Ⓒ Ⓓ Ⓔ	30. Ⓐ Ⓑ Ⓒ Ⓓ Ⓔ	50. Ⓐ Ⓑ Ⓒ Ⓓ Ⓔ
11. Ⓐ Ⓑ Ⓒ Ⓓ Ⓔ	31. Ⓐ Ⓑ Ⓒ Ⓓ Ⓔ	51. Ⓐ Ⓑ Ⓒ Ⓓ Ⓔ
12. Ⓐ Ⓑ Ⓒ Ⓓ Ⓔ	32. Ⓐ Ⓑ Ⓒ Ⓓ Ⓔ	52. Ⓐ Ⓑ Ⓒ Ⓓ Ⓔ
13. Ⓐ Ⓑ Ⓒ Ⓓ Ⓔ	33. Ⓐ Ⓑ Ⓒ Ⓓ Ⓔ	53. Ⓐ Ⓑ Ⓒ Ⓓ Ⓔ
14. Ⓐ Ⓑ Ⓒ Ⓓ Ⓔ	34. Ⓐ Ⓑ Ⓒ Ⓓ Ⓔ	54. Ⓐ Ⓑ Ⓒ Ⓓ Ⓔ
15. Ⓐ Ⓑ Ⓒ Ⓓ Ⓔ	35. Ⓐ Ⓑ Ⓒ Ⓓ Ⓔ	55. Ⓐ Ⓑ Ⓒ Ⓓ Ⓔ
16. Ⓐ Ⓑ Ⓒ Ⓓ Ⓔ	36. Ⓐ Ⓑ Ⓒ Ⓓ Ⓔ	56. Ⓐ Ⓑ Ⓒ Ⓓ Ⓔ
17. Ⓐ Ⓑ Ⓒ Ⓓ Ⓔ	37. Ⓐ Ⓑ Ⓒ Ⓓ Ⓔ	57. Ⓐ Ⓑ Ⓒ Ⓓ Ⓔ
18. Ⓐ Ⓑ Ⓒ Ⓓ Ⓔ	38. Ⓐ Ⓑ Ⓒ Ⓓ Ⓔ	58. Ⓐ Ⓑ Ⓒ Ⓓ Ⓔ
19. Ⓐ Ⓑ Ⓒ Ⓓ Ⓔ	39. Ⓐ Ⓑ Ⓒ Ⓓ Ⓔ	59. Ⓐ Ⓑ Ⓒ Ⓓ Ⓔ
20. Ⓐ Ⓑ Ⓒ Ⓓ Ⓔ	40. Ⓐ Ⓑ Ⓒ Ⓓ Ⓔ	60. Ⓐ Ⓑ Ⓒ Ⓓ Ⓔ

AP U.S.
GOVERNMENT & POLITICS
PRACTICE TEST 3

ANSWER SHEET

1. (A) (B) (C) (D) (E)	21. (A) (B) (C) (D) (E)	41. (A) (B) (C) (D) (E)
2. (A) (B) (C) (D) (E)	22. (A) (B) (C) (D) (E)	42. (A) (B) (C) (D) (E)
3. (A) (B) (C) (D) (E)	23. (A) (B) (C) (D) (E)	43. (A) (B) (C) (D) (E)
4. (A) (B) (C) (D) (E)	24. (A) (B) (C) (D) (E)	44. (A) (B) (C) (D) (E)
5. (A) (B) (C) (D) (E)	25. (A) (B) (C) (D) (E)	45. (A) (B) (C) (D) (E)
6. (A) (B) (C) (D) (E)	26. (A) (B) (C) (D) (E)	46. (A) (B) (C) (D) (E)
7. (A) (B) (C) (D) (E)	27. (A) (B) (C) (D) (E)	47. (A) (B) (C) (D) (E)
8. (A) (B) (C) (D) (E)	28. (A) (B) (C) (D) (E)	48. (A) (B) (C) (D) (E)
9. (A) (B) (C) (D) (E)	29. (A) (B) (C) (D) (E)	49. (A) (B) (C) (D) (E)
10. (A) (B) (C) (D) (E)	30. (A) (B) (C) (D) (E)	50. (A) (B) (C) (D) (E)
11. (A) (B) (C) (D) (E)	31. (A) (B) (C) (D) (E)	51. (A) (B) (C) (D) (E)
12. (A) (B) (C) (D) (E)	32. (A) (B) (C) (D) (E)	52. (A) (B) (C) (D) (E)
13. (A) (B) (C) (D) (E)	33. (A) (B) (C) (D) (E)	53. (A) (B) (C) (D) (E)
14. (A) (B) (C) (D) (E)	34. (A) (B) (C) (D) (E)	54. (A) (B) (C) (D) (E)
15. (A) (B) (C) (D) (E)	35. (A) (B) (C) (D) (E)	55. (A) (B) (C) (D) (E)
16. (A) (B) (C) (D) (E)	36. (A) (B) (C) (D) (E)	56. (A) (B) (C) (D) (E)
17. (A) (B) (C) (D) (E)	37. (A) (B) (C) (D) (E)	57. (A) (B) (C) (D) (E)
18. (A) (B) (C) (D) (E)	38. (A) (B) (C) (D) (E)	58. (A) (B) (C) (D) (E)
19. (A) (B) (C) (D) (E)	39. (A) (B) (C) (D) (E)	59. (A) (B) (C) (D) (E)
20. (A) (B) (C) (D) (E)	40. (A) (B) (C) (D) (E)	60. (A) (B) (C) (D) (E)

AP COMPARATIVE GOVERNMENT & POLITICS PRACTICE TEST 4

ANSWER SHEET

1. Ⓐ Ⓑ Ⓒ Ⓓ Ⓔ
2. Ⓐ Ⓑ Ⓒ Ⓓ Ⓔ
3. Ⓐ Ⓑ Ⓒ Ⓓ Ⓔ
4. Ⓐ Ⓑ Ⓒ Ⓓ Ⓔ
5. Ⓐ Ⓑ Ⓒ Ⓓ Ⓔ
6. Ⓐ Ⓑ Ⓒ Ⓓ Ⓔ
7. Ⓐ Ⓑ Ⓒ Ⓓ Ⓔ
8. Ⓐ Ⓑ Ⓒ Ⓓ Ⓔ
9. Ⓐ Ⓑ Ⓒ Ⓓ Ⓔ
10. Ⓐ Ⓑ Ⓒ Ⓓ Ⓔ
11. Ⓐ Ⓑ Ⓒ Ⓓ Ⓔ
12. Ⓐ Ⓑ Ⓒ Ⓓ Ⓔ
13. Ⓐ Ⓑ Ⓒ Ⓓ Ⓔ
14. Ⓐ Ⓑ Ⓒ Ⓓ Ⓔ
15. Ⓐ Ⓑ Ⓒ Ⓓ Ⓔ
16. Ⓐ Ⓑ Ⓒ Ⓓ Ⓔ
17. Ⓐ Ⓑ Ⓒ Ⓓ Ⓔ
18. Ⓐ Ⓑ Ⓒ Ⓓ Ⓔ
19. Ⓐ Ⓑ Ⓒ Ⓓ Ⓔ
20. Ⓐ Ⓑ Ⓒ Ⓓ Ⓔ

21. Ⓐ Ⓑ Ⓒ Ⓓ Ⓔ
22. Ⓐ Ⓑ Ⓒ Ⓓ Ⓔ
23. Ⓐ Ⓑ Ⓒ Ⓓ Ⓔ
24. Ⓐ Ⓑ Ⓒ Ⓓ Ⓔ
25. Ⓐ Ⓑ Ⓒ Ⓓ Ⓔ
26. Ⓐ Ⓑ Ⓒ Ⓓ Ⓔ
27. Ⓐ Ⓑ Ⓒ Ⓓ Ⓔ
28. Ⓐ Ⓑ Ⓒ Ⓓ Ⓔ
29. Ⓐ Ⓑ Ⓒ Ⓓ Ⓔ
30. Ⓐ Ⓑ Ⓒ Ⓓ Ⓔ
31. Ⓐ Ⓑ Ⓒ Ⓓ Ⓔ
32. Ⓐ Ⓑ Ⓒ Ⓓ Ⓔ
33. Ⓐ Ⓑ Ⓒ Ⓓ Ⓔ
34. Ⓐ Ⓑ Ⓒ Ⓓ Ⓔ
35. Ⓐ Ⓑ Ⓒ Ⓓ Ⓔ
36. Ⓐ Ⓑ Ⓒ Ⓓ Ⓔ
37. Ⓐ Ⓑ Ⓒ Ⓓ Ⓔ
38. Ⓐ Ⓑ Ⓒ Ⓓ Ⓔ
39. Ⓐ Ⓑ Ⓒ Ⓓ Ⓔ
40. Ⓐ Ⓑ Ⓒ Ⓓ Ⓔ

41. Ⓐ Ⓑ Ⓒ Ⓓ Ⓔ
42. Ⓐ Ⓑ Ⓒ Ⓓ Ⓔ
43. Ⓐ Ⓑ Ⓒ Ⓓ Ⓔ
44. Ⓐ Ⓑ Ⓒ Ⓓ Ⓔ
45. Ⓐ Ⓑ Ⓒ Ⓓ Ⓔ
46. Ⓐ Ⓑ Ⓒ Ⓓ Ⓔ
47. Ⓐ Ⓑ Ⓒ Ⓓ Ⓔ
48. Ⓐ Ⓑ Ⓒ Ⓓ Ⓔ
49. Ⓐ Ⓑ Ⓒ Ⓓ Ⓔ
50. Ⓐ Ⓑ Ⓒ Ⓓ Ⓔ
51. Ⓐ Ⓑ Ⓒ Ⓓ Ⓔ
52. Ⓐ Ⓑ Ⓒ Ⓓ Ⓔ
53. Ⓐ Ⓑ Ⓒ Ⓓ Ⓔ
54. Ⓐ Ⓑ Ⓒ Ⓓ Ⓔ
55. Ⓐ Ⓑ Ⓒ Ⓓ Ⓔ

AP COMPARATIVE GOVERNMENT & POLITICS PRACTICE TEST 5

ANSWER SHEET

1. (A) (B) (C) (D) (E)
2. (A) (B) (C) (D) (E)
3. (A) (B) (C) (D) (E)
4. (A) (B) (C) (D) (E)
5. (A) (B) (C) (D) (E)
6. (A) (B) (C) (D) (E)
7. (A) (B) (C) (D) (E)
8. (A) (B) (C) (D) (E)
9. (A) (B) (C) (D) (E)
10. (A) (B) (C) (D) (E)
11. (A) (B) (C) (D) (E)
12. (A) (B) (C) (D) (E)
13. (A) (B) (C) (D) (E)
14. (A) (B) (C) (D) (E)
15. (A) (B) (C) (D) (E)
16. (A) (B) (C) (D) (E)
17. (A) (B) (C) (D) (E)
18. (A) (B) (C) (D) (E)
19. (A) (B) (C) (D) (E)
20. (A) (B) (C) (D) (E)

21. (A) (B) (C) (D) (E)
22. (A) (B) (C) (D) (E)
23. (A) (B) (C) (D) (E)
24. (A) (B) (C) (D) (E)
25. (A) (B) (C) (D) (E)
26. (A) (B) (C) (D) (E)
27. (A) (B) (C) (D) (E)
28. (A) (B) (C) (D) (E)
29. (A) (B) (C) (D) (E)
30. (A) (B) (C) (D) (E)
31. (A) (B) (C) (D) (E)
32. (A) (B) (C) (D) (E)
33. (A) (B) (C) (D) (E)
34. (A) (B) (C) (D) (E)
35. (A) (B) (C) (D) (E)
36. (A) (B) (C) (D) (E)
37. (A) (B) (C) (D) (E)
38. (A) (B) (C) (D) (E)
39. (A) (B) (C) (D) (E)
40. (A) (B) (C) (D) (E)

41. (A) (B) (C) (D) (E)
42. (A) (B) (C) (D) (E)
43. (A) (B) (C) (D) (E)
44. (A) (B) (C) (D) (E)
45. (A) (B) (C) (D) (E)
46. (A) (B) (C) (D) (E)
47. (A) (B) (C) (D) (E)
48. (A) (B) (C) (D) (E)
49. (A) (B) (C) (D) (E)
50. (A) (B) (C) (D) (E)
51. (A) (B) (C) (D) (E)
52. (A) (B) (C) (D) (E)
53. (A) (B) (C) (D) (E)
54. (A) (B) (C) (D) (E)
55. (A) (B) (C) (D) (E)

Appendices

APPENDICES

Appendix A

IMPORTANT HISTORICAL ANTECEDENTS TO THE U.S. CONSTITUTION

Magna Carta (1215) – The Great Charter challenged the tyrannical acts of an absolute monarch (King John) and established the rule of law. It paved the way for trial by jury, written constitutions, due process of law, and no taxation without representation.

Virginia House of Burgesses (1619) – The Virginia Colony elected 22 burgesses (representatives) by male suffrage to consult with the governor's council to make laws for the colony. This was a first step towards self-government by establishing an elected legislative assembly.

Mayflower Compact (1620) – This was a covenant signed by 41 men binding them to make "just and equal laws." This accord recognized and respected the concept of, and the deference to, majority rule established by the consent of the governed of the newly-formed Plymouth Colony. The document represented the first written agreement for self-government in the English Colonies.

The Fundamental Orders of Connecticut (1638-39) – This was the oldest written constitution in the English Colonies. Its purpose was to legitimate Connecticut's effort (under the leadership of Thomas Hooker) to establish a separate colony from the Massachusetts Bay Colony.

Two Treatises of Civil Government (1689) – John Locke challenged the Divine Right of Kings Theory by propounding that the sole legitimate purpose of government was based on protecting, preserving, and defending one's natural rights of "life, liberty, and estate." Locke's influence was clearly evident in both the Declaration of Independence and the Constitution.

English Bill of Rights (1689) – Among other things, this document validated citizen rights, representative government, parliamentary supremacy regarding power of the purse (raising revenues), and protection from the arbitrary suspension of Parliament's laws. Parts of this document were to resurface in the U.S. Bill of Rights.

The Spirit of the Laws (1748) – Clearly reflected in the Baron de Montesquieu's work was his belief that the fusion or concentration of powers in the same hands ultimately led to tyranny and the trampling of human freedoms. Consequently, he advocated the separation of powers into three separate and distinct branches of government: legislative, executive, and judicial. Madison's essay **Federalist #47** directly alluded to Montesquieu's influence on the framers of the Constitution, an influence that was embodied by the first three articles of the Constitution (the legislative, executive, and judicial branches, respectively).

Virginia Declaration of Rights (1776) – Signed two months before the Declaration of Independence, and drafted by George Mason (who was an unrelenting advocate of a bill of rights), this document was influential in the writing of the Declaration of Independence and, subsequently, in the Bill of Rights drafted by fellow Virginian James Madison.

Declaration of Independence (1776) – This was the classic natural rights document drawn from John Locke's political writings. Justifying the right to revolution when government usurps its role to protect, preserve, and defend one's natural rights, Jefferson (who was the primary author of the Committee of Five which drafted this hallowed parchment) underscored the principles of popular sovereignty, limited government, the consent of the governed, and self-determination.

Articles of Confederation (1781–88) – The first official form of self-government of the United States. Drafted in 1777 and ratified in 1781, it provided for a weak central government (partially in response to the centralized unitary form under British rule) and treated the individual states as thirteen separate sovereign entities. The Articles became increasingly discredited and eventually imploded due to economic problems regarding taxation and trade, the inability to maintain "domestic tranquility" (e.g., Shays' Rebellion), and political paralysis (e.g., the unanimity requirement to amend or change any structural or procedural feature of the Articles of Confederation).

The Articles of Confederation vs. the Constitution: A Comparison

Weaknesses of the Articles of Confederation	Consequences	U.S. Constitution (Constitutional Remedies)
1. No separate executive branch to cary out the laws of the Confederation Congress, or to speak with one voice in foreign affairs.	1. Lack of coordination of national policy – domestic and foreign.	1. Separate coordinate executive branch established to enforce the Constitution, and to "faithfully execute" the laws enacted under it, and to conduct foreign policy.
2. No separate national judicial branch, only a system of state courts (which proved inadequate when there were disputes between states).	2. No final judicial authority – only nonbinding and, at times, conflicting state court decisions that often proved unenforceable.	2. A separate judicial branch was established, headed by a supreme court that would act as the final arbiter of the Constitution and on all "cases and controversies" brought before it.
3. Inability to directly levy and collect taxes to fund the expenses of the central government.	3. Confederation Congress could only request tax contributions from the states – which often ignored such requests with impunity, resulting in a central government continually on the brink of bankruptcy.	3. Article I, Section 8 gave the Congress the specific power to levy and collect taxes – thus removing its reliance upon voluntary state contributions to finance governmental operations.

→

The Articles of Confederation vs. the Constitution: A Comparison (cont'd)

Weaknesses of the Articles of Confederation	Consequences	U.S. Constitution (Constitutional Remedies)
4. Inability to raise and support an army and navy. AOC could not directly induct men into the armed forces – but only request support of the state militias.	4. States often ignored requests for troops – thereby leaving the Confederation Congress unable to enforce national law or to "provide for the common defense."	4. Article I, Section 8 authorized Congress to raise, provide, maintain, and support an army and navy – from tax powers.
5. The states and the Confederation Congress both had the power to coin money. The AOC could not control or regulate the printing or value of money in circulation.	5. Competing foreign and domestic currencies. AOC paper money not backed by gold or silver, and various exchange rates between states led to economic chaos and confusion.	5. Only Congress was given the authority to coin money and to regulate its value. One uniform national monetary standard was established as legal tender.
6. Inability to regulate interstate and foreign commerce.	6. Protectionist trade barriers caused interstate trade to languish. No common foreign trade policy to promote national economic development.	6. Article I, Section 8 gave Congress the power to regulate interstate and foreign commerce – thus a national trade policy, based on enforceable trade treaties, could evolve.

→

The Articles of Confederation vs. the Constitution:
A Comparison (cont'd)

Weaknesses of the Articles of Confederation	Consequences	U.S. Constitution (Constitutional Remedies)
7. It was difficult to pass most laws since 9 of the 13 states were required to approve such things as borrowing and coining money, setting the budget, making treaties, and fixing the size of the armed forces.	7. Sporadic attendance by delegates. States often voted by blocs (e.g., 5 smaller states vs. 8 larger ones).	7. The law-making process required that bills passed by Congress only needed a simple majority vote in each house to become laws.
8. Unanimous consent of all 13 states were required to amend the AOC.	8. Amendment procedure was so rigid and impractical that the AOC was never amended regarding any basic structural or procedural change.	8. Article V provided an easier amendment procedure that required a two-thirds vote of Congress and ratification by three-fourths of the states.
9. No power to enforce Confederation laws upon the states – since, ultimately, the states were sovereign.	9. The AOC could only advise and request that states comply with Confederation laws.	9. "Supremacy Clause" affirmed that Constitution was the supreme law of the land, notwithstanding any federal or state laws to the contrary.

Appendix B

THE CONSTITUTIONAL CONVENTION: AN "ASSEMBLY OF DEMIGODS"

PREFATORY NOTE

Much has been written about this august assembly that gathered in Philadelphia between May and September 1787 to revise or amend the flagging Articles of Confederation. The attendees were a very unrepresentative demographic sampling of the American people. They included a veritable "who's who" of American society—a fact that prompted Thomas Jefferson to refer to them as an "assembly of demigods." Almost without exception, they were men of substance and social position representing the upper economic and social classes. Their attributed motivations have elicited much debate among historians as to whether their primary motivations were essentially their own personal aggrandizement and enlightened self-interest or, conversely, the promotion of the general commonweal. Notwithstanding this debate, a clear consensus emerged among the delegates that the Articles of Confederation were beyond salvation and that they had to be replaced by a stronger central government. Republican in form, but predicated on the principles of popular sovereignty, the new Constitution was designed to prevent the "excesses of democracy" feared by Alexander Hamilton, as well as to prevent tyranny by dividing power among the legislative, executive, and judicial branches of government and providing them with a system of reciprocal checks and balances. The product of their collective labor, delicately crafted from the constitutional crucible in Philadelphia, became the nucleus of that remarkable document that has endured for over two centuries.

THE CONSTITUTIONAL CONVENTION: A PROFILE

- Seventy-four delegates were appointed, 55 delegates attended, and 37 delegates signed the final draft. All were white and male.

- All 13 states were represented by delegates—with the exception of Rhode Island.

- The ages of the delegates ranged from 26-year-old Jonathan Dayton from New Jersey to the respected elder statesman, 81-year-old Benjamin Franklin from Pennsylvania. The average age was 42 years, with 6 under 31 years and 12 over 54 years.

- Thirty-nine delegates had previously served in the Congress, 7 had been governors of their respective states, 3 were professors, and 2 had been college presidents—yet, interestingly, only 8 out of the 56 signers of the Declaration of Independence were at Philadelphia.

- The delegates were primarily merchants, manufacturers, planters, lawyers, and bankers—specifically, there were 40 delegates who held government securities, 14 were land speculators, 24 were bankers or money lenders, 15 were slave owners, and 11 were in manufacturing and shipping.

- Conspicuously absent were small farmers, city mechanics, and indentured servants (and, of course, women, African-Americans, and Native Americans). Also absent were some of the notable fiery radicals of the American Revolution (e.g., Patrick Henry, Samuel Adams, John Hancock, Thomas Paine). John Adams and Thomas Jefferson were both in Europe at the time, serving in diplomatic roles.

KEY PLAYERS AT THE CONSTITUTIONAL CONVENTION

George Washington – a Virginia delegate who lent his enormous prestige and presence, was unanimously elected President of the Convention. He rarely participated in the discussions or debates.

James Madison – known as the "Father of the Constitution," this Virginia delegate wrote the Virginia Plan, was the scribe of the Philadelphia Convention who took the only systematic and detailed notes of the daily sessions, was a major contributor to *The Federalist Papers,* and drafted the Bill of Rights (which was added in 1791).

Benjamin Franklin – utilized his role as the "elder statesman" to act as a conciliator, to provide timely counsel and advice, and, through his wit and wry humor, to promote harmony and compromise when conflict threatened to scuttle the Convention's sessions.

Alexander Hamilton – while spotty in attendance and participation as a delegate from New York and despite offering an unpopular plan to create an extremely centralized national government, Hamilton's main contribution was as chief essayist in *The Federalist Papers* (which outlined and extolled the nature, design, purpose, and advantages of the new Constitution).

George Mason – representing Virginia, Mason forcefully advocated the need for a written bill of rights—as well as arguing, less convincingly, for a plural executive.

Gouverneur Morris – an eloquent and aristocratic delegate from Pennsylvania, Morris addressed the Convention more frequently than any other member and was given the task of writing the final wording and draft of the Constitution.

Roger Sherman – broke the deadlock over the nature of representative government bitterly dividing the larger and smaller states by proposing the Connecticut (Great) Compromise that appeased both sides.

Appendix C

WEIGHING 3 PLANS OFFERED AT CONSTITUTIONAL CONVENTION

THE HAMILTON PLAN: MOST CENTRALIZED

- Proposed by Alexander Hamilton, delegate from New York.

- Lower house of the bicameral legislature to be directly elected by the "people" for a 3-year term (N.B., Keep in mind that there were considerable suffrage restrictions in the states at that time that greatly limited those who could actually vote).

- Upper house of the bicameral legislature indirectly chosen by electors to serve for terms of good behavior (most likely, lifetime).

- The executive, indirectly chosen by electors, was to serve for a term of good behavior (N.B., Hamilton's reference to an "elective kingship," reminiscent of the British monarchy, generated opposition by those fearful of a dictatorship).

- Supported the concept of judicial review by a national supreme court.

- Commerce would be controlled by the national government.

- Slaves would not be counted regarding population criteria.

Effect: A much too conservative, centralized, and nationalistic proposal to be accepted by the mainstream Convention delegates.

THE VIRGINIA PLAN: MORE CENTRALIZED

- Written by James Madison, but presented by Edmund Randolph, this plan reflected the views and interests of the larger and more populous states.

- Recommended a bicameral legislature consisting of a lower house based upon wealth or the total number of the free population for a fixed term and an upper house chosen by the lower house from nominees of state legislatures for a fixed term.

- The executive would, in turn, be indirectly selected by both houses of the bicameral legislature for a fixed term.

- Bicameral legislature would also provide for a national court system to act as a "council of revision" which would be empowered to veto/override the acts of the legislature.

- Commerce would be controlled by the national government (by implication)

- Slaves would not be counted regarding population criteria.

Effect: This plan caused great alarm among the smaller and less populous states because they felt that their interests and concerns would be given short shrift by the larger and more populous states.

THE NEW JERSEY PLAN: LEAST CENTRALIZED

- Introduced by William Paterson, this plan represented the views and interests of the smaller and less populous states, which felt threatened by the Virginia Plan's proposals.

- Sought to retain a unicameral legislature (similar to the Articles of Confederation) where each state would have one vote (based on state equality) and which would now be bolstered with additional taxation, commerce, and treaty enforcement powers.

- Unicameral legislature would appoint a plural executive (executive committee).

- Unicameral legislature would also create a single national supreme court to supervise the interpretation of national laws by the state courts.

- Commerce would be controlled by the national government.

- Slaves would be counted as three-fifths of a person for taxation purposes.

Effect: Deadlock between the larger and smaller states, and the threat of withdrawal by the smaller state delegations from the Convention, led the Virginia Plan proponents to acquiesce. A "committee of eleven" was formed to break the impasse and resolve the outstanding differences. The end result was the "Great (Connecticut) Compromise" engineered by Roger Sherman.

Appendix D

THE U.S. CONSTITUTION: PRODUCT OF COMPROMISE (5 EXAMPLES)

COMPROMISE #1: FEDERALISM

Rejecting the confederal form of government under the Articles of Confederation, which essentially decentralized authority and conferred sovereignty upon the states, and repudiating the British unitary system of centralized power from which the American Colonies had just emerged, the Constitution represented a federal model of "shared sovereignty" where power was to be divided between the national government and the states. Specifically delegated, expressed grants of power were enumerated for the national government (Article I, Section 8), concurrent powers were provided for both the national and state governments, and powers were reserved for the states that were not specifically denied nor prohibited (10th Amendment).

COMPROMISE #2: REPRESENTATIVE GOVERNMENT

The bicameral Congress that finally emerged from the Convention's debates was itself a compromise between the Virginia Plan (supported by larger states which wanted a lower house based proportionately on population) and the New Jersey Plan (supported by smaller states which wanted a unicameral legislature where each state would have one vote based on the idea of state equality regardless of population). The Great Compromise, which reconciled elements of both plans, provided for a two-house legislature that gave the lower house (House of Representatives) representation on the basis of population and the upper house (Senate) representation on the principle of state equality (two senators per state). Subsumed under this compromise was an additional quid pro quo on direct elections for the people's chamber (House of Representatives) versus indirect elections for the more aristocratic upper chamber (Senate). (N.B., The Senate was indirectly elected by state legislatures until 1913 when the 17th Amendment was ratified providing for direct popular vote).

COMPROMISE #3: SLAVERY

Potentially a very divisive issue between the slave states and the "free" states, was the "peculiar institution" of slavery and how it would impact on representation in the House of Representatives—as well as the ancillary matter of direct taxation (e.g., slaves were a form of property). The slave states wanted slaves fully counted as part of the population in determining the number of seats they would be entitled to in the House of Representatives. Conversely, they wanted slaves not counted at all as a form of taxable property. The free states, on the other hand, wanted slaves to be counted fully as taxable property, but not to be counted at all for purposes of representation in the House of Representatives. In the end, the Three-Fifths Compromise, a solution agreeable to both sides, broke the impasse by counting each slave the equivalent of three-fifths of a free person for both representation and taxation.

COMPROMISE #4: COMMERCE/SLAVE TRADE

The North wanted Congress to have full authority to regulate interstate and foreign commerce (including the slave trade), while the South, fearful of a potential numerical majority of the North, worried that the more industrial North would control the regulation of trade to the detriment of the South in such matters as the export of agricultural goods (tobacco, cotton, indigo, sugar) and the slave trade. To assuage the South—even though the Congress could regulate interstate commerce by a simple majority—the Congress was prohibited from levying export taxes, interfering with the slave trade until 1808, or imposing an import tax exceeding ten dollars per slave. Furthermore, a two-thirds majority of the Senate would be required to ratify any commercial treaty, thereby giving the South additional safeguards and leverage to protect its economic interests.

COMPROMISE #5: THE PRESIDENCY

Neither the parliamentary-type creature suggested by the Virginia Plan's proposal that the executive be selected by the Congress, nor Alexander Hamilton's monarchical "elective kingship," nor even the New Jersey Plan's plural executive by committee came to fruition. The disparate views on the presidency were ultimately resolved by the final language of Article II (and later by the 12th Amendment) of the Constitution. The executive was to represent a separate, equal, and coordinate branch of government to be independently elected by electors chosen by the people for a fixed term of four years and with no restrictions on re-election. (N.B., This was to be changed in 1951 with the subsequent ratification of the 22nd Amendment, which imposed specific term limits).

Appendix E

CONSTITUTIONAL OMISSIONS AND OTHER ILL-DEFINED FEATURES

SUFFRAGE

The original Constitution was particularly vague about identifying any specific nationally endorsed or recognized standard relating to voting eligibility. On such matters as age, gender, or other sundry qualifications relevant to suffrage, the Constitution was silent. These matters were initially left as reserved powers of the states—and, as a result, there was no single consensus evidenced by the states. In fact, a great diversity of qualifications existed with respect to age, residency, literacy tests, poll taxes, property requirements, etc. The addition of various constitutional amendments over time clarified this matter significantly by defining the issue of suffrage with greater specificity and detail (e.g., the 15th Amendment expanded the suffrage to include African-American males; the 19th Amendment extended the suffrage to women; the 24th Amendment abolished poll taxes in federal elections; and the 26th Amendment established the national voting age at 18 years for the election of President and congress).

POLITICAL PARTIES

Political parties were never mentioned or legitimated in the original Constitution—nor were they subsequently included by revisions or amendments later on. Originally regarded in pejorative terms in Madison's **Federalist #10** (1787-88) and in Washington's Farewell Address (1796), these so-called "factions" (embryonic political parties deriving from the Federalist/Anti-Federalist conflict over the adoption of the Constitution, and which later coalesced around the personalities and ideas of Jefferson and Hamilton) were perceived as the progenitors of evil and baneful effects that divided rather than unified the country. Notwithstanding the alleged divisive and discordant nature of these "parties," they became the nucleus of the emerging two-party system that evolved. They became the interest-aggregation vehicles that traditionally nominated candidates and contested elections at various specific intervals. Nowadays, the historical legacy and legitimacy of mainstream political parties are rarely, if ever, questioned and they have acquired widespread de facto constitutional acceptance.

FEDERAL COURT SYSTEM

Article I, Section 8 and Article III of the Constitution were particularly brief and sketchy as to the specific structure and design of the judicial branch beyond the Supreme Court. In fact, Congress was authorized to "ordain and establish" such inferior courts as it deemed necessary from time to time. Fulfilling its constitutional charge, the Congress passed the Judiciary Act of 1789, the Judiciary Act of 1801, the Circuit Court of Appeals Act of 1891, and numerous other enactments between 1789 and the present that have helped to define the parameters of the judicial branch regarding such matters as types of courts, size, jurisdiction, and operational costs of courts, number of judges, judicial salaries, and perquisites. Moreover, the House/Senate Judiciary Committees were established by Congress as standing committees to oversee the judicial branch and to suggest reforms and recommend changes as needed.

PRESIDENT'S CABINET

While the word *cabinet* is never explicitly stated in the Constitution, a cognate reference to "executive departments" is (Article II, Section 2). Due to the de facto needs of the presidency, George Washington unwittingly established the precedent by forming the first "cabinet" when he asked Thomas Jefferson (Secretary of State), Alexander Hamilton (Secretary of the Treasury), Edmund Randolph (Attorney General), and Henry Knox (Secretary of War) to assist his administration and lend their expertise in their specific portfolio assignments. This became the historical precedent that has subsequently acquired its own institutional legitimacy since 1789. By 2002, the Cabinet had grown from its original four positions to fourteen executive departments, plus the addition of cabinet rank officials which have subsequently been created to assist the President (e.g., Administrator of the Environmental Protection Agency, Director of the Office of Homeland Security, Director of the Office of Management and Budget, etc.).

BILL OF RIGHTS

One of the most glaring omissions of the original Constitution that emerged in September 1789 was the conspicuous absence of a bill of rights. See Prefatory Note on the next page for a full explanation and treatment of this vital component of the Constitution.

The Bill of Rights: Prefatory Note

To allay the objections of the Anti-Federalists (those who opposed the adoption of the Constitution)—and such Convention delegates as George Mason and Elbridge Gerry—a written bill of rights was drafted by James Madison. It had become abundantly clear that a number of states would only conditionally accept the Constitution on the understanding that a bill of rights designed to protect and safeguard individual liberties would soon be added. Thomas Jefferson's admonition that a written bill of rights "is what the people are entitled to against every government on earth" did not go unheeded. In 1791, 10 of Madison's original 12 amendments were ratified and added to the Constitution. These amendments, which were envisioned to become a bulwark against tyrannical government, are now considered to be an integral part of the original Constitution.

1st Amendment **Five Basic Freedoms**	1) Freedom of (or from) Religion "Free Exercise Clause" and "Establishment Clause," 2) Freedom of Speech, 3) Freedom of the Press, 4) Freedom of Peaceable Assembly, 5) Freedom of Protest (Petition).
2nd Amendment **Right to Keep and Bear Arms**	Because they retain the right to have state militias subject to national and state regulation, the people also have the right to keep and bear arms.
3rd Amendment **Quartering of Troops**	Government cannot require citizens to house soldiers in their homes during peacetime—and only in a manner prescribed by law during wartime. (This amendment addressed colonial grievances stemming from the Revolutionary War when colonists were obliged to house and feed British troops.)

4th Amendment **Search & Seizure**	Right of citizens to be protected against unreasonable searches and seizures—and establishing procedures for legal searches and seizures (e.g., warrant procedures, probable cause standard, particularity provision). (N.B., This amendment also addressed colonial grievances against the British writs of assistance, which were ill-defined, all-purpose general search warrants that violated colonial rights to privacy and property.)
5th Amendment **Rights and Protections** **of Accused Persons**	–Right to grand jury in cases of serious crimes (indictment process) –"Double jeopardy clause" protection –"Self-incrimination clause" protection –"Due process clause" regarding life, liberty, and property protection –Eminent domain protection regarding private property seizure by government
6th Amendment **Substansive and Procedural** **Rights Regarding a Fair Trial**	–Right to a speedy and public trial –Right to an impartial jury –Right of accused to be informed of specific charges –Right to confront prosecution witnesses –Right to have compulsory process to produce witnesses –Right to the assistance of counsel –Right of citizens to a jury trial in civil cases –Applicable where the principles of common law apply

7th Amendment **Trial By Jury/Civil Cases**	Right of citizens to a jury trial in civil cases where the principles of common law apply. (N.B., the common law is the body of law inherited from England through judicial decisions based on custom and precedent.)
8th Amendment **Fines/Punishments**	Right of citizens to be protected against excessive bail and fines—as well as cruel and unusual punishment.
9th Amendment **Unenumerated Rights of the People**	Unspecified or unenumerated rights—other than those explicitly stated—may also deserve constitutional protection.
10th Amendment **Reserved Rights of the States and the People**	Official recognition of the divided sovereignty implicit in the U.S. federal model where power is shared between the national government and the states—all other powers neither specifically prohibited nor denied belong and are reserved to the people.

Appendix F

AN ANATOMICAL SUMMARY OF THE CONSTITUTION OF 1787

Preamble – The official statement of the constitutional framers outlining six major purposes and goals for the new document.

ARTICLES (I-VII)

I. Established the Legislative Branch (Congress)

- Composition of House of Representatives and Senate
- Terms/Qualifications/Elections
- Internal Organization/Meetings
- Law-Making Powers
- Specifically Enumerated Powers/Elastic Clause
- Powers Denied the National Government
- Powers Denied the States

II. Established the Executive Branch (President, Vice-President, Executive Departments)

- Term/Qualifications/Election
- Powers
- Duties
- Impeachment

III. Established the Judicial Branch (Supreme Court)

- Federal Courts
- Term/Compensation of Federal Judges
- Jurisdiction of Federal Courts
- Jury Trials/Venue
- Definition of Treason

IV. Relations Among States

- "Full Faith and Credit Clause"
- Extradition Procedures
- Admission/Creation of New States
- Congressional Control Over Territories
- Guarantee of a Republican Form of Government
- National Government Protection Against Invasion or Domestic Violence

V. Amending the Constitution

- Provided Several Methods for Amending the Constitution

VI. Role of National Government

- Honoring the Public Debt
- "Supremacy Clause"
- Requisite Oaths of Office to Support Constitution
- No Religious Tests as a Requirement to Hold Public Office

VII. Ratification

- Outlined Process for the Adoption of the Constitution

AMENDMENTS (1-27)

See preceding section for greater detail on the Bill of Rights (Amendments 1-10). These amendments were collectively ratified and added to the Constitution in 1791.

AMENDMENT 11 (1795)

— Established that state courts are the proper venue for lawsuits against states by citizens of other states (or foreign states).

AMENDMENT 12 (1804)

— Election of the President/Vice-President
— Procedures of the Electoral College

AMENDMENT 13 (1865)

— Abolished slavery and involuntary servitude (except as punishment for a crime).

AMENDMENT 14 (1868)

— Defined citizenship and the rights of citizens
— "Due Process Clause" (binding on the states)

— "Equal Protection Clause" (binding on the states)
— "Penalty Clause" (for abridging rights of citizens)
— Former Confederate leaders prevented from holding high public office
— Civil War debts from the Union honored and recognized
— Civil War debts from the Confederacy repudiated

AMENDMENT 15 (1870)

— Suffrage extended to black male citizens
— Right to vote cannot be denied on the basis of "race, color, or previous condition of servitude."

AMENDMENT 16 (1913)

— Established the right of the national government to levy an income tax.

AMENDMENT 17 (1913)

— Changed the method by which senators were chosen, from indirect election by state legislatures to that of direct popular election.

AMENDMENT 18 (1919)

— Prohibition (forbade the manufacture, sale, transportation, importation, or exportation of alcohol).

AMENDMENT 19 (1920)

— Suffrage extended to women (known also as the Susan B. Anthony Amendment).

AMENDMENT 20 (1933)

— "Lame Duck Amendment" shortened the intervening time between the election of Congress and the President and the actual installation of the next Congress and President.

AMENDMENT 21 (1933)

— Repealed the 18th Amendment (Prohibition) (N.B., So far, this is the only example where a subsequent amendment was used to repeal a previous one).

AMENDMENT 22 (1951)

— Limited the number of presidential terms to two full elected terms (eight years)—or to one full elected term (four years), if the President was serving more than two years of his predecessor's term.

AMENDMENT 23 (1961)

— Provided for three electors to represent the inhabitants of the District of Columbia in the election of President and Vice-President.

AMENDMENT 24 (1964)

— Abolished poll taxes as an impediment to voting in all federal elections.

AMENDMENT 25 (1967)

— Provided for specific procedures to deal with the issue of presidential disability and succession of the President and Vice-President.

AMENDMENT 26 (1971)

— Extended the right to vote to all citizens over 18 years.

AMENDMENT 27 (1992)

— Congressional salaries cannot be raised until an intervening election shall take place in the House of Representatives first (known also as the "Madison Amendment," which was originally proposed, but not ratified, in 1789).

Appendix G

CHECKS & BALANCES AND SEPARATION OF POWERS

PREFATORY NOTE: PHILOSOPHICAL UNDERPINNINGS

In **Federalist #10**, Madison presented an articulate defense of the establishment of a widely extended, geographically decentralized, numerous and diverse non-tyrannical republic. Recognizing the need to further protect the polity from the danger of tyranny, he proposed additional safeguards to that end, namely an intricate system of both formal and informal checks and balances. Woven into the constitutional fabric and based on the Madisonian notion of human nature expressed in **Federalist #51**, men were pejoratively regarded as flawed beings subject to the frailties and corruption that led to the ultimate detriment of the commonweal. To combat the avarice and competing ambitions of men, and to safeguard the polity from recurrent abuses of power, internal and external controls would be necessary. Referred to by Madison as "auxiliary precautions," these were to become the bedrock principles encapsulated in the constitutional design of the new document.

Also inherent in the constitutional design was Lord Acton's admonition, written about a century later, that "power tends to corrupt, and absolute power corrupts absolutely." Fearful of the concentration of power in the hands of the one, the few, or the many, the Framers sought to fragment and divide power in a myriad of ways—so that no one person, group, branch/level of government, or institution would have unbridled or sovereign power. The idea of balanced government set forth in the writings of John Adams, as well as the notions advanced by the Newtonian principles of harmony, symmetry, and equilibrium in the physical world, heavily influenced the final constitutional product and design. As a result, the Constitution formally created three separate but coordinate branches of government in Article I (Legislative), Article II (Executive), and Article III (Judicial). By trifurcating the powers of the national government into three separate branches, the Framers were hopeful that a delicate equilibrium could be established that would deter tyranny. Moreover, as an additional immunity against tyranny, the dispersion of power was further fragmented and sub-divided by the principle of federalism. Accordingly, power would also be vertically shared by different levels of government—national, state, and local—as well as each level being horizontally divided into its respective three branches of government. In the final analysis, similar to the system of checks and balances, the principle of separation of powers, both horizontal and vertical, became a fundamental and indispensable construct of the new Constitution.

THE LEGISLATIVE BRANCH (ARTICLE I)

Checks on the Executive (Examples)
— Congress can override presidential vetoes by a two-thirds majority
— Congress can impeach, try, and remove the President from office
— Senate can refuse to confirm presidential appointments
— Senate can refuse to ratify treaties
— Congress can place limits on President's war-waging powers as Commander in Chief (e.g., War Powers Act of 1973)
— Congress can regulate President's impoundment power (e.g., Budget and Impoundment Act of 1974)
— Congress has staggered electoral terms of two and six years—which are not always congruent with a presidential election
— Congress can use legislative tactics, such as the rider or filibuster, to impede or frustrate presidentially-sponsored legislation

Checks on the Judicial (Examples)
— Congress can create or eliminate all inferior (lower) federal courts
— Congress can determine the personnel, size, salaries, and jurisdiction of lower federal courts
— House of Representatives can impeach and the Senate can try and remove federal judges (justices) from the bench
— Congress can change the size of the Supreme Court (but not its jurisdiction)
— Senate can reject judicial nominations submitted by the President
— Congress can propose constitutional amendments to bypass judicial rulings

THE EXECUTIVE BRANCH (ARTICLE II)

Checks on the Legislative (Examples)
— President can veto bills (both regular and pocket)
— President can appeal directly to people by lobbying in the mass media for his legislative program
— President can initiate legislation (e.g., State of the Union Address, "Administration bills" receive special priority)

— President is the head of his political party (which may control one or both houses of Congress).

— President can call special sessions of Congress.

— President can make executive agreements (rather than a treaty) to circumvent the Senate's treaty ratification power.

— President can claim "executive privilege" to protect executive confidentiality or secrecy from congressional scrutiny (e.g., withholding information from Congress and its committees).

— President can commit U.S. troops abroad as Commander in Chief without a formal declaration of war (e.g., for a short duration).

— President can curtail Congress's power of the purse by ordering deferrals and rescissions.

— President can issue executive orders (ordinance power) (e.g., Franklin Roosevelt's internment of Japanese-Americans, Harry Truman's desegregation of the armed forces).

— President could briefly use the line-item veto (1996-98) until the Supreme Court ruled it unconstitutional in 1998.

Checks on the Judicial (Examples)

— President can nominate individuals to fill judicial vacancies in the federal court system.

— President can grant clemency, reprieves, amnesties, and pardons.

— President can fail to vigorously and "faithfully" enforce court orders with which he disagrees.

THE JUDICIAL BRANCH (ARTICLE III)

Checks on either/both the Legislative and the Executive (Examples)

— Supreme Court has the power of judicial review to declare laws/treaties passed by the Congress and signed by the President to be unconstitutional.

— Supreme Court has the power of judicial review to rule executive actions to be unconstitutional.

— Federal judges (and Supreme Court justices) serve for terms of "good behavior" (essentially lifetime terms)—thus providing some degree of judicial independence against undue political coercion.

— Congress may not diminish the salaries of judges (another safeguard to promote judicial independence).

Appendix H

THE ALLOCATION OF CONSTITUTIONAL POWERS: ENUMERATED, IMPLIED, CONCURRENT, RESERVED, AND DENIED

PREFATORY NOTE

In accordance with the precept advanced by the Framers that sovereign power must be divided and fragmented in a multitude of ways as a means to prevent tyrannical and/or abusive government, the Constitution diffuses power in such a manner that no one source exercises all of it. In fact, there was a fine line in the Constitution reflecting an ambivalence towards the need for strong national power to maintain order and stability, and yet a concomitant fear that such power could be misused, usurped, or abused by the national government. To placate critics, such as the Anti-Federalists, the Constitution recognized the nature of this seemingly intractable problem by creating a means of dividing power between the national government and the states. The solution was to define the parameters of national versus state power in a delicately calibrated balance—it was called Federalism.

Enumerated/Specifically Delegated Powers
to the National Government
(Article I, Section 8) (Examples)

— Levy and collect taxes
— Borrow money on the credit of the United States
— Establish lower (inferior) federal courts
— Regulate interstate and foreign commerce
— Coin and print money

— Declare war
— Grant patents and copyrights
— Raise and support an army and navy

Implied Powers (Not Specifically Delegated to the National Government (Article I, Section 8, Clause 18)

— "Necessary and Proper Clause" (N.B., This is also known as the "Elastic Clause")

The aforementioned clause expands the power of Congress to matters that may not have been initially delegated or provided for in Article I, Section 8, Clauses 1-17, but derive from, or are connected to, those specifically enumerated powers in some way. For example, while the Constitution cites Congress's role concerning national defense (army and navy) and declaring war, it doesn't mention anything about an "air force" (since air forces didn't exist at the time). The "elastic clause" implies that Congress's purview over defense matters in general is proper and appropriate even if it is not explicitly stated.

Concurrent/Shared Powers Exercised by the National Government and the States (10th Amendment) (Examples)

— Levy and collect taxes
— Establish and maintain courts (federal, state, local)
— Borrow money
— Eminent domain
— Charter banks
— Make and enforce laws
— Promote public health and welfare
— Maintain public roads and highways

Powers Reserved to the States (10th Amendment) (Examples)

— Regulate intrastate commerce
— Establish the state's educational system

— Set up and regulate local governments

— Ratification of constitutional amendments

— Conduct and regulate elections

— Establish suffrage requirements not in conflict with the Constitution

DENIED POWERS OF THE NATIONAL GOVERNMENT AND THE STATES (ARTICLE I, SECTIONS 9 AND 10)

Prohibitions on the National Government (Article I, Section 9) (Examples)

— Cannot place a tax on exports

— Cannot issue titles of nobility

— Cannot impose bills of attainder

— Cannot pass ex post facto laws

— State boundaries cannot be changed without the consent of the states involved

— Cannot violate the Bill of Rights

— No preference can be given to one state over another in matters of commerce

Prohibitions on the States (Article I Section 10) (Examples)

— Cannot place a tax on imports or exports

— Cannot issue titles of nobility

— Cannot impose bills of attainder

— Cannot pass ex post facto laws

— Cannot enter into treaties with foreign nations

— Cannot coin money

— Cannot violate the U.S. Constitution

Appendix I

THE AMENDMENT PROCESS—ARTICLE V

PREFATORY NOTE

There have been only twenty-seven amendments to the original Constitution from 1789 to 2002. While the formal amendment process has been used only sparingly, the Constitution is, in fact, a product that has been revised, defined, and redefined through a variety of other means, including but not limited to congressional acts (e.g., using the "elastic clause"), presidential practices (e.g., executive agreements, executive privilege, ordinance powers, etc.), and Supreme Court decisions predicated on the principle of judicial review. The evolving "living Constitution" has continually evidenced a dynamic and ever-changing document that has endured for over two centuries.

After the addition of the Bill of Rights (Amendments 1-10) in 1791, there have been only seventeen subsequent amendments in the following 211 years. While the formal amendment process technically provides for four different variations of amending the Constitution, all of the amendments since 1791, with one exception, have utilized one particular method for the amendment process (N.B., The anomaly was the 21st Amendment, which involved the repeal of Prohibition).

The formal amendment process involves a bifurcated procedure: *1. Methods of Proposing Amendments*—followed by: *2. Methods of Ratification.*

Method #1 (Used for 26 out of 27 amendments)

Method of Proposal:

Two-thirds vote of each house of Congress

Method of Ratification:

Ratification by three-fourths of the state legislatures (38)

Method #2 (Used only for Amendment 21)

Method of Proposal:

Two-thirds vote of each house of Congress

Method of Ratification

Ratification by three-fourths of the state conventions (38)

Method #3 (Not Used)

Method of Proposal:

National nominating convention called by Congress at the request of two-thirds of the state legislatures (34)

Method of Ratification:

Ratification by three-fourths of the state legislatures (38)

Method #4 (Not Used)

Method of Proposal:

National Constitutional Convention called by Congress at the request of two-thirds of the state legislatures (34)

Method of Ratification:

Ratification by three-fourths of the state conventions (38)

INDEX

Index

Y

Z

REA's Test Preps
The Best in Test Preparation

- REA "Test Preps" are **far more** comprehensive than any other test preparation series
- Each book contains up to **eight** full-length practice tests based on the most recent exams
- **Every** type of question likely to be given on the exams is included
- Answers are accompanied by **full** and **detailed** explanations

REA publishes over 70 Test Preparation volumes in several series. They include:

Advanced Placement Exams (APs)
Art History
Biology
Calculus AB & BC
Chemistry
Economics
English Language & Composition
English Literature & Composition
European History
French Language
Government & Politics
Latin
Physics B & C
Psychology
Spanish Language
Statistics
United States History
World History

College-Level Examination Program (CLEP)
Analyzing and Interpreting Literature
College Algebra
Freshman College Composition
General Examinations
General Examinations Review
History of the United States I
History of the United States II
Introduction to Educational Psychology
Human Growth and Development
Introductory Psychology
Introductory Sociology
Principles of Management
Principles of Marketing
Spanish
Western Civilization I
Western Civilization II

SAT Subject Tests
Biology E/M
Chemistry
French
German
Literature
Mathematics Level 1, 2
Physics
Spanish
United States History

Graduate Record Exams (GREs)
Biology
Chemistry
Computer Science
General
Literature in English
Mathematics
Physics
Psychology

ACT - ACT Assessment

ASVAB - Armed Services Vocational Aptitude Battery

CBEST - California Basic Educational Skills Test

CDL - Commercial Driver License Exam

CLAST - College Level Academic Skills Test

COOP & HSPT - Catholic High School Admission Tests

ELM - California State University Entry Level Mathematics Exam

FE (EIT) - Fundamentals of Engineering Exams - For Both AM & PM Exams

FTCE - Florida Teacher Certification Examinations

GED - (U.S. Edition)

GMAT - Graduate Management Admission Test

LSAT - Law School Admission Test

MAT - Miller Analogies Test

MCAT - Medical College Admission Test

MTEL - Massachusetts Tests for Educator Licensure

NJ HSPA - New Jersey High School Proficiency Assessment

NYSTCE - New York State Teacher Certification Examinations

PRAXIS PLT - Principles of Learning & Teaching Tests

PRAXIS PPST - Pre-Professional Skills Tests

PSAT/NMSQT

SAT

TExES - Texas Examinations of Educator Standards

THEA - Texas Higher Education Assessment

TOEFL - Test of English as a Foreign Language

TOEIC - Test of English for International Communication

USMLE Steps 1,2,3 - U.S. Medical Licensing Exams

Research & Education Association
61 Ethel Road W., Piscataway, NJ 08854
Phone: (732) 819-8880   **website: www.rea.com**

Please send me more information about your Test Prep books.

Name _____

Address _____

City _____ State _____ Zip _____